THE ADMIRAL'S
WOLF PACK

THE ADMIRAL'S WOLF PACK

by JEAN NOLI

TRANSLATED BY J. F. BERNARD

Doubleday & Company, Inc.
Garden City, New York, 1974

Originally published in France by Fayard Publishers as *Les Loups de l'Amiral* © Librairie Arthème Fayard 1970

ISBN: 0-385-00372-2

Library of Congress Catalog Card Number 72–89338

Translation Copyright © 1974 by Doubleday & Company, Inc.

This book is dedicated to the
seamen of all nations who were
lost at sea during World War II

The only thing that really frightened me
during the war was the submarine threat.

—WINSTON CHURCHILL

CONTENTS

Part One

THE WOLF

1

On October 12, 1939, a Norwegian tanker lay approximately 180 miles northeast of Scotland, latitude 58° North and longitude 2° West, en route to Aberdeen.

On the tanker's bridge, the men on watch were dulled by fatigue and noise. The sea was so rough that there were moments when the deck seemed to drop out from under their boots. In total darkness, its bridge and superstructure swept by the wind, the ship dipped slowly, heavily into the waves. Its squat hull creaked and moaned, and its prow sent up great heaps of black-ish foam onto the forward deck. Then, with tons of water rolling from its decks, the vessel's dark mass slowly righted itself and, rolling from side to side, fell once more into the waves in its slow forward movement. It was 2 A.M. The sky was a black ceiling of clouds billowing across the sea from horizon to horizon as the wind grew in violence and intensity.

The tanker's crew were not apprehensive about the rising storm. To the contrary, they found it reassuring, and, curled up in their hammocks, they dropped off to sleep comforted by the thought that, in such weather, there was little chance that a German submarine would discover their ship.

Several miles from the tanker, in the midst of the giant waves stirred up by the south-southwest wind, which occasionally reached a force-nine velocity, lay a slender gray shape which had just emerged from beneath the surface in search of its prey: a U-47 submarine, type VII C, 517 tons, with a length of 61 meters and a beam of 6 meters, armed with ten torpedoes.

In the submarine's conning tower was the port watch, Wil-helm, battered by the waves and the wind, wrapped in a leather coat, his sou'wester pulled down around his ears so that only his eyes, and his five-day growth of beard, were visible. Though wet to the bone, he remained alert; and he spotted the tanker immediately. He touched the shoulder of Endrass, the second officer, and pointed to the ship, scarcely visible in the darkness. Instantly, the night glasses of the other three men on watch swung in the direction indicated by Wilhelm, while Endrass leaned into the conning tower and, supporting himself with one hand against the interior handrail, gave the alarm: "Tanker to port! Distance, 2 miles. Speed, 7 knots. About 8,000 tons."

The alert immediately sounded below, throughout the submarine. On the conning tower, the watch unbuckled their safety belts, ready to go below for the dive as soon as Endrass gave the order.

Endrass, however, was waiting for the U-47's commander, Günther Prien, to reach a decision. The men around him, never taking their eyes from the tanker, as though they were afraid that it might slip away from them in the night, also waited for the order, which they expected momentarily, to dive and attack. But the order, when it came, its words barely audible through the loudspeaker over the roar of the wind and sea and the torrent of rain which had begun to fall, was not what they had expected.

"Set course for 180," the commander's voice spoke. "Full speed ahead."

The Grey Wolf had changed its course.

No one aboard the tanker ever knew of their miraculous escape from destruction. They never suspected that they had come face to face with death, and that death had spared them.

On the U-47's conning tower, the men looked furtively at one another.

"It's happened again," Wilhelm grumbled as he licked away the salt water which had dripped from his forehead and nose to his mouth. Then he spat. "That's the second time that we run away!"

"Fasten your belts," Endrass ordered. "And don't let me hear any complaints about orders."

"Excuse me, Lieutenant," Wilhelm said. "I wasn't complain-

ing." Then, with his mouth close to Endrass' ear, he continued:
"I was only saying we're in a submarine that doesn't like to fight
much."

"Shut up, Wilhelm."

Relations were already strained between Endrass and Wilhelm, and they had been so ever since Endrass had overheard
the sailor telling other members of the crew that "the second
officer is so small that we're going to have to get him a step-
ladder. When he's on the conning tower, he can barely see over
the railing." And the others had laughed.

Endrass had not forgotten. In his book, Wilhelm was an in-
subordinate loudmouth. The sailor prided himself on being a
"tough guy" because he had belonged to the submarine service
since its inception in 1936, at Wilhelmshaven. He had taken the
examinations to become a petty officer—and failed. Since then,
he had had an unyielding grudge against all officers. He was a
squat, muscular man, with a square head hunched down between his shoulders, and with the fixed, unblinking look of an
animal.

Now, Endrass returned Wilhelm's stare. "Shut up!" he ordered
sharply.

Below, Commander Prien had gone back to bed immediately
after the end of the alert had sounded. While the crew had
rushed to their battle stations, he had announced his decision:
"We will not attack."

Then, his orderly had brought him a cup of coffee which he
had drunk slowly, calmly. Afterward, he had spoken with Spahr,
the navigator, and studied the chart. The U-47 was in the open
sea off the Orkney Islands. Without saying a word, he had returned to his cabin, pulled the curtain across the doorway, and
stretched out with his white commander's hat within easy reach.
He had fallen asleep immediately, despite the rough sea.

He was the only one aboard to do so. Everyone else was in a
state of high excitement. If Commander Prien refused to attack
the tanker, it must be because they were on a special mission.
And a special mission, with a man as determined as Prien in

command, might well turn into a suicide mission. No one knew what lay ahead; and no one felt at ease in the face of this uncertainty. The crew lay in their narrow, hard bunks, some of them flat on their backs and staring into space, others propped up on their elbows, all of them in the grip of that indefinable fear of men who face the unknown. The rumbling of the diesels, the pitching and rolling of the U-47, the rattling and sliding of unsecured gear inside the lockers and, occasionally, across the metal deck, made sleep impossible.

Elsewhere aboard the submarine, the men of the next watch were preparing to begin their tour. They drank their coffee, ate their three eggs and sausages; out of habit, they offered elaborate insults to the cook.

Then, in boots and leather coats and sou'westers, they made their way toward the conning tower, steadying themselves by holding onto the bunks and pipes which ran the length of the vessel's narrow hull. Amidship, they found von Varrendorf, the third officer, waiting for them, clutching the rungs of the steel ladder which led to the upper deck. The officer's eyes, still swollen from sleep, were like two red balls in his round, plump face. Von Varrendorf was twenty-one years old; and he disliked intensely being exposed to cold and to water.

The officer began climbing the ladder leading up into the open air. His four men followed, wrinkling their noses under the unaccustomed weight of the red-tinted glasses which regulations required that they wear below, before beginning a watch, in order to accustom their eyes to darkness. "The torture of the glasses," von Varrendorf thought to himself. He had never been able to wear the glasses without bruising his nose. For the thousandth time, he wondered what had ever possessed him to volunteer for U-boat service.

A spash of water through the conning tower's open hatch drenched the officer and brought him to full wakefulness.

With the third watch on deck, the fourth watch went below. Lieutenant Endrass, the last to leave the deck, closed the hatch behind him as his men, water running in rivulets down their coats and hats, struggled out of their outer garments and, in the process, sprinkled liberally the men lying in the surrounding bunks. There was an immediate and loud protest.

Wilhelm, having draped his coat and sou'wester over a pipe, shouted for coffee. He knew that, with his reputation as a fighter, none of his mates would tell him to shut up.

"Quiet in here!"

The order echoed through the compartment. Wilhelm recognized the voice. He turned, steadying himself against a table with one hand, and came face to face with Endrass. Wilhelm towered over the first officer, dwarfing him by his enormous bulk. Yet, the look on Endrass' face silenced him. Furious at himself, he lowered his eyes.

Endrass turned and left the forward compartment. Wilhelm remained silent. He made faces for the benefit of the men around him, but no one smiled.

In the control room Endrass found Hansen, the duty officer. "That one's a son-of-a-bitch, isn't he?" Hansen remarked.

"Yes, he sure is," Endrass answered. "But he's also an expert gunner." Then, turning to the sailor on duty there, he said: "Wake the captain at dawn; and me, too."

A few seconds later he was stretched out on his bunk. He had changed from his dripping uniform into another uniform—a damp uniform, for nothing really dries aboard a submarine. From a packet he pulled the damp, wrinkled photograph of a woman with dark hair. She was not very pretty, and her expression was serious. Endrass looked at the photograph for a moment, then replaced it carefully in his pocket, and closed his eyes.

The third watch had only a few minutes left of its tour. The *U-47*, pitching and rolling, its engines wide open, continued to move along the surface at 12 knots through the tossing, churning sea. A second-torpedoman named Peterei rolled out of his bunk onto the deck and sprained his wrist. Commander Prien got up, wrapped the man's wrist tightly in a long bandage, and then returned to his bunk. Hermann Staub, at nineteen the youngest man aboard, on his first combat mission, was sick as a dog. As part of the clean-up detail, he had tried to sweep out the crew's quarters; but, under the effect of the vessel's unceasing roll, he suddenly turned white as chalk, and then vomited on the deck. Someone shouted: "Why don't you go to the head, you filthy bastard!"

Staub looked imploringly at the man who had spoken, and then crumpled to the floor. No one dared look at him, let alone touch him, as the young sailor lay there in his own vomit, his hair plastered to his forehead with sweat. Staub moaned, asking for help.

Wilhelm said loudly: "With guys like that aboard this tin can, we'll be lucky if we don't all end up on the bottom."

It was October 13, 1939.

At 6 o'clock in the morning, before the man on duty in the control room had had the chance to awaken him, Prien was already dressed and standing next to Spahr. The navigator had not slept, and his eyes were puffy with fatigue.

"Where are we?" the captain asked.

"Off the Orkneys, sir."

"Good," Prien answered. He turned to Endrass, who had also risen early and was standing behind him. "Prepare to dive."

As the horn sounded, men tumbled from their bunks. The conning tower hatch was closed and locked. The rumble of the diesels ceased as the electric engines took over, and the hiss of the ventilators became more strident. Twenty-five seconds after Prien had given the order, the *U-47* disappeared below the surface.

As the submarine sank deeper into the water, the noise of the waves breaking against the decks faded and the rolling ceased as the vessel regained its stability. Staub, still lying in a heap, began to revive. The deck beneath him no longer pitched and rolled. Painfully, he rose to his feet. No one said a word. Then Wilhelm spoke:

"Change your uniform. I'll clean up this mess." The other crewmen looked at one another in astonishment.

There was a silent shock aboard the U-47, followed by a creaking and groaning. The submarine was now lying on the bottom in 150 feet of water.

"Assemble the crew in the forward compartment," Prien ordered. It was 6:38 A.M.

Endrass' voice came over the intercom: "The captain will address the crew in the forward compartment."

After a few minutes, Prien, followed by Endrass and the other officers, went forward. It was a narrow compartment, its bulkhead painted white and perpetually sweating in the ubiquitous dampness, glistening in the glare of the grilled lamps. The narrow upper and lower bunks, mattressed by a green, foamlike substance, had been folded back against the bulkhead. The men waited, leaning against the ladders and pipes and bunks, confident that they were going to be told where they were going, that they would be freed of their burden of uncertainty.

Prien had prepared a short speech beforehand. Now, he looked around at the members of his crew, one after the other—forty-two men, each of whom had a precise technical function to perform. He decided not to make his speech. It would serve no purpose. Instead, in his clear, precise voice, he announced: "Tomorrow, we will enter an English shipping lane, the Scapa Flow."

2

Lying on the bottom 3 miles from the entry to Scapa Flow, under the very noses of the British destroyers patrolling continuously in the area whose ASDIC* were capable of detecting the smallest object beneath the surface, the U-47 played dead.

"Men on watch must wear soft-soled shoes," Endrass ordered.

---

* Acronym for Allied Submarine Detection Investigation Committee—an ultrasonic underwater detection device.

"Everyone else, into your bunks. No moving—and try to use as little oxygen as possible. There must be absolute silence. Reveille at 1600 hours. We attack at 1900 hours."

The submarine lay in total silence. The only sounds audible within were the creaks of the vessel as it rolled slightly on the sandy bottom, and the soft whistling of the air vents running on low speed.

Stretched out on his bunk in the motionless steel submarine, Commander Prien, for the first time, was worried. Behind the green curtain separating his quarters from the rest of the ship, out of sight of his officers and crew, he struggled vainly to subdue his anxiety. His was the sole responsibility for the lives of his men. They depended for survival upon his judgment, his coolness, his intelligence. And never had that responsibility seemed so enormous, so unbearable, as at this moment.

"War is war," Prien repeated to himself for the hundredth time. He tried to feel as certain of himself as he always had, as detached from doubt and emotion. The captain of a ship stands alone, and he has but one duty: to carry out the orders received from his superiors. The duty required that he be ready to risk everything. Whether his crew lived or died should be a matter of indifference to him; for, in war, success justified all things. Or, at least so he had been taught in the school at Danholm. And yet, the fact that the lives of these men were in his hands was a source of torment to him, and it prevented him from concentrating totally on his mission.

He passed his hands over his face, lined with fatigue from sleepless nights, from hours spent on watch. In a few hours, his submarine would be in Scapa Flow, the hitherto inviolate lair of the Home Fleet. It was situated at the northernmost point of Scotland, within the confused maze of Orkney Islands, and protected by an extraordinarily strong current.

Prien knew that his was, for all practical purposes, a suicide mission. During the First World War, two U-boats—one commanded by Emsmann, the other by Hemmings—had attempted the same mission. They had succeeded in entering the shipping lane, but they had both been sighted and, since they had been unable to make speed against the current, they had been sunk. Every man aboard his submarine, Prien knew, was aware of the fate of their predecessors. He knew, too, that his own engines would barely be strong enough to carry the *U-47* against the fatal current.

"Well, we'll see," he told himself.

So far as the mechanics of entering the lane were concerned, he was not worried. He knew precisely what to do in order to avoid the nets, the mines, and the depth charges which the British had deployed. The location of these traps was graven upon his memory. Commodore Karl Doenitz' headquarters had done an excellent job.

It had begun the preceding month, in September, a few days after the beginning of hostilities. And it had happened almost by accident. A small submarine (250 tons) was on a mission of surveillance to the east of the Orkneys, off Pentland Firth, in the stretch of water separating the islands from the Scottish mainland. It was a dangerous area because of the violent and unpredictable currents; and, as it turned out, the submarine's engines were unable to cope with these currents. The vessel's captain, taken unawares, allowed the submarine to be swept into the strait of Pentland Firth, and then he could do nothing but let the submarine drift among the innumerable underwater reefs. During this forced navigation in enemy waters, however, the captain was able to make some extremely important observations. His report, taken in conjunction with the information already obtained from spies and through aerial reconnaissance, made it possible for Admiral Doenitz and his staff to draw an exact map of the Scapa Flow port and of its defenses. As the result of a series of interminable conferences and studies of these maps, the project of a submarine raid was born. Doenitz then decided that the moment had come to execute the project.

On October 5, 1939, Prien, then a lieutenant commander, had

been summoned aboard the *Wechsel*, the flagship from which Commodore Doenitz masterminded the operations of the fifty-six U-boats which comprised his submarine command at the opening of hostilities.

Prien had no idea of what was behind the order to report to Doenitz. He was, in fact, uneasy about the whole thing. As he himself often admitted, a seaman on land was always apt to get into trouble, and he never had an easy mind except when at sea. As he climbed the gangplank of the *Wechsel*, he searched his conscience for an explanation, but found none. He had not offended any of his superiors. He had committed no blunders on his last mission off the Norwegian coast. And, above all, he had not engaged in any political activity. Politics, for that matter, held no interest for him. What, then, could Doenitz—the man whom submariners all called "the Lion"—possibly want with him?

Prien had been ushered into Doenitz' quarters immediately, and had stood facing the chief of the Grey Wolves and his assistant, Captain Godt. On Commodore Doenitz' desk was a thick folder. The walls were lined with maps showing the positions of Doenitz' submarines in their respective combat zones.

Doenitz had been affability itself. "Come in, Prien, come in. Sit down."

Then, when the young officer was seated, the chief went on: "Let me tell you that this is all going to be completely off the record." He had smiled, almost affectionately. "What I am going to say to you will be strictly among the three of us. Your answer, even if you say no, will be no reflection upon your honor or courage; and it will have no effect upon your career."

Doenitz was silent for a moment. Prien still had no idea what the commodore had in mind. He had not been certain that the Lion was not going to give him a reprimand of some kind, and Doenitz' words, while they relieved him, also increased his puzzlement.

The commodore stared briefly and hard at his young subordinate—Günther Prien was only twenty-four at the time—and

then smiled again. It was as though he was assuring himself that
he had chosen well; that Prien was the man best suited to the
job he had in mind, for he was the most levelheaded, as well as
the most determined and daring of all his submarine commanders.
Then he spoke: "Captain Godt will explain what this is all
about."

Godt, with a long wooden pointer in his hand, went to one
of the wall maps. He was a large, dark man, with an air of remote
gentleness about him. His black eyes were constantly in motion,
observing, recording. He was Doenitz' right hand and confidant.
In a low, almost monotonous voice, he explained that Prien
was being offered the opportunity to undertake a secret mission:
to enter the Scapa Flow, to do as much damage as possible to
British shipping there, and, if possible, to return alive.

Prien listened in silent astonishment. He tried to commit to
memory every detail of what he saw and what he was told. At
the same time, he tried to grasp all the implications of the
audacious enterprise described by Captain Godt.

"Do you think you'd be able to do it?" Doenitz asked. Then
he added immediately: "I'm not asking you to answer right away.
Take the next forty-eight hours to study the charts and our
intelligence reports—and to think about it calmly. Then let me
know your decision."

"Thank you, sir."

Prien saluted and left the commodore's office hurriedly. He did
not trust his ability to conceal his emotion and his joy. And his
fear.

As soon as he had left the *Wechsel* he began walking quickly
toward the room he occupied near the U-boat base. Distract-
edly, he returned the salutes of the sailors he encountered. He ran
into Lieutenant Commander Schepke, captain of the *U-100*—
on his way to the flagship, Prien guessed, to receive the usual
reprimand over some affair with a woman. He paused only
briefly, for he was eager to be alone in his room with the thick
folder which Doenitz had handed to him with the words, "Here,
you'll find everything that we know on Scapa Flow." It was a

heavy cardboard envelope, a corner of which had somehow been crushed, and it bore no exterior markings.

Once in his room, Prien threw his cap and overcoat over a chair, but he did not remove his jacket. He prided himself on always being in full uniform, even in his own quarters.

He sat at his desk, lit a cigarette, then slowly opened the folder and removed the photographs and maps which he spread over his desk and, when there was no more room, on his bed and, finally, on the floor. As he studied them, his forehead wrinkled, and the seaman's lines around his mouth and eyes deepened. He was astonished at the amount and precision of the information before his eyes, and at the perceptive comments, in Doenitz' own hand, scrawled in the margins. It was obvious that the commodore attached great importance to the success of the Scapa Flow mission. It was equally obvious that a striking U-boat victory at Scapa Flow would be of enormous help to him in arguing his case for submarines with the naval High Command. It would enable him once more to take the matter directly to Grand Admiral Erich Raeder. It might even open doors directly to Hitler himself. For Doenitz was convinced that the Führer did not realize the decisive role that U-boats could play in the war.

Until then, no one had listened to Doenitz. Neither Raeder, nor Goering, nor Hitler were willing to believe that a sufficiently large U-boat fleet alone, given Britain's naval might, was capable of bringing England to her knees. Since 1936, Doenitz had bombarded the naval High Command with memoranda on the subject, arguing that a fleet of three hundred submarines could, in case of war, give a decisive victory to the Third Reich.

But, on September 3, 1939, at 1540 hours, when war was declared, the chief of the Grey Wolves still had only fifty-six U-boats at his command. And, of these, ten were either training vessels or were laid up for repairs. Of the forty-six remaining vessels, only twenty-two were able to operate in Atlantic waters, since the cruising range of the others restricted them to the North Sea. The Atlantic was 450 miles away—so far that hardly more than a third of Doenitz' U-boats were capable of effective operation in those waters.

This situation was not without its effect on the temper of the Lion. Whether aboard the *Wechsel* or in the villa somewhere among the fields Swinemünde at Wilhelmshaven, where he had established his headquarters, Doenitz was in a constant fury. "The whole world imagines that we have hundreds of submarines scattered throughout the seas," he complained. "They are therefore afraid of us. The truth of the matter is that we're like an old lion who still looks ferocious, but who has lost his teeth." And he concluded: "Yet, the people at the Führer's headquarters expect us to cut Great Britain off from the rest of the world and starve her into surrender. Well, they're either ignorant—or mad."

More than once, Prien had heard Doenitz express his feelings with respect to the Nazi party and to Grand Admiral Raeder in bitter and dangerous terms. For Raeder, only the surface fleet, with its battleships and cruisers and destroyers, had any importance or striking power. Doenitz had once overheard him explain his philosophy of submarines to Hitler himself. "I don't deny that they're useful," he had said, "but we shouldn't exaggerate their importance."

The difference of opinion between Raeder, Goering, and Hitler on the one side, and Doenitz on the other, was so fundamental that it had degenerated into a real, though hidden, conflict. On the occasion of Doenitz' last visit to the Chancellery, Hitler had confined his remarks to Raeder and Goering and had pointedly ignored the little naval officer who dared maintain that there were forms of blitzkrieg other than the rumble of tanks and the scream of Stukas.

Prien knew all of this. He also knew that the Grey Wolves had got off to a bad start in this war. On September 4, 1939, a *U-30*, under the command of Captain Lamp, had torpedoed a ship traveling outside of the usual lanes. The vessel had been in total darkness and had been following a zigzag course, and Lamp had assumed it was a cruiser. It turned out, however, that his target had been a British passenger ship, the *Athenia*, with 1,400 people aboard. Hitler had been furious. He interpreted Lamp's error as a blow to his plan to preserve, in the war against Great Britain, an outward appearance of chivalrous conduct; and he personally disavowed the hapless U-boat captain. In this circumstance, Prien knew that only a dramatic military success would redeem the submarine service in Hitler's eyes and bring it recognition as an effective and separate combat arm. And this was the reason why, if he accepted the Scapa Flow mission, he wanted to be certain of succeeding; or, at least of having the qualities necessary for success. He had already decided that if he had any doubts about his qualifications for the command of such a mission, he would decline the offer so that some other, more qualified officer could undertake it.

By that evening, he knew the Scapa Flow file by heart. He knew every chart, every bottom, and the location of every enemy defense. He had weighed and analyzed everything with that maturity of judgment characteristic of men who spend their lives on the sea, and with that degree of seriousness which proceeds from the knowledge that the sea does not make allowances for human error.

Doenitz had given him forty-eight hours to decide. Prien did not have to wait any longer. He had already made up his mind. He replaced the documents in their folder and then put the folder in a drawer which he locked.

Now, as though relieved of a heavy burden, he realized that he was hungry. And, even though he usually did not drink, he felt in the mood for a glass of schnaps. He took his cap, put on his overcoat, and went out into the street. A light drizzle was falling, but it was hardly visible in the blackout which enshrouded the town of Wilhelmshaven. On foot, with a brisk step, Prien made his way to the Officers' Club. Upon entering, the first person he saw was Schepke. As usual, he was surrounded by several beautiful, laughing women.

The orchestra was playing a slow, romantic popular melody.

At a table to one side of the room, Prien saw Lieutenant Commander Kretschmer seated with several other officers. Kretschmer, as usual, was quiet, reserved, aristocratic. At other tables throughout the room were elegant and handsome women, some of them without escorts. Prien looked at them one after the other, his face impassive, his eyes cold. Women were his weak point. With them, he was uneasy, withdrawn. Many women found him attractive; but his air of aloofness always kept them at a distance.

Prien walked over to Kretschmer's table and sat down. He liked Kretschmer. He felt they understood each other, and he found him an agreeable companion. Kretschmer was slightly older than he; a cultivated man, always calm and rational. Prien and Kretschmer sometimes sat for hours together, with neither man saying a word.

At 9:30 A.M. on October 6, Prien stood at attention before Doenitz on the bridge of the *Wechsel*. But the chief of the submarine service did not look at his visitor. His eyes were on a report on his desk. Prien could see two large veins pulsing on Doenitz' forehead: a sign of tension, or of fatigue. It was well known that the commodore never slept more than three or four hours a night.

Suddenly, Doenitz raised his eyes and looked searchingly at Prien. His question was precise and to the point: "Well? Yes or no?"

"Yes, sir."

Doenitz rose and walked around his desk. He stood directly in front of Prien and asked: "You've thought it over?"

"Yes, sir."

"Very good. Then prepare your ship to get under way," Doenitz ordered. Then he clasped the hand of the young commander.

By afternoon, preparations were well under way aboard Prien's *U-47*; and the crew were already asking questions.

"Why are we taking on so little drinking water, Lieutenant?" Wilhelm asked Endrass.

"Why don't you ask the captain?"

"Because he wouldn't answer me if I did."

"Then do your work and don't ask any questions."

The crewmen working on the deck and below deck were wondering what kind of mission they were about to undertake. And, everywhere, Wilhelm was repeating, in a tone of perennial pessimism, "I've never seen a submarine take on so little food and fuel, and so many torpedoes."

By nightfall, the *U-47* was ready.

At 4 o'clock in the morning, on October 8, an automobile drew up to the gate of the submarine base. The sentry checked the identification of the occupants and then raised the gate. The automobile moved slowly onto the pier and stopped when it reached the gangplank of the *U-47*, where Lieutenant Endrass stood at attention. Commander Prien climbed out of the car, and Petty Officer Hanchlitt, a tall, thin Bavarian, raised his whistle to his lips and, to its strident notes, Captain Prien was piped aboard the waiting vessel.

"Everything is ready, sir," Endrass announced as he saluted.

Prien climbed rapidly aboard the submarine. His orderly handed him his leather coat. He stood on the conning tower and gave the order: "Loose all lines."

"All lines loosed, sir."

On the deck, hardly visible in the rain which had begun to fall, the crew busied themselves manipulating boat hooks and retrieving fenders. Then, a shudder went through the *U-47* as its diesels started up.

The *U-47* made its way slowly out of the port of Wilhelmshaven, wending its way past the great walls of the Banter Ruine to the left, and the oil tanks of the Groden ferry to the right. Once it had passed the main pier, the Kaiser Wilhelm Bridge, and Lock 2, the submarine was in the waters of the North Sea.

As the four men on watch scanned the sky through their infrared binoculars, the *U-47* began its precautionary trek toward

Scapa Flow, navigating on the surface at night in order to recharge its batteries, and beneath the surface during the day in
order to avoid being sighted by British ships.

This had been five days earlier.

3

In the forward compartment, behind the torpedo room, the
members of the crew were twisting and turning in their bunks.
No one slept. Now that they knew what their mission was, they
felt the weight of fear growing heavier as their submarine neared
its objective. The hardest thing to bear was the impossibility of
escaping from one's own thoughts. No one was allowed to move,
to talk, to engage in that humorous and sometimes indecent
small talk which was necessary to relax on board a submarine.
It did not help matters any that the heads had been placed off
limits.

Endrass did not sleep either. Stretched out on his bunk, he
thought of his fiancée. She lived in Hannover. The morning
before the *U-47* had left Wilhelmshaven, he had received a
telegram from the girl's mother: SYBIL VERY ILL. MUST ENTER
HOSPITAL IMMEDIATELY. STATE CRITICAL. But Endrass had not
been able to visit her. Since he was in charge of the loading of
the vessel, it was impossible for him to leave the pier. Now,
before him, was Scapa Flow.

In the crew's quarters, Wilhelm was also awake. The red-
haired giant was suffering. He twisted and clenched his teeth to
keep from moaning. The evening before, he had gone to a submariners' hangout near the base. He had intended to drink a
little; but, above all, he had wanted to find a girl. Girls were
very important to Wilhelm. Aboard ship, however, his acute
need for women was beneficial rather than otherwise. When the
submarine was in danger, he had only to think of a woman—of
her lips, her thighs—and, in an instant, he was free of the terror
which paralyzed everyone else aboard. No one knew why, at

the moment of the greatest danger, Wilhelm always seemed to remain calm and fearless.

Today, however, Wilhelm had two fractured ribs. His last night ashore had not had a happy ending. The girl he had chosen, it turned out, had been also selected by three other sailors before Wilhelm arrived, and they claimed priority over him. The three seamen—"minesweeper types," Wilhelm called them in his mind—had jumped him and, since Wilhelm had been alone, it had been a brief battle. A few punches, a few kicks, and Wilhelm was down. Then, a giant boot had descended with improbable swiftness and struck the submariner on the side. He had felt something crack in his chest, and there was a streak of unbearable pain. At that point, Wilhelm had fainted.

Anyone else would have been unable to move, but Wilhelm was like a force of nature. After a few hours of sleep, he felt almost like his old self again. Later, however, as he was climbing down the conning tower ladder, a sudden roll had sent him crashing against a handrail, and the pain in his side had re-awakened with a fury. During Prien's address to the crew, Wilhelm had almost fainted again. Unobtrusively, he had turned toward the bulkhead and extracted a small bottle of schnaps from the rock-hard pillow on his bunk. But the alcohol had done no good. The pain continued unabated; and now, because of the lack of oxygen aboard, an upset stomach added to his other discomforts.

By 3:57 in the afternoon, Prien could no longer lie still. He rose, put on felt-soled shoes, and walked through the submarine to see how his men were getting on. By 4 o'clock, he was in the control room. The men were taking turns standing, but everyone was groggy because of their prolonged immobility and because of the lack of fresh air. Slowly, noiselessly, they put on their damp green uniforms smelling of mildew. But then, everything aboard smelled of mildew, as it did in all submarines. Even the bread had the same smell, but no one threw it away. They kept it like a treasure, to dip in their soup.

Toward the end of the afternoon, Günther Prien gave an order which delighted the crew and helped them bear the tension of waiting. To the cook, he said: "Tonight, the holiday menu!"

At 6 o'clock, the men, some sitting on the lower bunks, some leaning against the table, and some crowded into the central compartment, ate in silence their double ration of sausages, eggs, cabbage, cheese, and preserved fruit with dry cake. Then Prien personally distributed vitamin-enriched chocolate and caffeine pills. Everyone would need them, Prien reflected, to fight against sleep, fatigue, and discouragement.

At 7:15, the crew were ordered to go to their battle stations. Their faces were drained of color, and there were many who could not conceal the trembling of their lips and their knees. No one spoke. In the control room, the engineering officer was busy getting the U-47 under way again. The submarine's decks vibrated, the hold pumps rumbled, and the electric engines started up. The Grey Wolf stirred gently, lazily. Like a sleeper who had just awakened, it rolled slightly and shuddered as it returned to life. The scraping of the keel against the sandy bottom combined with, and then was drowned out by the sound of water being expelled from the ballast tanks. The U-47 began to rise.

Prien, standing in the cramped control room, his white cap spotted with grease and oil, ordered: "Rise to periscope depth."

The engines turned slowly so as to avoid disturbing the water as the submarine rose toward the surface. At a depth of 45 feet, the engineer announced: "Periscope depth, Captain."

It was a critical moment. It would have taken very little for the appearance of the periscope to signal the U-47's last moment of life. If there were destroyers patrolling the surface; if the rising of the periscope caused bubbles; if the sonar devices of the British gave their piercing *ping-ping* warning, then it would be all over for the submarine. It would be sighted and immediately fired upon and destroyed.

Everyone aboard the U-47 knew that their lives hung in the balance during those few intolerable seconds of time. Everyone cringed, instinctively, pulling their heads down toward their shoulders in a childish and utterly useless gesture of self-protection.

Prien glanced at his men. He knew what they were going through. Therefore he lost no time. The sailor on duty had already pressed the lever and the periscope rose in its sheath of steel. A green light went on, signaling that the eye of the U-47 had broken the surface.

Prien, both hands on the periscope's handles, made a rapid, detailed, and precise survey of the horizon. Then, with his right hand, he adjusted the mirror to 70°: the sky was empty. Quickly, he lowered the eye to the level of the surface: it was also empty. With his left hand, he deftly manipulated the lever which made the periscope rise and fall in keeping with the height of the waves and the movement of the submarine.

Then Prien smiled, intentionally, so that everyone could see him; and the men, who had been holding their breath, heaved a collective sigh of relief.

"The English are asleep," Prien announced over the intercom, so that the message would be heard throughout the vessel.

The sailors looked at one another and smiled. The first moment of danger before the attack had passed without incident.

"Surface," Prien ordered.

The four men who, in a few minutes, would be on watch above, were standing ready next to the metal ladder, wearing their red-tinted glasses and nervously wiping the lenses of their binoculars. Prien, when the time came, also put on his glasses.

Fear had now faded aboard the U-47. The men were all concentrating on their jobs. Each one of them was aware that the least distraction, the slightest error on his part, might well cause the loss of the submarine and, consequently, his own death.

"Conning tower above the surface, Captain," the engineering officer announced.

When the time required for decompression had passed, Prien opened the hatch, and, closely followed by the watch officer, von Varrendorf, he went above. Both men immediately scanned the horizon once more. Their minute scrutiny revealed only

emptiness. It was true. Northern Scotland's most important war-
time port was without protection. Everyone, apparently, was
asleep.

"It's incredible," Prien muttered. Then he ordered: "Keep a
sharp eye out. Start up the engines!"

The electric engines were silenced, and their hum was replaced by the roaring of the diesels, which shortly was drowned
out by the noise of the wind and waves.

"With all this damned light," Prien groaned, "it will be a
miracle if we're not sighted." He was right. The huge bay, surrounded by steep, black mountains, was illuminated and outlined with fatal clarity by the aurora borealis. For a moment,
Prien seriously considered postponing the attack. But he decided
against it. It would be impossible. The next night, the currents
would be even stronger than they were then. And, above all, the
nerves of the crew would never survive another twenty-four
hours of waiting.

"All engines, half speed ahead," he ordered.

The U-47 moved toward Scapa Flow. It passed Holm Sound,
and there was still no sign of the British Navy or the Royal Air
Force. But, although the aurora borealis lighted the bay brightly,
visibility was poor beyond the bay's perimeter. Then Prien's
heart stopped. A dark, threatening silhouette emerged from the
darkness about a mile away: a destroyer.

Luck was with the U-47. Before Prien had had time to give
the order to dive, the destroyer was swallowed up again by the
darkness out of which it had come.

But there were other, and perhaps greater dangers. The U-47,
pitching and rolling among the waves, was suddenly seized
with terrifying violence by the current of the Orcades. Prien,
without taking his eyes from the bow of the submarine, ordered
von Varrendorf to go below. "I will stay on deck alone," he
explained.

Von Varrendorf disappeared through the hatch without a word,
but with a terrifying sight graven upon his memory. Directly
ahead of the U-47, he had seen the barrier which the British
had erected to protect Scapa Flow—a barrier composed of sunken

ships, floating mines, and steel nets. And the submarine, in the grip of the current, was being carried at full speed toward this deadly array.

The *U-47* was tossing like a cork in the water. It required all of Prien's ability, all his knowledge of the charts confided to him by Doenitz, to keep his vessel on course so as to avoid instant destruction. Giving orders to the helmsman, and aiding the rudder by variations in speed, he slalomed like an experienced skier among the sunken British ships.

Then, without warning, a tremendous crash reverberated throughout the hull of the submarine. Below, everyone blanched with fear. Had they run into a net? Immediately, the bulkheading was searched for signs of leaks while the men held on, as best they could, to anything which was bolted down.

The *U-47*, in maneuvering to avoid a net, had struck the anchor chain of a sunken ship, and the submarine, carried along by the current, had leaped entirely out of the water. When it fell back, there was an ominous cracking sound. Prien, holding on with all his strength to the railing of the conning tower, was certain that his submarine must either break in two or capsize.

But the Grey Wolf's luck had held. The near-catastrophe was followed immediately by a calm and silent sea. The howling of the wind and waves ceased, and the *U-47* was once more on course. The current of the Orcades had loosed its grip.

Prien sighed with relief. He had won the first round. He leaned over the hatchway and spoke through the acoustical tube to the crew whose terror he sensed, understood, and shared:

"We are in Scapa Flow."

It was 11:15 P.M.

4

Wilhelm, smiling his big smile, pulled out from under his shirt a piece of silk as light and filmy as a spider's web. It was a woman's stocking, which he had found floating on the water several weeks before. The stocking had become the good-luck piece of the *U-47*. The men passed it back and forth among themselves, some of them squeezing it, and a few of them kissing it. Even the officers did not refuse to hold it when it was passed to them. Then, when everyone had touched it, Wilhelm carefully replaced it under his shirt.

The immense bay was as silent as though abandoned. Prien decided to make a half circle, in the direction of Cava. To the south, not a single ship was sighted. Prien then chose to skirt the coastline in returning toward the north; and through his binoculars he was able to make out the dark, looming forms of ships.

"Full speed ahead," he ordered.

Since entering Scapa Flow, Prien had never ceased wondering why the English had not been alerted to his presence by the noise of the submarine's diesels. It seemed a miracle that no sentinel and no watch officer had seen the dark, slender silhouette of his vessel.

Furtively the Grey Wolf drew near its prey. Two large ships, with enormous superstructures, were perfectly visible against the bright sky. Prien's heart missed a beat when he recognized them. They were both battleships. One was the *Royal Oak;* the other, the *Repulse*. There was only one thing wrong. They were lying at quincunx, with the *Royal Oak* hiding a part of the *Repulse*.

Prien took only an instant to make his decision. At slow speed, the *U-47* glided toward the *Repulse*.

"Prepare to fire," the captain ordered.

"Ready, Captain."

"Tubes 1 to 4. Simultaneous firing."

It was the second officer, Lieutenant Endrass, who took aim through the periscope. He saw the *Repulse* clearly outlined against the trigger hairs, and immediately pulled the firing lever.

"Fire!"

The *U-47* shuddered as the four torpedoes sped from their tubes.

Prien, still above on deck, mentally followed the course of the projectiles through the water and counted the seconds. The torpedoes, invisible in the black water, sped toward their target as Prien and Endrass prayed for them to strike the mark.

Suddenly, there was an enormous explosion, and an incredible column of water rose from the surface. The forward section of the *Repulse* was thrust from the water like a great and mortally wounded beast. Then, the British battleship began listing rapidly as it was enveloped in flames. The water around it began to boil furiously.

Neither Prien nor Endrass took pride in their accomplishment. They were overwhelmed by the realization that the three other torpedoes, those aimed at the *Royal Oak*, had missed their target. What had gone wrong? Had they been badly aimed? Or was it because the torpedoes themselves, once more, were defective? At the thought, Prien was overcome by a blind rage.

The explosion which was to sink the *Repulse* took place at 58 minutes past midnight. It was now two minutes past 1 A.M. and, incredibly, there was still no sign of life among the British. Silence lay once more over Scapa Flow, and the warships still lay quietly at anchor. The British did not seem to realize what had happened.

"Well," Prien said, "let's take advantage of the situation." He knew that the enemy's reaction might come from one instant to the next. At any moment, the bay might be swept by searchlights, and the *U-47* would be a sitting duck from the big guns of the destroyers and the coastal batteries.

Prien, knowing the risks, gave the order: "Reload tubes 1 to 4."

"Tubes 1 to 4 ready, Captain."

This time, Prien wanted to take no chances. He brought the submarine to within 450 yards of the *Royal Oak*. And Endrass, as soon as he saw the battleship in the periscope's sight, pushed the firing lever.

"Fire!"

The suspense was brief. This time, two giant columns of water rose, and two tremendous explosions reverberated over Scapa

Flow. The torpedoes had been on target, and the debris of the battleship's superstructure, pieces of its guns, fragments of its plate armor, and human bodies, were thrown into the air by the violence of the explosions. They fell back into the bay around the *U-47*.

The port was finally alerted to the presence of the enemy. Lights suddenly appeared on the ships, horns and sirens echoed through the night, and frantic signals were sent out in Morse code.

The submarine's torpedo tubes were now empty, and Prien knew that it was time to leave. Already searchlights were sweeping over the water. The headlights of an automobile, coming from Kirkwall and traveling along the shore, struck the conning tower of the *U-47* for an instant as the vehicle continued along its route.

Had they been seen? Prien dared not even consider the possibility. Time was wasting. He had to get his vessel out of these dangerous waters before it was discovered by the cruisers, destroyers, corvettes, and gunboats.

"Full speed ahead!"

The submarine moved forward rapidly toward the passage leading out of the bay, the same passage the entry through which it had barely survived. This time, however, the difficulty was the reverse of what it had been earlier. Coming into the bay, Prien had had to struggle not to be taken by the current. Now, he had to fight to go against the current.

"Maximum speed! Let's get as much as we can out of the engines!"

The propellers spun wildly, and, on each side of the submarine, the water boiled and foamed. The vessel trembled, groaned in its struggle against the current. Prien kept his eyes on the reference point he had established for himself: the wreckage of an old coasting vessel. He bit his lips in rage and frustration. The *U-47*'s engines were not powerful enough to make headway against the current. The submarine seemed not to have moved an inch. It was as though it were stationary in its remote corner of the bay.

Suddenly Prien turned. The sound of two guns firing from the east split the night. And the sound was coming closer. It was a destroyer. "Maximum power!" he shouted down the voice tube.

"Captain," a subdued and shaking voice replied, "we're already running at full power." Then the voice added: "The engine room reports that a seam is coming loose."

The destroyer's guns seemed to be zeroing in. Their projectiles were landing only a half mile away. Then, suddenly, the ship's great floods cut through the night, sweeping over the water.

"Well," Prien said to himself. "This is it. It's all over." He was overcome by disappointment and disgust. He had done the impossible; and now, to finish like this, without being able even to fight back. It was too stupid to be borne; too unjust.

Like a tongue of flame, the port searchlight of the destroyer licked for a moment at the U-47's deck and then continued its sweep over the waves. Prien could see that the ship was drawing closer and closer. Then, he gave an order: "Load the gun!" Since we're going to die anyway, he told himself, we had just as soon go down fighting.

Wilhelm appeared on deck and, despite the rolling and pitching of the U-47, made his way quickly to the 105, closely followed by the second gunner.

Then the miracle occurred. The destroyer was no more than 200 yards behind the submarine when it suddenly changed course and began making for the entry to the bay.

"Go below!" Prien shouted to the gunners who stood on the forward deck, paralyzed by astonishment as they watched the dark silhouette of the destroyer disappearing into the night.

"I said, go below!"

Like men in a dream, Wilhelm and his assistant obeyed after a final glance at the wake of the enemy ship which was now moving through the passage. Behind the U-47, clusters of foam bore witness to the speed of its engines in the white-crested sea.

They're bound to come back, Prien thought. His throat was dry.

Prien, distracted by the destroyer, had lost sight of his point of reference. Now he found it again, and noticed that its position relative to the U-47 had changed. The submarine was making progress, albeit slowly, against the current. At a speed of 14 knots, it was moving painfully forward, yard by yard, toward escape.

A sudden scraping noise to port made Prien jump. The U-47's hull was sideswiping a huge wooden pontoon floating, half submerged, in the passage. He paled; and the men below, their foreheads bathed in sweat, their hands moist with tension and fear, looked at one another. But neither the captain nor the crew had time to do more than register an initial reaction. For, at that instant, the terrible current loosed its hold on the submarine, and the U-47 plunged forward at full speed into the open sea, like a dog who, by straining on its leash, finally succeeds in breaking it. There was a great lurch, and the men below were thrown to the greasy, oily deck. Prien, on the conning tower, lost his balance and was thrown against the periscope. There was a sharp pain in his back, but he rose immediately, leaned toward the voice tube, and ordered: "Maintain full speed."

Behind the U-47, the Scapa Flow bay was an inferno of detonations and explosions. The British could not believe that the Grey Wolf had escaped from the trap, and the cruisers, destroyers, gunboats, and coastal batteries were bombarding the center of the bay and launching depth charges blindly. To the north, two immense bonfires were visible, the flames rising into the night sky: the *Repulse*, and the *Royal Oak*, both of which were listing as they burned. On their decks, half-naked men milled about in terror. Some of them had been wounded. Some jumped over the side, while others tried to lower the lifeboats.

Suddenly, the U-47 was sighted by a coastal battery, and immediately all guns were trained on the submarine and opened fire. Prien maintained his course at full speed, and however threatening the salvos booming across the water, the shells fell harmlessly in the wake of the submarine.

The U-47 was now five miles to the east of the bay's entry, and Prien gave the order for a turn to the north. In a few seconds, his submarine was hidden in the shadow of the mountains surrounding the anchorage of the Home Fleet.

The Grey Wolf's luck had held to the end.

The sea was very rough, and the U-47 rolled violently in the waves. Prien, alone on the tower, with a wool cap on his head, shivered with cold and tension. Finally, he could bear no more. He was too numb even to protect himself from the sheets of icy water which swept over the tower and drenched him. He leaned toward the voice tube: "This is the captain," he said. "We've left Scapa Flow—and we're still alive. We've sunk one battleship and damaged another." As he spoke, he glanced at his watch. It was 3 o'clock in the morning. It had taken an hour and a half for the U-47 to work its way out of Scapa Flow and into the open sea.

From every compartment of the submarine, a great shout went up. The crew, finally free of the anguish which had held them in its grip for the past twenty-two hours, sent up a mighty hurrah. It was a strange shout, almost inhuman; a cry which delivered the forty-two men aboard of the fear with which they had lived.

Prien turned away from the tube. In the distance, far beyond the crests of the mountains, he could see the red glow over Scapa Flow.

"Prepare to dive," he ordered.

5

On the morning of October 16, the sea was gray and turbulent; the weather, cold and dry. Endrass, with a container of red paint and a brush in his hands, appeared on the forward deck. Making his way to the conning tower, he began painting on the gray steel surface as several sailors watched him curiously from the hatch.

"What on earth are you doing?" Prien asked in astonishment.

"Well, sir," Endrass answered, "the men saw a drawing in one of the magazines they were reading during our mission. It was a bull—a bull with its horns lowered, and jets of smoke coming from its nostrils. It struck them that the U-47 resembled that bull. It, too, is full of courage, and ready to attack. They'd like the animal to become the emblem of our submarine, and that from now on the U-47 be known as 'the Bull of Scapa Flow.'"

"An excellent idea," Prien said. And, after he had carefully examined Endrass' work, he added: "You are not without a certain artistic talent, Lieutenant."

At 2:27 P.M., on October 17, the Bull of Scapa Flow entered its home port of Wilhelmshaven. As it moved slowly toward its pier, it received the salutes of the warships at anchor: a deafening chorus of sirens, horns, and whistles. Sailors on the piers and decks tossed their caps into the air in a gesture of welcome.

On the conning tower of the U-47, Prien, with Endrass and the men on watch, savored these moments of glory. On the rear deck, several of the crew stood smartly at attention.

When the submarine reached its pier, the gangplank was lowered and Prien descended to meet the crowd of superior officers from the *Kriegsmarine*, the Luftwaffe and the Wehrmacht who were waiting for him in their dress uniforms, glittering with braid and decorations.

Commodore Doenitz was there, standing slightly forward of the others, waiting. Prien stopped before his superior and saluted. Doenitz returned the salute, and as the band began playing the national anthem, all the officers and men came stiffly to attention. When the anthem was over, an overwhelming shout of enthusiasm, a giant hurrah, rose from a thousand throats and echoed through the port.

Doenitz then went aboard the U-47. Smiling, and obviously

moved, he presented each officer with the Iron Cross, First Class, and each sailor with the Iron Cross, Second Class. As he distributed the decorations, he clasped the hand of every man aboard, and said: "Thank you."

When the commodore went down the gangplank, the men grinned and nudged one another proudly. They were heroes. They knew that there was not a sailor in port that day who did not envy them.

Prien's voice suddenly came through the loudspeaker: "This is the captain. I want every man to be standing on the pier in five minutes. I've just been handed a message. A Luftwaffe plane is going to fly us to Kiel, and then to Berlin. The Führer is expecting us tomorrow at the Chancellery."

When the forty-two men landed at Kiel, they were led to a large building and each of them was handed a bar of perfumed soap, a towel, and shaving equipment. Then they were shown to the shower room. Before being allowed to enter, however, they were required to pass through a production line consisting of several master tailors and their assistants, who took the measurements of every man, and seven barbers—all working at top speed. Then the heroes were hustled into the showers and told that they had twenty-five minutes to rid themselves of the smell of oil and mildew which had been with them since October 7.

An hour and twenty minutes later, scrubbed and outfitted in new uniforms which had been altered to their individual measurements, the men of the U-47 were on their way to the airport. Three hours later, they landed in Berlin and were taken by bus to the Kaiserhof, the city's most prestigious palace.

The sailors had hardly settled into the unaccustomed luxury of their accommodations when they heard the shouts of a large crowd of people outside of the hotel, demanding to see the heroes of Scapa Flow. When the men appeared on the steps of the palace, they were mobbed by admirers who broke through the police lines to see, touch, and, if possible, to embrace, the men of the U-47.

It was 2:30 in the afternoon. For the forty-two men, their contact with the worshiping crowd marked the beginning of an afternoon and evening of unadulterated pleasure and unprecedented respect. No sooner was any one of them recognized on the street than he was subjected to a barrage of invitations. Wilhelm, for his part, went from one girl to another. Never before had he been so successful in his favorite pursuit.

Meanwhile, back at the Kaiserhof, an SS captain sank slowly into despair. His orders were to prepare the sailors for their audience with the Führer, and especially to coach them in the answers to Hitler's questions, in what to say about the Nazi party, and—above all—to order them not to mention that, during any phase of their mission, they had felt the slightest fear. But the men had disappeared into the welcoming mob before he had been able to talk to them. The captain, in other words, had not been able to carry out his orders. And, for an SS officer, this was very serious indeed. So, he paced in anguish within the glittering Kaiserhof, waiting for the heroes to return.

He was still there when the men began to drift in, or rather to be carried in, between 3 and 6 o'clock the following morning. Some were brought back by the civilian friends with whom they had caroused all night. Some were hustled in, shouting and singing, by the military police, who treated their charges with unaccustomed gentleness. And a few walked in under their own power, accompanied by women from whom they were separated only with the greatest difficulty and over the vehement protests of the women. Whatever their condition, they had, one and all, to be ordered to go to bed.

At 9 o'clock in the morning, in the Kaiserhof, Prien inspected his crew as they stared back at him through red, swollen eyes. Then he gave them a blistering lecture on military comportment. Afterward, he led them into an adjoining room for breakfast, where photographers, cameramen, and journalists were waiting. The cameras snapped away, the film rolled, and the journalists scribbled. But no questions were asked. The SS captain had forbidden anyone to speak to the exhausted heroes of Scapa Flow.

By 9:30, eleven gray army convertibles were waiting in front of the Kaiserhof. As soon as the men were seated in the vehicles, four to a vehicle, with Prien and Endrass in the lead automobile, the convoy began to move through the streets of the capital toward the Chancellery. It was a triumphal procession in the classic sense. Arches of flowers had been erected, and the streets were lined by shouting, cheering people. The ovation continued until the convoy reached the Chancellery. Only one man had not enjoyed the parade: a young sailor named Staub, who had a stomach ache and fell asleep against Wilhelm's shoulder in the car. An enterprising photographer snapped a picture of the scene, but two policemen quickly confiscated his camera and exposed the film.

At the Chancellery, the Führer's guard of honor, uniformed in black, presented arms as Prien, followed by the officers and men of the U-47, entered the building. They were received in the Grand Salon by Doenitz and his chief-of-staff, Commander Godt. A few feet away from him, surrounded by high-ranking officers of the Navy and the other branches of the service, were Grand Admiral Raeder, *Reichsmarschall* Goering, Dr. Goebbels, and General Keitel.

After a few moments, two carved wooden doors were thrown open and the Führer himself entered the room. Escorted by Raeder and Doenitz, he inspected the now world-famous crew of the U-47. He shook the hand of every man and, his eyes fixed upon theirs, he spoke to each of them, inquiring about their families and their plans for the future.

Never before had the Führer's officers seen him so happy and so much at ease. They were familiar with his quixotic changes of mood, his instant transitions from amiability to rage without warning and without apparent reason. Yet, with the submariners he was a model of sustained cordiality.

To Endrass, Hitler said with enthusiasm: "I envy you for belonging to this elite group. How I'd love to share the excitement of your work—to leap upon the enemy as you do. Submariners are models of what our fighting men should be. I'd like for every one of our soldiers to have the same courage and determination that you do!"

Doenitz then addressed the Führer. Ordinarily, when he spoke, it was to recite figures and statistics, or to give a technical explanation. But on this occasion he spoke with obvious emotion as he said: "My Führer, the deeds of these men of the *U-47* demonstrate the value of the submarine service. You've said you admire their courage, which has indeed been exemplary. But their courage would have been to no avail if they had not each been able to win a difficult and individual victory beforehand— a victory over fear and over death."

At these words, Hitler frowned. He disliked any talk of fear. Soldiers should never know fear; and they should be willing to accept death in combat. That, after all, was part of the soldier's contract.

The men of the *U-47*, however, were touched by the commodore's words. They knew that Doenitz understood what they had experienced; for, in 1918, he had known the same fear. And, perhaps worse, he had been a prisoner in England. They were aware, above all, that Doenitz knew every one of them, and that he suffered deeply whenever one of his crews was reported missing. There, in the Grand Salon of the Chancellery, standing among the highest dignitaries of the Third Reich, Prien's men felt that they were a group apart; that they were truly what Goering, with thinly veiled contempt, had called them: "Doenitz' bunch."

"I can see that you have a high regard for your men," Hitler replied to Doenitz. "That is as it should be. This is a great day for us. The fighting men of Germany have shown the world that they are capable of great deeds, and I want to show my appreciation for what you have accomplished. Therefore, I hereby promote you to the rank of vice-admiral."

Everyone in the room applauded.

"As for Commander Prien," the Führer continued, "I bestow

on him the Knight's Cross, with palms. He is the first combat soldier to receive this supreme distinction in the present war."

Hitler then took Prien by the arm and led him into his office, with Doenitz and Raeder following. The rest of the men were taken in charge by a group of SS officers who led them on a tour of the Chancellery. The tour was to take an hour, and, afterward, they were to regroup in the Grand Salon for a final word with the Führer.

As the tour began, Wilhelm asked the officer who was his guide, "Isn't there anything to drink around here?"

"The Führer doesn't smoke or drink. Therefore, no one in the Chancellery smokes or drinks."

At the end of the tour, the men returned, as planned, to the Grand Salon. There, they found Doenitz and Prien waiting for them. Everyone else had disappeared. Prien explained that the Führer had been called away on a matter of urgency, and that he sent his apologies.

That was not quite the truth. The fact was that the interview in Hitler's office had not gone well. After the Führer had listened to Prien give a detailed report on his mission to Scapa Flow, he had turned to Doenitz and asked: "Well, Admiral, what do you plan next?"

As a tactician and leader of men, Doenitz was widely admired and respected. But, as a diplomat, he left something to be desired. "Miracles," he answered bluntly, "are never repeated. From now on, the task of the submarine service is going to become more and more difficult to accomplish."

Hitler scowled, but Doenitz pushed on: "The mission of our U-boats is simply to sink enemy ships faster than replacements can be built. But, with the small number of submarines at our disposal, I cannot promise that we will be able to carry out that mission in the months ahead. I must call your attention to the fact that, since 1937, I have been asking for an increase in the number of our submarines. And I submit that no one has listened to me. So, I must tell you now that, unless we increase our production of submarines, I cannot give you any guarantees of success for the future."

Hitler, his face somber, his hands clasped behind his back, said not a word. Prien had the impression that he was trying to maintain control over his temper. For several very long minutes an ominous silence filled the room. Then the Führer turned to Raeder. "Tell the admiral," he said, "that he shall have his submarines. And tell him," he added in a scathing tone, "that submarines are not the only thing that I have to worry about."

Then Hitler turned on his heel and stomped out of the room, without another word, slamming the door behind him. Grand Admiral Raeder, with a disapproving glance at Doenitz, followed him, leaving Doenitz and Prien alone in the room.

"Don't repeat a word of what you've just seen and heard," Doenitz cautioned Prien.

"You have my word," Prien answered. And then he added familiarly: "If you ask me, Admiral, it would be a good idea for us to take a few of these gentlemen along with us on our next mission. Maybe then they'd have a better understanding of what it's all about."

Doenitz smiled sadly and said in a strained voice: "Prien, you've learned something today: that, in time of war, the enemy is not always the greatest danger we have to face. To beat England today, I'd need a hundred submarines in simultaneous operation. At the moment, I have six."

Part Two

THE WOLF PACK

6

There was no autumn in 1939, the first year of the war. Instead, winter came early, bringing with it an unbroken series of storms. For months, Admiral Doenitz' U-boats were tossed and covered by waves as they pitched and rolled among the crests, fighting against the swell in the howling wind. It was a difficult time for the submarine crews, but they lived up to Doenitz' expectations of his Grey Wolves in their eagerness for combat. The U-boats were playing an important role in the war, despite the skepticism of Grand Admiral Raeder and of Hitler himself. The Grey Wolves had scored their first important success exactly one month and four days before the *U-47's* great victory at Scapa Flow.

On September 17, 1939, about 200 miles southwest of Ireland, the *U-29*, under the command of Lieutenant Commander Schuhart, had sighted the aircraft carrier *Courageous,* escorted by four destroyers. Thanks to a particular maneuver on the part of the *Courageous,* the submarine suddenly found itself in a good firing position. Two commands were given aboard the U-boat: *Rohr ein . . . Torpedo, los! Rohr zwei . . . Torpedo, los!* The two torpedoes streaked through the water, striking their target with deadly accuracy. In six minutes, the *Courageous* had disappeared beneath the surface, taking five hundred men down with her. The explosions had been of such force that the *U-29*, lying a thousand yards from the carrier, had been tossed about violently. And then, the submarine was sighted by the escort destroyers and subjected to a depth-charge assault which lasted for six hours.

The remarkable victories of Schuhart and of Prien had enraged the British Admiralty, and it had been decided immediately to evacuate Scapa Flow and the northern ports. Winston Churchill, First Lord of the Admiralty, explained to Commons that "Our primary effort must be aimed at the destruction of the German submarines. We must take urgent and draconian measures if England is to regain her freedom of movement on the seas."

The success of Doenitz' Grey Wolves was not the only matter of grave concern to the Home Fleet. The Germans had perfected a new naval weapon, a magnetic mine, and Doenitz had dispatched his U-boats to lay almost 250 of these devices across the lanes and passes of the North Sea. The result was an undeniable disaster for the British.

Every night, the U-boats slipped into the entries of British ports themselves, into the bays and even into the mouths of rivers, laying their deadly mines. There were thirty-four such missions, and the results were spectacular: 115 British ships sunk, totaling 395,000 tons of shipping. On December 4, 1939, the battleship *Nelson* and the cruiser *Belfast* were seriously damaged by magnetic mines laid in the Firth of Forth by a submarine under the command of Captain Frauenheim. At the same time, the Grey Wolves continued their attacks on British and French shipping, sinking some 199 ships, totaling 700,000 tons between September 3, 1939, and February 29, 1940.

Despite the spectacular success of his tiny submarine fleet, Doenitz remained pessimistic. "This war," he told his officers with a conviction so impressive that the memory of it still remained thirty years afterward, "will be a long one. And the best that Germany can hope for in the end is a negotiated peace."

Convinced nationalist that he was, and devoted soldier, the admiral did not allow his doubts to affect his life's work. He was the creator of Germany's submarine fleet, and his duty was clear; to do the impossible so that his Grey Wolves might help his country attain victory—and to carry on with his task no matter what the shortcomings and errors of the political leaders of the Reich.

"In Berlin," he explained to Commander Godt, his chief-of-staff, "they don't understand that we can't give the British time to get sufficiently organized to survive these first, very difficult months of the war. The British have almost inexhaustible naval resources. They make use of these resources only gradually, but they always finish by winning. We must strike the death blow immediately. If we wait, then it will be too late."

During the first months of the war, Admiral Doenitz was obsessed by two goals. The first was to obtain, as quickly as possible, a sufficiently large number of submarines to strike a decisive blow against Great Britain. The second was to make optimum use of the few Grey Wolves actually at his disposal. And, for the latter, he depended heavily upon the skill and courage of the U-boat crews which he had trained before the war.

Then, suddenly, he had a new concern: the effectiveness of his torpedoes.

On September 17, 1939, the *U-39*, under the command of Lieutenant Commander Glattes, had sighted the carrier *Ark Royal*. Three torpedoes, equipped with magnetic fuses, had been fired —and all three had exploded before striking their target. The *U-39* had then been discovered and sunk by the carrier's escort destroyers.

Had it been merely an incredible coincidence that all three torpedoes had misfired? Any doubt that Doenitz may have had on that score was banished by an incident which occurred on October 30. On that day, a message was received from the *U-56*, commanded by Lieutenant Commander Zahn: "10 o'clock, sighted *Rodney, Nelson, Hood* and ten destroyers . . . Fired three torpedoes. Misfire due to faulty fuses." The captain and crew of the *U-56* had been wholly mystified. They had clearly heard the torpedoes strike the hull of the *Nelson*—but there had been no explosions. And, as it happened, the deadliest enemy of the Third Reich, Winston Churchill, had been aboard the *Nelson* that day.

When the *U-56* returned to Wilhelmshaven, its captain, suffering from severe depression, had had to be taken to a hospital and placed under observation. Zahn, an experienced combat officer who had dared attack the *Nelson* as the carrier nestled securely among its twelve escort destroyers, was crying like an infant.

The commanders of the Grey Wolves, despite their eagerness for contact with the enemy, were beginning to ask themselves: "Why take such risks when our torpedoes are so shoddy that we'll only get ourselves killed?"

Under cover of darkness, the *U-100* of Lieutenant Commander Schepke was cruising about 12 miles off the English coast. Schepke could see the flat, low-lying coastline despite a light fog. Suddenly, a sailor nudged Schepke and pointed. The captain raised his binoculars in the direction indicated by the sailor and was able to make out the long, dark shape of a destroyer on a course which would soon bring it squarely between the U-boat and the coast. Immediately, the alert was sounded, followed by the order: "Prepare tube 1!"

"Tube 1 ready, Captain."

There was a lapse of a few seconds; then—"Fire!"

The torpedo sped through the night as Schepke followed its wake with his binoculars. He saw it strike the destroyer slightly under the keel. But there was no explosion. A chorus of curses rose from the captain and the crew of the U-boat. Another fuse had malfunctioned! Then an explosion shattered the night and echoed interminably over the sea. The torpedo had indeed exploded, but not on target. Deflected by the steel hull of the destroyer, it had turned aside and plunged toward the shore, striking and destroying a fishing boat on the beach.

Schepke and his second officer immediately turned toward the destroyer. The U-boat had been sighted, and the white foam from the destroyer's prow was clearly visible from the conning tower as the British ship sped toward the *U-100*. Its floodlights moved over the surface and its guns fired the first salvo at the Grey Wolf.

"Dive! Dive!" Schepke shouted, and the men on deck rushed toward the hatch. Anyone who climbed down the ladder too slowly was in danger of being kicked in the head by the man following him.

Schepke himself was the last to go below. After securing the hatch, he dropped into the control room and threw himself on the deck as the U-100, its nose dangerously low, began a crash dive to the bottom.

"We're taking on water!" the engineering officer shouted.

The U-100 dropped like a stone, and its nose struck the bottom violently. Under the impact, the hull cracked ominously, and the electrical system went out. Trickles of water ran down the bulkheads of the control room. Schepke could hear the noise of the destroyer's engines as the vessel approached, passed overhead, and then continued on its way. Everyone was silent. They knew what to expect, and everyone held on tightly to whatever fixed object they could grasp. Then it began. Depth charges exploded around them without cease, and the U-100 tossed and turned on the rocky bottom. Paint detached itself in sheets from the hull. Numb with terror, the men of the U-100 felt as though they were trapped within a cyclone.

Five hours later, at dawn, Schepke's U-100, under cover of a dense fog, managed to limp away from the spot which had almost become its tomb—all because of a torpedo which had not worked properly.

The winter of 1940 finally ended, and the thick layers of ice which had covered the Baltic and the North Sea, transforming the watch into a torture, melted. The arctic wind, which had so long lined the faces and burned the eyes of those on watch, grew gentler. Life once more became bearable aboard Doenitz' U-boats. For months, it had required an enormous expenditure of energy to continue their combat missions off the coast of Norway and in the fjörds. The temperature on the surface was sometimes —25°; and, below the surface, 5° above zero. In such conditions, the most ordinary operation became arduous and dangerous. The hulls of the U-boats were covered with a layer of ice several inches thick, and this added considerably to the weight of the vessels. The diving mechanism worked sluggishly, and the propellers stalled and turned unevenly. The air hoses and the ballast blow-off were often blocked, and the rapid dives became a dangerous undertaking.

And yet, the U-boats had pursued their mission. Despite the British patrols and defenses, they had continued to lay mines and to lay in wait night and day in shipping lanes. But, when a U-boat returned to its base after weeks at sea, many members of the crew were not on deck to receive the greetings and congratulations of officials and friends. They remained below, lying on their bunks, with hands, feet, ears, or nose frozen.

With the coming of spring, Doenitz was preparing to send his Grey Wolves out into the Atlantic when he was ordered to place his fleet at the disposal of Operation Weserübung—the invasion of Norway. It would be an excellent opportunity to take on the Allied fleet which was also preparing to land in Norway. An explosive confrontation was in the making.

Doenitz, serious and silent, was at his headquarters studying reports from the U-boat commanders:

"April 14. Launched torpedoes unsuccessfully at the *Warspite* and two destroyers. *U-48.*"

"April 16. Fleet of ships anchored in Bydden-Fjord. Launched eight torpedoes. Not a single hit. *U-47.*"

"April 19. Fired torpedo at the cruiser *Emerald*. Premature detonation after twenty-two seconds. *U-65.*"

When Doenitz, as was his habit, went to the piers to welcome U-boat commanders returning from a mission, he found them pitiful with their growth of several weeks' beard, thin under the leather coats spotted with oil and whitened with salt. Günther Prien, commander of "the Bull of Scapa Flow," told him on one such occasion, on behalf of his fellow commanders: "Admiral, if you want us to go into combat again, you'll have to give us something better than wooden guns."

Doenitz' reaction was so violent that Berlin, finally, was moved to action. The technicians of the *Kriegsmarine* dug out of their files Doenitz' increasingly bitter series of complaints, and

Grand Admiral Raeder ordered the formation of a court of inquiry into the question of the malfunctioning torpedoes. The guilty were found and haled before courts-martial. And, finally, in June 1940, the order was given to abandon the magnetic torpedo.

From that time, malfunctioning torpedoes became very rare. The "new" torpedo made use of a percussion system which had been developed earlier—in 1918. What this meant in theory was that a U-boat would have to use several torpedoes to sink an enemy ship; and this would proportionately reduce the range and self-sufficiency of submarines on a mission.

Yet, in practice, the fortunes of war compensated for this dis-advantage. On July 7, 1940, at 11 o'clock in the morning, the *U-30* moved slowly into the port of Lorient. It was the first German U-boat to enter a French port to take on fuel and supplies since the capitulation of France in the preceding month. Things would no longer be the same as before.

September 1. A black automobile drew up to 18 Boulevard Suchet in Paris. The two German sailors standing guard pre-sented arms as Admiral Doenitz arrived to take possession officially of his new *Befehlshaber der Unter-See-Boot,* or B.D.U. —headquarters of the new German submarine bases on France's Atlantic coast.

Doenitz, his hands behind his back, stared out of the window at the red autumn leaves on the trees. Godt, his chief-of-staff, Fuhrmann, his ordnance officer, and Hartmann, his liaison chief, stood silently behind him, waiting for him to speak. The admiral turned. "The surrender of France," he said, "is a great stroke of luck for us. We've finally broken out of the 'wet triangle' of the Baltic which was such a handicap during the First World War. Now that we have France's Atlantic ports, our submarines will be able to go into action much more swiftly. The fact that they'll no longer have to start from Wilhelmshaven and Kiel will greatly increase their operating range."

Doenitz looked at his staff, then added: "For the first time since this war began, and despite our inadequate means, I believe in the possibility of a German victory."

Several days before, the admiral had undertaken a detailed inspection of his new base at Lorient. Everything was almost ready to begin servicing vessels arriving from the Atlantic. The workmen of the *Germania Werf* had done a good job. And yet, Doenitz was not happy when he returned to Paris. "Here, in Paris," he told his staff, "we're very comfortable. The only thing is that we're too far away from our men. The strength of our service is that we are *with* them, as it were. We're there when they leave, and we're there when they return. It's a bad thing for us to be so far away from them now."

Doenitz was never a man to hesitate over a decision. Turning to Fuhrmann, he told him: "I want you to find me a headquarters close to the base. Paris is an ideal city for a submariner on shore leave; but it's no place for a man my age."

At this time, Berlin had decided finally to abandon Operation Sea-Lion—the proposed invasion of the British Isles—since Raeder did not have a sufficient number of surface ships to transport the men and supplies required by such an undertaking. Thenceforth, it was Hitler's plan to isolate and suffocate Britain. There was nothing, therefore, to keep Doenitz in Paris, and, on October 16, his *Junker* took him to Kernevel, where he installed himself in a villa, belonging to a sardine merchant, which Fuhrmann had requisitioned.

The admiral's staff and equipment had preceded him, and everything was already in place: the maps and charts, communications equipment, the supplies for the officers' mess and staff quarters. It was from this den that Doenitz would direct the greatest submarine battle in history.

That same evening, after having inspected a detachment from the submarine base, Doenitz and Godt walked on the beach at Larmor. A light rain, like that so often seen in Brittany, fell without interruption. It was high tide, and the long, gray sandy waves were in temporary possession of much of the beach.

Doenitz watched the waves. The veins standing out on his temples told Godt that his superior was lost in thought. The admiral, in fact, was thinking of a decision recently announced by Churchill; a decision which would put a new face on the war at sea. The Prime Minister had told the officers of the Defense Committee and of the Battle of Atlantic Committee of three unusual steps to counter U-boat attacks. First, merchantmen would now be armed and equipped with depth-charge launchers. Second, merchantmen, whenever they sighted a German submarine, would attempt to sink it by depth charges or by gunfire. And finally, commercial vessels would henceforth be escorted by cruisers, destroyers, frigates, or gunboats.

Standing on his Breton beach, Doenitz was analyzing, once more, the implications of Churchill's decision.

On the road back to the villa, he said to Godt: "Churchill thinks that he can muzzle us by adopting the same system of convoys which defeated us in 1918. Well, we're going to respond with the *Rudeltaktik* [wolf pack tactic] which we developed in 1937 during the Baltic exercises."

A new phase of the war was about to begin for the U-boats. The procedure adopted was as follows: a submarine, upon sighting a convoy, would radio the enemy's position and course to the B.D.U. It would maintain contact and wait for the arrival of other submarines in order to form a "pack." Then, the pack would attack. Afterward, they would scatter, and thus escape the pursuing destroyers and the five hundred vessels of the British Coastal Command.

The Battle of the Atlantic had begun; and it was to be a battle in which neither side would give quarter. Despite their small numbers (eight or nine operational units since the occupation of their French bases), the U-boats would group at nightfall, forward of a convoy, and then attack simultaneously and overwhelm the escort vessels. When a sufficient number of cargo ships had been turned into giant torches in the sea, the pack would disperse and flee, only to regroup again forward of the convoy. Then, just before dawn, they would launch another attack.

Doenitz, the inventor of the wolf pack tactic, richly deserved the nickname conferred upon him by his submariners: "The man who makes the oceans temble."

7

October 5, 1940. The long swell of the Atlantic was like a series of mobile but ever-renewed hills which reduced visibility to almost zero. The *U-46* rose and fell on the surface; and, whenever it fell, the line of the horizon was blocked from the view of the men on watch. The wind, blowing in squalls from the northwest, was like ice; and Lieutenant Endrass, wearing a leather coat, a turtleneck sweater covering his chin and a wool cap pulled down over his ears, was still cold—cold, and also tense. The great joy he had experienced when Doenitz, after Scapa Flow, had named him captain of the *U-46*, had been transformed into a gnawing impatience. Since sailing from Lorient nine days earlier, he had seen little but the empty ocean. On the day of his promotion there had been a reception at Kernevel, and Doenitz had proposed a toast wishing him good fortune. The champagne had been excellent; and yet, fortune seemed to have turned her back on Endrass.

On the *U-46*'s second day out, about 150 miles northwest of Brittany, it had been attacked by a British plane which, hidden by clouds until the last minute, had taken the submarine unawares. The U-boat had made an emergency dive, but its stern had still been on the surface when the first shells exploded. They had missed, but not by far; and the submarine had been violently shaken.

Endrass had been in his berth next to the control room when the alert had sounded. He had rushed to the side of the engineering officer, who was working frantically to keep the submarine from assuming too steep an angle in its dive. Then he had looked around at his men, about whom he knew, as yet, practically nothing. Some of them were gnawing on their lips. Others had their mouths open, as though they had difficulty in breathing. And the eyes of some were glazed in terror. For the latter, this was the first combat experience; and, Endrass concluded, they had performed satisfactorily during their baptism of fire, all things considered.

The *U-46* had not been damaged. But, when the danger was past, Endrass summoned to the control room the four men who had been on watch. The first to arrive was Will Leitzer, who was obviously still shaken. He had been closely followed by Paul Winckepeg. Both men were twenty-one years old, and they had been close friends since childhood. They were always together. Years earlier, when Will had decided that he had had enough of school and went to work in a shipyard at Königsberg, Paul had made the same decision. When Will was fired because of a brawl, Paul had quit and joined Will as a hand on a coasting vessel. They chased girls together, drank together, and shared the same room near the slaughterhouses. Then, one day in 1939, Will had told Paul: "You can do whatever you want, but I'm going to sign up for the U-boats."

Paul had not been overly enthusiastic. The U-boats—the microscopic, closed, and dangerous world of the submarine—did not appeal to him. Still, he was unwilling to let Will go without him, and he had enlisted with his friend. When they signed their enlistment papers, they had asked to be assigned to the same unit.

During their four-month training course in the Baltic, Paul thought that he would never recover from seasickness. When he went ashore, he was so weak that his legs trembled like those of an old man. "Forget it," Will told him. "Ask to be transferred to the infantry. Do you want to die of exhaustion?" But Paul's friendship with Will accomplished a minor miracle: he had finally got his sea legs, and seasickness became nothing more than an unpleasant memory.

The third man on watch had been a small, dark man with a

scraggly black beard, a large body, and long, swimmer's muscles: Karl Delelmo. Delelmo, of Italian origin, was nervous and a perennial malcontent.

The fourth man, Horst Mandel, was the least engaging of the four. He was a chronic drunk who suffered greatly from the lack of alcohol aboard ship.

Endrass came directly to the point. "I want to know," he said drily, "which one of you did not see the plane in your sector."

"It was me, Captain," Will said.

"No, sir," Paul interrupted. "It was me!"

Endrass looked at them closely. He knew nothing of their lives, but his experience with men had told him, the first day aboard, that these two men would stand together until death.

"All right. No more nonsense. Which one of you was it?"

"Me," Will answered.

"No, I tell you I did it. The plane was in my sector," Paul insisted.

Endrass sensed that Paul was the guilty one. But he also knew that it would be useless to try to separate the two men. "All right," he said. "I'm going to put you both on report. When we get back to the beach, you can both spend two weeks in the brig."

Then he raised his voice and spoke to the crew. "Listen to me, all of you. You're not on maneuvers now. This is a war, and we're in a combat zone. We were lucky this time. But you've all got to understand once and for all that, aboard a U-boat, the slightest distraction, the least error, the smallest degree of panic on the part of any one man, can lead to only one thing: the death of everyone aboard."

It was 3 o'clock in the morning. A storm had risen, and for six hours the *U-46* had been fighting against wind and waves. The vessel leaped among the crests, pitching and rolling. Despite the weather, a group of men, not on watch, were standing at the rear of the conning tower deck, on the metal platform on which the 20-mm. machine gun was located—a spot which the

submariners had christened "the winter garden." In spite of the
waves which were constantly crashing against the conning
tower, the men were smoking, shielding their cigarettes within
their cupped hands. They were allowed to remain on deck only
five minutes; then they were replaced by another group who
climbed topside in order to enjoy a breath of fresh air and to
escape the pestilential stench of mildew, oil, and garbage
which reigned below. Attached to the railing by safety lines, a
group of men on detail were washing soup containers in the sea
and dumping garbage. The hatchways on the forward and rear
decks, which were ordinarily open in order to provide fresh air
for the interior of the submarine, were now closed because of
the weather. Whatever fresh air there was came through the
conning tower hatch.

"Smoke to starboard," the watch officer shouted.

Endrass, who had been plotting a course with the navigator,
rushed to the conning tower. For several seconds, he could see
nothing in the darkness.

"Over there, Captain," the watch officer said, pointing.

Then Endrass saw them, and he tried to count the thin, dark
columns of smoke rising against the stormclouds. "A blasted convoy!" he shouted. Then he turned to the voice tube: "Sparks!
Notify B.D.U. of the enemy's position and course. Tell them that
we will maintain contact, and that we're waiting for instructions."

"Watch out, Captain!" someone shouted.

Endrass ducked in time to avoid being struck by a solid
sheet of water which broke over the conning tower and then
drained off through the portholes. Then he was back at the tube:
"Full speed ahead!"

He could barely control his impatience. "We must catch up
with that convoy," he kept repeating. "We *must.*"

A long and exasperating chase began. At times, it seemed to
Endrass that he was gaining on the convoy; at others, he was
certain that the submarine was being outdistanced.

The watch was changed twice; but Endrass refused to go below. Soaked to the skin, his teeth chattering with cold, his eyes

red from lack of sleep and from the wind and water, his determination never flagged. The wind had increased its velocity,
and the *U-46* pitched alarmingly as the waves grew higher. But,
under Endrass' orders, the U-boat's engines were maintained at
full speed.

Hendig, Endrass' orderly, appeared on deck wearing a raincoat. "Coffee, Captain?"

"Yes. Thanks." Clutching the railing, Endrass drank the steaming liquid as best he could. Most of it sloshed onto the deck
before he could drink it.

"God, that's good," he told Hendig. "How's everything going
below?"

"Well, nobody's sleeping," the orderly answered. "A few men
have been knocked around, but nothing serious." He explained
that several men had been thrown from their bunks by the
rough seas. One of them had fractured a rib. Another had split
open his knee. And a third had a sprained thumb. "Nothing
serious"—as he had said.

The heavy rain reduced visibility to practically zero. Endrass
piloted his U-boat by instinct, praying the whole while that the
course he had chosen was the same as that of the convoy. If
the ships had made even a slight turn eastward, then he would
never find them.

The coffee had done him good, and he felt better. But he
knew that its stimulating effect was only temporary, and that
soon he would once more have the bitter taste in his mouth
which came from too little sleep and too many cigarettes. His
hands and feet were already numb, but he firmly refused to go
below and enjoy a few minutes of warmth and of sleep. It
would soon be dawn; and then he would know if he had set the
right course.

At 6:45 A.M., the relief watch emerged on deck, and the old
watch unfastened their safety belts and disappeared down the
hatchway, shivering, wet and exhausted, into the moist warmth
of the submarine.

The sky was beginning to clear. The watch reported:

"Forward starboard, nothing to report."

"Forward port, nothing to report."

"Rear starboard, nothing."

"Rear port, nothing in sight."

Endrass closed his eyes for a second. He was overwhelmed by frustration. It had all been for nothing. He opened his eyes and looked around. There was only the sea and the sky. The convoy had disappeared, and the horizon was empty, with only the clouds and the gray sea blending where they met into a single hostile element.

"I'm going below to get some sleep," Endrass said. "Wake me if you sight anything."

"Right, Captain," the watch officer answered. "Sleep well."

A few seconds later, Endrass collapsed onto his bunk. He was too exhausted to remove his soaked clothing, or even his water-filled rubber boots. Hendig gently and deftly removed his clothing, turning him over as he worked, and then replaced the sodden clothing with a dry uniform. Then, Endrass slept like a dead man, his face waxen, his eyes circled with black and sunken into his skull.

Meanwhile, the *U-46*, vibrating, cracking, sweating within, its diesels roaring, continued on course throughout the morning.

At noon, Endrass awakened. His mouth was dry; his eyelids, swollen. He rubbed his hands over his stiff body, and then, steadying himself against a handrail, made his way to the control room. Several crewmen turned when he entered and smiled a bit condescendingly but with friendliness in their eyes.

"Sleep well, Captain?" the navigator asked.

"I swear I could sleep for a year," Endrass said.

The crewmen smiled again. If the captain was making jokes, it meant that he was feeling better and that everything would be all right.

Endrass went to the voice tube. "This is the captain. Anything to report?"

"Nothing, sir. Except that it's wet up here."

Endrass felt a sudden rage. I've *got* to find them, he told himself, even if it means running those diesels at full speed until they burn out; even if it means that we'll all drop in our tracks from fatigue. I've got to find them.

He tried to calm down a bit in order to concentrate on the next step in this exasperating hunt. The convoy, he reasoned, was following a zigzag course at 7 knots. But I've been straining my engines to travel at 12 knots. If the convoy has disappeared, it must mean that those ships have changed course. Now, they were heading toward the south of England, and I know that they haven't made a half-circle. Therefore, they must have decided to go north, and then head east again. We probably passed behind the convoy during the night. If that's so, we must now change our course to east-northeast.

He turned to the navigator and explained what he had in mind. "Figure all this out for me," he ordered. Then he put on his raincoat and his boots. He had already begun climbing the ladder to go above when the engineering officer spoke to him: "Captain, one of our cooling pumps is giving me trouble. Could we cut our speed for a few hours to give it a rest?"

"No," Endrass snapped. "Absolutely not. I'm afraid you'll have to find another way to fix it. I don't care how you do it. If we have to, we'll just have to run without the pump."

At 5:20 P.M. Endrass was back in the control room, boiling with rage. As though he didn't already have enough to worry about, the radio was now out of order, and it was impossible to send or receive messages from the B.D.U.

Considering that this is my first mission as captain, Endrass reflected, I'm really out of luck!

Then another bit of bad news: a man in the forward compartment was violently seasick. It was Paul Winckepeg. But, at the same time, there was a message from the communications officer to the effect that the radio was now operating and that no more trouble was anticipated. Endrass thanked the

officer warmly, but the expression on his face was still one of
ill humor. Where in the hell could they have *gone*, he wondered.

"Watch officer to captain. Smoke to starboard, about 6 miles
away!"

"It's them, by God! Engineer!"

"Captain?"

"Engineer, listen to me. I don't give a damn about your pumps
or anything else. I want you to give me everything that we've
got. We have to be in position to attack five hours from now, at
very latest. Do you understand? Five hours. Not a minute more!"

Through a sea of foam the *U-46* leaped forward with renewed
vigor. Suddenly, everyone forgot their exhaustion. They forgot
about sleep, hunger, and cold.

The communications officer appeared with a message. The
B.D.U. acknowledged receipt of Endrass' message and informed
him that five other U-boats were now heading for a position
forward of the convoy. There was a postscript from Doenitz
himself, urging Endrass not to let the convoy out of his sight,
and telling him not to spare the torpedoes.

Endrass immediately went topside and remained there. He
had not taken the time to put on his leather coat, and he
shivered from the cold. The *U-46*, by an adroit maneuver, was
now almost two miles forward of the convoy; and everyone
aboard the submarine, from the captain down, was infected with
the excitement of the chase.

Darkness fell quickly, but a graying light filtered through
the clouds and provided sufficient visibility for what Endrass
planned. He had decided that the *U-46* would attack on the surface.

At 10:10 P.M. he gave the order: "Prepare tubes 1 to 4."

"Tubes ready, Captain."

Now, Endrass told himself, if only we can take advantage
of the darkness to get as close as possible to the convoy without
being sighted.

At that moment, he saw an escort destroyer, which had been
cruising forward of the merchantmen, turn toward the *U-46*.

From the conning tower, Endrass could see the foam around its prow widening as the destroyer drew nearer. Then, suddenly, it changed course, like a sheep dog who has picked up the spoor of a wolf but is not quite sure in what direction to go. In turning, the destroyer carelessly presented its side to the *U-46*, at a distance of no more than 2,500 feet.

"Let's attack!" Endrass shouted. It took only a few seconds to get the ship in his sights. *"Rohr ein. Feuer!"*

The detonation was deafening. The torpedo struck the destroyer amidships, at the level of the munitions room, and the ship disintegrated in a burst of fire and a chain of explosions which cast a reddish hue over the dark sea. Pieces of steel and debris showered down into the water. When all was quiet once more, there was no longer a trace of the U-boat's victim, and the ocean had resumed its accustomed rhythm.

Meanwhile, the other ships of the convoy had been seized with panic. The heavy, slow-moving cargo ships, sirens screaming and horns blaring, began to scatter, crossing over one another's wakes.

"Full speed ahead," Endrass ordered.

The efforts of the merchantmen to escape from their invisible attackers were in vain. Soon, more explosions rent the air and echoed interminably over the sea as flames rose high over the surface and turned it into a red pool of blood.

"The other U-boats!" Endrass remarked.

The wolf pack had been punctual at the rendezvous. They now attacked the convoy from different directions and then scattered and fled, only to return a short while later to launch a new salvo of torpedoes. By then, the *U-46* was no more than 800 yards from the disorderly and terrorized convoy. Endrass brought his vessel close to a heavily loaded ship which had just completed an evasive maneuver. At first, he could see only the ship's prow, which rose and fell heavily in the sea, like the chest of a hunted animal who falls exhausted to the ground and waits for the death blow.

Endrass waited until the ship's flank was toward him, then he ordered: "Tube 2, fire! Tube 3, fire!"

There were two sharp whistles. The *U-46* lurched, and the torpedoes cut through the water. Endrass, torn between satisfaction and pity, saw a half-naked man on the cargo ship's deck pointing frantically over the side to the wake of the approaching torpedoes.

There were two explosions, and two columns of water were thrown into the air. Once more, flames mounted toward the sky. Endrass saw the dark forms of men running on the rear deck of the cargo ship and throwing themselves into the sea. Then the ship's engines exploded with a colossal noise, and the *U-46*, which lay 400 yards from the cargo ship, was raised in the water as by a giant fist. It rolled and shuddered as though it had struck a solid object, and Endrass and the watch clutched frantically at the handrail. They were thrown to the deck and scrambled to clutch the periscope. When they were able to rise, the cargo ship had disappeared beneath the indifferent waves.

One explosion followed another in a continuous series. The *U-46* passed 200 yards from a tanker which burned as it sank. There were black figures in the water around the doomed ship: survivors. Their eyes and lungs scorched by the burning oil, their faces black and shining, they cursed and shook their fists at the *U-46* as it passed in search of new prey.

Will and Paul could not take their eyes from the destruction and tragedy around them. "Will, it's horrible—horrible," Paul repeated over and over again.

Will did not answer. His throat was dry as he watched the bodies of the dead floating face down in the sea, their life preservers around their chests, their eyes no doubt open and staring into the depths.

Karl Delelmo put his hands over his ears to shut out the curses of the dying. He was trembling, his face haggard, and he seemed on the verge of tears. He prayed. He prayed for forgiveness for the death of these unknown men of whom he had been one of the executioners.

"Reload," Endrass ordered.

The *U-46* cruised in a half circle to reach its firing position forward of a tanker of 10,000 tons. Endrass saw its port clearly silhouetted against a burning ship to starboard.

Now, he thought, if only it doesn't turn to starboard.

He looked around the deck. Will and Paul were still shaken. He would have to talk to them, to bring them to their senses. Or maybe the simplest thing would be to have two other men relieve them. But there was no time to do anything. The tanker, as though eager to meet its fate, turned fully to port. In a few more seconds, it would be squarely in the U-boat's sights.

"Prepare tubes 1 and 2."

"Tubes 1 and 2 ready, Captain."

The tanker was now in direct line of fire.

"Fire 1! Fire 2!"

There were two loud whistles, almost simultaneous. Two barely perceptible wakes. An explosion, a column of water, and flames.

My God, thought Endrass, one of the torpedoes didn't explode!

The operative torpedo had struck the cargo ship in its bow, and although it was taking on water, it continued on course, turning now to starboard.

Well, old friend, Endrass told himself, I'm going to get you, one way or the other.

Just then, one of the tanker's guns fired a salvo. The shot was long, striking the water several hundred yards behind the submarine. A machine gun began firing tracer bullets above the conning tower, and the gun fired a second shot. This time, it came closer, falling behind the *U-46* slightly to port.

"20 degrees to starboard, full speed ahead," Endrass ordered.

The submarine listed to starboard as it made a sharp turn intended to carry it across the tanker's bow and thus to re-establish its firing position.

Endrass shouted a curse. The captain of the tanker had been

taken unaware by Endrass' maneuver, but he quickly recovered and was now making a hard turn to port.

"Radio message for the captain."

"What is it?"

"The enemy is sending out an S.S.S.* to the escort destroyers of the convoy."

Endrass looked to starboard, where he could see what was left of the decimated convoy. He could still hear explosions and see columns of flame.

The destroyers have enough to keep them busy as it is, he told himself.

Endrass ordered a change of course. Instead of trying to intercept the tanker, he now planned to take up a position off its stern and fire as best he could from that less than ideal location. It was all he could do, for the destroyers might arrive at any moment.

The chase was a short one. The tanker, taking on water in its forward compartments, was traveling at considerably reduced speed.

"Its engines have stopped," Will informed the captain.

"Good. They're going to try to launch their lifeboats."

The U-46 followed a curving course until it was facing the tanker's flank. Endrass and his watch could see the ship's prow low in the water, and the crew rushing about the deck toward the lifeboats and life rafts.

"Do you think we're going to sink her before they can get off?" Paul asked Will in a trembling voice.

"Shut up. How do I know what we're going to do?"

Both men waited in silence for their captain's decision. Endrass was on the horns of a dilemma. He knew that if he fired his torpedoes immediately, it was unlikely that any of the men aboard the doomed ship would escape with their lives. To fire, then, would be the equivalent of wholesale murder. Yet, if he waited a moment too long, he would be increasing the chance

---

* Communications code for "We are being attacked by submarines."

of an attack by escort destroyers and thus compromising the lives of his crew and the safety of his ship.

He reached a decision. "Prepare tubes 3 and 4."

"I can't look," Paul whispered, and turned his head away.

"Hand me the megaphone," Endrass ordered.

The captain's sharp tone brought Paul out of his horrified stupor. He found the megaphone and handed it to Endrass. Endrass turned toward the tanker, raised the megaphone to his mouth, and shouted in his approximate English: "I give you three minutes exactly to leave your boat! After, I bomb you!"

His amplified voice echoed lugubriously over the water. Aboard the tanker, lifeboats loaded with men were being lowered over the side. Some of them capsized as soon as they hit the water, and the men in them began to fight savagely among themselves for places in other boats. Life rafts had also been launched, and sailors jumped over the side and swam desperately toward them.

"One minute more," Endrass shouted.

The lifeboats and rafts began rowing frantically away from the ship.

The U-46's engines were thrown in reverse to increase the distance between the tanker and the submarine.

When they were 500 yards apart, Endrass gave the order: "Fire 3! Fire 4!"

The tanker was raised out of the water by the force of the explosions, and roaring flames from the ship leaped a hundred yards into the air as fragments of metal and wood were showered in all directions. Then, as the submariners and the survivors in the lifeboats and rafts watched in horrified fascination, the tanker turned on its side, like a great beast in agony, and sank slowly into the flaming sea.

As the U-46 pulled away from the scene, it passed two lifeboats. The men on deck could see the faces of the survivors, faces distorted by fear and hate. No one spoke.

Endrass' voice broke the silence. "We have more work to do.

Full speed ahead! We have to try to find the rest of the convoy."

He looked at the men around him. Only a few hours ago, before the sea had been transformed into a place of suffering and death, they had been hardly more than children. Most of them were still in their 'teens. But now they had lost their look of fresh youthfulness and eagerness. Their eyes were somber, and their lips no longer smiled. Their faces suddenly bore the hard lines of war. They were veterans.

The first wolf pack mission had been a success.

On the deck of the U-46, Karl Delelmo came timidly toward the captain, steadying himself against the railing. He was obviously embarrassed and did not know how to stand, or how to begin. Finally, he spoke.

"Captain, the men and I would like to thank you for letting those men get off the ship before firing."

Endrass was silent for a moment. "You know," he said, "I think what we all need is a good cup of hot chocolate."

It was 4:30 A.M. The sun would be up in two hours. Endrass decided to sleep for a while. "Wake me as soon as you sight the rest of the convoy," he told Hermann Steher, his third officer.

Steher let the captain sleep well into the morning. The convoy had disappeared once more, and the U-46 sighted nothing more than corpses and the debris of ships in the sea.

8

At 4:42 A.M. the signal for battle stations resounded through the U-46. Steher's excited voice came over the intercom: "Destroyer at 500 yards—and heading our way!"

Endrass was in the control room in an instant. "Dive to 350 feet," he ordered. "Quick! Send some men forward!"

Water was sucked into the ballast tanks and the U-46 began its dive. The men on watch above had made a hurried descent into the control room by sliding the railing and dropping to the deck below. Steher, the last man down, had secured the hatch and simply jumped down.

"Dive! Dive!" Endrass shouted. "Dive before that bastard is right on top of us!"

"I'm picking up its engines," the radioman announced.

Almost immediately, eight depth charges exploded simultaneously, dangerously close to the *U-46*. The submarine tossed and cracked under the impact of the explosions. Lamps were smashed, and everything that was not secured crashed to the deck and rolled forward. The crew, surprised and terrified, were thrown off balance and clutched at railings or fell one on top of the other. The sound of depth charges grew louder. Some of the sailors lighted their flashlights, and the beams swept over the bulkheads and over the faces of their friends.

"Report," Endrass barked.

"Rear compartment secure, Captain."

The engine room reported: "The exhaust valves are leaking, Captain. We're taking on water."

The submarine continued its dive. Overhead, the men heard the sound of propellers.

"Several destroyers, sir," the radioman said in a shaky voice.

"I don't want anyone to make any noise," Endrass warned. Then he turned to the engineering officer. "Where do we stand?"

"The main pressure gauge is working, but the rest of them are out. The alert equipment and the hold pump are not working either. The magnetic compass is out. We'll have to use the emergency lighting system."

"Stop all engines," Endrass ordered. "It's time for our siesta, anyway."

In the light of their flashlights, the men looked at one another. The captain's voice had reassured them. Here we are, they told themselves, 400 feet down, with our ship about to cave in on our heads, and he's still making jokes. Things can't be all that bad.

The explosions began again, but this time they were farther away.

"They're looking for us," Endrass said. "That's a good sign. It means that they don't know our exact position."

The *U-46* had now come to a full stop, with its nose slightly down.

"All right, electricians," the engineering officer ordered, "you can begin working on the emergency lighting—but don't make any noise."

There was a new series of explosions in the distance. The destroyers had not given up their search. Everyone aboard the submarine listened, nerves tense, eyes closed, to the continuing explosions.

The emergency lighting came on, and everyone relaxed a bit. The chief electrician, however, quickly extinguished all but four night lights.

Meanwhile, the destroyers circled overhead, each pass was followed by new explosions of depth charges—the *Wasserbomb*, or as they were known to the submariners, *Wabos*.

The silence of the submarine was suddenly shattered by a terrified shriek from Paul Winckepeg.

"For God's sake, shut that man up!" Endrass whispered harshly.

Three men jumped on Paul; but the sailor, suddenly endowed with the strength of his hysteria, fought like a madman, shouting: "Will! Where is Will?! They left him topside! The bastards! They left him topside!"

The engineering officer struck him sharply on the chin with his fist, and Paul crumpled to the deck.

Endrass went quickly into the forward compartment. "What did he mean?" he whispered. "Where is Will Leitzer?"

"Leitzer's not aboard," someone answered.

"What?"

"He's not here, Captain. And neither is Karl Delelmo."

"Are you out of your mind?" Endrass asked. "Who was the watch officer?"

"I was, Captain," Steher said. And then the twenty-one-year-old midshipman burst into tears.

"There's no time to cry! What happened? You know that the officer is supposed to be the last one down. What happened?"

Steher, sniffling, wiped his eyes on his sleeve. "Captain, I swear I thought all the men had gone below. When I came down, there was no one on the deck. I swear it!"

Above on the surface, riding on the swell, Will Leitzer was trying to remove his water-filled boots and to stay afloat. He was in desperate straits. The water was icy, and he was already half paralyzed with cold. Even though he kept in constant motion, he was shivering violently. A wave swept over him. He succeeded in thrusting his head above the surface and took a deep breath. Along with the air, he swallowed sea water and began choking and coughing in an effort to clear his lungs.

His waterlogged clothing made it almost impossible for him to swim, and he was almost at the end of his strength. He struggled to concentrate on swimming. It was not more than an hour since the U-46 had dived, but to him it seemed that his struggle for survival had lasted an eternity.

A wave caught him and raised him so that, for an instant, he could see around him, and he caught sight of a plank. And on the plank was Karl Delelmo.

"Karl," Will shouted as loudly as he could. "Karl!"

Delelmo did not hear him. The wind, the roaring of the sea drowned out all other sound. His numb fingers grasped the plank and his breath came in gasps. He was almost frozen, and his strength was gone.

If only I can reach that plank, I'll be rescued, Will told himself over and over. And, now that he had an objective, he somehow found the strength to begin swimming desperately in the direction where he had seen Delelmo. He made steady but maddeningly slow progress. He was only 50 or 75 yards from Delelmo when his strength gave out entirely. Overcome by cold and fatigue, he realized that he would never make it. He stopped swimming, hoping to be able to catch his breath. Another wave washed over him, pulling him beneath the water. He struggled to the surface, gasping, and managed to take several deep breaths. Immediately, he felt better, and called out to Karl as loudly as he could.

The bastard! he thought. He's pretending he doesn't hear me so he won't have to share his plank with me!

But Karl had heard Will's last shout, and the sound of his own name had served to awaken him from his torpor. He raised his head and looked around.

They've come back for me! he told himself.

Then he saw Will, almost unrecognizable in the water, waving his arms. In spite of his own exhaustion, Delelmo, using his arms as oars, began frantically paddling his board toward Will. When the plank reached him, grazing his cheek, Will clutched at it with such desperation that Delelmo fell into the water.

"Thank you, Karl," Will gasped, "thank you. I'll never forget this—"

"Don't be a fool!" Delelmo shouted. "Listen. There isn't room for both of us on here. We're going to have to take turns. We'll each get five minutes on, and five minutes off. It's your turn first. You climb on the plank, and I'll hang on to the edge."

Painfully, but with a sense of intense exaltation, Will climbed onto the plank and lay flat. Almost immediately, his whole body began trembling uncontrollably. He felt colder now than before. The plank, carried by the swell, was almost constantly covered by waves.

"Karl!" Will cried. "We're going to die!"

Then he lay still, tossed by the sea, almost unconscious. His numbed mind was obsessed by a single thought: soon he would have to turn the plank over to Karl. Instinctively, his hands clutched it harder to his body. He never wanted to go down into the water again. Never.

The men watched in helpless silence as, a mile away, two English destroyers circled, dropping their depth charges. It was a miracle that they were still alive. Almost immediately after Steher had given the order to go below, they had been in the water. And at that instant, they had been convinced that they were going to die. The destroyer had rushed toward them as they treaded water only a few yards from the U-46, but the wave from its prow had carried them out of the way of its propellers. Therefore, by the time the depth charges had begun to explode, they had been well out of range. Otherwise, they would surely have been blown apart.

"It's my turn," Karl gasped through chattering teeth. His lips were blue, his eyes sunken.

"Not so soon," Will begged, frantic at the thought of giving up the plank. "Let me stay on just a minute more!"

"It's my turn!" Karl screamed. "You're lucky I let you on at all!"

Will shook his head, crying. "Just a little longer," he begged, "just a few seconds!"

Karl, mustering his last ounce of strength, gave the plank a violent shake, and Will, with a shriek, fell into the water. He swallowed water, coughed, and, half drowned, flailed his arms in the water. By chance, he succeeded in grasping the edge of the plank.

In the distance, the men could hear explosions. The destroyers were continuing their hunt for the U-46.

Will was now totally exhausted. He could no longer move his legs, and his hands and fingers were without feeling. This time, he told himself, he would not be able to hang on. He was going to die.

"Karl," he said, "Karl, I've had it. I can't make it." Then his hands slipped from the plank.

In an instant, Karl had caught him by the arm and tried to hold him above the water. "Try to climb up, Will! Try!"

Will shook his head. What was the use? he thought. He was going to die. He couldn't even move. He would freeze to death if he didn't drown before.

"Let me go, Karl," he whispered, his eyes closed. "I've had it. Let me go."

Karl tightened his knees to steady himself on the plank and

used both hands to hold on to Will's motionless body. "Will!"
he shouted, "Will! Don't give up! You know Endrass! When he
finds out we're not aboard, he's going to come looking for us.
You know that, don't you? So come on! Climb up here. It's
your turn on the plank!"

Will did not answer. Karl's mouth was next to his ear, but he
barely heard what he was saying.

"I'm going to die," he managed to say. He could hardly move
his lips. Karl slapped him twice, hard, and Will's head moved
under the force of the blows. With an immense effort, he opened
his eyes and looked at his shipmate. Karl saw a cry of help in
those eyes, and, at the same time, a reproach, as though Will
were saying: "Why don't you let me die? Why do you want me to
suffer?"

"Come on, Will," Karl shouted. "Let's try to sing something."
Holding on to Will's collar with both hands, he began to sing,
in a thin, toneless voice, the first notes of a melody by Zarah
Leander. He stopped and began to shake Will, shrieking, "Sing,
you son-of-a-bitch! Sing, goddammit! You're not going to die like
this! You're not going to leave me alone out here!"

Will shook his head and whispered: "Go fuck yourself. I'm
going to die."

"No!" Karl screamed. He refused to lose his shipmate. He
needed him. He knew that if there were two of them, he would
somehow find the will to fight to the last breath. But if he lost
Will, he would have lost the last thing that still bound him
to mankind in this gray, hostile, and terrifying vastness. Then,
he knew, he would be lost. Without Will, he would be afraid.
Therefore, he was determined to save Will in this tug-of-war
with death. Frantically, he tried to pull Will's limp body onto
the plank. "Help me, you bastard," he shouted.

Will heard him, but he could not answer. He opened his
eyes, and it was as though he were looking through a dense
fog. He closed his eyes. His legs and arms floated freely in the
swell. Only his head and shoulders were above the water, held
there by Karl, who had thrust his hands under Will's collar.

By now, the British destroyers had disappeared. Dawn was breaking, and a fine, stinging rain was falling. The wind had abated, and the swell was less powerful. Karl stretched out on his plank, held firmly to Will's motionless body. "Why did we do it?" he asked himself. "What came over us?"

Karl and Will had been on the *U-46*'s deck. Endrass had just gone below, and they were waiting to be relieved on watch. A dense fog, common in the Atlantic, had just risen, and it was impossible to see for more than 500 yards. Karl had been next to Will, leaning against the periscope superstructure which concealed them from Steher and the other two men on watch. Both had been thinking of the horrors of that night, of the bodies they had seen floating on the waves. Steher's frightened shout had recalled them to the present: "Destroyer at 500 yards!"

They had seen the dark shape of the enemy ship appear suddenly out of the fog, already huge, and draw rapidly nearer.

"They're going to get us!" Will had shouted, and then, as Karl had watched helplessly, he had run toward the "winter garden," climbed over the railing, and jumped into the sea. Karl had looked over his shoulder at the enormous shape of the oncoming destroyer. It seemed to him that nothing could save the *U-46* now. The destroyer was going to ram it, head-on. And he had followed his shipmate over the side.

When Karl had returned to the surface, he remembered having heard an incredible noise. The *U-46* was no longer in sight. Then, he had been covered by enormous waves and thrust down beneath the water, and it had seemed forever before he reached the surface again. When he had been able to breathe once more, he had seen the destroyer's rounded stern in the distance, as the ship circled and dropped its depth charges. When the first explosions came, Karl had felt as though he were caught in a vise which was slowly squeezing his trunk and his neck. He had lost consciousness and sunk beneath the surface, but the cold water on his face had revived him, and he had struggled back to the surface. He had swum as long as he could, wondering how long it would be before he drowned, when, miraculously, he had struck a plank drifting toward him. He had climbed onto it, almost unable to breathe, and limp with terror and fatigue. His greatest fear was that the *U-46* had been sunk. The repeated passes by the destroyers, however, and the continuing launching of depth charges, had given him hope. Since they're still looking for it, he had reassured himself, it's because they haven't found it yet.

Then he lay on his plank, motionless and uncaring, until he had heard Will call his name.

Now, Karl shook Will. There was no reaction. The other man's face was greenish, and his eyes were closed.

"You bastard," Karl shouted, "you're lucky I don't let go. It would serve you right."

Karl could no longer feel his arms or hands or fingers. And yet, he was able somehow to hold onto Will. "Tell me that you're not dead," he begged his motionless shipmate. "You're still alive, aren't you?"

He crawled slightly forward on the plank until his ear was against Will's mouth. Will was still breathing.

Karl closed his eyes for what seemed only a second. When he opened them again, he had a disagreeable feeling of lightheadedness. Then he looked around. It took a few seconds for him to realize what had happened.

"Will! Will!" he shouted. "Where are you?!"

Karl raised himself on his elbows and looked at the water around him. He saw Will drifting about 50 feet away from the plank.

I must have fallen asleep, he told himself. But it couldn't have been for very long. He's so close—

He began paddling with his arms, shouting, "Will, Will you bastard! Come back! Come back! Don't leave me!"

When he reached Will he clutched him to the plank, laughing and crying with joy. "You wanted to get away by yourself, didn't you?" he asked the unhearing Will. "Well, you should know by now that I'm not going to let you go. We're buddies, you and I, and we're never going to be separated!" Karl laughed. "We're like Siamese twins—united forever!"

Then he stopped laughing. What if he fell asleep again? What if he didn't awaken in time and Will was lost?

Twisting and turning on the plank, he managed to remove his belt; then he looped it under Will's armpits and tied the loose end to his left wrist. "Now," he told Will, "even if I fall asleep, you won't get away."

He laughed again, and his staring eyes, burned by the salt and the wind, swept over the horizon. He sang the words of a song, but the sounds which came from his throat had nothing human about them. Then he put his head down and slept, still clutching the collar of Will's pea coat.

9

"I think they're gone," Endrass said.

He walked toward the forward compartment. Paul lay on the deck, tied and gagged, as tears filled his eyes and rolled down his adolescent cheeks.

"Untie him," Endrass ordered.

There was a long silence, unbroken except by the sound of water lapping as the submarine's hull rolled on the rocks which littered the sandy bottom.

Paul stood, red-faced and reeling. A dark bruise was beginning to form on his chin, where the engineer had struck him.

"We should be going after the convoy," Endrass said softly. "I'm sure I'll catch hell from the old man, but we're not going to do it. We're going to go back to the surface to look for our two lost idiots. I don't have much hope that we'll find them, but I promise you that we'll keep looking until we know for sure that it's hopeless."

Paul said nothing.

"Prepare to surface!"

The electric motors hummed. The *U-46* budged, rose from the bottom, and began to rise.

"Periscope depth," Endrass said.

A few minutes later, he was sweeping the horizon through the periscope. There was nothing in sight.

"Surface!"

On the surface, Endrass climbed the conning tower, closely followed by the watch officer and men, and by Paul. It was 1:25 P.M. The destroyers had abandoned their search two hours earlier. And Will and Karl had been missing for eight hours and seven minutes.

Endrass walked toward the navigator, who was trying to get a reading despite the clouds. "Taking into account such factors as drift, the currents, and the time lapse," he asked, "can you give me an idea of where we should start looking for Leitzer and Delelmo? If they're still afloat, that is. We're still at about the same position that we were when they were lost."

The navigator made a quick calculation, and passed the results on to Endrass. The *U-46* then began its search. It was not an easy task. Submarines, because of their reduced height, have poor visibility—generally not more than 5 miles. Still, a dozen men standing in the "winter garden" and on the conning tower scanned the sea through binoculars for three hours. Several times, they sighted dark objects floating on the surface; and, each time, investigation disclosed that the object was nothing more than debris from the battle of the preceding night.

It would soon be dark again, and discouragement reigned aboard the *U-46*. Everyone knew that, when darkness fell, it would be useless to go on. And, as time passed, the chance of finding the men even now grew less and less.

"A dark object to forward port!" someone shouted, and all eyes were immediately turned in that direction as Endrass gave the order which sent the *U-46* speeding through the waves toward the object.

In the dim twilight, it was difficult, even through the binoculars, to make out what the object was as it rose and fell with the waves, disappearing and then reappearing on the surface.

"It's two men!" Endrass shouted hoarsely, his voice shaking with emotion. "Stand by with the grappling irons."

Some of the sailors on the deck went toward the rear as the submarine drew near the men at reduced speed and then maneuvered into a position alongside it. The grappling irons hooked onto the plank and drew it against the U-boat's side.

"It's them!"

Karl Delelmo was humming in a monotone when he was brought aboard. His eyes were open, wild, and he recognized no one. He was carried gently down to the forward compartment, where his clothing was changed. Then he was strapped into his bunk.

Will Leitzer was hoisted onto deck. His eyes were wide open, but he saw nothing. He was dead.

Paul, without a word, without a sound, went below to find the canvas sack which would serve as a shroud for his childhood friend. In the darkness which had now descended upon the Atlantic, in the biting wind, Endrass read the prayers for the dead. The quartermaster's whistle shrieked its strident notes and Will Leitzer's body, heavily ballasted, was lowered into the sea as his shipmates stood at attention in a final salute.

The *U-46* now resumed its search for the convoy. Karl, strapped into his bunk, continued to hum. From time to time, he was shaken by chills; and, in his delirium, he shouted Will's name. About 4 o'clock in the morning, Hendig heard him mumble: "Will, we must have been out of our minds to jump overboard!"

He immediately reported Karl's words to Endrass. The captain, despite his almost total exhaustion, called the crew together and asked Steher also to attend. "I would like everyone to know that Lieutenant Steher is in no way responsible for the tragedy we experienced yesterday." Then he shook Steher's hand and returned to bed.

For several days and nights, the *U-46* continued its search for the convoy, without success. They did not even sight the life-boats and life rafts with the survivors from the earlier attack. Visibility was continuously blocked by a dense fog which lay, like a ball of cotton, over the sea. Finally, realizing that he was low on fuel, Endrass resigned himself to returning to Lorient.

It was a mild, sunny fall morning when the *U-46*, flying the pennants of the ships it had sunk, reached its Atlantic port. Doenitz and a part of his staff were waiting on the pier for Endrass and his men. The quartermaster's whistle blew, and there were fanfares, salutes, and handclasps. Then Doenitz, scarcely able to contain his impatience, asked: "Well, Endrass, where did you disappear to? Everyone thought that you were lost. All the others arrived a couple of days ago."

"I had a little trouble, Admiral."

"Oh? You'll have to tell me about it. Was it serious?"

"Serious enough."

"But why did you keep radio silence? We've been trying to contact you for the past week."

"The radio was not operating, Admiral. We repaired it, but it broke down again."

"I see. Well, go change your uniform. I can smell the oil a hundred yards away. Then come have lunch with me, and give me your report."

"Yes, sir."

Twenty minutes later, a Red Cross ambulance, sirens blaring, pulled up at the foot of the *U-46*'s gangplank. Three nurses boarded the submarine. A few minutes later, two husky sailors appeared on deck. Between them, on a stretcher, was Karl Delelmo. His beard was unkempt, and he appeared filthy. He spat continuously, as though trying to rid his lungs of sea water; and he groaned unceasingly, sometimes gutturally and some-times stridently. When they reached the ambulance, two of the nurses, with the help of the stretcherbearers, strapped him into a straitjacket.

Paul stood on the pier, lost and alone. He wanted to join one of the groups of his shipmates returning to the base, but he had no idea of how to go about it. His life in the past had centered exclusively around Will. He hardly knew anyone else. And no one dared speak to him and ask him to join them. Paul, therefore, waited until everyone had left; and then he picked up his sea bag, hoisted it onto his shoulder, and walked slowly toward his quarters.

Endrass stepped into his bath. With a deep sigh of satisfaction he lowered himself into the hot, almost boiling water. It felt as though, for the first time in weeks, his pores were breathing. He closed his eyes to concentrate on what he would tell Doenitz, and his mind wandered off onto an increasingly vague and non-sensical series of disconnected thoughts. He was asleep. He awakened with a start. Depth charges! No, he reassured himself. Just the sound of someone pounding on the door. He looked up at the blue ceiling and remembered where he was.

"It's me!" a voice shouted. "Schepke! Are you sleeping?"

"Yes, I was," Endrass admitted.

"Well, come on. Get a move on. The Lion's waiting for you, and he's biting his claws with impatience. He wants to know what happened to your men. And I wanted to remind you that I am taking the train to Paris tonight."

Schepke walked around the bathroom and, as Endrass dried himself and put on a robe, continued with his accustomed volubility. "I'm going to have an orgy to end all orgies. I'm going to bury myself under women, under a great pile of women. And I'm going to drink champagne like no man has ever drunk champagne before. How about coming with me?"

"Sorry, I can't. If I can get permission from the admiral, I'm going to Hannover. I have a fiancée, remember?"

The napkins, tablecloths, and curtains were checked in red and white. Fishermen and local people leaned against the bar, sipping a bitter local *apéritif* made of artichokes, or else a local beer as light as water. The drinkers were, for the most part, sullen, silent. Their faces were blank, if not actually hostile. Not one of them deigned to glance toward the large dining room. On either side of the door, armed German sailors stood guard. The atmosphere of sadness and bitterness which pervaded the bar was broken only by the sound of voices and laughter which occasionally drifted from the dining room.

Within, Doenitz, Godt, and a dozen other officers were having a banquet. For their convenience, the owner's wife had placed five small tables together. On the menu were oysters from the Gulf of Morbihan, lobster and langouste, leg of mutton aux flageolets, salad, cheese, fruit, and Breton prune pudding. The champagne, specially ordered by Admiral Doenitz, had come from Paris.

"If I could be sure of such a feast every time I come back from a mission," Schepke shouted, "I'd fight much harder!"

Admiral Doenitz, smiling and relaxed, rose to his feet. There was an immediate silence. "Gentlemen," he said, "our wolf pack tactic has put us on the road to victory. In the month of October 1940 we've sunk more vessels than ever before since the beginning of the war: sixty-three vessels, representing 362,407 tons of shipping.

"Two factors make our success even more striking. The first is that the English shipyards can turn out only 200,000 tons of shipping a month—which means that we are now sinking more ships than the enemy can launch. The second factor, gentlemen— and I am happy to say so—is your own effectiveness. The average tonnage for each of our Grey Wolves has never been so high: 920 tons for every day at sea, for every one of our submarines, during the month of October. This is almost twice as much as before we began operating from French bases on the Atlantic."

The room was filled with applause. The admiral continued in the same, quiet voice. "I must warn you, however, against too much optimism. I can tell you already that the English shipyards are now building faster and more heavily armed destroyers. These, along with the aircraft of the Coastal Command, will be formidable adversaries.

"Do not forget, gentlemen," Doenitz concluded, "that we are at war against the greatest naval power in the world. And the English never turn and run in the middle of a battle."

10

His features set in a frown, his left hand clutching a small package containing his toothbrush, razor, dirty socks, underwear, and toothpaste, Wilhelm saluted the sentries on duty and then heaved a great sigh. He was free. The great iron door of prison closed behind him. Regulations required that he report immediately to his base for assignment to a new ship. The *U-47*, commanded by Prien, and manned by Wilhelm's shipmates, had left three weeks earlier on a mission. During that time, Wilhelm had been in a cell, on bread and water. Now, as was his habit, he spat on the ground in a gesture of anger and defiance. The idea of being assigned to a new ship, with a new captain and new shipmates, infuriated him.

"They'll be waiting for me at the base," he told himself. "Hell with them. They've gotten along without me for three weeks, so they can get along a while longer. I'm going to have a drink."

He crossed the main square of Lorient, paved with stone and still damp from a recent rain, and entered the Café de l'Arsenal. He had hardly closed the door behind him when he noticed that the few customers in the bar had huddled together in a group, with their backs toward him, as soon as he had entered. They were fishermen, for the most part, and a few laborers. A young woman, plump and sturdy-looking, wearing a bright green sweater, her eyes bright and alert, stood behind the counter.

"*Guten Tag*," she said.

"*Guten Tag*," Wilhelm answered. "*Vin*." The word was one of the few that the sailor knew in French.

"No wine," the girl said with an air of vague disappointment. "Coupons for wine. Germans take all the wine."

Several of the customers looked away. Others hurriedly paid and left.

Wilhelm knew that the girl was lying, but the last thing he wanted now was trouble. He had just finished paying for the last time. Three weeks earlier, the night before the *U-47*'s departure, he had been involved in a fight over a girl who, after having invited him to her room, had asked an exorbitant price for her professional services. Then she had begun screaming insults that Wilhelm did not understand. Two tall, husky men had rushed into the room, and a fistfight had begun to the accompaniment of the girl's shrieks. The French police had arrived almost immediately and taken everyone down to the station. An hour later, they turned over a bloody Wilhelm to the *Kriegsmarine*. Prien had come to see him in his cell and, his eyes cold, his voice cutting, he had not minced his words: "You deserve everything that you're going to get. The only good thing about this situation is that everyone aboard will be happy to be rid of you. Let me make myself clear: if you haven't changed your attitude and your outlook by the time you get out of jail, I will not allow you to set foot on my ship again."

Prien had left almost immediately, leaving Wilhelm crushed. But the captain was no sooner out of sight than Wilhelm began shouting Prien's name. His voice reverberated through the long corridors and echoed from the ancient stone walls. A guard had come running. "Shut up in there!"

"Listen," Wilhelm said hurriedly, "run after the captain and ask him to come back. I have something important to tell him. Come on, be a nice guy."

"Sorry. You should have talked to him when he was here instead of standing there like an idiot."

"You bastard," Wilhelm screamed, wild with rage, his face pressing against the bars of the opening in his door. "Call him back. It's important! It's urgent!"

The door of the opening slammed shut, flattening Wilhelm's

nose. He wandered around the cell for a few moments, then slumped onto the bunk. "They're going to have bad luck," he mumbled. "God, if you're listening, let them come back from this mission. If they don't, I'll kill myself."

His giant hand fumbled in his blouse and pulled out the silk stocking which he always carried. He looked at it, and caressed it dumbly.

The next morning, the *U-47* had sailed on its mission into enemy waters, leaving its good-luck piece ashore in a cell.

"Then give me some lemonade," Wilhelm said.

"That, we have," the girl answered, standing on tiptoe and reaching for a shelf. "It's good, too. Made with saccharine."

She poured the liquid into a slightly dirty glass.

Wilhelm began to drink, taking very small swallows. "Tastes like shit," he said to himself. "I wonder how these frogs can drink it."

He did not finish the lemonade. He threw a bill of occupation money on the counter and, without waiting for his change, picked up his package and walked out of the bar. As the door closed behind him, he heard the sound of conversations resumed, and of laughter.

Without even pausing, he began loping like a large animal toward the base.

Once past the main gate, his nostrils picked up the familiar smell common to all submarines. He walked over to the dock, where four submarines were moored for repairs. Then he reported for reassignment, and was ordered aboard the *U-46*. He shook his head in resignation when he learned that the new captain of the *U-46* was Endrass.

In a foul mood and, at the same time, apprehensive for a reason he did not understand, Wilhelm began walking toward his barracks. The faces of the sailors and officers he encountered seemed strained, serious. Wilhelm sensed that something was wrong. The whole base seemed under a heavy, oppressive cloud.

"Hello, Wilhelm."

The sailor turned. It was Lieutenant Spahr, navigator aboard the *U-47*. Wilhelm drew himself to attention and saluted smartly. He liked Spahr, whom he regarded as a competent, calm, level-headed officer. He noticed now, however, that the lieutenant seemed discouraged, listless.

"What's going on, Lieutenant?"

"You mean you haven't heard? I guess not. We got the news only a couple of hours ago." Spahr's voice quavered. And Wilhelm knew. His heart pounded like a hammer in his chest. He did not want to hear any more; but Spahr's voice went on relentlessly: "The *U-47* has gone down with Prien and all of our shipmates aboard. There are no survivors. It happened three days ago, on the eighth, south of Ireland."

"Who did it, Lieutenant?"

"A destroyer, the *Wolverine*. You and I, Wilhelm—we're the only ones left of the Scapa Flow crew. I owe my life to my age, I suppose. Somebody checked through my records and noticed that I was twenty-eight—too old for a mission, they said. So I was given shore duty; taken off the *U-47* and assigned to Wilhelmshaven to train recruits. But how about you, Wilhelm? To what do you owe your life?"

"To the fact that I'm an asshole, Lieutenant."

Late that night, shortly before lights-out on the base, a weeping man walked alone to one of the docking slips. He took a small, dark ball from under his blouse and hurled it violently into the water. The silk stocking unfurled and floated on the green water among the glimmering blue spots of oil.

11

At 3 A.M., March 17, 1941, the tanker *Korsham* sank beneath the surface of the violently roiling sea. The *U-99*, under the command of its captain, Kretschmer, had, with its last torpedo, literally cut the *Korsham* in two; and, 40 seconds after the explosion, nothing but debris remained on the surface.

The tanker was the eleventh victim from the convoy which Kretschmer's *U-99* and Schepke's *U-100* had tracked for ten days. For four hours, almost without interruption, explosions had resounded lugubriously over the Atlantic to the south of Ireland.

Aboard the cargo ships of the convoy, the crews were so exhausted by watches, by continuous calls to battle stations, and by the terror from which they were never free, that they had reached the point of wishing for death to release them from this nightmare. For endless days, they had neither eaten nor slept. Constantly bombarded and straffed by German Condors overhead and torpedoed by the Grey Wolves in the surrounding waters, they reacted like robots to the orders of their officers. They no longer felt either pity for their fallen comrade, or pain at their own wounded. Broken by fear and fatigue, they simply waited destruction.

The surviving ships of the convoy, their sirens shrieking, maneuvered frantically in a red sea illuminated by tankers blazing like gigantic torches. In their frenzied attempts to escape, they rammed torpedoed ships, swamping survivors in the water and thus cutting short their agony.

Aboard the destroyer *Walker*, flagship of the protective escort, Commander Donald MacIntyre, a husky blond Scotsman, paced the bridge furiously, scrutinizing the surface through his binoculars and firing questions at the ASDIC technicians. MacIntyre was in despair. Since the beginning of the attack, he had been compelled to stand by helplessly as the convoy confided to his care was exterminated. The *Walker*, followed by another destroyer, the *Vanoc*, was sailing in large, continuous circles to port of the convoy, where lay the unseen attackers. But it was all in vain. Except from a few ASDIC contacts, of brief duration, the Grey Wolves remained elusive. About an hour earlier, a man on watch aboard the *Walker* had sighted the phosphorescent silhouette of a U-boat on the surface. Immediately, the *Walker* and the *Vanoc* had given chase; but the submarine, despite continuous salvos from the destroyers, had succeeded in diving. For a half hour, the two ships had seeded the surrounding water with depth charges, but with no result.

"It's enough to drive a man crazy," MacIntyre raged.

The hurried footsteps of the radioman distracted him from his anger. "A message from the captain of the *Vanoc,* sir. ASDIC has picked up a submarine."

"If we get hold of that son-of-a-bitch—" MacIntyre swore. "What's his position?"

"At 310°, sir."

"Full speed, all engines," MacIntyre ordered. Then, turning to his second officer, he said: "Instruct all gunners to fire on sight and at will."

The prows of the two destroyers cut a white swath through the sea. They had gone scarcely more than a mile when the watch officer called out, "Over there, Captain! A submarine, over there!"

"We've got the bastard," MacIntyre shouted. "Sparks, send a message to the *Vanoc:* 'He's yours. Ram him!'"

The diesels of the *U-100* were running at slow speed. From the conning tower, Commander Schepke and the watch saw two ships emerge from the darkness. It was impossible to dive. An hour later, the *U-100* had been sighted by the *Walker* and the *Vanoc*. In the depth-charge bombardment which had followed, the U-boat had suffered considerable damage and major leaks. Schepke, his cap at its customary jaunty angle, had announced gaily: "Surface! We're going to plug up our holes, men!"

The men had been inspecting the ship fore and aft for damage when they were sighted for the second time. Now, the men on deck could see the *Vanoc*'s prow emerging from the fog and growing rapidly larger. It was no more than 100 yards away. They watched in terror, their eyes wide, as the monster charged out of the darkness. Screaming, they began to throw themselves into the water.

"Hard to starboard!" Schepke ordered. Then, turning to his

men, he shouted, "Don't panic! She's going to miss us! We're going to be all right!—"

At that moment, the steel mass of the *Vanoc* struck the *U-100*'s starboard at the level of the "winter garden," and Schepke's last words were drowned out as the destroyer passed over the submarine. The *U-100* cracked and was thrust beneath the surface, as though it had been struck by a titanic hammer blow. Schepke emitted one long, inhuman scream as the twisted, torn steel plates from the conning tower housing crushed him against the periscope superstructure. The hellish noise drowned out his second cry, the shriek of a man driven mad by pain. Handsome Schepke, easygoing Schepke, had had both legs pulverized. He felt his strength draining, but, like an animal caught in a trap, he fought to free himself. Then he lay still. He knew that he would die. His head fell forward. Next to him, two men of the watch were torn from the conning tower by the passage of the *Vanoc*. They did not have time to scream as their torn bodies were washed into the sea.

Engulfed by an incredible noise, his eyes wide with pain and horror, Schepke watched as the stern of the *Vanoc* passed over the broken rear deck of the *U-100*. Above him, he saw the destroyer's propellers churning. Then the *Vanoc* passed beyond his line of vision. The steel plates, loosened by the destroyer's thrust, gave way, and Schepke was able to move. What remained of one leg was still pinned between two of the plates. At the moment that Schepke saw, as through a fog, a head appear in the hatchway, the *U-100* gave a great leap, and then capsized. The captain was thrown into the water. His leg was torn from his body and remained between the steel plates.

The men on the *Vanoc*'s deck saw Schepke's bloodless face in the water. He still wore his white cap. The young German commander raised an arm, as though in a final salute, then was covered by a wave and disappeared from sight.

As the *Vanoc*'s searchlights scanned the surface for survivors from the *U-100*, the communications officer aboard the *Walker* announced to MacIntyre: "ASDIC contact, Captain, to starboard."

MacIntyre was startled. He had thought that there was only one U-boat in the area. "Hard to starboard," he commanded.

Aboard the *U-99*, the radioman, Josef Kassel, announced: "The sound of propellers, sir."

"Quick dive to 200 feet!"

The *U-99* had been at 65 feet for only a few minutes. After the sinking of the *Korsham*, Kretschmer had decided to break off combat. He had barely returned to the control room when the alert had sounded. Within a few seconds, the Grey Wolf had dived. And it was the dive that had irritated Kretschmer.

"We were picked up by a destroyer, Captain," the watch officer, Peterson, explained.

"So?" Kretschmer responded drily. "Why couldn't we escape on the surface?"

Kretschmer was furious. He was certain that he would have been able to escape without submerging by taking advantage of the darkness and making full use of his powerful diesel engines. Now, they would have to undergo a depth-charge attack—a prospect which the crew relished no more than Kretschmer himself. He was especially angry, however, because he had been unfair. Peterson's decision was justified. He had simply made use of what he had been taught during training in the Baltic. Moreover, there was no doubt that a submarine on the surface was no match for a destroyer traveling at full speed.

But Kretschmer was tired. He had known for several days that Prien was reported missing. He and Prien and Schepke had all been good friends. In 1936, they had all joined the submarine training fleet, and, together, they had formed the cadre of the had been unfair. Peterson's decision was justified. He had simply future commanders of the Grey Wolves. They were quite different one from another. Prien was a "loner," shy, and yet audacious. Schepke was irreverent, devil-may-care, daring. And Kretschmer himself, a Prussian from Upper Silesia, was a rigorist, always calm, but intensely self-willed. He was nicknamed Otto *der Schweiger*—the silent. It was Kretschmer who had developed the new tactic for attacking convoys. Certain officers were of the opinion that the only way to attack was from beneath the surface, by launching groups of two or four torpedoes at a target. But Kretschmer had come up with the idea of attacking at night, on the surface. He took a position to the rear of the parallel lines of a convoy, following the convoy, then, from the surface, chose his victim and launched a single torpedo—two, if necessary—at each ship. During their last session at Kernevel, Doenitz had agreed that it was an excellent technique. The *Korsham*, which Kretschmer had just sent to the bottom, brought the total enemy tonnage which he had destroyed since the beginning of the war to 325,000 tons—fifty ships.

There were three U-boat commanders, Kretschmer knew, whom the English would have paid any price to neutralize: Prien, Schepke, and himself. Prien was their first great victory.

Kretschmer stood silently in the control room, chewing intently on an unlighted cigar. His eyes were bloodshot, his nerves taut with the fatigue, the strain of combat, and the continuous dives of the past ten days. The crew of the *U-99* was likewise at the end of its strength. When the last torpedo was sent on its way, Kretschmer had announced: "We're heading home to Lorient." He sensed the relief of his men. His own reaction, however, was one of gloom. No one else aboard knew it yet, but the *U-99* was to be Kretschmer's last command. Doenitz, after many attempts at persuasion, had finally ended by ordering Kretschmer assigned to his staff.

"You're tired, Kretschmer," the admiral had said. "You've been at sea for almost a year. You'll have to learn to take care of yourself."

"I'm in excellent health, Admiral."

"People always say that. Then, one day, because a man is tired, he makes a small mistake—one that costs a great deal. No, this time it's going to be different. I've already decided. I want you with me at headquarters."

The Lion's decision was irreversible.

"More propeller noises," Kassel reported. "There are two of them." His hydrophones had just picked up another enemy ship.

Almost immediately, Kretschmer heard the detonation of depth charges. He counted twelve of them. The *U-99* reared, pitched, and rolled crazily from the shock of the explosions. "I've never heard them so close," Kretschmer said to himself. "Their accuracy is remarkable."

Suddenly, the *U-99* was in darkness. The men fell to the deck, holding onto their stations as best they could.

"Three hundred and fifty feet," Kretschmer shouted.

Flashlights threw their narrow beams on the control-room dials. Then, another series of explosions: fourteen, this time. The *U-99* was shaken with extraordinary violence, and the men who had been hurt in falling began to scream. Finally, the emergency lighting system was activated. Kretschmer looked around at his crew. Terror was on their faces. The engineer crawled over to him: "Captain!"

"Yes?"

"The depth-indicator is out of commission."

Kretschmer paled. The loss of that instrument in the present situation was critical. It was no longer possible to know the submarine's depth.

"Rear compartment, Captain."

"Report."

"Fuel leakage from the aft tanks, sir."

"Forward compartment, Captain."

"Report."

"We have a ruptured turbulure, sir. We're taking on water rapidly."

As the *Wabos*, the depth charges, exploded and tossed the submarine about, Kretschmer concentrated on reaching a decision. Already, the entire vessel was ankle-deep in a slimy mixture of fuel and sea water. With every pitch and roll, the mass of liquid rushed fore and aft and from side to side, making the *U-99* list dangerously.

"Torpedo room, Captain."

88   THE ADMIRAL'S WOLF PACK

"Report."

"There's a depth-indicator in here that seems to be working."

"What's our depth?" Kretschmer shouted.

"You're not going to believe this, Captain—"

"Give me the goddam depth! Fast!"

There was a brief silence. Then: "Six hundred feet."

The men exchanged horrified looks. Their vessel was more than a hundred feet deeper than the depth at which a submarine's hull can be crushed by the pressure of the water.

"Electrician, Captain."

"Report."

"Our propellers are barely turning, sir."

Kretschmer threw down his cigar. "If this keeps up," he told himself, "then it's the end." He was acutely aware that a submarine deprived of speed during a dive is doomed: it sinks.

"Forward compartment, Captain. We're now at six hundred and fifty feet."

A sailor standing near Kretschmer, his eyes wide with fear, whispered: "We're dead."

"One more word," Kretschmer replied, "and I'll beat the shit out of you."

Kassel was still at his hydrophone station: "Propellers coming closer, Captain."

Kretschmer knew then that there was only one thing he could do: surface. No matter what the cost. Regardless of the destroyers waiting there to finish him off.

"Surface," he ordered. "Empty all tanks."

A petty officer waded through the mixture of fuel and water and grasped the lever controlling the compressed-air valve. He reddened with the effort of trying to move it, but it would not budge. Panic was on the faces of the men. If the lever did not work, it was the end. It was as simple as that.

"Aft torpedo room, Captain. We're taking on water here."

Kretschmer did not answer. Instead, he rushed toward the lever, pushing the petty officer aside roughly. "Here, help me!" he ordered.

The two men braced themselves against the lever and pulled with all their strength.

"Six hundred and seventy-five feet, Captain," the forward compartment announced.

Kretschmer, face scarlet, teeth clenched, fingers white, continued pulling. Suddenly, the lever unjammed and air whistled into the ballast tanks. The U-99 shivered, and the noise of her propellers became more distinct.

"Six hundred feet," Peterson announced. "Five hundred and seventy-five feet . . . five hundred and sixty feet . . . We're rising . . . We're rising . . ."

At 200 feet, Kretschmer ordered Schröder, the engineer, to bring the ship to an even keel. There might still be a chance, he thought, to escape the destroyers waiting above. But the submarine's propellers had been disaligned by depth-charge explosions, and the batteries of the electric engines were almost dead. There was nothing to do but take the U-boat to the surface.

As soon as it broke the surface, Kassel transmitted the U-99's last message to Kernevel: "Two destroyers . . . depth charges . . . 53,000 tons . . . captivity . . . Kretschmer."

Then the crew was ordered to don their life preservers.

The first thing that met Kretschmer's eyes when he went above was the dark, towering flank of the *Walker*. "By God," he told himself, "if I had a torpedo, I'd show them!"

But there was no possibility of further combat. The U-99 was in a sorry state. It was almost a total wreck, listing badly to starboard, its propellers ruined, its diesels out of commission. It lay there, rising and falling in the swell, totally exposed to the destroyer's guns.

Aboard the *Walker*, Commander MacIntyre was in a quandary. For several seconds, he did not know what to do. The officers around him on the bridge were still in shock at the sudden appearance of the submarine on the surface. "If they fire a torpedo," a sailor observed uneasily, "we're done for."

The sailor's comment shook MacIntyre out of his indecision.

He would follow the orders of the British Admiralty: "Attempt by any means to capture a U-boat intact for technical study."

"It's easy to give such orders," MacIntyre muttered. "But how does one go about capturing a submarine?" He stared intently at the Grey Wolf rolling and pitching, its engines dead, 200 yards away. Then he reached a decision.

"Sweep the tower and the deck with machine-gun fire," he ordered. "Gunners, zero in on the sub, but don't hit it. We must force its crew to abandon ship."

To the *Vanoc*, whose own propellers had been damaged, he dispatched a message: "Keep your distance. Keep your guns on the enemy, but open fire only at my command."

Machine-gun fire and salvos of artillery filled the night as the *Walker* moved at reduced speed along the port side of the dying Grey Wolf.

Kretschmer, hunched down in the conning tower housing, was in despair. He knew that the death agony of the *U-99* was beginning. Rising, and protected from the machine-gun fire by the list of his vessel, he went to the voice tube: "Captain to crew: We are no longer in a position to fight. Prepare to abandon ship. As you come above, remain to port. Prepare explosives to scuttle."

Kretschmer was silent for a moment. Then, determined and imperturbable though he had always been, he was overcome by deep emotion. In a rough voice, he spoke again. "I regret that I've not been able to get you home again. We've spent a long time together. You've been the best crew that a man can ask for. To every one of you, I say: Courage, and good luck. And may God have us in his keeping."

The crew of the *U-99* climbed topside through the fore and aft hatches and then scrambled to port, where they were sheltered from the constant fire of the destroyer's machine guns. Holding onto the storage compartments, or else lying flat on the decks as their sinking vessel drifted slowly in the sea, they kept their eyes on a small red glow which alternately brightened and

dimmed on the conning tower. It was Kretschmer's cigar, which
he puffed calmly as he sat awaiting the end. The orderly had
just brought him his dress cap, startlingly white, which he
jammed onto his head. The *Walker*, now stationary 250 feet to
the submarine's port, continued its fire; but Kretschmer refused
to take any action until his men were all topside. Meanwhile,
Volkmar Koenig, the midshipman, was distributing cigarettes to
the men on deck. "Take a lot of them while you can," he en-
couraged them. They all lighted three or four cigarettes at a time
and puffed rapidly.

Suddenly, von Knebel-Döberitz, the second officer, appeared
in the hatchway. "Captain, the scuttle detail can't get started.
The door to the compartment where the explosives are stored
is jammed shut."

As Kretschmer was about to answer, the *U-99*'s prow rose from
the water. The men aft were thrown into the sea. Peterson, with
a scream, tumbled down the open hatchway into the flooded
control room. Kretschmer, oblivious to any danger, threw away
his cigar and plunged down the hatchway. Peterson was fighting
against the current as he was dragged toward the aft compartment of the vessel. Kretschmer shouted: "Give me your hand!
Hold on! Try to get a grip on me!"

Holding onto the ladder with his left hand, he used his right
to feel frantically in the darkness. He felt Peterson's two hands
grip him; then, straining every muscle, inch by inch, he pulled
the man through the water in the rolling, sinking submarine until he was safely on the ladder.

In the water around the U-boat, sailors were swimming about,
calling to one another, trying to form a circle. Only a few yards
away, Volkmar Koenig floated in his life jacket, so exhausted that
he was fast asleep.

Kretschmer, as soon as he had brought Peterson topside, felt
around the conning tower housing until he found what he was
looking for: his signal lamp. It still worked. "Peterson," he ordered, "send a message to the British: 'Captain to captain. Save
my men. I am sinking.'"

The response was immediate. The *Walker*'s searchlights began sweeping the sea for survivors, while three lifeboats were put down to rescue the shipwrecked German seamen.

Commander MacIntyre's mind, however, was elsewhere. He was obsessed by a single idea: to capture the *U-99*. He turned to the second officer. "I think it's time for us to board her and try to secure a towline," he said. "Assemble a boarding party and let's try to get alongside her."

As the boarding party grouped on the *Walker*'s deck, the destroyer began a cautious approach to the Grey Wolf.

Meanwhile, Kretschmer, pale with rage, had guessed the enemy's intentions. The *U-99* was sinking, but not fast enough to avoid capture.

"We have to do something to keep them from coming aboard," he roared.

Schröder, who was standing nearby, answered immediately: "I'll do it, Captain. I'll go below and open the ballast sluices so that the water can come in faster—"

"Out of the question, Schröder! It's up to me to do it," Kretschmer shouted, as he grabbed Schröder by the arm and attempted to push him away from the hatch.

But Schröder, for the first time in his career, disobeyed his captain. He broke away from Kretschmer and plunged into the control room. The flank of the *Walker* was now no more than 200 feet away, and the British boarding party was preparing to leap aboard the dying submarine.

There was a long, strident whistling sound. Schröder had opened wide the sluices, and the air was rushing out of the ballast tanks. Now, the *Walker* was 100 feet away. Kretschmer could see sailors on her foredeck, holding grappling irons and lines.

"Schröder," he shouted down the hatch. "Schröder! Come up! Schröder, I *order* you—!"

It was too late. The *U-99* was suddenly shaken by a violent shiver. There was a sound like a deep sigh, or a death rattle.

The submarine's prow reared vertically out of the water, pointing proudly toward the heavens. Kretschmer and Peterson were thrown into the sea. When they regained the surface, the swell had already dragged them more than 50 feet from the submarine. Kretschmer turned for a last look at his vessel. There was another sigh, deeper this time, heavier. The prow seemed to rise even more, as though it would leap from the water. Then the U-99 disappeared forever into the sea which had been the scene of so many of its missions and so many of its battles.

Kretschmer swam toward the *Walker*, which had now come to a full stop. A boarding net had been installed to starboard. The survivors of the U-99 were climbing laboriously to the destroyer's deck. Kretschmer was the last man to begin. He found that he no longer had the strength to climb. The weight of his boots, filled with water, was too much for him. He was utterly exhausted. The fatigue induced by the past ten days of battle, the terrible strain of losing his ship, all that he had been through, suddenly overwhelmed him. And, as the *Walker* resumed its course, he remained hanging from the net. A few moments more, and he knew that he would have to let go. His eyes were closed, and his breath came in gasps. He was preparing himself for death when he felt a hand clutch at him. It was his boatswain who, from the destroyer's deck, had seen Kretschmer's plight and had scurried down the net to save him.

"It's the captain!" he shouted.

On the destroyer's deck, the German seamen, surrounded by guards, let out a loud and joyful hurrah.

Slowly, supported by his boatswain, Kretschmer dragged himself up the net, step by step, until finally he stood aboard the *Walker*. He had not had time to catch his breath when he felt a pistol against his chest. Before him was a British officer, holding the weapon in his right hand as, with his left, he removed the binoculars still hanging from Kretschmer's neck. Kretschmer stared at him for an instant; then, before the astonished eyes of the British seamen who had witnessed his capture, he burst out laughing.

A few minutes later, Commander MacIntyre, who had come to see what a U-boat commander looked like, returned to his bridge. He was both irritated and disillusioned. Kretschmer, tall, blond, with cold eyes and, for all of his waterlogged appearance, an aristocratic demeanor, had greeted MacIntyre with a smart military salute. It irritated MacIntyre that he had instinctively returned the salute. Then, when the German commander said, "I'm grateful to you for having rescued my men," MacIntyre, an officer of His Majesty's Navy, and in full sight of his crew, had answered politely, as though he were sitting quietly in his club in London: "Not at all. It was the thing to do."

On March 18, MacIntyre received a message which read: THIS IS THE BEST NEWS I'VE HAD SINCE THE BEGINNING OF THE WAR. It was signed: WINSTON CHURCHILL.

12

From Kernevel, a radio message went out continuously every fifteen minutes: "U-99 and U-100, report your position." "U-99, report your position." "U-100, report your position."

At Kernevel, no one rested, and sleep was rare. It was a giant message center, constantly receiving information from Doenitz' submarines and unceasingly transmitting orders to them. There was a continuous coming and going of couriers bringing other messages: messages transmitted by enemy surface vessels and intercepted and decoded by the German Navy. There were also intelligence reports received from agents of the *Abwehr;* and some—though these were too few—obtained by air reconnaissance.

Daily, Doenitz faced the same questions: "What shipping lanes will the enemy use?" "How can I find out?" And: "How can I intercept this shipping?"

For the answer to these questions, the admiral could rely only on his own talent for analysis and on his instinct. Indeed, other than the daily reports transmitted to him by his U-boats whenever they were cruising on the surface on a mission, he had no major, organized source of information. On one occasion, he had taken advantage of a hunting party hosted by *Reichsmarschall* Hermann Goering to ask Hitler for twelve aircraft—aircraft which would be directly under his orders and the function of which would be to reconnoiter the surface and alert U-boats of enemy ships. In order to convince the Führer, it had been necessary for him to cite only two figures: "An aircraft flying at 10,000 feet, in one hour, can reconnoiter 60,000 square kilometers of ocean. A submarine, in one hour, can reconnoiter 400 square kilometers."

Hitler, impressed by the argument, had replied: "All right, Admiral, take the planes. But the *Reichsmarschall's* going to be furious, and you'll have to settle with him."

Goering's fury was not long in making itself felt. Immediately after the hunt, he had summoned Doenitz and Godt to the train station at Pontoise and received them in the luxuriously decorated drawing-room car of his personal train. The interview had gone badly. Goering, enraged by Doenitz' courteous but firm refusal to give him back his planes, had used terms of extraordinary vulgarity, even for him. Doenitz had not backed down an inch. On leaving the train, however, the admiral said to Godt: "I'll bet you anything that the Fat Man is going to move heaven and earth to get even. Since 1935, he's been saying: 'Everything that flies belongs to me.'"

The Fat Man, as Goering was known to the submariners, indeed refused to accept defeat, and had gone to Hitler and threatened to resign. Hitler, irritated, but preferring to avoid the extended period of sulking which was one of the *Reichsmarschall's* stratagems, had intervened in person to settle the affair. "I have a compromise that will satisfy everybody," he had announced. "The planes will remain at the disposal of the submarine command, but will belong once more to the Luftwaffe."

It goes without saying that, with few exceptions, Doenitz had never been able to make use of the planes as he wished. German pilots, unaccustomed to the sea, were unable to report the positions of convoys with exactitude. And Goering's inability to build long-range planes effectively deprived the Grey Wolves forever of the "eyes" which they needed so badly.

Doenitz had another serious worry. Britain was rapidly constructing a fleet of fast, heavily armed destroyers which, when added to the vessels of the Coastal Command, would virtually prevent his U-boats from venturing within 200 miles of the British coast. The Grey Wolves, depending solely upon the code-breakers of Doenitz' Section B, and upon the admiral's singular intuition, would therefore have to find their prey in the open sea. Day or night, whenever a message was received from a U-boat reporting the sighting of a convoy, Doenitz himself—sometimes wearing his pajamas and a robe—took personal charge of operations. First, he signaled all of his available craft and ordered them to set a course for the convoy. Then, he waited, nervously and with great impatience, for news from his commanders. The first reports arrived: "Contact established"; "Enemy sighted. I am attacking"; "I am in the area indicated"; "I see the smoke from their stacks." After a long delay for the gathering and classification of such messages, the admiral was in a position to work out a preliminary situation report on what was happening far out in the Atlantic.

Often, the reports received were discouraging: "Contact lost"; "Attacked by aircraft. I am diving"; "Short on fuel; must return to base"; "Engine trouble; am abandoning the hunt."

And sometimes, despite the admiral's insistent command, "Report position, Report position," a submarine remained utterly silent. On such occasions, Doenitz was constantly stalking into the communications room and asking—gruffly, in order to hide his concern—"Still no news?"

"No, Admiral."

Doenitz would then lock himself in his office and himself write to the families of the missing men.

Doenitz knew what these families were going through. After the disappearance of Prien, Schepke, and Kretschmer, his own son-in-law, Lieutenant Commander Hessler, had been assigned to the wolf pack patrolling the African coast in May 1941, off the port of Freetown. There, submarines had sunk seventy-four ships in the convoys arriving from the Cape of Good Hope and South America.

The admiral's two sons were also in the *Kriegsmarine*. One had chosen to serve on a vedette boat; the second was assigned to a U-boat.

Suddenly, it seemed that the seas were empty.

In the map room next to the operations room—which Doenitz called "our museum"—there was a chart reflecting submarine strikes. It showed a sharp drop: forty-five ships in July and August 1941; that is, only half the number of ships sunk in October 1940.

"This is impossible to explain," Doenitz told his staff, his voice shaking with anger. "For two months, our vessels have been unable to locate convoys. And, what is even more strange, they no sooner sight a convoy than they report contact has been lost."

The admiral, hands clasped behind his back, paced the length and width of the map room. "Gentlemen, I am convinced that the British have developed a system of radio goniometric detection which enables them to discover the position of our submarines at very considerable distances, whether they are on or beneath the surface.

"The British must be intercepting messages from our units. All they need then is a goniometric triangulation, computed on the basis of stations scattered over the ocean, to locate our wolf packs and to know what forces are at our disposal."

The admiral stopped before the graphs covering the walls. "You see, Godt," he said to his chief-of-staff, "these curves speak for themselves. Once more, we have proof that in time of war we must pay for our peacetime negligence. If we had had a hundred submarines operating in the Atlantic at the beginning of the war, we could have brought the English to their knees.

"Even now, the only response that would be able to neutralize the enormous technical progress made by the English would be for us to scatter twenty wolf packs throughout the Atlantic. As it is, all we can do, since we do not have enough submarines, is to order the few that we have to maintain radio silence as much as possible and try to direct them into what we believe are combat zones. I will never be able to understand why, at the very beginning of the war, we did not initiate a massive submarine-construction program."

Following Commander Prien's victory at Scapa Flow, Hitler had given in to Doenitz' demand that his Grey Wolves be given priority in construction. But various factors had rendered the Führer's promise worthless. For one thing, the Naval High Command had insisted upon pursuing its construction of surface vessels. For another, a shortage of copper had delayed work on new submarines. And, above all, the time required for construction of a U-boat had risen, first to nineteen months, and then to thirty. Instead of the nineteen submarines per month that Doenitz had been promised, he got only two per month during the first half of 1940, and six per month during the second half. This was at a time when submarine losses—during the first months of the war, before the wolf pack tactics had been developed—were particularly high. By September 1, 1940, for example, twenty-eight new submarines had been delivered; and twenty-eight submarines had been reported lost. After one year of war, "the man who made the ocean tremble" was in command of the same number of Grey Wolves as at the beginning of the war. It was only during the second half of 1941, after two years of war, that there was an appreciable increase in the size of the submarine fleet, with twenty vessels being delivered every month.

The launching of a submarine, however, did not mean that it was ready to strike out into the Atlantic. First, crews had to be trained. "Italian submarines," Doenitz pointed out to Godt, "sink an average of 20 tons of shipping every day, per submarine. Our figure is 1,000 tons a day. If our crews are capable of a return fifty times greater than that of the Italians, it is because we spend five months training our men in every aspect of seamanship and combat. Man, after all, is an alien in the sea; and submarine warfare is the most demanding kind of warfare. In a submarine, there is no time for on-the-job training."

The admiral was silent for a moment. Several hours earlier, he received a message which had brought him to the peak of fury. Then, with a last glance at the graphs, he announced: "Here are the latest orders from Berlin. In order to alleviate our difficulties, the higher-ups have decided to accelerate the training of our crews and officers in the Baltic. I did everything I could to oppose such a move; to make them understand that five months is the absolute minimum of training necessary in order to prepare a man, morally and physically, for combat. I was wasting my time. The Führer now orders that the training period not exceed two months. 'Practice,' he says, 'can be acquired in combat.' And he also says—as though the two could be compared—'A good infantryman takes even less time to train.' So, once more, we are obliged to ignore both our priorities and what we have learned from experience. There is nothing I can do but obey.

"So, gentlemen, a few days from now, five U-boats are going to arrive—manned by sailors trained under the new accelerated program."

The admiral was silent once more. The last rays of the setting sun fell suddenly on his expressionless face, making it a study in light and shadow. In the twilight which filled the operations room, there was not a sound. Then Doenitz spoke again, in a hollow voice: "May God help our German sailors!"

13

At 7:12 A.M., Rudy Geften, medic of the *U-570*, staggered toward the ladder leading topside. His face was green with seasickness, and he felt that he could not take another step. The submarine was permeated by a pestilential stench: from kitchen garbage, which no one bothered to throw overboard; from stopped-up toilets that no one was willing to repair; and from pools of vomit that seemed to be everywhere on the deck. To these nauseating odors were joined those of stale fuel-oil and humidity. The entire crew was sick and incapable of performing their duties competently. Orders, when they were carried out at all, were done so haphazardly.

Geften, clutching the ladder, heard one of his shipmates, Faurmann, from his bunk, growl in his raucous voice: "That son-of-a-bitch is going to kill us all. The bastard is staying on the surface on purpose!"

An approving murmur erupted from the other bunks.

The "son-of-a-bitch" was Commander Schmitt,* the "old man" of the U-570.

Since its departure from Wilhelmshaven, the U-570 had had one disaster after another. The training of its crew was suddenly broken off, and the vessel was ordered to Lorient—the last of the five U-boats which Doenitz was expecting. When the order was received, the men had been disturbed and incredulous. Walter Faurmann—called "Shrimp" because of his diminutive size—had expressed everyone's opinion: "They're out of their minds! What do we know about submarines? We hardly know how to make the goddam thing move!"

The most disturbed of all, however, was undoubtedly the captain of the U-boat. Schmitt, when a messenger handed him an envelope from the commander of the training fleet containing orders to set sail on his first *Feindfahrt* (search-and-destroy mission), had turned pale. "This must be a joke of some kind," he shouted. "They can't mean this!"

"I don't think it's a joke, sir," the messenger replied, before executing a smart about-face.

For a time, Schmitt was stripped of the arrogance and haughtiness which had made him an object of contempt among his fellow submarine officers. He lost no time in reporting to the

* A pseudonym.

commander of the fleet. "It's not possible to carry out this order, sir," he pleaded. "My crew has had only two months of training. They are absolutely in no condition for a combat situation."

The commander said nothing, and Schmitt rushed on in a voice strident with alarm. "This order is nothing more than a warrant for our death."

The commander, with great deliberation, crushed out his cigarette in an ashtray. Then, in a voice of ice, he replied: "Commander Schmitt, you have received orders to report to the Western Fleet at Lorient. It should not be necessary for me to remind you that orders are not open to discussion."

"Then at least give me a few experienced men—"

"You will weigh anchor at 5 o'clock tomorrow morning, Commander. Dismissed."

Returning to the *U-570*, Schmitt had ordered his second officer, Lieutenant Bundt: "See that we have the proper ammunition. Tomorrow morning, at 5 o'clock, we sail for Lorient."

"You're joking," the astonished officer replied.

Schmitt did not bother to answer. Standing on deck, silent, gloomy, he had watched the torpedoes being brought aboard. The obvious lack of enthusiasm among his men, and their muttered comments, deeply angered him. "With men like these," he told Bundt, "we're not ready for Lorient. They're not seamen. They're cattle."

He was not far wrong. The *U-570* was barely into the open sea before the medic approached the captain. "Sir, there are nine men *kaput*."

"Well, look after them," Schmitt replied, with an air of disdain. "They'll soon be ten."

"You don't know what it's like below, sir," Geften ventured, swallowing with difficulty. "It's a real cesspool. It's enough to make anybody sick—" Then he walked hastily toward "the winter garden," and under the stares of the men on watch, vomited, moaning.

That night, toward midnight, the sea became rough. The

U-boat pitched and rolled among the waves. At times, her prow was below the line of the horizon. The port watch was stricken and crumpled against the superstructure, shaken by continuous spasms.

"Take that man below," Schmitt ordered, and then watched contemptuously as the inert, vomit-stained figure was dragged through the hatch.

The third officer had appeared on deck shortly afterward. "Captain—"

"What is it now?"

"Sir, the men would be very grateful if you'd give the order to dive, so that they'll have a chance to get their sea legs."

"Tell the men," Schmitt answered sarcastically, "in case they've never been told, that the mission of a submarine is to search for the enemy on the surface. And, if they need another reason, explain that a submarine must recharge its batteries. We'll dive at dawn, and not before."

For five interminable hours, the crew's quarters echoed with obscenities, moans, gagging, threats, and curses.

Then, at the first light of dawn, Schmitt's voice came over the intercom: "Prepare to dive!"

Schmitt had no sooner closed the hatch than he was overwhelmed by the stench. His stomach overreacted, painfully.

He looked around the control room. The men on duty were on their feet, clutching levers to support themselves, their faces greenish, their uniforms soiled by vomit. In the bunks, and even on the decks, human figures lay, oblivious, gasping for breath. At almost regular intervals, groans escaped from the prostrate forms. And everywhere was the incredible, all-pervading, nauseating odor.

"Clean this place up," Schmitt ordered, beside himself with rage. "It's like a pigpen!"

A detail of men dragged themselves forward painfully, armed with buckets and mops and brooms. But these men, too, soon fell to the deck, moaning.

Four days had passed since sailing from Wilhelmshaven; four days of nightmare for the forty-two men of the *U-570*. On the second day out, the submarine had run aground, the crew was terrified. It was two hours before they were able to resume their course. There had been moments of panic which Schmitt, his officers, the engineer and the medic had had to overcome by beating, with their fists, the delirious men who tried to leave the submarine through the hatchways while the vessel was aground at a depth of 125 feet. Then, there was an error in navigation that brought everyone's exasperation to the boiling point. The *U-570*, it was discovered, was too far north, and lay only 120 miles south of Ireland.

Schmitt, after punishing the navigator by placing him under arrest for fifteen days, then decided to surface. The looks of the men, when they heard his order, were venomous. Since running aground and going off course, the men had lost all confidence in their captain.

Schmitt himself was overcome by fear. He sensed that the slightest provocation could now unleash a full-fledged mutiny. His revolver never left his side. He no longer slept, and when he was topside he kept one eye constantly on the hatch. He half expected to see it swing shut, and then to feel the submarine begin its dive, leaving him to drown among the waves.

The *U-570* had been cruising on the surface for approximately one hour when the radioman's head appeared through the hatchway. "Message from headquarters, Captain."

Schmitt jumped. "Give it to me!"

In the rising northwest wind, he had scanned the text: WHAT ARE YOU DOING THERE STOP EXPLAIN STOP YOU ARE LONG OVERDUE STOP.

The Lion was waiting for him at Lorient, and Schmitt had no illusions about what his treatment would be there. Certainly, he was in for a severe reprimand. It was not impossible that Doenitz might even relieve him of his command.

On the foredeck, a clean-up detail had just completed its work. Despite the overcast sky, the sea shone with a silvery light that seemed to stretch out into infinity.

The navigator appeared on deck. He had just calculated the position of the U-570. "Our position, Captain: 32°42′ N. and 58°55′ W."

"I hope that this time you're not mistaken," Schmitt growled.

"I hope not, Captain."

Schmitt's eyes swept over the horizon. Then he ordered: "Prepare to dive."

Commander Schmitt had just secured the hatch when, 2,000 yards away, out of the clouds, a reconnaissance plane from the naval base at Reykjavik emerged in search of a convoy which had gone off course in a storm. The pilot sighted the U-570 as it was sinking beneath the waves, and, a few moments later, he was over the patch of foam stirred up by the diving submarine. At that instant, the pilot pressed his release button. Nothing happened. The depth charges with which his plane was armed were jammed in their bays. The pilot cursed briefly, then circled back. By then, the submarine had disappeared. He sent a message back to his base: HAVE SIGHTED U-BOAT. AM LOW ON FUEL. SEND OUT RELIEF.

At 9:27 A.M. Schmitt rose from his bunk. There was a brassy taste in his mouth. His eyelids were swollen from lack of sleep, and his temples throbbed with fatigue. He passed a dry tongue over his lips, stretched. His orderly brought coffee. As he drank, the captain walked toward the navigator's post. He had formed the habit of checking the navigator's calculations—and with good reason, he reflected.

The clean-up detail had completed their work two hours earlier, and the air below was now breathable. The condition of the crew had also improved. There were still a half-dozen men sick, but, generally, they were beginning to get their sea legs. The engineer saluted and announced: "Everything shipshape, sir. This sub is really a honey."

Schmitt responded with a gesture. He closed his eyes for a moment, and then opened them wearily. The throbbing, pounding headache had been with him for the past twenty-four hours. He sensed the dangerous tension that persisted aboard the U-570. The morale of the crew, who had been sorely tried by conditions aboard the submarine and also by their own and their officers' lack of experience, was alarmingly low. He looked around at his men. Their faces were set in an expression of discouragement and simmering anger. "When a man is seasick," he had heard during a discussion at the officers' mess at Kiel, "there is absolutely nothing that you can do with him." He grunted.

Schmitt's headache was becoming more unbearable. He looked at his watch. It was time to surface so as to be able to receive any messages sent out by headquarters. Perhaps an hour of fresh air would do him some good. If the headache continued, he would take a few more pills. He had taken too many of them already in the past twenty-four hours, without much result.

"Surface!" he ordered, then climbed into the airlock.

"Tower above surface," the engineer announced.

Schmitt opened the hatch and emerged topside, taking great gulps of fresh air into his lungs. Suddenly, he stiffened and his eyes grew wide. There was a plane heading straight for the submarine.

"Dive! Dive!" he shouted, and then plunged down the hatchway, frantically pulling the hatch closed behind him. He had not finished securing it when the plane was directly overhead.

Group Captain Thompson, of the 269th Squadron, threw a quick look across the cockpit of his Hudson and rested his thumb on the release button. He pressed, and four depth charges fell into a neat frame around the U-570, exploding with a force which shook the submarine violently from stem to stern.

For the men of the U-570, it was their baptism of fire. It was also their initiation into the terror of combat.

"Two hundred and fifty feet!" Schmitt ordered, and the submarine plunged crazily into the depths.

"Forward compartment, Captain. We're taking on water here," reported a quavering voice.

"Electrical control, Captain!" another voice shouted in panic. "Chlorine fumes!"

Schmitt was in a panic of indecision. He was torn between an impulse to surface, and the urge, equally strong, to dive even deeper. He was agonizing over the dilemma when a line of men, fingers clutching at their chests, their bodies racked by continuous coughing, their breath coming in gasps, their eyes glazed, approached the captain and asked permission to report to the infirmary.

Schmitt began to tremble uncontrollably. He felt the hostile stares of his crew on him, and he was seized with such fear that a cool judgment was impossible. In such a situation, he had been taught, the captain should order repairs to be made; he should continue diving ever deeper, for only in the depths was there safety for his men and his ship. But he was exhausted and his judgment was clouded by sleeplessness and tension. In a trembling voice, he gave an order which he would live to regret: "Surface."

The *U-570* had hardly broken surface when Group Captain Thompson dived straight toward it, his 7.7 machine guns blazing. Schmitt, and the two men who had followed him topside, threw themselves flat on their stomachs. They had not even had time to see that the plane was still directly overhead. The machine-gun rounds struck the plates of the hull with a continuous staccato ping, and the roar of the plane's engines was clearly audible within the U-boat. The crew, in a panic, jostled one another in their frenzy to reach the forward and aft hatches which they were trying desperately to open.

In the Hudson's cockpit, Thompson boiled with rage. He had not a single bomb. Unaware of what had occurred aboard the submarine, he was certain that, in a moment, it would disappear once more beneath the surface. His machine guns alone were incapable of inflicting serious damage to the German vessel. He had already radioed his base for assistance, and he was increasingly disgusted that, as yet, there was no sign of other planes.

"All right, boys," Thompson told the three airmen who comprised his crew, "let's do it again!" But, as the Hudson circled for its third pass, preparing to rake the tower and the afterdeck of the U-boat again with its seven machine guns, Thompson countermanded his order:

"Hold your fire!"

The group captain had seen a German seaman waving a shirt, as a white flag, from the conning tower.

Thompson and his men were now at a loss. "This is the first time I've ever heard of a sub surrendering to a plane," the co-pilot said. "How the devil are we going to get it back to base?"

"This is a hell of a situation," Thompson muttered. "Navigator," he ordered. "Send them a message with the mirror: 'Do not go near your gun. Do not attempt to scuttle. All men on deck. At the slightest movement, we will open fire.'"

There was an immediate answer from Schmitt: "I am unable to scuttle." The fact was that, at that moment, Schmitt was no longer in command of his crew. For his men, this surrender without a struggle represented liberation from the terror with which they had lived since the first day of their *Feindfahrt*. Now, they climbed up on deck and, despite the rolling and pitching of the submarine, began joyously waving their handkerchiefs and caps at the circling plane. Among the men who were still below, a short fight occurred. A mechanic surprised the radioman in the act of sending a message. Unable to raise headquarters, he was sending out a continuous distress signal.

"Look at that son-of-a-bitch!" the mechanic shrieked. "He's going to screw us all!"

Three sailors leaped upon the radioman, who was in the midst of transcribing a message received from a nearby U-boat: WE ARE COMING AT FULL SPEED. REPORT YOUR POSITION— But he did not finish. He was torn from his seat and beaten until he was unconscious.

It was noon. Two Catalina seaplanes arrived in response to Thompson's latest message. Their mission was to land, take aboard the German officers, and place a boarding crew on the submarine. The sea was too rough, however, to allow them to set down, and they, too, in turn, began circling endlessly overhead. As the British airmen watched, the German submariners, perched on the conning tower and in the "winter garden," ate a leisurely lunch. Only one man did not eat: Commander Hans Schmitt.

Toward 1700 hours, an armed Norwegian trawler, the *Northern Chief*, diverted from its course by the British Admiralty, appeared. Its mission was to take aboard the enlisted men of the *U-570*. But the sea continued rough, and it could not safely draw alongside the submarine, or let down small boats, to do so.

Meanwhile, night was approaching, and no one, either aboard the *Northern Chief* or in the British Admiralty, doubted for a moment that the Germans would take advantage of darkness to attempt to dive and thus make their escape. The captain of the trawler brought his ship as near as he dared to the U-boat, and announced, through a megaphone: "The captain of your submarine is ordered to board my ship. Otherwise, I will fire and sink you."

Schmitt replied: "The sea is too rough. It is impossible."

"It is up to you to find a way. You have five minutes to come aboard. Otherwise, I will open fire." Then, in order to give proof of his intentions, the Norwegian captain ordered his guns to be trained on the submarine. From his bridge, he could see a bizarre disturbance on the U-boat's deck. Grinning, he turned to his second mate. "I have the feeling," he said, "that if that Kraut captain delays in coming, his men are going to throw him overboard."

He was correct. On the *U-570*, the sailors had only one wish: to see Schmitt go aboard the trawler. And they were prepared to take whatever action was necessary to save their own lives and keep the Norwegian ship from firing upon them.

Schmitt, trapped against the conning tower housing, face to face with his hostile and determined crew, for the first time since the beginning of the disastrous mission, attempted to use reason in dealing with his men. But it was too late for reason, and his arguments were unavailing. One sailor, less panic-stricken than the others, approached Schmitt and said, in obvious embarrassment: "Captain, they're serious about throwing you overboard. Listen, save yourself. Do what the ship says."

"Very well," Schmitt replied. He called Bundt. "Lieutenant, have an inflatable raft lowered. From this moment, you have command of the *U-570.*"

As the men prepared the raft, Schmitt went below to his quarters and packed his toothbrush, razor, and a few items of clothing into a bag. Then he removed his pistol from its holster and stared at it for a few moments. There was a strong temptation to put a bullet into his brain and be done with it. He raised the weapon to his mouth, and the touch of the cold steel sent a chill through his body. Brusquely, he threw the pistol onto his bunk and quickly climbed topside. As soon as he appeared in the open air, the captain of the trawler, which was now motionless twenty yards from the submarine, announced: "The five minutes are up. Either you come aboard immediately, or I give the order to open fire!"

Schmitt looked around at his men. He would have liked to say a few final words, to give them the customary advice regarding captivity; and also to wish them good luck.

"For Christ's sake," a voice near him growled, "move your ass!"

He went down to the foredeck where three men, with great difficulty, were holding a tossing raft against the submarine's flank. A line had been shot from the trawler and secured to one of the raft's cleats. Schmitt threw his bag into the tossing craft and stepped aboard. At that moment, a gust of wind tore the white cap from his head and sent it spinning away. In his at-

tempt to retrieve it, he lost his balance and fell into the bottom of
the raft. The men released the line and, from the trawler,
Norwegian sailors began hauling the light raft, tossing like a
cork, toward the *Northern Chief*. Over the wind and the roar of
the waves, Schmitt, as he was being dragged toward captivity,
heard a voice from behind him yell in German:

"Good riddance!"

14

It was night. Aboard the *Northern Chief*, the Norwegian captain
leaned against the railing of the bridge chatting with his officers.
At a distance of fifty yards, the U-570, its lights shining in the
darkness, followed meekly in the trawler's wake.

"I'm absolutely convinced," the captain said, "that the Germans
are going to try to get away. It's impossible for them not to try to
dive."

"If they do," a young midshipman asked, "what can we do
about it?"

"Nothing. Absolutely nothing. You can make up your mind
that as soon as we see the Krauts' lights go out, it will already
be too late for us to do anything."

"Well, can't we do something beforehand?"

"Do what? Look at that thing. Look at the way it's pitching.
Anytime it wants to dive, all it has to do is open its tanks and it'll
be beneath the surface in a few seconds. How can we tell the
difference between a dip in its prow because of the waves and a
dip that turns into a dive? And even if we could tell, how
would the gunner have time to take aim and fire? Believe me,
if that submarine decides to escape, there is nothing that we'll
be able to do about it. And, since we don't even have depth
charges, we'll just have to wish them *bon voyage*. How do you
say that in German, I wonder?"

"*Gute Reise*, Captain."

"O.K. *Gute Reise.* You know, I can't understand why the British Admiralty hasn't at least sent a plane . . ."

Throughout the night, even when they were not on watch, the officers of the *Northern Chief* remained on the bridge to observe the *U-570*. On several occasions, there were cries of, "There she goes! She's diving!" But, to everyone's astonishment, the U-boat always rose again above the foaming crests of the waves, following tamely behind the Norwegian vessel as though it were being towed. Finally, at 2 A.M., the exhausted captain went below and dropped into his bunk.

Hours later, he was awakened by his orderly. "Two British torpedo boats are reported directly ahead, Captain."

The captain yawned, blinked, and sat up in his bunk, rubbing his hand audibly over his rough beard.

"What about our friends back there?"

"Still there, sir. A half hour ago they asked us if we had any tea."

"What did you do?"

"We sent them some. That powdered stuff, Captain; not our good tea."

Aboard the *U-570*, the German sailors, although tossed about by the wind and waves and not entirely free of seasickness, were discussing the victory they had won earlier in the night.

It was about 2 o'clock in the morning when Lieutenant Bundt, the second officer appointed by Schmitt to replace him as captain, followed by the third officer, the radioman (his face still swollen from the beating he had received), and the medic, entered the crew's quarters. The engineer had remained in the control room to make certain that the submarine remained on course; but he had assured Bundt: "I am under your orders, sir." Bundt had thanked him, then gone to speak to the men.

He looked around the compartment, cleared his throat, and began: "Men, what happened several hours ago aboard this submarine is unworthy of the *Kriegsmarine.* I have no intention of criticizing the behavior of Commander Schmitt. I will say only that the conditions under which we operated since the beginning of this mission may explain the panic that took control of some of us.

"Now, the time has come for us to get a grip on ourselves again and take steps to avoid the humiliation of capture. The ship that we are following can do absolutely nothing to us. If we are fast enough, and determined enough, there is no doubt that we can escape."

A disapproving murmur spread through the compartment, but Bundt went on hurriedly: "In the present situation, there would be no risk in diving. The enemy ship, I can assure you, is not carrying depth charges.

"Gentlemen, consider: this is our chance to regain our honor; to meet our comrades who are waiting for us at Lorient and who are fighting for the final victory of the Third Reich."

At this point, Bundt's exhortations were interrupted by vehement protests from the enlisted men. One of them took it upon himself to answer for all: "That all sounds very nice, Lieutenant. The only trouble is that we've had it so far as the service is concerned. A few hours from now, we're going to be safe and warm in an English camp; and we're going to be fed better than we were by that son-of-a-bitching cook of ours with his goddam dried food. If you want to go on fighting, then go ahead. Take a raft and your pistol and go fire a few rounds at the trawler. If some others want to regain their honor, as you call it, and end up drowned or stuffed with lead when we're only a few hours from dry land, then they can go too. But as far as we're concerned, we've had it up to here. We're just not fighting men. And if you want to dive, then go ahead and try. Only, don't count on us to help you. And if you do try, we'll probably be able to find a way to make it hard for you."

The other men muttered their approval of their shipmate's words. Bundt, pale, turned and returned to the control room. Now, he realized, he and the other officers would be under constant surveillance by the crew. It occurred to him that perhaps he was too young and inexperienced for the command of a submarine; and at that moment he decided to give up trying to impose his will on the crew. Bundt, who only the day before had silently condemned Schmitt's lack of authority, realized that he himself had been weak and cowardly before his men.

An hour later, Otto von Klügering, the third officer of the U-570, pushed aside the curtain of Bundt's bunk. Bending down, his eyes shining, he whispered: "There's still one thing we can do."

"What?" Bundt replied in a loud voice.

"Shhh! Not so loud! I have an idea. We could set the explosives to scuttle the ship. Then, a few minutes before they go off, we could tell the men and give them time to evacuate the ship."

Bundt propped himself up on his elbows. He knew that Klügering's plan was perfectly feasible. But Bundt had neither the strength nor the will for it. A while before, in speaking to the crew, he had used up his last reserves. Now, as far as he was concerned, they could all go to hell.

"Leave me alone," he told Klügering. "This is not the time to play the hero. It's all over."

But the third officer was too young to understand Bundt's state of mind. He persisted: "I tell you my plan will work! Listen, if you give the word, I'll do it alone. I'll volunteer for the job. We can't let a U-boat fall into the hands of the British intact—"

"Lieutenant von Klügering," Bundt shouted, "I order you to get out of here!" Then, with a quick movement, he pulled shut the curtain of his bunk.

On the *Northern Chief*, the Norwegian captain, freshly shaved, strode onto the bridge. Perched on his head, at a rakish angle, was a bowler hat—in olden days, the headgear of merchant-marine captains. The officers smiled at his appearance, but saluted respectfully.

"Good morning, gentlemen," he responded. "I always wear this hat when it seems that Lady Luck, for all her perversity, has finally played into my hands. Just a few hours ago, I would have

bet my pension and all my fishing gear that, by now, our submarine would be miles away."

"You would have lost, Captain."

"Yes, you're right. It looks like, even aboard U-boats, there
are sons-of-bitches without a hair on their ass."

A few hours later, the *U-570* tied up in a channel near
Barrow-in-Furness, in Morecambe Bay. It was now officially a
part of His Majesty's Navy, and received the name of *Graph*.

Its capture was a matter of considerable importance to the
British. The submarine was first turned over to British technicians, who discovered with surprise not only that the U-boat's
diving capacity was incredibly superior to that of their own
submarines, but also that the watertight compartments within its
hull greatly reduced its vulnerability. So much so that submarines of this type—VII C—were capable, without severe damage,
of withstanding explosions the force of which, according to
British calculations, should have destroyed them. The Admiralty now understood why, despite intensive and repeated depth-
charge attacks, most of Doenitz' U-boats managed to escape destruction. Immediately, the Admiralty ordered a change in the
manufacture of depth charges. TNT would now be replaced by
an explosive infinitely more deadly: Torpex.

15

In the Cumbrian Mountains of England, overlooking the valley
and lake of Winder Mere, there lies the enormous estate of
Grizedale Hall, once the property of a wealthy nobleman who
lived only for sailing, fishing, and hunting.

During the afternoon of September 27, 1941, a military truck
drew up to the main gate of Grizedale Hall, under the large
sign which read: *OFFICER PRISONER OF WAR CAMP NO. 1.*
After the formalities of identification at the guardhouse, the
truck moved slowly toward the quarters of the camp com-

mander, Major James Veitch of the Queen's Grenadiers. Upon arrival, a man in navy uniform climbed down and, escorted by an armed corporal, entered Major Veitch's office. After clicking his heels and saluting, he identified himself according to regulations: "Lieutenant Heidrich Bundt of the *Kriegsmarine.*"

"Good afternoon, Lieutenant," Veitch answered politely. "I hope that your trip has not been too uncomfortable." Then, after explaining the rules of the camp to the newcomer, he added: "I sincerely hope that you will abide by our regulations. If not, I shall be obliged to be rather firm. But you understand that, of course. Everyone loves the food here—much better than submarine rations."

The major paused and filled his pipe with meticulous care. Finally, he continued. "There are approximately one hundred officers confined here, from the air and naval forces of your country. One of these officers, because of his character, rank, and age, has been appointed to supervise the activities of his fellow officers and to organize their entertainment. He is Commander Otto Kretschmer, captain of the *U-99.*"

At the mention of Kretschmer's name, Heidrich Bundt turned white.

Still accompanied by the corporal, carrying the canvas bag containing his personal effects, he walked the three hundred yards to his barracks. On the way, he passed several German officers, all of whom stopped to stare at him in silence.

A few minutes after arrival at his quarters, Bundt found himself face to face with Kretschmer in a small room which the former commander of the *U-99,* as ranking officer in the camp, used as his office. Kretschmer remained standing, hands behind his back, his features cold, immobile. "It is customary," he said in a biting voice, "for me, as the moral leader of this camp, to bid welcome to our unfortunate comrades who have been taken in combat. However, before integrating you into our group, Lieutenant, you will have to explain the circumstances of your capture. Read this."

Kretschmer threw an English newspaper onto the desk.

"Read it, Lieutenant. You read English, I suppose?"

Bundt read an article, circled in red, relating the circumstances of the U-570's surrender. Kretschmer had been given the paper by a friendly guard.

"What do you think of that?"

Under Kretschmer's implacable eyes, Bundt, who had not yet recovered entirely from his experience aboard the U-570, coughed noisily before replying. "Sir," he said, "sometimes there are unforeseeable situations in the face of which a man is powerless—"

Kretschmer interrupted in a voice which, to Bundt, seemed more gentle. "Listen, Lieutenant. I must tell you that you are held in universal contempt here. That contempt is based solely upon this newspaper article. I must also tell you that I, personally, would never—*never*, do you understand?—have surrendered as you did. Nonetheless, it is not for me to judge you. As prisoners of war, we have neither the authority nor the means to organize a court-martial. However, in order to give you the opportunity to explain and justify your conduct, we have convened a court of honor composed of German officers. Tomorrow morning, in absolute secrecy, you will appear before that court. We have all done so upon arrival here. If we find your explanation satisfactory, your honor will be restored. Are you willing to answer the questions of that court?"

"Yes, sir."

"Very well. Until then, you may be assured that no one here will treat you differently from any other officer."

In a building at the far end of the camp, four submarine officers sat with Kretschmer at a dining table. Before them, alone on a bench, was Heidrich Bundt. No one else was in the room.

"Before beginning, Lieutenant, let me point out something very important: no member of this court of honor has any intention of asking questions for the purpose of trapping you. Our sole purpose is to allow you the opportunity to free yourself from a situation which appears to be inconsistent with your honor as an officer. And, finally, your right to speak will in no way be curtailed. We hope for nothing more than to hear everything that you may wish to say in your own defense."

Kretschmer was silent for a moment. Despite his Prussian stiffness, despite his own strict concept of honor, he hoped that Bundt would be able to find arguments to convince the court.

"The first question, Lieutenant. Isn't it true that, as second officer, it was in your power to oppose the wishes of your captain when he decided to surrender? You could even have placed him under arrest, couldn't you?"

"Yes."

"Why did you not do so?"

"I was taken unawares by events."

"Why, then, after Schmitt had left his ship and turned command over to you, did you not attempt to fight?"

"The morale of the crew was so low that it was impossible to do so."

"Do you mean that you were not in a position to give orders aboard your own ship?"

After a brief hesitation, Bundt replied in a low voice: "Yes."

"You did not try to restore discipline, by the use of arms if necessary?"

"I could count only a handful of men—seven or eight, at most. But the crew were not the only ones to blame for the collapse of their morale. They were poorly trained, weakened by seasickness, and without any combat experience. They simply could not go on. It's difficult to explain all of this. It was—"

"Very well. We accept that the situation was as you have described it, and that it was a situation for which you were not responsible. But, in that case, Lieutenant, you must be aware that the code of the *Kriegsmarine* expressly forbids the surrender of a ship to the enemy—especially a ship which is still intact."

"Yes. I know it."

"Then why did you not attempt to scuttle your ship?"

"I was confused. I had only one thought: to preserve the lives of my men."

"The enemy trawler would have taken them aboard."

"No, it couldn't have. The sea was too rough at the time."

"Didn't it occur to you," one of Kretschmer's four associates asked, "that the surrender of your vessel would reveal technological secrets to the enemy? Could you have not been aware that this meant the destruction of countless submarines and the death of hundreds of German seamen?"

In a choked voice, Bundt replied: "I was concerned only with the safety of my men."

"If I understand you correctly, you are saying that you considered the lives of your men, and even your own, to be more valuable than the lives of the men who were still at sea and who would be exposed to the enemy after your surrender?"

"Yes," Bundt said, his voice barely audible.

Standing in the middle of a huge esplanade which had been converted into a football field, Kretschmer communicated the decision of the court of honor to the other officers in the camp. It was slightly before noon. The court had just concluded its deliberations and reached a verdict: Lieutenant Bundt was guilty of cowardice in the face of the enemy.

"When Germany invades England," Kretschmer told the assembled officers, "we will turn this man over to the occupation forces for trial by court-martial. Until then, he will live in complete isolation. He will take his meals alone. He will be excluded from the life of the camp. No one will speak to him. Gentlemen," he concluded in a tone which allowed of no reply, "from this moment on, Lieutenant Bundt does not exist so far as we are concerned."

One October evening, several days after the verdict which made an outcast of Bundt, a Luftwaffe lieutenant named Moll ran toward the athletic field where Kretschmer was supervising the organization of football teams. When he arrived, Kretschmer was disserting on various plays to be used. He interrupted his lecture at the sight of Moll. From the Luftwaffe officer's expression, it was obvious that he had important news. "Well, old man, what is it? You seem excited."

"There's good reason for it, Commander. And believe me, once you hear what I have to say, you'll be more excited than I. I just found out that the U-570 is tied up at Barrow-in-Furness, where the English are going over her with a fine-toothed comb."

"Are you certain of this information?"

"If the newspapers can be believed, then we can believe this news. I read it myself in a newspaper that one of the guards was holding."

Kretschmer was accustomed to quick decisions. He knew that Barrow-in-Furness, on the Irish Sea, was no more than twenty-five miles from Grizedale Hall. If a prisoner managed to escape and make his way to the port, and if he could get aboard the submarine, he would be able to scuttle it. It was an insane idea, Kretschmer knew, with only a minimal chance of success. Nonetheless, it must be attempted.

Someone asked: "What do we tell the guards if they ask why we're all gathered here?"

"A good question," Kretschmer answered. "Let's tell them that we called a meeting for the purpose of—of what? For the purpose of organizing a glee club. That's it. To organize a glee club!"

In the officers' club of the camp, Major Veitch relaxed in an easy chair, his legs stretched out, his eyes half closed, and puffed tranquilly on his pipe.

"Major," a young lieutenant asked, setting down his whisky glass, "don't you think they sing remarkably well?"

"Devilishly well."

"I wouldn't change places with them for the world, but if I should—heaven forbid!—I doubt that I'd feel much like singing."

"Nor would I, my dear fellow. Nor would I. Strange chaps, these Germans."

In the prisoners' barracks, the German officers, sitting on the chairs, beds, tables, and even on the floor, had been singing as loudly as they could for almost half an hour. Kretschmer raised his hand for silence.

"Gentlemen," he said, with a quick smile, "I suggest we take a short break and discuss a matter of interest to us. You've all heard Lieutenant Moll's news. I don't have to tell you how essential it is that we do something. I have given the matter much thought, and I've come to the conclusion that we do not have many ways to choose from. There is, in fact, only one way to destroy the submarine. One of us will have to get to the U-570. The man who goes will have to be a submariner, because only a submariner has the necessary training to scuttle a submarine efficiently."

The officers murmured their approval.

"Now," Kretschmer continued, "whom can we send on this mission? With your permission, I would like to suggest a name. Two days ago, Lieutenant Bundt underwent a change in attitude. Isolated as he was, he was able to see his error, and he asked me for permission to kill himself in order to restore his honor. I think that if we entrust him with this mission we will accomplish two things. First, we will achieve the necessary destruction of the U-570. Second, we will give Bundt the opportunity he seeks to redeem himself."

"Commander," someone asked, "will he have the guts to do this job?"

"A man who wants to redeem himself is capable of the most foolhardy deeds," Kretschmer replied. "So, are you all in favor of having Bundt do it?"

There was not one dissenting vote.

"Good. Go get Bundt," Kretschmer ordered.

Bundt, when he entered the room, seemed extremely nervous. He advanced timidly toward the table where Kretschmer was sitting. Face to face once again, the two men looked at each other in silence. Seconds passed—an eternity for Bundt, who had no inkling of why he had been summoned. Then, in a loud voice, Kretschmer spoke: "Lieutenant, we have decided to give you the opportunity you have requested."

At these words, Bundt began to tremble uncontrollably. He

felt the eyes of the other prisoners on his back, accusing, judging. "They're going to ask me to kill myself," he concluded. Then Kretschmer spoke again, softly, so that no one outside the room could hear or guess what was being said, and explained the mission to Bundt. He finished with a question: "Do you accept?"

The lieutenant's voice was hoarse with emotion. "Yes, sir."

"I should tell you, Bundt, that when you come up before a court-martial, your conduct tonight will be taken into consideration."

"Thank you, Commander."

"There's no reason to thank me, Bundt. I'll let you know when everything is ready. Good evening, Lieutenant."

In the days that followed, a group of Luftwaffe officers established two routes on a map, both leading to Barrow-in-Furness. One was through the countryside; the other, along a road. A second group of officers was putting together civilian clothes for Bundt. A third was engaged in the most demanding task: forging identity papers for the lieutenant. These papers were copied from an identity card and a ration card stolen by a German pilot from the jackets of two British soldiers.

When all was ready, Kretschmer summoned Bundt. The young lieutenant, since he had discovered what was in store for him, had regained something of his former spirit. The guards were astonished at the vast amount of time he had spent, in the past few days, walking briskly back and forth across the prison compound.

"Well, Lieutenant," Kretschmer said, "here are your papers and your clothing. Now we'll have to work out the story you're to tell if you're stopped on the way to Barrow. Cigarette?" Kretschmer extended a half-full pack. It was his first friendly gesture toward the former second officer of the *U-570*.

"Since you speak fluent English," he went on, "there's no reason why you shouldn't be able to pass yourself off as English. So, if there are any questions, say that you're a British seamen on pass, returning from London. You know London, I believe?"

"Yes, sir. I was a student there."

"Good. In London, you lived it up and spent all of your money. In order to return to your ship at Barrow-in-Furness, you are obliged to travel as best you can—by walking, or getting rides on trucks going in your direction. So far as the details are concerned, I think we can depend on your imagination."

Bundt turned to go. "One moment, Lieutenant. It's possible that you'll have to leave here in a hurry and that I won't see you again. I wish you good luck. Long live Germany!"

"Long live Germany, Commander!"

It was a mild mid-October evening. After dinner, the prisoners had wandered, one by one or in small groups, to an area near the barbed-wire fence. It had not rained for several days, and the ground was dry. When everyone was there, some sitting on the grass, some kneeling, some standing between the watchtowers, they began to sing. It was late, and the guards in the towers were weary. They leaned out, the better to observe and hear the unusual spectacle. Out of sight, at the foot of a tower, two men were silently at work. Armed with wire-cutters, they clipped through the strands one by one and then carefully folded back the ends to make a sizable opening in the fence.

Meanwhile, in the barracks directly opposite the tower, Bundt was waiting. He adjusted his clothes for the last time, and checked to make certain that he had his identity papers. Then he glanced at the map drawn inside his shoe. He had decided to cut across the countryside rather than follow the road to Barrow.

Outside the barracks, a prisoner tapped on the windowpane. It was the signal. A pilot opened the door. Bundt did not hear his whispered, "Good luck." He was already outside, running in a crouch, toward the hole in the fence. He hardly heard the singing which rose in the night. A few of the prisoners saw him, moving like a shadow. Then, he was through the opening. He ran for several yards, stopped, and ran again as he counted in his mind: "17, 18, 19, 20." At 20, he threw himself to the ground. The beam of a searchlight passed over him and then receded into the distance. He now had twenty seconds before the beam returned. He must cross a clearing to reach the shelter of a small woods bordering the camp to the southwest.

Panting, Bundt crossed the open space, stumbling occasionally over the uneven ground but always regaining his balance quickly. 17, 18, 19, 20. He threw himself to the ground once more, and then was up and running again. He reached the trees and paused to rest. Little by little, his breathing became normal again. He looked at his watch: it was a few minutes past eleven. If everything went according to schedule, he would be in Barrow at 6 o'clock in the morning.

Immediately upon rising the next morning, everyone was hungry for news. The prisoners tried in every way they knew to glean information, but it was useless. Even those who had cultivated friendships with the guards were unable to discover anything. The British, ordinarily courteous, seemed angry and unusually silent. It was impossible to get a word out of them.

"Do you think he's succeeded?" Kretschmer heard the question a hundred times. He had no answer to it; but he derived considerable satisfaction from the nervousness and silence of the British.

"We can only hope," he replied. "If everything has gone well, by this time the U-570 is lying on the bottom."

At 9 o'clock, the prisoners gathered on the athletic field. Their faces were wreathed in smiles. A Luftwaffe captain walked up to Kretschmer, who was standing in the midst of a group of officers. "Commander," the captain said, "I believe it's safe now to offer the congratulations of the Luftwaffe. I think we can conclude that Bundt has succeeded. Otherwise, they would already have brought him back to camp."

Kretschmer did not have time to answer. Carried by the wind, there came the muffled sound of distant rifle shots.

Only Kretschmer spoke: "They got him."

Late in the afternoon, Kretschmer was ordered to report to Major Veitch's office. The British commandant was very serious.

"Commander, the courageous escape of your officer has ended in tragedy."

Kretschmer stiffened. His face expressionless, he asked: "May I know what happened?"

"Surely. Early this morning, a British patrol found a man walking rapidly across the fields. The patrol stopped him, and the man claimed to be a seaman. After checking his identity papers and listening to some vague story about a pass in London, they were preparing to release him when the officer-in-charge, for some reason, had a moment of doubt. He asked the man to accompany him to headquarters for another identity check, and offered to have him driven to his ship afterwards.

"The man seemed reluctant, but he accepted nonetheless. The patrol was returning to its vehicles when he pushed one of the soldiers aside and made a break for it across the fields. The usual warnings were given, but he did not stop. Thereupon, the patrol opened fire. The man was struck in the back. He was taken immediately to a nearby house, where he died a few minutes later."

The major rose and walked to within two feet of Kretschmer. Staring him in the eyes, he went on. "We found a map on Bundt, Commander. A map showing, in amazing detail, the precise location of the U-570's mooring. We also found some remarkably convincing identity papers—forged, of course. Is it possible for you to clarify these points, Commander? It seems to me that there must surely be some connection here. This man was an officer whom you had placed in quarantine—please don't deny it. And the submarine that he tried to reach was the same submarine which he, as second officer, surrendered to a virtually unarmed Norwegian trawler."

Kretschmer did not hesitate. He raised his head and answered: "Major, I was in complete ignorance of Lieutenant Bundt's intentions and plans."

"I thought that would be your answer, Commander. Nonetheless, I should tell you that London is informed of what has happened. It is not unlikely that certain sanctions will be applied against you and your comrades."

"Major," Kretschmer protested, "it is the duty of every prisoner of war to make use of any means to escape!"

"And it is my duty, Commander, to see that he does not escape."

In the cemetery of Ambleside, a tiny hamlet near Grizedale Hall, a grave had just been dug. The ranking German officers of the camp, wearing all their decorations, were standing at attention. Opposite them, a squad of British soldiers fired three volleys as the coffin of Heidrich Bundt was lowered into the grave. When Major Veitch asked Kretschmer if he wished to give the eulogy, the German commander shook his head.

After the burial, Kretschmer summoned his fellow prisoners. They stood in the rain which was rapidly transforming the camp into a mudhole. Kretschmer spoke: "Gentlemen, the charge of cowardice against Lieutenant Bundt must be stricken from our minds. Henceforth, the memory we retain of this officer must be that of a comrade who, in death, has regained his honor as a soldier."

16

Doenitz learned of the surrender of the U-570 from a British newspaper supplied by the *Abwehr;* the same issue that Kretschmer had shown to Bundt. He was deeply affected by the news. And, as always, when troubled by events, he locked himself in his office for a while. Later, when he reappeared before his staff, his features had regained their customary glacial calm. He paced the operations room, his hands clasped behind his back. Suddenly, he stopped. "Fuhrmann," he said to his aide, "prepare another memorandum to *Kriegsmarine* headquarters, again asking that the training period for crews be extended to five months' minimum. Be firm, but polite so as not to offend the sensibilities of those gentlemen at headquarters. I'm afraid at this point that I'm incapable of doing it myself."

Peter Cremer was combing his hair before a mirror. He was blond, with very light gray eyes, of medium build. Incapable of inactivity, in love with life, he was one of the young officers who had taken the places of Prien, Schepke, and Kretschmer.

As Cremer adjusted his cap, he heard a voice calling his name in the hallway. Footsteps approached his door. It was Hermann Rasch, captain of the *U-106* and Cremer's closest friend. Ordinarily, Cremer delighted in Rasch's company. Sometimes the two men spent days together, discussing art, music, and painting. But tonight he was in a hurry. He looked at his watch. It was 11 o'clock. "Hermann," he said, "I'm sorry, but in a few minutes I have a very important appointment in the hotel bar."

Rasch smiled. "Well, you'd better get it over with in a hurry, because I was sent to get you."

"What do you mean?" Cremer asked uneasily.

"The Lion has invited us to dinner."

"Oh, God!"

In the experience of the two young officers, dinners with Admiral Doenitz were a form of torture. Despite the admiration and affection in which they held their chief, it was the consensus of the submariners that—except when celebrating the return of a victorious crew—the admiral's dinners were absolutely inedible.

Doenitz, indeed, despite the privileges of his rank, made it a point to eat no better than an ordinary German soldier, and he expected his guests to follow his example. Therefore, the food at the headquarters officers' mess left a great deal to be desired.

Cremer made his apologies to the young woman waiting for him in the bar and then followed Rasch to the navy vehicle waiting for them in the street. "Before going to the mess," he ordered the chauffeur, "take us to the Auray Road." Then turning to Rasch, he asked: "How many of us will be there?"

"About fifteen, I think."

"Fine," Cremer said, settling back into his seat and lighting a cigar.

"Gentlemen, please be seated." Doenitz himself took a place at the long, broad table around which fifteen of his officers—members of his staff or submarine commanders between missions—were grouped. Voices rose in animated conversation and drowned out the footsteps of the waiters who entered carrying dishes. The admiral was served first. With a preoccupied air, he took a few boiled potatoes, some carrots, and a slice of dried ham.

As the others were being served, Doenitz reached for a pitcher of water before him on the table. His hand remained suspended in midair, and his eyes opened wide in astonishment. Godt, Fuhrmann, Cremer, Rasch, and his other guests had served themselves silently, but in abundance. And the food on their plates bore not the slightest resemblance to the ham and boiled vegetables on his own, Doenitz', plate. Each of the officers had a plate piled high with eggs, shrimp, salad, and cheese.

The waiters approached the table with bottles of Bordeaux, and the officers looked down at their food and, their faces blank, began to eat in silence.

The admiral's face was somber, but he said nothing.

It was Cremer who broke the silence. "It's absolutely delicious!" he shouted.

Everyone looked at Doenitz, who was trying to swallow a piece of boiled carrot. Then, unable to contain themselves any longer, they burst out laughing.

"Don't eat that mess, Admiral," Cremer shouted in the hubbub.

Doenitz muttered a few incomprehensible words, but when the waiter approached him with a plate containing the same fare as his officers', he too began to laugh. He pushed aside his watery vegetables and dried meat and said: "Well, you gave me a good scare. I thought I would be the only one eating that mess, and I had just about decided to have you all transferred to the infantry. I suppose that we're obligated to our good friend Cremer for this feast?"

"Naturally, Admiral."

"I thought so. May I ask, Peter, how you managed to get hold of this food?"

"Certainly, sir. There's a farm about 12 kilometers from here, out in the country, which belongs to the Wehrmacht. Rasch and I went out there and requisitioned a few things intended for the infantry officers' mess."

"But how did you do it?"

"It was very simple, sir. We went in, took what we wanted, and then left."

"There was no—no difficulty?"

"Well, almost none. A military-police patrol stopped us. Rasch, well known for his talent as a diplomat, negotiated with them. Even so, they were suspicious and asked to search our automobile. We agreed. We were very polite. Of course, they found our food. 'What is this?' they asked. 'It's food,' Rasch answered. 'Where did you get it?' Rasch said: 'Not so loud! This is black-market stuff.'

"You should have seen them, Admiral. They were so delighted at having caught a couple of submarine officers *in flagrante* that they could hardly control themselves. They told us that we were under arrest. 'All right,' we said, 'we'll follow you.' One of them wanted to ride with us, but our car was so full—there were the two of us and the chauffeur, as well as all the food—that he had to give up the idea, so he went back to his own car in a huff.

"Well, we got into our car and drove off. They couldn't follow us, of course. While Rasch was talking to them I had let the air out of their rear tires."

The antics of his irrepressible young officers provided no permanent distraction for Admiral Doenitz. The strategic situation which preoccupied him seemed wholly without a solution. It was true that the submarine construction program was beginning to bear fruit, and the Lion now had a hundred Grey

Wolves under his command. But, at the same time, his operational field had so expanded that it was wholly disproportionate to the means at his disposal.

He and Godt, at the admiral's suggestion, were accustomed to taking long walks in the woods and on the beaches of Brittany. On one such outing, Doenitz confided to his chief-of-staff: "You see, Godt, Hitler understands absolutely nothing about the sea. He's said so himself. And the naval high command is afraid to risk losing its beautiful ships. So, they use our U-boats for just about anything, no matter where or what."

Doenitz was not exaggerating. His submarines were being used even as escort vessels and meteorological ships and were scattered throughout every theatre of operations. By such means, the life's blood of the Grey Wolves as a striking force was drained out, drop by drop. On June 22, 1941, Germany had invaded Russia, and Hitler had immediately ordered six submarines dispatched to the Arctic Ocean, even though there were no convoys in the Arctic at the time. Then, Rommel had gotten into trouble in Africa because 70 per cent of his supply ships were being sunk by the British Mediterranean Fleet; and six Grey Wolves were sent to supplement the Italian submarines operating in that theatre. Their expertise had quickly re-established the situation: on November 13, the U-82 of Commander Guggenberger sank the aircraft carrier *Ark Royal*; on November 25, Baron von Tiesenhausen's *U-331* sent a battleship, the *Barham*, to the bottom; and on December 14, the cruiser *Galates* suffered the same fate at the hands of Lieutenant Commander Paulsen. But Doenitz knew the price that he would have to pay for these striking successes. For submarines, the Mediterranean was a trap. It was extremely difficult to navigate the Strait of Gibraltar beneath the surface when entering the Mediterranean; and it was almost impossible to do so when leaving the Mediterranean, because of the currents.

Thus, the admiral exploded in anger when he received an order to send ten more submarines to the eastern Mediterranean, and permanently to commit fifteen more on either side of the

Gibraltar strait. "These fine gentlemen," he told Godt, "think only of victory on land. They've forgotten the essential principle of the art of war: Be as strong as possible at the critical spot. No one in Berlin thinks of the Battle of the Atlantic. I doubt that the higher-ups even know that there is such a thing."

The admiral's own convictions, however, had never changed. He believed wholeheartedly that only the Battle of the Atlantic could bring England to her knees; that only the Grey Wolves could prevent the United States from becoming the arsenal of the Allies. But, for that battle, the Lion had only fifty-five U-boats at his disposal, of which barely ten were in continuous operation. The rest were either laid up for repairs and modifications or en route to and from missions.

Doenitz, therefore, had good reason to be worried. His few submarines were no more than tiny points in the immense expanse of water stretching from Greenland to the Azores. He moved these few about unceasingly, from the North Atlantic to the South Atlantic, from Iceland to Africa; but, after each success of his wolf packs, the sea was emptied of ships. In August, in the North Atlantic, the U-boats encountered no ships; only planes. The admiral ordered his vessels to move westward; and finally, on September 11, they encountered a convoy, the SC-42, and sunk sixteen ships. But that same month of October 1941 marked the beginning of the "ebb tide" of the Grey Wolves. The climatic and technical conditions in which they operated presented such insurmountable problems that their efforts no longer met with success. In the South Atlantic, however, where Doenitz had dispatched six submarines, two won a brilliant victory: the *U-105* and *U-106*, commanded respectively by Lieutenant Commander Schewe and Lieutenant Commander Oesten. After a chase which went on for more than a week and which led from Sierra Leone to the Canary Islands (over 1,300 miles), the two submarines caught up with a convoy, sinking ten cargo ships and damaging seven more. Oesten even attacked the battleship *Malaya*, placing two torpedoes squarely amidship. The other U-boats in the South Atlantic—*U-38*, *U-103*, *U-105*, and

U-124—together sent sixty-eight more cargo ships to the bottom. But these were successes for which a high price was exacted, for the reaction of the British was as immediate as it was violent. In order to prevent German U-boats from attacking in mid-Atlantic—where the convoys were especially defenseless, since they were too far from land to have the advantage of aerial protection—the British fleet began attacking German surface supply vessels. In one clean-up operation, the *Esso,* the *Gedania,* and the *Belchen* were sunk—a terrible loss for Doenitz, who had only a very limited number of ships available to supply his submarines, in the open sea, with fuel, food, and torpedoes. It was a new demonstration that the British possessed a highly developed detection system which now covered the entire Atlantic.

Two thousand kilometers west of Lorient, in mid-Atlantic, the *U-93* of Lieutenant Commander Cläuss Korth had just passed its lines and hawsers to the petroleum supply ship *Egerland.* Large hoses, buoyed by floats, were laid between the two vessels. It was through these that the U-boat's precious fuel flowed from the supply ship into the *U-93*'s enormous tanks. Meanwhile, boxes of food, drink, cigarettes, and a mail pouch were hauled by rope from the ship to the U-boat and hurriedly stowed in any available space. In the midst of the refueling operation, a sailor on watch aboard the supply ship gave the alarm: "Enemy destroyer! Enemy destroyer!"

"Loose all lines!" Korth shouted. "Dive!"

A few seconds later, the Grey Wolf plunged into the shelter of the sea while, overhead, the first salvos from the destroyer zeroed in on the supply ship. The *U-93* continued its descent to 150 feet, then stabilized and prudently continued on its way for several miles.

"Periscope depth," Korth ordered.

As soon as the submarine's eye had broken surface, Korth looked in the direction of the *Egerland.* It had suffered several hits and now was no more than a bonfire. Its crew was already in lifeboats, rowing frantically to escape the inevitable explosion which they expected momentarily and to avoid the whirlpool created by a sinking ship.

Korth watch the death agony of the ship. When the smoke had cleared, there was nothing left of it on the surface but a gigantic spot of oil. In the distance, he saw smoke from the stacks of the British destroyer. It was moving away without attempting to rescue the survivors from the *Egerland*. Korth knew why. The British had sighted the submarine at the time of their first salvo and were fearful of exposing themselves to a torpedo attack.

For several seconds, Korth scanned the surface in all directions. Other than the lifeboats, and the debris from the *Egerland*, the sea was clear.

"Surface!"

On the surface, the *U-93* proceeded, at slow speed, toward the tossing lifeboats. One after another, the survivors climbed aboard. There were fifty-seven of them. With the submarine crew, there were ninety-nine men occupying a space calculated exactly to house no more than forty-two. To move from one compartment to another, it was necessary to step carefully over and around the men sitting and lying on every square inch of deck not occupied by equipment. The cook was unable to prepare hot meals any longer, and he served only cold sausages and dried foods. The red lamps of the toilets were lighted night and day, and finally Korth was obliged to issue an order limiting the time of occupancy to a maximum of three minutes per person. It was also necessary to initiate the newcomers into the mysteries of the complex flushing mechanism.

In the center compartment, the captain of the sunken ship chatted with Korth as the men around them listened to his story. "This is the second time I've been sunk," he told Korth. "The first time, it happened pretty much in the same way. There was one difference, however. While the submarine was taking on fuel, its captain asked me if I had a bathtub aboard. He said that the one thing he needed most in the world was to smoke a cigarette while soaking in a hot tub. So, I had a bath prepared for him, and he was still soaking and smoking when the shells began to explode around us. His second officer, of course, immediately gave the order to dive. And, a few minutes later, my ship went down. After a while, the submarine surfaced to pick up its captain, who was naked as a jaybird and completely covered with oil. When he climbed aboard, the second officer yelled out: 'Sir, you need a bath!' The captain answered: 'Thank you, but I've already had one today.'"

"What became of you and your crew?" the U-93's engineer asked.

"Oh, we ended our voyage in real luxury. We were picked up by a German steamer which happened to be passing."

The U-93, overloaded and overcrowded, was cruising northward when, one night, the watch gave the alarm: "Convoy to port at 7 miles!"

"Dive!"

In the control room, the second officer asked, "Are we going to attack, Captain?"

Korth turned to the engineer. "What do you think?"

"Well, with all these people aboard and the extra weight that we're carrying, it seems to me that it would be very dangerous, Captain. We don't have our usual maneuverability or speed. If we run into any difficulty, it could turn into a disaster." Then, looking around at the men piled around the compartment, almost stacked one on top of the other, the engineer added: "I've never heard of a can of sardines attacking a convoy."

The convoy was therefore allowed to continue peacefully on course. But the welcome Korth got from Doenitz back at Lorient was far from peaceful. For the first time, Doenitz' voice could be heard in the outer office as he roared and pounded his fist on his desk. "Why," he stormed at Korth, "do you think we work twenty-four hours a day trying to locate convoys? We investigate the slightest lead! We stay up all night trying to guess where the British are going to send their ships! And you! You stumble over a convoy and you let it get away!"

"But, Admiral—"

"Be quiet! I know what you're going to say: that you couldn't attack because of the number of people you had aboard. Good God, Korth! When I give you a submarine and send you out into the Atlantic, it's to make war, do you understand? To fight! Do you think you're the hostess at a garden party? The least you could have done was to maintain contact with the convoy—if only to pass the information on to your comrades who are out there right now, patrolling day after day, trying to find enemy ships to sink!"

The storm which broke over Korth's head had been a long time in the brewing. Doenitz was totally exasperated by the lack of positive results from his submarines. For, despite the establishment of a new service known as "systematic co-ordination" which was supposed to collate information on enemy movements and communications, the convoys remained invisible.

"When one of our U-boats finds one," the admiral complained, "it's pure luck. And we can't fight a war on the basis of luck."

The evidence was there. Thanks to a detection network laid squarely across the ocean, the British each day knew more and more about the movements of the U-boats. The convoys now had only to sail around the waiting wolf packs.

Part Three

A CLASH OF CYMBALS

17

On December 19, 1941, Admiral Doenitz received shocking news. Endrass had been lost in the Mediterranean, after a furious week-long battle with a convoy heading for Egypt. In the course of the same battle, the *U-571*, under Lieutenant Commander Bigalk, had succeeded in sinking the carrier *Audacity*.

As Doenitz mourned the loss of his subordinate, six U-boats were preparing to sail from their French bases. Among these were the *U-123* of Lieutenant Commander Hardegen; the *U-66* of Commander Zapp; the *U-130*, Commander Kals; and the *U-103*, Lieutenant Commander Winter. Their mission: to reach the coasts of North America and position themselves like the teeth of a gigantic rake from the St. Lawrence to Cape Hatteras.

The Lion's instructions to his commanders were simple: "Sink everything that passes before your torpedo tubes," he said, as he drank a toast to their future victories. "Woe to the man who comes back emptyhanded! And don't attack anything of less than 10,000 tons."

For ten days, Germany had been at war with the United States, and Doenitz was determined to strike a telling blow at the second greatest naval power of the world, whose fleet at the time consisted of some 1,300,000 tons of shipping. Operation Pankenschlag—Clash of Cymbals—as it was known, was about to begin. The admiral had every intention of taking revenge for all the difficulties caused thus far by the American Navy.

In September 1940, the United States had ceded fifty destroyers to England. In February 1941, the Americans had set up their Atlantic Fleet, under Admiral Ernest J. King, and announced that it would operate in a "security zone" which comprised four-fifths of the Atlantic. After the adoption of the Lend-Lease Act of March 11, they had, on June 7, assumed responsibility for es-

corting convoys as far as Iceland, thus freeing a large number of
British ships for other combat areas. Then, on June 20, the U-203
had encountered the battleship *Texas* well within the blockade
zone surrounding the British Isles. Hitler had immediately issued
formal orders: his U-boats were authorized to open fire—but only
if they were attacked.

"How long," Doenitz had protested, "will we have to put up
with this impossible situation?"

"You must be out of your mind," the Führer answered. "Don't
tell me that you want to take on the second most powerful Navy
in the world!"

But now, the moment of reckoning had come. Now, the Lion
was no longer limited to defending himself. He could attack;
and he was determined to do so with all the means in his
power.

"What do you find so interesting?" Lieutenant Commander
Hardegen asked one of the seamen on watch. "You haven't put
down those binoculars for the past fifteen minutes."

"I'm watching some women dancing, sir. There are several
blondes—well, if they decide to go swimming, I'll be happy to
join them."

"Where are they?" asked Horst von Schroeter, the second
officer. Then, after a long look through his infrared binoculars, he
let out a long, admiring whistle. "You're right. There are some
choice pieces there."

The U-123 had surfaced a short while earlier off the port of
New York, and the men on watch, and even their captain, could
not take their eyes from the city. For, despite the war, it was
lighted by thousands of signs which glowed in the night like
some incredible fairyland. Even without binoculars, it was easy
to make out the headlights of automobiles moving along the
coast.

"It's absolutely unbelievable," Hardegen said. "I have the feeling that the Americans are going to be very surprised when they
find out where we are . . ."

This was on January 13, 1942, at midnight, the moment designed by Doenitz for the beginning of Clash of Cymbals.

"Ship to port, Captain."

All binoculars swung quickly to port. "At least 10,000 tons," Schroeter estimated.

"Well," Hardegen decided, "let's find out if our torpedoes work at the western end of the Atlantic as well as they do at the eastern. Ten degrees to starboard. Full speed ahead.

"Load tubes 1 to 4."

"Tubes 1 to 4 loaded, sir."

Several minutes passed while the *U-123* drew nearer to its target and took up its firing position.

"*Rohr 1. Torpedo los!*"

"*Ein ist los.*"

"*Rohr 3. Torpedo los!*"

"*Drei ist los.*"

Two great explosions ripped through the night. On deck, the men watched in fascination as giant flames rose into the sky and turned the water into a sea of red.

The U-boat's radioman announced, "Captain, the torpedoed vessel is sending out a distress signal. You won't believe what it is. They say: 'We have struck a mine south of Long Island.'"

"What?" Hardegen shouted. "You're certain that they're saying 'mine'?"

"Yes, sir. They're sending in the clear."

"A mine!" Hardegen was incredulous. "What assholes!"

He leaned toward the voice tube. "Captain to crew. Listen to me, everyone. We're here like a wolf in the middle of a flock of sheep. We've just sunk a tanker, and the Americans still haven't realized that there's a submarine in the area. So much the better for us. Let's take advantage of the situation. Radioman, since the Americans are making it easy for us by sending in the clear, monitor all of their communications. No doubt they'll tell us exactly what their positions are and what they intend to do."

"Ship to port, Captain!"

The *U-123* turned quickly to face its new victim. Eleven minutes later, another explosion resounded over the sea, and forty seconds afterward, the 10,000-ton tanker sank beneath the surface. It had not even had time to send out a distress signal.

Hardegen, smiling with satisfaction, turned to his second officer. "If we keep up like this, we're going to build a wall of sunken ships across this port."

There was still no sign of a reaction from the Americans. Hardegen meditated for a minute, then reached a decision: "All right. Let's live dangerously. We'll take her in closer."

Silently, the *U-123* followed the line of buoys marking the port's entry. A seaman stood on the prow, taking frequent soundings. The water was shallow: about 60 feet. If the Grey Wolf was sighted, it would be impossible to dive.

The second officer was uneasy. "This is really foolish," he whispered to Hardegen.

"God, my friend, protects drunks and fools."

"I hope God knows it," the officer replied, his throat dry.

It was 2:30 A.M. Through the darkness, the watch sighted a small cargo ship of about 5,000 tons coming toward the *U-123* from the south. Hardegen took aim at its bow and fired a torpedo. It did not explode. "Christ!" he muttered. "We'll have to try again."

At that instant, the watch officer reported: "Lights to starboard, Captain."

"They're all coming at once," the captain grunted. "What a happy hunting ground after all the chasing and waiting we did in the North Atlantic!"

The *U-123* made a half turn and set out in pursuit of the ship. "It looks like a big one to me, Captain," the second officer observed. "It has four hatchways . . . At least 10,000 tons."

"All right. Reload the tubes."

"All tubes already loaded, sir."

Hardegen smiled. What luck to have a competent crew.

Suddenly, the tanker made a turn which considerably shortened the distance between the two vessels. Hardegen saw its side, looming darkly at no more than 500 yards.

"Ahead, slow," he ordered. At this distance, he reflected, the *U-123* should be visible from the tanker's bridge. Yet, it seemed that the Americans were not yet willing to recognize that they were at war. He watched in fascination as the ship moved directly in line with his torpedo tubes. The U-boat would not even have to maneuver into firing position.

"It would be different if these were English ships," someone muttered.

"Quiet!" Hardegen ordered.

The tanker was now in a perfect position for Hardegen's torpedoes.

"Torpedo 1, fire! Torpedo 2, fire!"

A few hundred yards away, there was a deafening explosion. Pieces of canvas, wood, and steel shot into the air and fell back around the submarine. A buoy landed on the deck with a loud clang, and everyone ducked. When Hardegen peered over the tower housing a few moments later, he saw the tanker's prow pointing toward the sky.

It was almost dawn when two U.S. patrol boats appeared to the north, their searchlights sweeping over the sea.

"Let's head eastward," Hardegen ordered, "and get some sleep."

During the daylight hours, the *U-123* lay silently on the bottom in 100 feet of water off Wimble Shoal, several miles to the south of New York. All day, the radioman reported: "The sound of engines overhead, Captain."

Hardegen was almost wild with impatience. He had never seen or heard so many ships. The naval traffic off the port of New York was incessant. "God!" he kept saying, "can you imagine what we could do with twelve U-boats here?"

For the next two nights, the *U-123* was pitiless in attacking everything that came within range. Now, finally, the Americans had come to realize that there were Germans in the area. Radio broadcasts announced that "several German submarines" were prowling in the waters off New York.

American destroyers patrolled around the clock, but their crews and their officers, unaccustomed to naval combat and lacking experience, were unable to detect the whereabouts of the *U-123*. Hardegen's radioman noted with vast amusement that the destroyers passed overhead according to an unvarying schedule, always following exactly the same course, and still transmitting in the clear.

Aircraft also circled overhead all day long, but without spotting the Grey Wolf.

At dusk, on January 18, when the destroyers had come and gone on their appointed rounds, the *U-123* rose to the surface and proceeded at slow speed. The second officer climbed topside to remind the captain that there was only one torpedo left. Hardegen was in a rage, and needed no reminder. He could not bear the thought of leaving the area where targets were constantly available in incredible numbers, and without escorts.

"We are not going to leave this U-boat paradise without doing a little more damage," he announced. To the northwest, he saw the lights of New York glimmering brightly in the night, almost beckoning.

"Ship to starboard," a voice reported.

Hardegen and Schroeter turned quickly. It was a cargo ship of about 8,000 tons.

"Christ!" Hardegen cried. "Well, we still have our gun."

The second officer looked at him in shocked disbelief. "A gun? Here? Practically in New York?"

"I don't give a shit about New York or anything else." The captain leaned toward the voice tube. "Gunners! Battle stations!"

As the gunners climbed topside, carrying boxes of ammunition, the *U-123* headed straight for its intended victim.

"Engine room, Captain. One of our refrigeration tubes has come loose. We're soldering it now."

The sailor had not quite finished his report when one of the diesel engines came to a full stop. "Son-of-a-bitch!" Hardegen swore. "She's going to get away!" He turned to Schroeter. "Don't tell me I'm crazy or that I expect the impossible. We're going to fire on her from the rear. I know that it's contrary to all artillery principles, but we don't have any choice."

The second officer did not share Hardegen's determination. He knew that, at any moment, a destroyer might be upon them. The Americans might not know what they were doing, but there was no point in pushing one's luck.

Hardegen was deaf to his arguments. Despite its crippled diesel, the U-123 was gaining on its prey. It was now only 300 yards away. Everyone waited tensely. A few moments later, the second officer gave the order: "Gunners! Distance, 250 yards. Eight rounds. Fire!"

The first rounds struck with a deafening roar. "You've got it," Hardegen shouted. "Keep firing!"

Flames were now visible on the stricken ship, and it came to a full stop.

"Finish it off!" Hardegen ordered. "Aim for its tanks . . . !"

There was another series of explosions. The ship listed and began slowly to sink.

One of the sailors on watch called out: "Captain! Look!"

Hardegen swung his binoculars toward shore. He could see hundreds of automobiles. They had stopped, facing the sea, their headlights glaring eerily over the water as the occupants gaped at the spectacle of the burning cargo ship.

"They must think this is a movie," one of the sailors commented.

The U-123 was almost abreast of the sinking ship. From the deck, Hardegen could make out the name: the Noress.

"Tanker to starboard, sir!"

"Engineer! How are we doing on that diesel?"

"It'll be another half hour, Captain."

"Half turn," Hardegen ordered. "Let's try to get our money's worth out of the last torpedo."

At reduced speed, the Grey Wolf took up a position intercepting the course of the tanker, which seemed to be taking no precautions against attack. And there was still no sign of any American destroyer.

"I just don't understand these people," Hardegen said in amazement. "They know damned well we're here. They can see one of their ships burning. And they don't even bother to zigzag. Well, it just makes our job that much easier."

A few minutes later, the *U-123* fired its last torpedo, and a new explosion shook the Atlantic. The tanker, struck amidship, was cut in two. The two sections of the vessel separated, rose partially from the water, and then fell back. Until the very last second of life, the radioman of the stricken tanker remained at his station, transmitting: "*Malaya*, attacked by submarine." Then there was silence.

"Hard to port," Hardegen barked. "Let's go get some more torpedoes and then see what we can find at Cape Hatteras."

Doenitz listened attentively to Hardegen's report. He did not speak for several moments. Then, his fingers nervously ruffling through a folder on his desk, he addressed his staff. His words came slowly: "The exceptionally favorable combat conditions encountered by our U-boats at present off the American coast must become a new opening toward the West. If I could do as I wish, gentlemen, I would immediately send practically our entire fleet to that area. It seems to me that it is much more profitable for us to sink the greatest possible number of tankers there than to spend our time tracking down cargo ships, carrying arms, in the North Atlantic. The climatic conditions there are too severe, both for our men and for our equipment."

His voice rose. "Can anyone tell me what good tanks and trucks and airplanes are if the enemy doesn't have fuel for them? Yet, the High Command can't see it. Once again, I've tried to explain the simple facts to them: our Grey Wolves are not the German Navy's handymen. Our sole mission should be to sink as much tonnage as possible, as quickly as possible, and in the place where we can do it most efficiently. Well, gentlemen, I've received an answer from the High Command: 'You are over-simplifying,' they say. It seems to me that these fine gentlemen have forgotten what Napoleon said: 'War is a simple art and consists entirely in performance.'"

18

"Shut up, for Christ's sake! You're going to give us away!" shouted Peter Lunar, chief electrician aboard Commander Rasch's U-106. Karl Moggerein, a husky Berliner, looked up at him. Moggerein pressed one hand against his swollen cheek, as though to push down the pain, and mumbled: "I can't stand it any more. The pain . . . You have to do something."

"There's nothing we can do here," Lunar replied. "You'll just have to keep your mouth shut. If you start yelling again, I swear I'll beat the shit out of you."

Unmoved by Lunar's threat, Moggerein twisted on his bunk and emitted a piercing shriek. His left cheek was puffed up to twice its normal size, and he had a burning fever.

The U-106, rolling slightly, was lying in 180 feet of water several miles off the Canadian coast. That morning, just before dawn, she had sunk a 12,000-ton tanker. But the ship, before going down, had had time to send out a distress signal giving its position. The signal had been picked up by two destroyers in the vicinity; and these two vessels were now overhead, searching relentlessly for the Grey Wolf. Several times, Rasch had attempted to escape; but the destroyers' improved ASDIC equipment was remarkably efficient. Too efficient, it seemed to the submariners. At the least movement of the U-106, the sound of the destroyers' engines was heard and the depth charges began to explode.

Tension aboard the submarine was extreme. Leaks had been repaired. Chlorine loss from the storage cells had been stopped in time. And all these repairs had had to be carried out in silence. Every time there was the sound of a hammer stroke, the *clang-clang* of the destroyers' propellers could be heard approaching rapidly.

Rasch took advantage of a short respite to address the crew: "Men, you know that we're in trouble. But it's not hopeless, by any means. We have enough oxygen to lie here until nightfall. So, we have no problem there. I'm convinced that the Canadians do not know our exact position, and I think that, once it's dark, we will be able to get away on the surface. But, until then, we'll have to play dead—absolutely no noise. So, lie down in your bunks, read, do whatever you want. But we must maintain complete silence."

He returned to the control room, where Nyssen, the second officer, and the engineer were drinking coffee. "I could use a cup, too," Rasch said. He had just raised the coffee to his lips when a piercing scream came from the crew's quarters. The three men jumped. Coffee spilled from the cups and scalded their fingers.

Rasch ran into the forward compartment. "Who was the son-of-a-bitch who screamed?" he whispered hoarsely, losing his temper for the first time. He did not have to wait for an answer. Karl Moggerein was seated on his bunk, rolling his eyes, holding his cheek with both hands.

"I'm sorry, Captain," he moaned. "But I can't stand the pain. I can't help it—it feels like a knife turning in my skull."

"Let me see," Rasch said, moving toward the seaman. "Come on, open up. Show me where it hurts."

"There," Moggerein mumbled, opening his mouth and pointing with his index finger.

Rasch shone a flashlight into the open mouth. "You have one hell of a cavity; and maybe even the beginning of an abscess from the looks of your gum."

He was still speaking when Moggerein screamed again.

"Shut up, for Christ's sake! Are you out of your mind? Do you want to get us all killed?"

"Propellers approaching, Captain," the radioman announced.

"Hell! Medic, keep this man from screaming."

"Yes, Captain."

When Moggerein opened his mouth to scream again, the medic and two sailors hurriedly pushed him flat on his bunk and covered his head with a rolled blanket.

"Propeller noise receding, Captain."

The medic removed the blanket which he had been pressing against Moggerein's face. It was not a moment too soon. The sailor had almost suffocated. His face purple, he gasped: "Are you crazy? You almost killed me, you bastards!"

"If you don't want us to do it again, keep your trap shut."

The medic had not quite completed his sentence when Moggerein let out a long, blood-curdling yell. Lunar, in a single bound, was on him, his fist raised, snarling: "Are you going to shut up, you bastard? Are you going to keep your filthy mouth shut? Or are you going to get us killed?" As he spoke, he grabbed Moggerein by the collar and began shaking him violently. Then he drew back his giant fist.

Rasch, his voice dry, commanding, spoke: "Let that man go." Lunar moved away. Rasch handed Moggerein some pills. "Here, take these. They'll ease the pain."

The sailor's face was a mask of suffering. Tears streamed down his swollen cheek, and he was trembling uncontrollably. He shoved the pills into his mouth greedily. Then, in the voice of despair, he asked: "Captain, when are we going home?"

"In a month."

Despite the pills, and the meager store of drugs aboard, Moggerein's condition grew worse. Nothing could keep him from screaming, neither threats nor the fear of the destroyers prowling the surface. The submarine was filled with the moans and cries of the suffering man.

In order to calm his nerves, Hermann Rasch carefully inspected once more the unbelievable cargo which filled every available inch of the *U-106*. The submarine was among those which had come to relieve six U-boats which had inaugurated

Clash of Cymbals. But it looked more like an Oriental bazaar than a Grey Wolf. There seemed to be everything aboard that could be needed in any conceivable situation: clothing, boots, fur-lined gloves; sun helmets, khaki shirts and shorts; salves for frostbite and lotions for sunburn; heaters, and electric fans. Under the lower bunks, reserve torpedoes were carefully stowed. Airtight compartments had been attached to the hull to increase the U-boat's resistance to water pressure; and these compartments also contained torpedoes. In addition, the torpedo tubes were already loaded. Additional supplies were stored everywhere within the submarine, often to the discomfort of the crew. The sailors, however, did not complain. To the contrary, they were openly in favor of keeping a supply of reserve fuel in the tanks which normally contained water for washing. It was impossible to move from one compartment to the next without climbing over and around boxes of ammunition and food.

"As long as we were going to fill the ship," Rasch commented, "we should have included a dentist's chair."

"Why don't we try to extract the bad tooth," Nyssen suggested. The men nearby overheard and nodded vigorously. "Go ahead, Captain. Do it. It'll hurt, but then it'll all be over."

"No," Rasch said firmly. "Absolutely not."

"Why not, Captain?" the engineer persisted.

"Let me tell you a story," Rasch replied. "When I was a midshipman, I went on a cruise on a training ship—a sailing ship—to Trinidad. In the middle of the Atlantic, I suddenly got the worst toothache I've ever had. I was in such pain that I literally begged the ship's doctor to pull the tooth. He didn't want to, but I kept at him until he consented. Well he tried, but it was worse than before. He wasn't a dentist, and he broke my tooth with the forceps, so that the nerve was exposed. I could see it in the mirror, throbbing! They had to shut me up in the hole so as not to hear me screaming, and they didn't let me out until we reached Trinidad—twelve days later. Believe me, there were times during those twelve days when I thought I would lose my mind. And that is why I refuse to pull Moggerein's tooth."

Another hour passed; an hour during which each of Moggerein's screams brought every man aboard one step closer to total exasperation and open hostility. One thought was in every mind: "God! If only he'd shut up!"

Finally, Rasch himself could bear it no longer. "Bring me the box of periscope tools," he ordered.

All eyes turned toward him, eyes which now glimmered with hope. "He's found a solution," the sailors whispered among themselves, as they moved silently in their felt-soled slippers and gathered around the captain.

Rasch inspected the tools carefully, removing them one by one from their case. Then he looked up. "Bring Moggerein. And somebody go get the bottle of cognac in my cabin."

Calmly, Rasch picked up a small electric drill and examined it from every angle. The officers and men of the *U-106* watched in silence. They now understood what Rasch intended to do.

"Lunar," Rasch said, "plug this thing in." Then he placed a metal stool under a bright light, as Moggerein, his features contorted with pain, watched.

"Sit down here," Rasch said kindly. "You know that I'm not a dentist, and I may hurt you. But this is the only way in which we can possibly help you. Here drink this, and don't worry about being polite." He held out the bottle of cognac.

Moggerein, exhausted by pain, groggily reached for the bottle and took several swallows.

"That's good stuff," he mumbled.

"Drink some more. Go ahead. It's good French cognac."

Moggerein drank, and then held out the bottle to Rasch.

"More," the captain ordered.

"But I'm getting drunk," the sailor protested feebly.

"Drink! That's an order. And don't worry about anything else."

Moggerein obeyed. When finally he put the bottle down, his head seemed loose on his shoulders, and his eyes were glazed.

"Stand up," Rasch said.

Moggerein rose, swaying. If Nyssen had not caught him, he would have fallen. "Everything's turning, Captain," he said, slurring his words. "I'm so dizzy—"

"Perfect. You're anesthetized," Rasch said. "Lunar, and you, Holtzphafel, hold him, and don't let him move a muscle. Nyssen, you keep that flashlight directly on our patient's mouth."

Moggerein, completely drunk, was singing softly. Rasch touched him on the shoulder with one hand, holding the drill in the other. He looked at Lunar: "Stand behind him and lock your arm around his neck, just tight enough to make it hard for him to breathe. That'll make him keep his mouth open wide."

"Yes, sir," Lunar replied with enthusiasm.

"Now don't strangle him, you understand?"

"Don't worry, Captain."

"All right. Let's get started."

The sailors craned their necks to see better, and everyone held their breath. One man nudged his neighbor and pointed with his chin to the bottle of cognac a couple of feet from them.

"The first man to touch that bottle," Nyssen growled, "will get his head bashed in with a hammer."

Rasch's face wore a look of utter concentration as the drill bored into Moggerein's tooth. The patient, half strangled by Lunar's brawny arm, his eyes wide and tearing, was in agony. After several seconds, Rasch removed the drill; after a pause, he began again.

"All right," he said finally, "let him breathe."

Moggerein gasped, inhaling deeply.

"Well," Rasch asked, "how does it feel?"

"I'm choking, Captain! That bastard Lunar is squeezing too hard—"

"What about the tooth?"

Moggerein's tongue prodded gingerly, exploring the infected tooth. A look of intense relief came over his face, and a sigh went up from the onlookers. "There's a great big hole," he said, "but it doesn't hurt as much. It aches, but it's not too bad. Captain, you did it! At the beginning, when I saw the drill, I was ready to crap in my pants!"

"So was I," Rasch confessed. "And I think I deserve a shot of cognac for a job well done, even though it's contrary to regulations . . ."

He took a long swallow, then held the bottle out to Moggerein again. "Here, take another drink, then go lie down on your bunk."

"Propellers, Captain," the radioman reported.

"Who gives a damn?" Moggerein giggled, as two seamen carried him carefully into the crew's quarters and deposited him on his bunk.

"Thank God," Nyssen said. "Now maybe we'll have some peace. Captain—"

At that moment, Moggerein's voice rose loudly, joyfully, and filled the compartment. Drunk as a lord, he was singing.

"For Christ's sake!" Rasch said angrily, "isn't he ever going to shut up?" He walked hurriedly toward the crew's quarters. By the time he reached Moggerein's bunk, the man was silent. Eyes closed, a beatific smile on his face, he was asleep.

At 11 o'clock that night, the *U-106* surfaced. Three miles away, the Canadian destroyers moved through the night, searching for a trace of the U-boat.

"Let's take her to the east," Rasch told his navigator, "and try to find a more peaceful spot."

With six submarines, scattered over several thousand miles of ocean, Doenitz confronted American naval power; and what his half-dozen Grey Wolves achieved was more than a victory. It was a slaughter. Every night, making use of the glare of shore lights from houses, night clubs, apartment buildings, and neon signs to discern the silhouettes of ships making their way in and out of the port of New York, the submarines took a heavy toll. During the month of January 1942 they sank sixty-two ships— 300,000 tons of shipping—to the bottom. In the face of such a threat, the U. S. Navy had only 125 airplanes at its disposal, none of which could be used at night, and about twenty out-dated destroyers supplemented by thirty-four English patrol boats hastily dispatched by the British Admiralty.

"Why," the U-boat captains asked themselves, "haven't the Americans adopted the blackout system? That would reduce our efficiency considerably. Why don't their ships travel in convoys, like the British?"

There seemed to be only one possible answer to such questions. President Franklin D. Roosevelt was unwilling to take measures which would bring home to the American people the fact that the war was at their doorstep, or that would cause them to worry.

"During the first phase of Clash of Cymbals," Doenitz estimated, "our U-boats have inflicted damage comparable to that of 80,000 bombers. If we engage all our Grey Wolves along the American coast, we will be able to bleed enemy shipping to death."

The evidence supported Doenitz' conclusions. At headquarters, every message received from his submarines was a communiqué of victory. All of the Lion's young commanders waited impatiently for orders to set sail for America. Berlin, however, stood in the way. Once more, Hitler's idea of how to wage war came into direct conflict with that of Admiral Doenitz.

At this time, early in 1942, the Führer was convinced that the Allies would attempt to land a force in Norway. He therefore ordered that twenty submarines be assigned to protect the German troops in that country; and even to transport supplies to them, for, to Hitler, nothing was impossible.

The Führer was naturally delighted with the results obtained by the Grey Wolves off the American coast. But he was unaware of how many submarines Doenitz had at his disposal; and so, six Grey Wolves, ready to sail for America, were diverted, by Hitler's order, to the Norwegian fjörds.

Doenitz protested. He demonstrated that submarines were not designed to take action against heavily protected invasion forces. He explained that the only way to keep the enemy from landing was to deprive the Allies of the shipping necessary to mount such an operation. He questioned the veracity of the reports relative to an invasion of Norway. But nothing was of any avail. The Führer's order stood: "Operations against convoys to and from Murmansk and Archangel have absolute priority."

And Doenitz, with death in his soul, could only obey. The only satisfaction left to him was that which he took in the performance of his U-boat captains. And, once more, the "intuition" of Germany's Supreme War Lord saved the free world from disaster.

19

In mid-February, at Kernevel, Doenitz, Godt, the officers of Doenitz' staff, and several U-boat commanders were having their after-dinner coffee. Doenitz suddenly rose and walked out onto the terrace, followed by the other officers. Everyone knew what the admiral was thinking. In a few hours, 4,000 miles away, the same moon would shine down on the Caribbean, where Doenitz had sent four of his Grey Wolves to prey on oil tankers. Their presence there would be as much a surprise to the enemy as their sudden appearance off New York had been. And Doenitz had also given them the job of using their guns at night to fire upon the oil storage tanks located on the coasts of Aruba and Curaçao.

Cremer broke the silence. "May I ask a question, Admiral?"

"What is it, Cremer?"

"Do you intend to send other submarines into those 'distant seas,' as Victor Hugo calls them?"

After a brief hesitation, Doenitz replied: "Still impatient, Cremer? Well, you'll be happy to know that I do intend to send more. And your ship is one of them. Is that all?"

"Not quite, Admiral. When do you plan for us to leave? I mean, of course, if you're at liberty to tell me."

"You are supposed to leave in nine days. Now, is that all, Cremer?"

"Well, no, sir."

Doenitz, and everyone else, knew that Cremer was working up to something.

"Well, I'm listening, Cremer."

In great embarrassment, the captain of the U-333 cleared his throat. "Admiral, I hear that a group of young officers, just out of school, is in Paris for a few days."

"That's correct."

"I was thinking that it might be useful—if you'll agree, of course—I mean, an experienced U-boat captain could give them some practical guidance, some pointers that would be useful in combat situations. I'd like to be considered for the job, sir. There. That's all, Admiral."

"An interesting suggestion, Cremer," Doenitz replied in obvious amusement. "Let's go to my office so you can tell me more about it. Godt, would you come with us, please?"

"Yes, Admiral."

As soon as he was seated behind his desk, his eyes fixed firmly upon Cremer's, Doenitz attacked: "What's this nonsense about giving pointers, Cremer? Do you take me for a fool? The idea of you as an instructor! Come on, let's have the truth!"

"But, Admiral, I assure you—"

"Bullshit. What is it that you want, exactly? Let me tell you what's behind your interesting proposition. You simply want to spend a few days in Paris and raise hell. Isn't that it?"

"Yes, sir," Cremer said in a weak voice.

"Then why on earth didn't you come out and ask me?"

"Well, because—because I don't have a mark or a franc to my name and I wanted to go at the Navy's expense."

Doenitz and Godt burst out laughing.

"Godt, give this miserable officer 4,000 francs from our black box. Well, Cremer, is that enough?"

"More than enough, Admiral. It's a pleasure to fight a war under your command."

"A pleasure, is it? I promise you that if you're not back here in six days, rested and ready for combat, I have another sort of pleasure in store for you. All right, take your money and get going."

"Yes, sir, Admiral. And thank you."

When Cremer had left, Doenitz, his face serious, turned to Godt. "Any news of the *U-156*?"

"Yes, Admiral. A message has just come in. The *U-156* is within sight of Aruba."

"All diesels, stop. Electric engines, full speed ahead."

Silently, invisible in the darkness, the *U-156* drew near the coast of Aruba. Two hours earlier, the U-boat's captain, Lieutenant Commander Werner Hartenstein, had received a message from headquarters: PRIORITY DESTRUCTION OF STORAGE TANKS. SHIPPING ATTACKS NOW SECONDARY. Hartenstein, slender and blond, loved cigars. One jutted from his mouth, below his hooked nose, as he reflected on Doenitz' orders. He knew the importance that the admiral attached to his mission: if the twenty giant tanks could be destroyed, the Russian Army would be paralyzed for months on the eastern front. "You absolutely must succeed, Hartenstein," Doenitz had told him with desperation in his voice. And Hartenstein was determined to succeed. It was not for nothing that his audacity in combat had won him the nickname of "Mad Dog."

He did not, however, embark on his mission without a fair idea of what was involved. Thanks to a protracted and perilous effort on the part of the *Abwehr's* agents, Doenitz was able to provide him with the approximate topography of the coastline. "Be careful," Godt had added. "Don't confuse the target tanks, which are probably camouflaged under painted netting, with the old tanks which have not been used for several years and which are slightly to the left of the docks."

Now, the *U-156* slipped through the dense fog along the waterfront, barely perceptible in the darkness. Impatiently, Hartenstein scanned the shore through his binoculars. There was no sign of activity. These people, he reflected, apparently were as careless as the Americans. They seemed totally ignorant of, or at least indifferent to, the protection offered by a blackout.

"There it is!" Hartenstein exclaimed. "And there are even some tankers!"

In his own way, and in different circumstances, Hartenstein intended to repeat the exploit of Günther Prien at Scapa Flow.

"All engines stop," he ordered. Then, as the U-boat moved forward on its own momentum: "Hard to starboard!"

The Grey Wolf, now facing the oil storage tanks, continued to move slowly forward until it was barely 800 yards from shore. "Hold her as she goes! Reverse, half speed!"

The U-156 came to a full stop and began to roll slightly.

"Gunners to battle stations!" ordered von dem Borne, the gunnery officer who would direct the artillery fire.

The gunners immediately appeared on deck, carrying boxes of ammunition, and took their places at the 105-mm. and the 37-mm.

"Twenty incendiary rounds. Ten explosive rounds," von dem Borne directed.

As the gunners prepared their charges, the gunnery officer was momentarily distracted by a disturbance on shore. "Did you see that, Captain?" he asked, turning toward Hartenstein. Fascinated, the two officers watched through their binoculars as a wedding party paraded through the streets of the town, preceded by a brass band, the members of which danced as they played, and followed by a laughing, singing, jostling throng of relatives and friends.

"Ready to begin firing," von dem Borne announced, after he had given his gunners the range and elevation.

"Fire!"

Hartenstein, in order to avoid losing his night vision because of the flame from the guns, closed his eyes. He heard an explosion and the screams of wounded men. He opened his eyes and saw two of the gunners drop to the deck, unconscious.

"Medic topside!" he shouted down the voice tube, and then made his way toward the two men who lay moaning and bleeding profusely. With great care, Hartenstein raised von dem Borne's head. "What happened?"

The gunnery officer, his eyes half closed, in agony from a shattered knee, whispered: "The bung—we didn't remove it from the gun . . ." Then he fainted.

"Of all the stupid—" Hartenstein roared. He examined the gun. Part of the barrel was twisted and partially melted. In despair, he realized that, because of a bit of inexcusable negligence, it was impossible to destroy Aruba's oil tanks.

The wounded men were carried below. A few minutes later, Hartenstein's voice came through the tube: "This is the captain. How are they?"

"Well, sir, the lieutenant will make it, but Büsinger is in bad shape. His abdomen was ripped open. He's in a coma right now."

Hartenstein had no time to brood. Searchlights from the port were already cutting through the night.

"Hard to starboard!"

The U-156 made a half-circle.

"Both engines, full speed ahead!"

The Grey Wolf moved off rapidly toward the open sea.

For the second time, he looked through all his pockets and through his wallet. Then he resigned himself to the fact that he had only a few francs left. With a weary sigh, Peter Cremer pushed across the table the bills which constituted his entire fortune.

In an icy voice, the waiter said: "Sir, it is not enough."

The three beautifully groomed women with Cremer fell silent, as though to disassociate themselves from a distasteful situation. Slumping carelessly in his chair, Cremer addressed the waiter in impeccable French: "I know very well that it's not enough. Nonetheless, it is all that I have."

"Sir, this is very awkward," the waiter said in obvious impatience.

"Sweetheart, what are you going to do?" asked the dark young woman on Cremer's left.

The officer laughed loudly. He was in his element. Then, putting on a serious expression, he turned once again to the waiter. "Call the manager. And then, wipe that glum expression off your face and bring us some more champagne."

"Sir, since you have no money—"

Cremer interrupted him in a sharp tone: "Do what I tell you!"

Angry, the waiter moved away and walked rapidly toward a door in the shadows. There was a sign on the door: MANAGER.

Cremer yawned. He looked at his watch. It was 3 o'clock in the morning. In four hours, he would have to catch his train back to Lorient. His six days in Paris had exceeded his wildest expectations. Once more, he had proved that there was no place like Paris for a man to relax. At night, that is; for Cremer had not once seen the sun during his visit. The daylight hours had been devoted to sleeping. Paris was also an expensive city, and the 4,000 francs from Admiral Doenitz' black box had somehow slipped through his fingers.

"Well, what *are* you going to do?" The woman who spoke was a blonde, though she owed her coloring more to a bottle than to nature. She had a harsh voice, which Cremer found extremely irritating. She leaned toward him and began to stroke his hand. "Do you think they'll bring us more champagne, my baby sailor?"

"Stop calling me your baby sailor."

"But you're so young, honey. You look like a baby. All you submariners are so young."

Cremer was about to retort angrily when the waiter returned, followed by an impressive man with gray hair.

"Here is the manager," the waiter said.

"I understand, Commander—" the manager began.

"Captain," Cremer corrected him.

"I'm sorry. I understand, Captain, that there is a question of payment?"

"That's correct. I'm confident that it's a question we can resolve. But not before I get the champagne I ordered."

"Certainly, Captain." The manager of the Schéhérazade left, only to return a few seconds later. "It's coming, Captain. Would you like a cigarette?"

Cremer shook his head. French tobacco was too strong for his taste. He found its smoke asphyxiating.

The champagne arrived. "Compliments of the house," the manager murmured, as the waiter filled the glasses. "*Prosit.*"

"*Tchin-tchin,*" Cremer responded.

"*Prosit,*" the three women repeated.

Everyone drank. The glasses were put down on the table. The manager, after he had delicately tapped his lips with an embroidered handkerchief, asked: "Captain, how do you intend to pay your bill—which, as you know, is quite high?"

"Nothing could be simpler," Cremer replied. He searched through his wallet and took out a calling card and his pen, and then wrote on the card: *Admiral Doenitz is requested to pay this bill. This card takes the place of an IOU.* He signed the card, dated it, and then handed it to the manager.

"What will the admiral say when he sees this bill?"

"He'll raise holy hell, but he'll pay. Don't worry."

"You're not worried about what he'll do to you?"

"By then, I sincerely hope to be far away."

On the train taking him to Lorient, Cremer closed his eyes and smiled. He was thinking of the admiral's expression when he saw the calling card.

He shifted into a more comfortable position, pushed his cap down over his eyes, and reflected that, after all, the chances of being within striking distance when all hell broke loose were very slim indeed. In a few hours, he would be leaving on his ninth combat mission. Not many U-boat captains survived so many. Perhaps, he thought, my ninth mission will be my last one.

His eighth had almost been the last. It seemed to Cremer, as he thought about it, with a shiver, that his return to Lorient on that occasion had been nothing less than a miracle. He had almost met his end off Freetown, at dawn. The *British Prestige,*

a 10,000-ton tanker, had suddenly appeared dead ahead of his
submarine out of a dense fog, at not more than 350 yards. Despite
the nearness of the target, Cremer had not hesitated for a moment.

"Battle stations!" he ordered. "Prepare to fire. Periscope depth!
All engines ahead, slow."

The distance was reduced still farther. Then, when the U-333
lay some 200 yards from the tanker, Cremer spoke: "Ready,
tubes 1 and 2."

"Tubes 1 and 2 ready, Captain."

"Fire!"

The torpedoes sped from the submarine with a force that made
her prow rise almost to the surface. "Stabilize the ship, engineer!
Quick!"

At the moment that the U-boat regained an even keel, two
fantastic explosions were heard. Cremer immediately raised the
periscope. What he saw made his blood turn to ice in his veins.

"Hard to starboard! Thirty yards," he shouted.

He was obeyed instantly, blindly. No one knew what danger
threatened.

"She turned," Cremer explained quickly to Willy Pöhl, his
second officer. "She was about to ram us."

The U-333 gained speed. In every compartment, the men could
hear the monstrous gurgling of the sinking tanker. "Will we be
able to get out of her way?" everyone wondered. "God, let us get
out of the way . . ."

There was a great impact; a shock of such force that everyone
was knocked to the deck.

Under the weight of the tanker resting on its forward deck, the
U-boat began to sink slowly into the depths.

The lights, which had gone out at the moment of collision,
went on again. But, with the submarine's stern raised high above
the level of her stem, it was impossible to stand in any of the
compartments. Cremer and his crew, clutching at any fixed object within reach, tried desperately to regain control of their
ship.

"Major leak in the forward compartment, Captain."

"Depth 375 feet, sir."

The tension in the control room was unbearable. How would they ever escape from the weight of the tanker which seemed bent on exacting vengeance by dragging down the submarine to its death?

Cremer's voice rang out: "All engines in reverse, full power! Rudder hard to port!"

"Hard to port, sir," answered the helmsman in a tight voice.

"Now, hard to starboard!"

"Hard to starboard, Captain."

As the helmsman's voice died, Cremer heard the scraping of metal against metal as the U-333 began slowly to free itself from the weight of the tanker, foot by foot, as its propellers spun wildly.

"475 feet, Captain."

Sweat poured down every face. A little deeper, and the U-boat would be crushed by the pressure of the water.

Slowing first one engine and then the other, increasing their speed in turn, working the horizontal rudder and the vertical rudder, Cremer struggled against defeat. Yet, the sinister cracking sounds of the hull under pressure announced that that battle could continue only for a few seconds longer.

Then, there was a final, mighty screech of metal. The U-333 shot upward as though thrown by a giant hand. It rose to within a hundred feet of the surface before the engineer was able to bring the ship to an even keel.

The men looked at one another, the traces of panic still in their eyes.

"Surface," Cremer breathed, wiping the sweat from his forehead.

On the surface, Cremer and his engineer inspected the damage. The superstructure was twisted, the handrail almost torn away, the periscopes disaligned. Worse, the forward deck, near the stem, was punctured by a yawning hole some 12 feet long. The engineer's report, after a close inspection, made Cremer pale.

'Another fraction of an inch, and the wall of the forward compartment itself would have been torn open and water would have rushed in and filled the Grey Wolf. There would have been no way to prevent it. It would have been the end.

"What a fucking mess," the engineer groaned. "The diesel mounts are cracked, the batteries are ruined—and to top it all, we have leaks in the ballast tanks. We'll have to keep pumping them out if we want to stay afloat—"

"Well," Cremer concluded, "I think the only thing to do is take her back to port."

As soon as the U-333 reached Lorient, Cremer had reported to Doenitz. Godt, the chief-of-staff, commented drily: "The very same thing happened to Rasch. Except that he was able to disengage his ship at a depth of a hundred feet."

And Doenitz, in a cold voice, added: "I hope you've learned not to fire your torpedoes at such close range."

20

"Put him down there—yes, that's right. Careful! Don't hurt him, for Christ's sake!"

Three sailors, supervised by Hartenstein, carried Büsinger to his bunk. The injured seaman's breath came in gasps. The face was chalk-white; his eyes, sunken. He moaned. The bandage on his wound was soaked with blood. His pulse was low, irregular.

It was 5 o'clock in the morning, and the men on watch were already sweating in the tropical heat as the U-156 proceeded at reduced speed.

"What do you intend to do, Captain?" the engineer asked. Then he saw the wounded man, and he gagged.

"I think he's done for," Hartenstein replied. "The only thing we can hope is that he doesn't suffer too long. His intestines are cut to ribbons."

The heat below was asphyxiating, and the small amount of

fresh air coming through the open hatch was woefully inadequate. The thermometer remained stationary at 92° F.

"Let's see about von dem Borne," Hartenstein decided. He walked toward the center compartment where the young officer was lying on a stretcher. Hartenstein bent down and touched the wounded man's knee. Von dem Borne shrieked in pain. Hartenstein turned to Remmert, the radioman who doubled as a medic. "I don't know anything about these things," he said. "You take a look at it."

Remmert, his throat dry, inspected the knee. Whenever he applied pressure, the officer screamed. "It's completely smashed, Captain."

"What would a surgeon do?"

"He'd—he'd amputate."

Several sailors heard Remmert's words and exchanged horrified glances.

Hartenstein meditated for a few seconds. He knew his men. He knew that it would be unwise to expose them to the sight and sound of the gunnery officer's prolonged agony. He reached a decision.

"Chief?"

"Yes, sir?"

"Do we have any hacksaws aboard?"

"Hacksaws, Captain? Yes, sir. But—"

"How many?"

"Seven, I think."

"All right. Divide the men into seven details. Then cut off the damaged section of the cannon."

"You mean saw the cannon, sir? Is that what you mean?"

"Yes, of course. You can do it, can't you?"

"Maybe. But it'll take hours. Maybe the whole day."

"We have lots of time, Chief. Until tonight. Then, we'll try to equilibrate it."

"Yes, sir, Captain."

As the petty officers divided the crew into seven groups, Hartenstein bent over von dem Borne and raised the blood-soaked gauze and cotton which covered his knee. He examined the wound carefully, then shook his head. "Listen, Dietrich," he said in a trembling voice, "I'm afraid I have bad news."

"I know, Captain," the second officer replied faintly. "My leg's going to have to come off—"

"That's right. Not all of it—and not now, of course. We're going to have to try to put you ashore somewhere. Meanwhile, Remmert is going to try to remove the fragments and patch you up as well as he can. Unfortunately, we don't have enough morphine aboard to anesthetize you. I'm afraid it's going to hurt pretty badly."

"If I have a choice, Captain, I'd rather have the cognac that you sneaked aboard—"

"Oh, you know about that, do you? O.K. It's yours."

A few moments later, Hartenstein returned to the compartment carrying the bottle. He filled a glass to the brim and handed it to von dem Borne.

Remmert was sterilizing his instruments in a pan of alcohol. "Captain," he whispered, "we're going to need some strong men to hold him down."

"I'll take care of it." Hartenstein climbed topside, chose four men from those lounging and smoking in the "winter garden," and sent them below.

A moment later, the second officer's head appeared in the hatchway. "Büsinger's dead, Captain. What should we do?"

Before Hartenstein could answer, a scream came from below, ending in a rattling sound. The captain and the second officer exchanged glances. Although accustomed to the sight of men in pain, they were both white, trembling. Hartenstein was the first to be able to speak: "Remmert has begun."

There was another scream. The grating sound of metal sawing metal, coming from the forward deck where the men had begun work on the cannon, ceased abruptly. "Son-of-a-bitch!" one of the men sobbed. "I can't take that screaming!"

"Shut up!" Hartenstein thundered. "Keep on with your work."

As he made his way down the hatchway, a shriek of agony

struck him like a fist in the stomach. He clutched at the steel handrail to steady himself.

In the central compartment, the four crewmen were holding down von dem Borne. They were unable to watch, and their eyes were shut tightly. In order not to hear the gunner officer's cries, they had stuffed balls of cotton into their ears. One of them had vomited on the deck.

The captain looked at von dem Borne's face. It was a mask of terror and agony. His eyes were rolled back into his head so that only the whites were visible. There was a yellowish foam on his lips, and his skin was so white that it seemed transparent. Yet, somehow, he had the strength to struggle frantically against the restraining arms of the crewmen.

As Hartenstein moved quickly toward von dem Borne, he heard a soft splash. He looked down. The gunnery officer's shoe had fallen off, into Remmert's wastebucket. Blood had splattered everywhere from the impact.

"How are you doing, Remmert?"

"I'm just doing the bandaging, Captain," the radioman reported shakily.

Hartenstein watched, his teeth clenched, as Remmert completed his work.

Suddenly, the radioman straightened. "All done, sir." He reached out to push away the bucket, and his eyes fell upon the shoe floating among the blood-soaked pieces of gauze and cotton. He looked around once at the men standing around him, and then, with a small gasp, he fell to the deck in a faint.

Hartenstein was giving directions for Büsinger's burial when Remmert, still shaken, reported back to duty. "Send a message to headquarters," Hartenstein ordered, "asking for permission to take von dem Borne to Fort-de-France. There's a French hospital there, and they can perform the amputation." Then, having announced that services for Büsinger would be at 8 P.M., Hartenstein climbed topside.

The men were still at work on the cannon, struggling to breathe, their naked torsos bathed in sweat. The teams worked in relays, one group relieving another every twenty minutes. The sun was so merciless, the heat so intense, that no one could use the saw for more than two minutes at a time.

When Hartenstein appeared on deck the engineer asked for news of von dem Borne. All eyes turned toward the captain. He replied laconically: "For the time being, he's doing all right."

"Is he in danger?"

"Well, gangrene—" Hartenstein sighed, shrugged, then walked forward. "How's the cannon coming, engineer?"

"Well, we're one hell of a long way from finishing, Captain."

Hartenstein touched the cannon at the spot where the saws had made a cut of a sixteenth of an inch. He withdrew his hand quickly. The steel was blistering hot. The sailors turned their heads aside to hide their smiles of satisfaction.

The captain looked at his watch, glanced at the sea and at the horizon on all sides. Then, smiling, he asked: "Anyone feel like going for a swim? This looks like a safe place."

There were shouts of enthusiasm. After the tension of the past few hours, everyone was eager to relax.

Hartenstein turned to the men on watch, proudly wearing their sun helmets. "Keep your eyes open, men."

In groups of ten, according to their assignments, the submariners swam and splashed in the cool water. If it had not been for the watch, and for the continual screeching of the saw, a casual observer would have thought they were vacationers on a pleasure cruise.

Several times, Hartenstein went below to see von dem Borne. The officer, running a high fever, was delirious. The captain then went to the officers' wardroom where Büsinger's body lay. The dead man, Hartenstein knew, was from Hamburg, the latest in a long line of seafaring men. One night, on watch, Büsinger had explained why he had asked for submarine duty. During the Norwegian campaign, he had been assigned to a troop transport, ferrying soldiers to the port of Narvik. He was a mechanic's mate; but whenever he was in the noisy, broiling engine room of the transport, Büsinger said, he was overcome by terror.

"I mean *terror*, Captain," he had explained. "I'm not ashamed to admit it. You can't imagine what it's like, knowing that at any minute you might be hit by a torpedo; and knowing that the odds are against your being able to get up on deck to escape. The fact is that if your ship is hit, you drown like a rat. I tell you, whenever I went into that engine room I started trembling."

But Büsinger had been lucky. On the return journey to Germany, his ship was torpedoed by a British submarine—while he was on deck, off duty. He saw the torpedo coming toward the ship, leaping through the waves like a gigantic tuna. Frozen with fear, he had waited helplessly for the explosion, telling himself that it was the end, that he was about to die. But, twenty minutes later, when the transport was lying on its side in the water and beginning to go down, he found himself floating in his life jacket a safe distance away. He had no idea how he got there.

The water was icy, and he was paddling about aimlessly, half frozen, unable to think clearly, when he felt two hands grab him by the collar of his jacket, lift him out of the water, and drop him like a sack of potatoes into the bottom of a lifeboat. For the next seventeen hours, he and the other survivors drifted in the boat, tortured by the cold, by hunger, and by fear. During the night, four sailors died. An officer held the rudder like a robot, without any idea of where the boat was drifting. Then, after dawn—Büsinger was not sure of the time—there was a terrified shout: "Submarine! Submarine directly ahead!"

Büsinger saw the periscope's wake; and, shortly afterward, in a rush of water, the vessel emerged. Aboard the lifeboat, fear was replaced by almost uncontrollable joy. "A Grey Wolf! It's one of ours!" the men had shouted as tears of relief coursed down their cheeks.

The U-boat had come alongside, and, from the tower, the captain promised to signal for help. Then, after passing over a huge pitcher of scalding coffee, some cans of food, cookies, and cigarettes, the U-boat prepared to submerge. "A *Kriegsmarine* patrol boat has acknowledged our message," the second officer told the survivors before leaving. "It will be three hours at most before it can get here. Try to maintain your position. Keep up your courage. And good luck."

The men heard the water pouring into the submarine's tanks. Seconds later, it disappeared beneath the surface. And, three hours later, Büsinger and his shipmates were picked up by the patrol boat.

"As soon as I reached Hamburg," Büsinger had told Hartenstein, "I decided to volunteer for submarine duty. I figured that it was the least I could do."

"Are you glad you did?" the captain asked.

Büsinger shrugged helplessly. "Captain, I'm even more scared now than before."

At 5 P.M., Hartenstein went below again to see von dem Borne. The interior of the submarine was like an oven, and the gunnery officer lay in his bunk, conscious but in intense pain. His face bore the marks of his agony. Hartenstein, as he drew near the bunk, made a strong effort to keep his expression from showing the intense revulsion he felt at the stench of sweat, filth, and sickness emanating from his subordinates.

"How are you feeling, Dietrich?"

"All right, Captain."

"Soon you'll be more comfortable. Headquarters has given us permission to take you to Fort-de-France."

"Captain?"

"Yes?"

"Don't let them throw my shoe away. I know I won't need it any more. But I'd like it to become the *U-156*'s good-luck charm."

It was night, and the air in the U-boat was slightly cooler. It seemed somehow easier to breathe.

The cook came to register a complaint with the second officer. "Lieutenant, the men refuse to eat. They say all they want is water and fruit juice."

"Well?"

"Well, at this rate we'll be without anything to drink in two days."

"What do you want me to do about it? You'll have to work something out yourself."

On the forward deck, the sawing detail had finally completed its work. The twisted section of barrel was off, and everyone heaved a sigh of relief. "We ruined five saws, Captain," the engineer reported. "The men had a rough time of it."

"All right," Hartenstein answered. "Listen, Chief. I have an idea."

The chief looked at him. What now? he asked himself.

Hartenstein explained: "I want you to weld a weight of some kind to the cannon as a counterbalance."

The engineer had already had enough of the cannon for one day. "But, sir," he protested, "if we try to weld at night they'll be able to see the light clear in London."

"I've thought of that," the captain replied. "I want you to put a tarpaulin screen around the cannon to cover the flame and the sparks. And I want the job to be done no later than 2 A.M. We're going to head back to Aruba before dawn."

It was 8 P.M. when Büsinger's body, enveloped in a canvas shroud and covered by the flag of the *Kriegsmarine*, was carried up on deck and placed on a board a few feet from the 105-mm. The entire crew, with the exception of the men on watch, were standing at attention on the deck or on the tower, to render final tribute to their dead shipmate.

Hartenstein took his place next to the body and read the prayers slowly, in a voice shaken by emotion. They were repeated by the men. After the prayer, Hartenstein saluted, and the boatswain's whistle rose sadly in the night. Then, as the crew sang *Auf einen seemansgrab da blühen keine rose*, two sailors raised one end of the board and Büsinger's remains slid into the dark sea.

By 5 A.M., the *U-156* was at Aruba. This time, however, the port was in total darkness. The authorities had learned to be careful since the attack of the preceding day, and they had ordered a strict blackout. Moreover, there were now five patrol boats cruising at the entry to the harbor, and their spotlights swept constantly over the water.

As the *U-156* lay hidden in darkness, Hartenstein chewed on an unlighted cigar in a frenzy of exasperation. Between the patrol boats with their lights and the coastal batteries, there seemed no chance for the U-boat to enter the port and fire on the oil tanks. To attempt to do so would be tantamount to suicide.

"The sons-of-bitches," he muttered. "The bastards! The whole thing has been for nothing."

The *U-156* made a half-circle while, below, Hartenstein described a new plan to his men: "We're going to lie low here for a few days and give them some time to let down their guard. Then we'll watch for the first opportunity to get in and get our job done. We'll pretty much play it by ear."

Early the following morning, the radioman woke Hartenstein. "Message from headquarters, Captain."

"What is it?" Hartenstein asked drowsily.

"It says: 'Abandon Aruba project.'"

Three days later, under a gray, threatening sky, the *U-156* put von dem Borne ashore at Fort-de-France.

On the way home, the U-boat sighted the *Oranjestad*, a cargo ship of 3,000 tons, and a 4,500-ton tanker, the *Pedernales*. It sank both of them—with its cannon. "At least," Hartenstein remarked, "we got something out of it."

21

"Convoy to port!"

The last word was almost drowned out by the alert which sounded immediately. Within the *U-106*, men ran to their battle stations, their heavy footsteps loud on the metal decks.

"Secure all hatches!"

In the center compartment, Commander Rasch turned to the radioman: "Notify headquarters of our position and course. I hope," he added, "that we have some friends in the neighborhood to give us a hand."

After giving instructions to adjust for firing the torpedoes at periscope depth, Rasch went above. There was a heavy swell, and the submarine was first raised on its crest, then plunged down into its depth. The men on watch had given up trying to protect themselves from the cutting wind and the spray which, in combination, felt like tiny darts of ice striking their faces with stinging velocity. Squinting, their eyes tearing, they were nonetheless alert, surveying the horizon. The fore- and afterdecks were continually awash in the waves. The sea was dark, somber, and looming black clouds overhead gave a sinister appearance to the sky and reduced visibility to near zero.

"Good job," Rasch said to Ritter, the man who had sighted the convoy. "You must have good eyes to be able to see smokestacks in this kind of weather."

Ritter smiled happily.

Rasch was satisfied. The *U-106* had sunk almost 100,000 tons of shipping off the Canadian and American coasts; and headquarters had asked Rasch, on his way back to Lorient, to follow a course that would take him to the south of Iceland "in case there is a convoy bound for Russia in that area."

And here it is, Rasch reflected contentedly.

There were about thirty smokestacks visible, and the convoy seemed to be moving at about 9 knots. It would take two hours at most for the U-boat to be in an attack position.

"What are you thinking about, Captain?" the second officer asked.

"I was thinking, Nyssen, that we're probably going to run into those damned English destroyers again. After our picnic with the Americans and the Canadians, it's going to be tough."

"Yes. No more fun and games."

The *U-106* had four torpedoes in its forward tubes, ready to be fired. Rasch was lucky to have them. A week before, headquarters had ordered another Grey Wolf to supply the *U-106* with the torpedoes. Getting them from one submarine to the other in a rough sea had not been easy. It had taken three hours; three hours in which the two U-boats, secured by lines between them, were sitting ducks for any enemy ship which might happen by as the torpedoes were being hauled on floats between the Grey Wolves. In such a situation, there would have been little chance of escape. But, as luck would have it, there had been no enemy ship, and everything had gone according to plan. At least on the *U-106*. On the other submarine, a sailor had broken his clavicle.

"This goddam weather," Rasch grumbled. "And now it looks like we're in for some fog."

"It's going to be a real pea soup, Captain," Ritter said. "I know this area from before the war. When you see fog coming, it means that in twenty minutes you won't be able to see your hand in front of your face."

Ritter was right. In a short while, the fog reached the *U-106*, and Rasch was compelled to navigate by instinct and in the hope that the convoy would not veer to the north. If it did, then there would be no chance of intercepting it.

"Navigator," Rasch asked, shivering, "how long will it be before we intercept?"

The navigator was silent as he did a quick computation. "Fifty-three minutes, Captain."

Rolling and pitching in the swell, the *U-106* forged ahead blindly, as Rasch chewed impatiently on his cigar. He did not like to trust to luck; and now his chances of finding the convoy depended entirely on luck. If the enemy ships should change course, or even increase or reduce their speed, the Grey Wolf would pass either in front of or behind the convoy.

"I can't even see the fore- or afterdecks," exclaimed one of the men standing next to Rasch.

"Quiet!" Nyssen ordered.

"I wonder where the hell they are," Rasch said, looking at his watch. "We should just be reaching them now."

Ritter's hoarse voice made him jump: "Oh, for Christ's sake! I can't—this is the funniest thing—"

Rasch and Nyssen turned in irritation and saw the man's long, thin face pushed forward, sniffing like a dog following a scent.

"What's so funny?" Nyssen asked.

"Well, Lieutenant, I know you're not going to believe this, but the smell around here—it's exactly the same smell as in the train station at Hamburg."

"Are you drunk, Ritter, or what?"

"I swear it's the truth. It's the exact same smell! Just like the railroad station. I have a good nose, Lieutenant. And I know what I'm talking about. I used to work on the railroad—"

Rasch was no longer listening. He was staring wide-eyed into the fog. "Full stop! Reverse all engines!" he yelled down the hatchway. "Rudder hard to port!"

Then the men on deck saw it: the impossibly huge, black silhouette of a cargo ship passing directly in front of them.

"Aft, Captain! Look!"

Rasch swung around. Another cargo ship, wrapped in dense fog; then another. As though by magic, the sea seemed suddenly covered with phantom ships.

"We're in the middle of the fucking thing," Ritter groaned.

Rasch was indeed on the horns of a dilemma. There were targets all around him. Yet, the first exploding torpedo would bring the convoy's destroyer escorts at full speed; and Rasch knew that the destroyers would not give up until they had bagged the attacker.

"We've had it," someone said, and the rest of the men on deck muttered in agreement.

When it seemed that everyone was on the point of resigning themselves to destruction, Rasch spoke in a voice so calm and confident that even he was amazed: "Engines ahead, slow."

The *U-106* crept forward, changing its course frequently under Rasch's direction, until it was almost touching the stern of a ship which even the most inexperienced seaman was able to identify from its shape: a destroyer.

"Ready tubes 1 and 2."

"What do you intend to do, Captain?" Nyssen asked hoarsely.

"Well," Rasch answered, "if we stay here, the chances are we won't be spotted. We'll fire our torpedoes, and then when all hell has broken loose we'll take advantage of the confusion to dive."

Several minutes passed as tension mounted aboard the *U-106*. Directly before the submarine, at a distance of approximately 600 yards, a cargo ship, which had lost its place in the convoy, was maneuvering back into line, its flank toward the U-boat. Still Rasch waited, as the men below looked nervously at one another. They could see nothing, but they were well aware that, at that moment, their lives were hanging by a thread.

"Fire 1! Fire 2!"

The instant that the torpedoes left their tubes, Rasch began to maneuver at full speed, leaving his position at the stern of the destroyer and moving toward the stern of a slow-moving cargo ship. It was a wise move. As soon as the torpedoes exploded, the destroyer began to move forward at maximum speed in search of the attacker. If Rasch had maintained his position, the submarine would have been left exposed and isolated in the middle of the convoy.

"Ritter, do you see anything?" Rasch asked anxiously.

"It seems to me that the ships are scattering," the seaman answered after a few seconds.

The boilers of the torpedoed cargo ship exploded with a roar, and the ship began to sink. The horns and sirens of the convoy ships screamed across the water, and, aboard some of the cargoes, gun crews began firing their machine guns wildly in every direction. In the midst of this pandemonium, the *U-106* left the tanker's stern and headed toward a transport ship which was turning to leeward at about 400 yards.

"Fire 3! Fire 4!"

"There's a destroyer heading for us," Ritter announced hoarsely.

"Relax," Rasch said without turning. "It probably hasn't even spotted us."

At the very instant that the torpedoes struck and the transport was cut into two sections, Rasch shouted:

"Dive! Dive!"

The destroyer, alerted by these new explosions, had turned toward the target ship, with the result that there was now a hole in the convoy's security ring. And Rasch headed at full speed toward that opening, aware that if the *U-106* was to escape this was its only opportunity—an opportunity that would last only a few seconds.

Before diving down the hatchway, Rasch satisfied himself that the transport ship was finished. When he looked, only the rear half of the ship was still afloat. Now, he worked frantically to secure the hatch. Water was already pouring into it. Then he jumped into the control room. "Chief! Deep dive! 375 feet."

In tense silence, the men listened to the water against the hull. There was a single thought in everyone's mind: "Will they find us?" They waited tensely for the sound of the first round of depth charges which would mark the beginning of terror.

Minutes passed. There was nothing more than the hum of

the electric engines and the sound of the water against the hull. Yet, no one dared breathe, and no one smiled.

"Propellers approaching, Captain."

Rasch winced. It had been too much to hope that they could escape without any trouble at all.

"Damn it! It's not *fair*," a young sailor whispered, biting his lips until the blood came.

"What about the men on the ships we just sank?" Lunar spat out. "Is that fair?"

"Ahead, slow," Rasch ordered. "Let's make ourselves as inconspicuous as we can."

The *U-106* had just slowed its engines when the radioman reported: "Propeller noise diminishing, Captain—"

No one made a sound.

Then the radioman, in a voice which had suddenly become stronger, said: "They're going away."

Rasch took a handkerchief from his pocket and wiped his sweating hands, pushed his cap back on his head, and gave a deep sigh of relief. "Men, it looks like we're going to get away with it!"

Two hours later, the *U-106* surfaced. The clouds were low over the gray, choppy water. The fog lifted momentarily to disclose an empty sea.

"Well, Ritter," Rasch asked, puffing on his pipe. "What does your nose have to report? Any trains around here?" Then, his voice suddenly serious, he turned to Nyssen. "I'm afraid," he said, "that Clash of Cymbals is the end of our holiday."

Part Four

THE CONFRONTATION

22

It was early in May 1942. There had been a British commando raid on Saint Nazaire, south of Lorient, and Doenitz had reluctantly transferred his headquarters to Paris. Hitler personally had insisted on it.

Still, the admiral had good reason to be satisfied. The half dozen or so submarines participating in Operation Clash of Cymbals had obtained unprecedented results off the American coast, proving once and for all that the submarine fleet was Germany's most effective combat arm.

After the first phase of the operation, American cargo ships began taking the southern route, hoping that the shallow water around Cape Hatteras would discourage submarine attacks. But it had been a vain hope. The Grey Wolves continued to attack fearlessly whenever and wherever they caught the scent of prey.

"It's absolutely extraordinary," Doenitz commented on learning that Hardegen had sunk eleven ships in water so shallow that it would have been impossible for him to dive if he had been attacked.

Clash of Cymbals was, in fact, the second Golden Age of Doenitz' U-boats. And his fleet continued to impose their reign of terror despite the beginnings of a defense organized by the U. S. Navy.

By April 1942 the situation changed. The U. S. Navy adopted the convoy system in American coastal waters. Doenitz, however, was equal to the challenge. He had a new means which enabled him to send out his Grey Wolves to seek and destroy enemy shipping in distant waters where vessels still cruised individually and without air protection. This device was given the unwarlike label of "the milkcow"—the name by which submariners referred to the supply submarine the prototype of which was launched in March 1942. The function of this new type of U-boat was to replace the surface supply ships sunk by the British. It was essentially a noncombat vessel of some 1,700 tons, and its only defense consisted of two machine guns, one 37-mm. and one 20-mm. It was capable of carrying from 500 to 700 tons of fuel, to U-boats operating at sea. It also supplied them with torpedoes, ammunition, spare parts, food, medical supplies, and mail. A physician was part of its crew.

From the end of April to the middle of June, the *U-459*, *U-460*, and *U-116*—as these submarines were designated—carried supplies to twenty of the thirty-seven U-boats operating in the Caribbean over an area of from 500 to 1,000 miles—4,000 miles from their home port of Lorient.

The Lion had finally been able to attain the goal set out in his motto: "To be the strongest where it really counts." In six months, his Grey Wolves sank 585 enemy vessels, totaling more than 3,000,000 tons of shipping. History would show that this achievement delayed the Allied landing in Europe by a year.

And yet, Doenitz was still not happy. "I don't care what Berlin thinks," he told Godt. "Our function remains what it has always been: to sink more tonnage than the enemy can launch." The fact was that that objective had been attained only in the first part of 1942. And Doenitz expected—he stated it clearly in a press conference on July 27—that there would be hard times ahead. He estimated that British and American shipyards would turn out more than 8,000,000 tons of shipping in 1942, and 10,000,000 tons in 1943.* And, to make things even more difficult, the Lion knew that never again would conditions in American waters be as favorable as they had been during Clash of Cymbals.

Already, in the eastern Atlantic, the British Navy was returning blow for blow. Now, the problem was not only to locate

* Doenitz was overestimating the Allies' production in 1942, but, like all German leaders, he was underestimating American industrial potential. Actual production in 1942 was 7,000,000 tons. But in 1943 it was 14,000,000 tons.

Allied convoys, but to get close enough to them to attack. After
the slowdown in construction during the difficult winter of
1941–42, the submarine-construction program began to show
results, and thirty new vessels were delivered every month. But
the hard fact remained that, as Germany was losing ground
during the winter months, Britain was gaining it by increasing
her production of destroyers and especially of aircraft. "It became much more difficult to attack convoys," Doenitz noted in
his memoirs. "Surveillance from the air reduced the mobility of
our submarines; and mobility was necessary for them to employ
our wolf-pack tactic. The presence of aircraft made it necessary
for them to remain submerged; and this obliged them to remain
more or less stationary."

Now, Doenitz was able to use his wolf packs only in mid-
Atlantic, where they were beyond the range of British planes.
The Grey Wolves' tactic was to locate a convoy as soon as possible after its departure from port, and then to alert all other submarines in the area of its position. During the next 24 to 48
hours, U-boats sped to the position indicated and, so long as the
convoy remained without air protection, they attacked unceasingly.

"And to think," Doenitz complained to his staff, "that we
could have had the means to overcome all these problems! As
early as 1937, I was asking Berlin to authorize the construction of
a fleet of the ultimate submarine: Professor Walter's submarine.
A submarine equipped with Walter's turbine engine—that is, a
submarine that could have attained a speed of 25 knots underwater, and could have been able to go to where the enemy
convoys are without the danger of being sighted from the air.
And after the attack, it could easily have gotten away from the
destroyer escorts. Destroyers and aircraft would have been
powerless against the *Walter* submarine!"

Unfortunately, no one had listened to Doenitz. The great
strategists of the *Kriegsmarine* laughingly dubbed Walter's an
"impossible dream"; and, when war had broken out, they had

insisted upon the construction of conventional submarines of proven performance.

The net result was that, as Doenitz awaited the arrival of the first *Walter* submarine—delivery had been postponed repeatedly, and was now scheduled for the end of 1942—the outcome of the Battle of the Atlantic depended upon factors over which Doenitz had little or no control: the correct guess regarding a convoy's course; the weather; the experience of a U-boat's crew; the competence of officers; the number of a convoy's escort destroyers; and, above all, the number of planes providing air protection.

In other words, the Grey Wolves had finally found a worthy adversary: the airplane.

The trouble began in February 1942 with the disappearance of three submarines: the *U-82*, the *U-537*, and the *U-252*. All three had been on their way back to Lorient and, as it happened, all were in the same general area, when a convoy was sighted. A few hours later, the three Grey Wolves had disappeared. Doenitz was convinced that there was a link common to the three lost submarines. At first, he believed that they had run afoul of some of the "trap-ships"—heavily armed warships disguised as cargo vessels—launched by the Americans. The *Eagle,* the *Atik,* and the *Asterion,* had been the first three of these; and the *Atik* had come up against an experienced U-boat captain, Hardegen, and gone down in 50 seconds. But many others had been launched since then, and now they presented a serious danger.

The more he thought about it, the less likely it seemed to Doenitz that this was the real explanation. The thought which had occurred to him when Prien, Kretschmer, and Schepke had all disappeared simultaneously, now returned to prey on his mind: What if the British had a secret weapon?

In support of this hypothesis was the fact that he was being flooded with reports of bizarre phenomena. Enemy destroyers now appeared suddenly, out of nowhere, and made for the exact location of submarines. On the darkest nights, a searchlight would suddenly flash on, one or two thousand yards away, and strike a surfaced U-boat squarely. Then the depth charges would begin.

"Is it possible," Doenitz inquired of Berlin, "for an aircraft to detect the presence of a submarine before it actually comes within sight of the vessel?"

"Impossible," the German technologists replied. "To detect an object as small as a submarine on the surface of the sea is very difficult and, in any case, cannot be done except at short distances."

The *Kriegsmarine* experts were wrong. The British had invented radar. And, as more and more of their escort destroyers and their aircraft were equipped with this new device, the confrontation between Doenitz' Grey Wolves and the British Navy took on an increasingly savage note.

23

2 A.M. At a depth of 175 feet, the *U-333* had just started up its electric engines. The only sound aboard was the whistle of the compressed air in the ballast tanks and the swish of water against the hull. Silently, the Grey Wolf rose to the surface. Its captain, Peter Cremer, was determined to enter the African port of Freetown, where several cargo ships, carrying both men and material from America, had assembled to form a convoy.

A suffocating, slightly nauseating heat reigned aboard the submarine. The crew's clothing was plastered to their skin, and everyone dripped with sweat.

When the U-boat reached periscope depth, Cremer scanned the horizon. The sea was empty.

"Surface," he ordered, and then began to climb the ladder up the hatchway. As soon as he was topside, he took a deep breath of fresh air. Around him, Willy Pöhl, his second officer, a petty officer, and the four men on watch, were already peering through their Zeiss binoculars. A refreshingly cool, steady drizzle was falling. As always in this area and at this time of the year, the sky was overcast, and the night was unbelievably dark.

"It's like being inside an inkwell," Pöhl observed.

"Yes," Cremer agreed. "I can't see a thing even at a thousand yards. I'd better go below and have a look at the charts. We can't be very far from the coast."

Cremer went down to the control room and, wearing his infrared glasses, asked the navigator for information on water-depth and the distance between his present position and Free-town. The chief torpedoman came up to report that the tubes were loaded.

The navigator straightened up from his table. "We're four miles away, Captain," he said.

At the same time, Willy Pöhl's voice came through the loud-speaker, tense, nervous: "Engines full speed ahead! Destroyer sighted! Captain topside!"

Before Pöhl had finished, Cremer was halfway up the ladder. When he emerged on deck, he heard a salvo of artillery and the insidious cough of heavy machine guns, which submariners called "pom-poms."

"There, Captain," Pöhl pointed as soon as Cremer was on deck.

"All right. I see it."

The dark, narrow silhouette of the destroyer was barely 150 yards away.

"How the hell did they spot us?" Pöhl blurted out, shocked at the sight of the enemy ship.

"This is no time for questions," Cremer said sharply. "Shut up, for Christ's sake!"

The bright streaks of tracer bullets and the flames of the blasting artillery pieces illuminated the night, and the machine-gun rounds fell like hail on the deck and the tower, forcing the men to take cover. Everything seemed to be happening at an incredible speed.

"Hard to starboard," Cremer shouted.

It was a maneuver inspired by desperation. As soon as he was on deck, Cremer understood the destroyer's tactic. H.M.S. *Crocus* intended to ram him. With a nerve-shattering roar, the destroyer's prow grew swiftly larger in the night.

The submarine was in the middle of its starboard turn when the *Crocus'* bow struck it with terrifying force. Under the impact of the collision, the Grey Wolf turned onto its side. Its tower touched the surface, while its afterdeck caved in with a great tearing and splitting of steel plates.

After several interminable seconds, during which it seemed that the *U-333* would capsize, the submarine slowly righted itself. Cremer, holding on to the handrail with all his strength so as not to be swept overboard, saw that the destroyer had ripped off ten feet of the afterdeck. Then a voice shouted: "Captain! Rudder twisted. Major leak in the aft compartment. Two torpedo tubes affected. We're taking on a lot of water. The pumps are working."

Cremer had no time to react. Under a steady rain of machine-gun rounds, he saw that the watch had been decimated. Holding with one arm to the periscope superstructure to steady himself, he bent toward Pöhl who lay curled in a pool of blood. Then he felt a stinging, burning pain in his left arm. He looked at it and saw blood running from several wounds.

He glanced at the rear to see the *Crocus* making a circle in the water. In two or three minutes at most, the destroyer would return and ram him again.

Cremer's mind moved at a speed that astonished him. He knew that he had to get his U-boat away immediately, before it was turned into a tomb. Already, the tower was a wreck from the machine-gun rounds and one well-placed shell; and the submarine's ability to steer properly, because of the torn aft section, was problematic. He could try an emergency dive; but he could not bring himself to abandon the six men on the tower, even though he suspected they were already dead. As he continued to watch the destroyer, he leaned down the hatchway and called: "Two men, topside! And hurry!"

He looked up. The destroyer was heading for the U-boat. He screamed as shrapnel struck him in the left knee and thigh. He fell, and screamed again as another sliver of metal grazed his forehead and then lodged in his shoulder. Frantically, he wiped the blood which was running into his left eye, blinding him.

On the bridge of the *Crocus*, Commander Holm of the Royal Navy put down his binoculars and turned to his officers. "I think she's had it," he said. "It's only a matter of time before she sinks. We'll make one more pass and use our machine guns. If only we could get far enough away, we could fire a salvo with our 102-mm.'s. But that blasted Jerry maneuvers so devilishly well that we can't touch him."

"That's right, Captain. As soon as we turn, he turns, and manages to stay abreast of us at a hundred feet."

"And if we use depth charges on him, close as we are we'll blow ourselves out of the water."

"Even so, we can't spend the entire night merely firing our machine guns at him."

Commander Holm scratched his head. "Have we asked for reinforcements?"

"Yes, sir. Freetown is sending out another destroyer."

The *Crocus* moved parallel to the submarine, machine guns firing, and Holm looked intently at the tower. "A devil of a man," he muttered admiringly. As he watched, the U-boat's captain, still wearing his white cap, and despite the continuous fire, was working desperately to drag his wounded men to the hatch, where there were hands waiting to carry them below. The last thing he saw, as the U-boat disappeared once more into the darkness, was the German commander falling to the deck with a scream. "He's been hit," Holm thought, almost with a feeling of regret.

Cremer felt shrapnel crash into his head, splintering his jawbone. He was losing too much blood, and he felt his strength ebbing. Screaming with pain, he dragged the body of the last man to the hatch, where it was taken by the two sailors waiting on the ladder. Cremer had forbidden them to venture on deck. Then, holding on to the periscope superstructure, the captain managed to pull himself upright.

"There's about a foot of water down here, Captain," the engineer reported, "and there are some chlorine fumes—"

"This is the captain," Cremer replied. "Put on your life preservers and your breathing apparatus. And remain calm. We're going to get out of this."

Despite the captain's assurances, a mechanic's mate lost his head. Trembling from head to foot, he watched the water rising higher and higher. When it reached his knees, he screamed: "He's going to kill us all. We're not going to get out of this! We're all going to die! I'm going to get out of here!" He made a break for the hatchway, but stopped dead in his tracks and crumpled to the deck as the chief mechanic's massive fist crashed into his face.

Standing on his one good right leg, Cremer decided to make a final gamble. He would lead the British ship to believe that the submarine was finished. He would let it come closer, and then, at the moment when it prepared to ram him again, he would dive. It was a trick which required split-second timing. If he was off by one instant, he and his men would all die.

"Engines ahead slow," he ordered. "Prepare to dive."

He felt a sharp blow to his chest, followed by a pain so intense that he could not even scream. A piece of shrapnel had struck his sternum. With a superhuman effort, he fought off unconsciousness and propped himself up on the superstructure. The unceasing rain revived him somewhat and helped him to clear his head. "Oh, God," he prayed with a fervor that he had never known before, "Oh, God, help me!"

The second officer of the *Crocus* spoke to Commander Holm: "Captain, she seems to be losing speed."

"Yes, she is. All right, now we'll finish her off. This time, we'll get her."

The destroyer's prow turned toward the Grey Wolf and began to move forward, gathering speed as the white wake rose higher along her flanks. On the bridge, Holm and his officers watched as the submarine grew in the darkness, their throats dry with emotion at the approaching death of men who, although the enemy, were nonetheless men.

"Ready to dive!" Cremer shouted.

The destroyer was now 100 feet away. 50 feet. 30 feet.

"Dive!"

There was a deafening crash as the U-boat's nose sank beneath the waves. The prow of the *Crocus* had struck the submarine's afterdeck once more. Cremer let himself fall through the open hatch, and, somehow, he found the strength to secure it.

"150 feet," he ordered, the note of command still strong in his voice. Then he lost consciousness.

When Cremer regained consciousness it was to the sound of exploding depth charges. The *U-333*, resting on a sandy bottom, had already been subjected to a 20-minute barrage. So far, there had been no hits; and now the explosions seemed farther away.

Painfully, Cremer dragged himself to his feet. Two sailors helped him to walk through the water to Pöhl's bunk. The second officer had been struck fifty-four times by shrapnel. A round had gone through his throat and lodged in his shoulder. Cremer clasped the wounded officer's hand for a moment. He knew that Pöhl's life hung by a thread, and yet he could do nothing for him but whisper, "Courage!"

"Help me get to the control room," he ordered the two sailors.

Cremer was half dragged, half carried through the narrow corridor to the control room and placed in the navigator's chair. He closed his eyes for a few seconds. The pain from his wounds was almost unbearable. But, more than the pain, he was tortured by the awareness that the left side of his body was now almost completely paralyzed. Yet, he did not dare reveal his condition to his men. He knew what they were going through. There was hardly a man aboard who was not convinced that the situation was hopeless. The electricians had been able to stop the chlorine tubes, but the U-333 was still taking on water.

Cremer opened his eyes. In spite of his broken jaw, in spite of the blood covering his face, he smiled. "Let's get up to the surface," he said.

At 4:39, the U-333 cautiously broke the surface. Chief Helmsman Schluppkoten, fear like a knot in his stomach, appeared topside and raised his binoculars. He was a small man, and had to stand on tiptoe in order to see over the railing.

"Well?" Cremer asked impatiently.

Schluppkoten, his words tumbling over one another, answered: "Enemy at between 900 and 1,000 yards, Captain. He's stopped over a pile of debris from our ship—"

"What's he doing?"

"He—he—" the helmsman stuttered with fear at the sight of the destroyer pitching gently in the darkness.

"What the hell's he doing?" shouted Cremer.

"He's turning on his searchlights and—and he's shooting off some flares, Captain."

"Has he spotted us?"

"Not yet, Captain."

"Good. Let's not give him the chance to." Cremer turned toward the navigator. "300 degrees," he ordered. Then, racked with pain, he clutched at his wounded shoulder. Sixty-two pieces of shrapnel were in his body. There were moments when his agony was so intense that he felt the blood was oozing out of his pores never to return and never to be replaced.

As the U-333 fled under cover of darkness, like a hunted animal, it occurred to Cremer, still seated in the control room, that he would probably die. He was aware of the frightened glances of his men. He knew that he was not a pretty sight. The blood from the wounds in his forehead and from his jaw had coagulated in his beard and had dried in dark spots on his face. His skin was of a corpse-like whiteness. Surreptitiously, his right hand tapped his left arm, then his left thigh, to ascertain whether there was any sensation, however slight. There was nothing. His entire left side was without feeling. It was as though half of him had already died. Then, his chin on his chest as though he dared not meet the eyes of those around him, he spoke, summarizing his suffering in the words: "I am paralyzed."

Spanberg, the engineer, was standing next to him. He bent toward Cremer's white, tortured face and, in a trembling voice, he said: "We thought so, Captain. But don't worry. We'll get you home."

Cremer tried to smile, but his wounded jaw would permit nothing more than a pitiful grimace. "Would you help me to my bunk?" he asked.

As two sailors gently lifted him to his feet, Cremer could not choke back a cry of pain. The wound in his forehead had begun bleeding again, and the blood soaked through the bandage, covered his face, blinded him, then dripped from his beard.

Once he was in his bunk, the medic gave Cremer a morphine injection. He felt instantaneous relief, as though he had returned to life from the tomb. He heard the diesels throbbing, and he felt the U-333, despite the damages it had sustained, moving through the water toward safety. His first thought was of his ship. "Will she hold together?" he asked Spanberg, who stood next to the bunk.

"Well, Captain, we're not in great shape, but I think we'll make it. As soon as we're safely away from here, we'll start the pumps again and do some welding."

"How is Pöhl?"

"He's breathing, at least for the moment."

Then, almost inaudibly, Cremer asked: "And the others?"

"All dead, Captain."

Cremer closed his eyes and said: "Take care of their burial, Spanberg—tomorrow night." Then he was asleep.

Spanberg, when he returned to the control room, heard the radioman reporting to the midshipman: "All right, Lieutenant. I've notified headquarters."

Three days passed. It was 8 o'clock in the morning, and for the past two hours the U-333 had been traveling at reduced speed. Streaks of white foam topped the gray waves as a north wind swept across the water. The watch, their teeth chattering, scanned the surface as it rose and fell in the rhythm of respiration.

Schluppkoten, whom Cremer had designated to supervise the watch, chewed on a water-soaked cigar butt. His eyes—said to be the sharpest aboard—searched the horizon with unaccustomed intentness. "Where the fuck are they?" he repeated over and over.

"They" was the U-459, a milkcow commanded by Lieutenant Commander von Wilamowitz. Doenitz had ordered the U-459 to change course so as to rendezvous with the U-333. And it was absolutely necessary that Cremer's ship meet the supply submarine. The U-459 was supposed to help Cremer's men make repairs on their U-boat—and it was also carrying a doctor. The condition of Cremer and Pöhl had grown steadily worse. The second officer, with a hole in his throat, was in a constant delirium. And for Cremer, every passing hour was a nightmare. He was unable to move his body. Only his mind remained active, and this despite a raging fever. From his bunk, his face almost hidden by his beard, he remained in command of his ship. Since he could not chew, his orderly fed him soup through a piece of lead pipe inserted between his teeth.

Suddenly, Schluppkoten's face brightened. There, directly ahead, west northwest, at about 4 miles, there seemed to be something dark among the waves. There it was again! There was no longer any doubt. It was the U-459.

"Vessel at 315 degrees," he announced.

The midshipman next to him swung his binoculars in the direction indicated. "Are you sure, Chief?"

"There's no doubt about it, Lieutenant," Schluppkoten answered, hurt that anyone could doubt his eyesight. To himself, he reflected: "This shithead can't tell the difference between a submarine and a destroyer; and he wants to command a ship."

The midshipman interrupted his thoughts. "You're right, Chief! It is the U-459. God, what eyes you have!" He leaned over the open hatch and ordered: "Engines, full speed ahead. Deck crew, prepare to put out our lines."

In the control room, Spanberg groaned. "Full speed ahead! Full speed ahead!" he muttered to himself. "The whole thing's about to fall apart, and he wants to run a race."

A half hour later, the two submarines were side by side, rolling violently in the waves. On their decks, the men on watch anxiously searched the sea and the sky.

As spare parts were passed from one submarine to the other, and as the milkcow's technicians helped those of the U-333 to weld, replace and repair damaged equipment, the doctor was working on Cremer. With professional deftness, he removed the most obvious pieces of shrapnel and fashioned a bandage to hold the captain's broken jaw in place. Then he gave the wounded man a series of injections.

"That's about all I can do for you, Commander. Keep up your courage."

The doctor then went to work on Pöhl and removed the round lodged in his shoulder. Finally, he replaced the bandage on his throat after having cleaned the wound, which showed signs of becoming infected. As the doctor worked, Pöhl groaned continually.

In the center compartment, the doctor asked, "Is there anyone else wounded?"

"Yes, sir, I am," a young sailor answered.

"What's the matter, son?"

"It's my head. Since the attack, my head hurts, Doctor, and it never stops."

As the sailor explained that he had been taking aspirin by the dozens, the doctor examined his skull, probing gently with his fingers in the sailor's thick hair. The doctor suddenly gave a gasp of surprise and looked at his finger. It was bleeding. He carefully parted one section of the man's hair and looked at the scalp. "Well, I'm not surprised that you have headaches, son. Look at this." The sailor had no time to scream. The doctor held out a sliver of metal. "This was in your scalp. I think you'd better continue taking aspirin for a while."

As the doctor replaced his instruments in his bags, he asked the sailor: "You didn't notice anything when you combed your hair?"

"Well, I noticed that my comb was losing a lot of its teeth."

Three hours later, the U-333 was more or less patched up, and it resumed its northward course, toward Lorient. Periods of watch followed one another monotonously. During the day, the U-333 navigated on the surface; at night, it moved more slowly beneath the surface.

On the morning of the fourteenth day of the journey, the U-boat had just completed her practice dive, which was mandatory for all submarines, and returned to the surface. Schluppkoten was on watch, scanning his sector with binoculars. The submarine was far to the west of the Gulf of Gascony, and the sea was rough and of a dark green, almost black color. As far as the eye could see, whitecaps danced on the crests of the waves. Cremer, although still paralyzed, was as lucid as ever, and he had ordered the watch to exercise the greatest vigilance. For some time, U-boats returning to their home bases had been subjected to air attack and had suffered serious losses.

Suddenly, Schluppkoten's attention was attracted by an unusual spectacle. Toward the west, he saw two dark objects, shining in the sunlight, leaping through the waves. "Look over there, you guys! Dolphins!" he shouted, laughing. Then the laughter died in his throat. He leaped toward the voice tube and shouted: "Hard to starboard! Quick!"

He straightened up, trembling, and his binoculars struck against his chest. He could hardly breathe. He moved quickly to the railing and looked over the side. At that moment, two bullet-shaped objects passed alongside the U-333, one on either side, a few yards away, leaving a white wake of foam on the surface. The men looked at one another in horror.

"Oh, shit," Schluppkoten said in a whisper, "we've gotten this far, only to—"

From below, Spanberg called: "What's happening?"

Schluppkoten, still shaken from what he had seen, his knees trembling, answered: "I thought I saw two dolphins jumping in the water—"

"Well, what about them?" Spanberg rasped. "Did they scare you?"

"Well—they weren't dolphins."

"What were they?"

"Torpedoes. A British submarine must have spotted us and tried to sink us."

"Oh, for God's sake! Get down here!"

The alert sounded immediately. The men on watch plunged down the hatchway. A few seconds later, the U-333 disappeared into the sea.

At the military hospital at La Rochelle, Lieutenant Commander Hessler, Admiral Doenitz' son-in-law, bent over Cremer's bed. Willy Pöhl lay in the next bed, unable to speak because of the bandages around his throat. He opened his eyes wide, as though this might help him hear what Hessler and Cremer were saying.

Hessler, and another officer from headquarters who was taking notes, had been with Cremer for a half hour. "So, what you are saying, Peter," Hessler asked, "is that the British destroyer could never have found you unless it had some kind of very highly developed detection device. Is that right?"

"That's right," Cremer answered. "I'm certain of it. As I've told you, visibility was absolutely zero. And the destroyer was not there by accident. It headed directly for us. It knew *precisely* where we were."

24

The prisoners of war from Grizedale Hall were comfortably ensconced on upholstered seats, enjoying the contents of a basket handed them by a soldier when they boarded the train. Curious as a group of tourists, they kept their eyes on Lake Ontario as they munched their sandwiches. The weather was magnificent, and in a few hours they would reach their destination, Camp Bowmanville. Before the war, Bowmanville had been a reform school for delinquent youths. It was only a few miles from Toronto, and it already housed some two hundred German officers.

Some of the men on the train drowsed in their seats. Others played cards. And others entertained themselves by signaling frantically at women whenever the train passed through a town. Only one man was silent, staring morosely at the impressive countryside: Kretschmer.

Kretschmer had changed considerably since being taken prisoner. He had lost nothing of his authority and intransigence, but he had grown noticeably older. There were deep creases in his cheeks; and his blond hair had grown thin and was now partly gray. During the Atlantic crossing, he had had one wish: that the transport ship carrying himself and his fellow prisoners would be sighted by a U-boat and sunk. His captivity, and his enforced inaction while his country was at war, irritated him constantly. When Major Veitch told him of the transfer to Canada, Kretschmer had turned pale. To those few officers who shared his confidence, Otto the Silent said: "How on earth will we ever be able to get back to Germany from Canada? If I have to abandon hope of ever being able to escape, I'll go crazy!"

Grizedale Hall was now far away; and Germany was even farther. For the first time, Kretschmer was discouraged. Even the good humor of his fellow officers irritated him, and he had to suppress the sharp words that rose to his lips when he heard them commenting enthusiastically on the quality of their food.

After numerous delays, the train finally came to a halt at a platform away from the station itself. There was a long delay, then the alumni of Grizedale Hall were led to a line of waiting buses. There were only the armed guards to remind the Germans that they were not, after all, going on a picnic. Kretschmer took a seat to the rear of one of the buses, so that he might be alone and undisturbed.

Bowmanville Camp finally came into view. After the comforts of Grizedale Hall, it was rather primitive: a series of stone barracks separated by lines of trees. The prisoners who watched the new arrivals climb out of the buses seemed resigned to their fate.

As soon as Kretschmer left the bus he was met by two Canadian soldiers who told him that the camp commander wished to see him immediately. Kretschmer put his bag on the ground and followed them to the commander's office.

As Kretschmer entered, a tall, thick-set man rose from behind a desk and came to meet him. "I'm Colonel Bull," he introduced himself. "Before your arrival, I received a report about you. So, I know what kind of man you are."

Bull stared fixedly at Kretschmer for a moment; and when the German did not blink, he turned and went to his desk. He took out a cigar, and as he removed the wrapper he went on: "I'm a peace-loving man, Commander Kretschmer. Very peace-loving, you might say. But I'm also very determined. I'm aware of your influence over your fellow prisoners, and I intend to hold you personally responsible for anything that they do. Do we understand each other?"

Kretschmer nodded.

"Very well, you may return to your quarters, Commander,"

Bull said, lighting his cigar and continuing to stare at Kretsch-
mer.

Within a few days, the prisoners, stimulated by the new arrivals, had transformed Bowmanville Camp. All of the barracks
were repainted, inside and out. Football fields and tennis courts
were laid out, and a swimming pool was installed. A Swiss
citizen, a man named Böschenstein who was director of Toronto's
YMCA, provided them with new uniforms and decorations,
which he imported from Germany by way of Switzerland. He
also rented them films, costumes for theatrical productions, and
musical instruments for the two orchestras—one symphonic, the
other popular—which were organized. Here, as always, Kretschmer had the final word in everything. Nothing was decided,
and nothing was done, without his consent. The pulse of life
in the camp, which before Kretschmer's arrival had slowed to
near apathy, now quickened.

In the midst of all this activity, Kretschmer was busy with
other, less overt business. He designated one group of men to
prepare maps of the area, and others to gather information and
to obtain false identification papers. One team specialized in the
manufacture of civilian clothing. A Luftwaffe officer, a Colonel
Hefele, headed another team which met every evening to work
out a long-range escape plan. For Kretschmer had no sooner
arrived at Bowmanville than he heard of the spectacular escape
of Pilot Lieutenant von Werra. "He got away one beautiful
sunny morning," Hefele told him. "One of our men was wearing
a sergeant's uniform stolen from a Canadian soldier's dufflebag.
He was with two other prisoners who were dressed as workmen.
One of them carried a can of paint, and the other carried a ladder. They spent some time daubing paint here and there, and
then the 'sergeant' led them to the main gate, where he shook
hands with them and then signaled the guard to let them
through. Carrying their paint and ladder, they walked casually
past the guards. A few feet outside the gate, one of them even
stopped to light a cigarette. Then they walked along slowly,

talking. A few hours later, one of them was brought back, kicking and yelling. But that was the last we saw of the other one, von Werra. From the American newspapers we managed to obtain, we learned that he succeeded in reaching Germany."

"How on earth did he do it?" Kretschmer asked.

"Well, von Werra is as slippery as an eel. He managed to avoid the search parties, and got to Montreal by hiding in the back of a truck. Then, he stole a small boat, rowed across the St. Lawrence, and entered the United States. This was last year, you understand, and we weren't at war with America yet. As soon as the American police got him, our ambassador was told about it and succeeded in having him released. He put von Werra on a commercial flight to Lisbon, and from there the *Abwehr* got him back to Berlin."

"Fantastic!" Kretschmer exclaimed, once more in high spirits. "It's different now, of course. We're at war with the United States. But von Werra's accomplishment shows that if a man really wants to escape, he can always find a way. All right, gentlemen. Let's get to work!"

"Colonel Bull wants to see you, sir."

Kretschmer put down his book and rose from his bunk. He buttoned his jacket, took his cap, and walked calmly through the camp, stopping occasionally to admire the flowerbeds laid down by the prisoners. As soon as he entered the camp commander's office, Bull said: "I have bad news for you and your friends."

"I'm listening."

"Following a Canadian commando raid at Dieppe, the Germans put handcuffs on the men they took prisoner."

"They must have had a good reason for doing so," Kretschmer interrupted.

"I doubt it very much, Commander," Bull retorted angrily. "Be that as it may, I've been ordered to put twenty prisoners in handcuffs, by way of reprisal. The prisoners' names have been selected in Ottawa. It's deplorable, I know. But I have no choice."

"It is utterly reprehensible!" Kretschmer exploded. "It is contrary to every international agreement to treat prisoners of war in this way!"

"Then you shouldn't have started it," growled the Canadian colonel.

"What makes you think that we started it? The English are no angels when it comes to war! They have no more sense of fair play on the battlefield than on the football field!"

"I will not allow you to speak to me in that tone of voice," Bull shouted.

"And I will not allow you to handcuff any of the prisoners here!"

"I am in command here, Commander," the colonel shouted, glaring at Kretschmer, his fists clenched at his side. "And you had better believe that there will be handcuffs."

"You'll have to put them on us, Colonel. And you're mistaken if you think we're going to let you do it," Kretschmer shouted back.

"Then I'll use force if I have to. But I intend to carry out my orders."

Kretschmer left the office in a rage. He walked hurriedly back to his quarters, stopping only to tell the prisoners he saw to pass the word to assemble in front of his barracks immediately.

When he entered his building, the officers in the room saw in his face that something serious had occurred. "Gentlemen," Kretschmer told them, "I have something important to tell you."

The prisoners stood silently waiting for him to go on.

"Gentlemen, Colonel Bull has just informed me that, as an act of reprisal, twenty of us are going to be put in handcuffs. I, in turn, have informed him that we will oppose such measures by every means in our power. It is unthinkable that a German officer be submitted to such dishonor!"

A murmur ran through the prisoners. "We must defend ourselves," someone shouted.

"That is precisely what I was going to ask you to do. We must organize our defenses and keep the guards from taking our comrades. Here's what I've decided. We're going to barricade ourselves inside the mess hall and Building No. 5. We'll also have to have weapons of some kind, so break up your chairs and tables and use the legs as clubs. Gather whatever stones and bricks you can find lying around. And let's not waste any time. Everyone to battle stations!"

The small crowd dispersed quickly. Shortly afterward, Kretschmer could hear the sound of chairs and tables being torn apart and of beds being dragged into piles against the doors.

It was Saturday, at 2 o'clock in the afternoon. "Here they come!" someone yelled.

Armed with billyclubs and bayonets, the Canadian soldiers advanced at a run to storm the mess hall. There had been no negotiations, since the position of the prisoners of war was inflexible. The two doors and six windows of the building were guarded like those of a fortress. Both sides shouted and yelled to spur themselves on. The clash was extremely violent. Kretschmer, clutching a huge copper pan by its handle, swung the utensil in a large circle, like a cavalry saber. At another window, Midshipman Koenig had leaned too far out, and two Canadians were trying to pull him through the window. Several prisoners grabbed Koenig's legs and attempted to pull him back into the building. The midshipman screamed like a madman as blows from clubs rained around him.

"Help them!" someone shouted, as the defenders of the window began to lose ground. Four of them lay unconscious on the floor. A dozen Germans ran to the rescue, and the seven Canadians were thrown back. There were shouts, moans, and the sound of breaking cartilage. The air was thick with stones, glasses, cans, and bottles which crashed indiscriminately against both friendly and hostile heads.

The screams of pain, the sound of clubs striking human flesh and bone, the shouts of encouragement—all were quickly drowned out by the Canadian NCOs' whistles signaling retreat. The mess hall was in ruins, and pools of blood on the floor bore witness to the determination of both sides. Standing in the clouds of dust, the German officers, out of breath but smiling happily, looked at one another.

"Look over there!" Koenig shouted.

About 200 feet away, the Canadians were in full retreat from Building No. 5, from which there issued a steady rain of stones and insults.

"Victory along the whole line," Hefele said. "But they'll be back. I think we should take advantage of the time we have to get a new supply of rocks. And the medics should see to the wounded."

The defenders of the mess hall were removing the barricade from the door when they heard the sound of men running.

"They're coming back!"

"Everyone to his station!"

But this time the Canadian assault was directed on the wooden barracks situated between the kitchen and the cinema, where several small pockets of resistance had formed. The Canadians attacked furiously with battering rams, and the fragile wooden doors splintered.

"Quick!" Kretschmer ordered. "Send some men up on the roof. Start throwing rocks at them, and anything else you can find!"

A group of prisoners climbed through a skylight in the ceiling. They had no need of rocks, however, they tore up the heavy roof tiles and began bombarding the attackers with them. Caught between two fires, the Canadians again beat a retreat; but not before capturing twenty of the prisoners of war.

No one had time to savor victory. Fire engines, summoned from Toronto, began arriving and took up positions directly outside the doors and windows of the two buildings which were the center of the revolt. Powerful jets of water that rose from their hoses quickly brought the battle to an end, and there was no way for Kretschmer's men, soaked and held helplessly against a wall by the water, to offer effective resistance as the Canadians moved into the buildings. There were a few more exchanges with clubs, a few shouts, and a large number of wounded men lying on the floor. At 7 o'clock, Colonel Bull entered, surrounded by a group of officers. He walked through the kitchen, inspecting the damage, then moved toward Kretschmer, his swaggerstick tapping against his boot. He stopped and looked at the German officer. A flicker of amusement passed over his face. The former captain of the U-99 was in rags. His shirt was ripped almost completely away, and his tanned face was covered with dried blood. Kretschmer raised his hand and gingerly touched his cheek. It felt as though he had a loose tooth. The two men looked at each other.

"This has been one of the most interesting and picturesque things I have ever been privileged to see," Bull spoke, in a loud voice. "But all good things must come to an end, Commander Kretschmer. For the last time, I order you to give me the twenty men who are to be handcuffed."

"Your men have already captured them, Colonel."

"We have indeed taken twenty men, Commander. But they are not the ones whose names are on the list prepared in Ottawa. Are you willing to turn over to me the men I want?"

"No."

"In that case, a special battalion of Canadian soldiers will arrive Monday to take them by force. These will not be middle-aged reservists, but young men trained for this sort of thing. Until then, you may all return to your quarters and look after your wounds."

The prisoners, as they left the building, passed in front of a Captain Brand of the Canadian Army. Brand held a swagger-stick in his hand, and as the Germans filed past he struck each one as hard as he could on the head or on the back.

The following day was Sunday. Kretschmer ordered Koenig to warn the guards that if Captain Brand were to enter the compound, there would be trouble. A number of the prisoners had sworn to take revenge for the humiliation of the day before. It added to their determination that, on returning to their barracks, they had discovered that the Canadians had taken their supply of beer, cake, cigarettes—and their decorations.

Two hours passed. Kretschmer was chatting with Peterson and Koenig outside his building when they saw Brand, accompanied by a guard, walking toward them with an air of utter defiance.

"Good morning," the Canadian said.

Kretschmer's fist struck him squarely on the chin, and Brand fell to the ground. At the same time, Peterson struck the guard with all his might.

"Help me," Kretschmer ordered.

Leaving the guard where he had fallen, the three Germans dragged Brand inside the barracks. When the Canadian regained consciousness, Peterson tied his hands behind his back with a piece of tattered chiffon and made him stand.

"And now, gentlemen," Kretschmer suggested, "let's take our prisoner and turn him over to the guards."

The Germans had intended nothing more than a stunt to make Brand look ridiculous. But the guards had already been alerted by the soldier who had accompanied Brand, and as soon as Koenig and Kretschmer stepped through the door, with Brand between them, they were met by a burst of fire from the nearby watchtower. Kretschmer pushed Brand to the ground and threw himself down next to him. Koenig swore once, then groaned. A ricocheting round had wounded him in the left thigh.

The firing continued. Crouching, Kretschmer and Peterson helped Koenig back into the barracks, leaving Brand lying facedown on the ground, his hands still bound behind him. As soon as the door was closed, the medic ran over to Koenig. "It's nothing," the midshipman said. "Just a flesh wound."

Meanwhile, Brand had managed to get loose and had run to the guardhouse at the main gate.

The rest of the day passed without incident. The Germans kept busy organizing their defenses and gathering stones.

Monday morning, at 8 o'clock, two companies of Special Canadian Commandoes, wearing helmets and full combat equipment, stood staring in fascination at the Germans before them. The latter were armed with chair legs and pieces of tables. And on their heads, attached by pieces of string, were skillets and kettle covers.

The commander of the detachment—a young captain built like a hockey player—turned toward his men. "I think what we ought to do, men," he said loudly, "is to beat the shit out of these Jerrys with our bare fists. Put down your weapons!"

Under the eyes of the soldiers in the watchtowers, the commandoes removed their cartridge belts, stacked their rifles, and began stretching their muscles.

Fifty yards away, Kretschmer understood what they were doing. "Men," he shouted, "put down your weapons. Let's show these pudding-eaters that we can hit as hard as they can!"

The Canadians came forward slowly. When their commander was a few feet away from Kretschmer, he delivered an ultimatum: "Either give us the twenty men we want, or we'll beat the hell out of you."

"Come and get them!"

The Canadian officer spat out his chewing gum. "Go ahead, boys!" he ordered, and the two groups of men rushed forward furiously.

For three hours, the battle raged. Peterson was badly beaten and wandered away, leaving a trail of blood. He found a faucet and allowed the water to run over his head for a few seconds. As he rested, a German and a Canadian rolled on the ground between his legs. The Canadian bit the prisoner's ear. The German screamed, then jabbed his fingers into the commando's eyes. Peterson grabbed a nearby pail and smashed it into the Canadian's head, while the German tried to staunch the flow of blood from his ear.

"Back to the barracks, men!" Kretschmer shouted. But in the noise and heat of battle, no one heard him. All around him, bruised and bleeding Canadians and Germans lay unconscious. Then, above the shouts and the moans there rose a siren. Reinforcements of four hundred Canadian infantrymen ran toward the barracks where the prisoners had barricaded themselves. It was the end of the battle. The Germans, discouraged, exhausted, their uniforms in tatters, their faces swollen and covered with dried blood, offered no resistance.

A loudspeaker in the quadrangle announced: "Commander Kretschmer to the commandant's office."

Kretschmer hurriedly washed the blood from his face and changed his clothing. Then, as lines of Canadians and Germans filed toward the waiting ambulances, he presented himself at Bull's office.

"Cigar, Commander?"

Kretschmer, surprised by Bull's affable tone, accepted. He had always had a weakness for cigars. The two men puffed in silence for a while, then Bull spoke again.

"Commander," he said, "you and I are both military men. We know that orders must be obeyed. And we also know that orders can be interpreted to suit oneself."

Kretschmer, drawing on his cigar, wondered what Bull was leading up to.

"My orders," the colonel continued, "do not specify that your fellow prisoners must wear handcuffs day and night. So, here is what I've decided. If you turn the twenty men over to me, all I will require is that they be wearing handcuffs when I see them at the morning and evening formations. The rest of the time, they can take them off and keep them in their pockets."

"But how will they be able to get them off, Colonel?"

"I've already told the guards to leave them unlocked."

25

September 12, 1941. 10:08 P.M.

"Ready tubes 1 and 3."

"Tubes 1 and 3 ready, Captain."

There was silence aboard the *U-156*; the tense and anxious silence which preceded every attack. Above, Werner Hartenstein gave the bearing and speed of the target ship he had been tracking for the past eleven hours.

"*Achtung!*"

Slowly, the dark form of the steamer moved into his sights.

"Fire 1!"

A few seconds passed, then a great explosion shook the South Atlantic.

"Amidships," Hartenstein announced.

The steamer cut its engines and now moved on its momentum.

"*Achtung!*"

Hartenstein took another look through his sights, and gave the order: "Fire 3!"

A second explosion shook the steamer, and it began to list.

"That should do it," Hartenstein said with satisfaction to his second officer, Mannesmann.

"Yes, sir. A big one, too—at least 15,000 tons."

"At least. All right, let's move toward her slowly and see the name of our victim. I wonder what she's carrying. Troops, probably."

In Paris, at five minutes past midnight, the headquarters of Admiral Doenitz was silent. In the message center, it was almost time to change shifts.

"What should we do?" the radioman on duty asked, holding out a message that had just arrived.

"We don't have much choice. I'm going to wake up the commander," the sergeant replied. He called the message-center orderly who was dozing in a chair. "Wake up Commander Hessler and tell him that we just received an important message from Melun. And then you'd better bring some coffee. I have a feeling we're not going to bed for a long time yet."

A few minutes later, Hessler appeared, partially dressed, his blond hair rumpled.

"Well?"

"Here, Commander," the radioman said, holding out the message.

Hessler took it and read. Then he turned to the orderly. "Quick! Go get Commander Godt."

The orderly left at a trot.

"What a mess," Hessler muttered.

Godt, the chief-of-staff, came quickly, his dark hair immaculately groomed, his eyes alert. Behind him followed a sailor carrying coffee and cups.

"What's going on?"

"It's Hartenstein," Hessler said, handing him the message.

Godt read attentively. "We have to tell the admiral," he decided. "This is a serious matter."

Once more the orderly set out. As he passed the guard stationed at the bottom of the main staircase, he whispered: "Next, they're going to tell me to go wake up the Führer!"

A few minutes later, Admiral Doenitz, his face pale, entered the operations room. Godt met him and, without a word, handed him the message. The Lion read: "9/13. Atlantic near Freetown. Sunk British *Laconia*, registry number FT 7-721 3,100. Unfortunately, was carrying 1,500 Italian prisoners. Have picked up 90 of them. Wind force 3. Request instructions. Hartenstein."

The admiral reread the message. The veins in his forehead began to throb.

"Bring me the copy of *British Shipping*," he ordered.

As Hessler sipped his coffee, Doenitz read: "*Laconia*. Launched, May 13, 1922. Home port, Liverpool. 19,695 tons. Length, 183 meters. Beam, 22 meters. Speed, 16 knots."

"Was it armed, Admiral?" asked his son-in-law.

"Yes! Two 120-mm. cannons, and twelve antiaircraft guns— 38-mm. and 76-mm."

"Well then, it wasn't a mere steamer. It was an auxiliary cruiser. Hartenstein was right to attack."

"That's not the problem, gentlemen," Doenitz replied. "What we have to decide is whether Hartenstein should risk his crew and his ship in continuing rescue operations. If so, we must send help; which means we must divert the wolf pack en route toward the Cape of Good Hope. Should we delay a military operation, gentlemen, and listen to our consciences? What do you think, Godt?"

The chief-of-staff thought for a moment. He knew that the Lion could not abide evasive answers. He required precise opinions from his staff.

"Hartenstein and the *U-156* are part of group *Eisbar* [Polar Bear], which also includes the *U-68*, the *U-504*, and the *U-172*. They've been out since mid-August. They're supposed to take on fuel and supplies from a milkcow—the *U-459* of von Wilamowitz-Möllendorf. Their mission is to patrol the South Atlantic coastal waters. These U-boats are all a good distance apart, and they're all between thirty and fifty hours away from the *Laconia*. If we send them to help in rescue operations, we'll be exposing them to enemy attack—as the *U-156* already is. My conclusion, therefore, is that Hartenstein should discontinue rescue operations and continue on, with the rest of the group, toward the Indian Ocean."

"What about you, Hessler?"

"My opinion is the same as the commander's, sir."

Doenitz, seated at the operations table, was silent for a few minutes. When he spoke, he had made his decision. "Which are the submarines closest to the *U-156*?"

"Würdemann's *U-506* and Schacht's *U-507* are about thirty hours away. Wilamowitz' is much farther."

"What is 'much farther'?"

"At least two days."

Doenitz reached for the message pad and his hand began moving over the paper. "Here," he said, "send this to Hartenstein."

The text read: "Inform me if ship has sent out distress signal. Are survivors in lifeboats? Give details on position of ship."

Then he wrote another message, to Würdemann and Schacht, ordering them to proceed at full speed toward the *U-156*.

At 3 A.M., as Doenitz waited for a telephone call to Grand

Admiral Raeder to be completed, so that he could inform his superior of the situation and his decision, answers from Würdemann and Schacht reached him. Their submarines were proceeding to Hartenstein's position; Würdemann was moving at 15 knots, and Schacht at 14 knots.

Turning to Hessler, Doenitz ordered: "Notify Admiral Parona to send his submarine, the *Cappellini*, which is in the vicinity, to help Hartenstein. It's to be expected that the Italians will want to take part in the rescue of 1,500 of their fellow countrymen."

At 3:28 A.M., Hartenstein was standing on the conning tower of the *U-156*, looking at the crowded fore- and afterdecks of his submarine. "How many of them are there?" he asked Mannesmann in a worried voice.

"Well, so far, Captain, there are 193. But they're still bringing more aboard."

"How is it down there?" Hartenstein shouted down the hatchway.

"We can hardly move, Captain," answered Wilhelm Polchau, the engineer.

Hartenstein looked at the water around him. In the darkness, he sensed, more than saw, the five lifeboats secured by lines to the Grey Wolf's stern. Altogether, they contained another two hundred survivors. He also knew that there were hundreds more still in the water, struggling among the waves to reach a lifeboat, a raft, a piece of debris—anything that could keep them afloat.

Cries for help came continually from all directions. Hartenstein was extremely uneasy. He had discovered that the *Laconia* was carrying not only British and Polish soldiers—that latter to guard the Italian prisoners—but also women and children. And, on that basis, he had determined that, whatever the risk, he would have to take aboard as many survivors as possible. The *U-156* cruised about constantly, picking up one survivor after another, until the submarine was so jammed that its stability was threatened. And the U-boat crew, despite their extreme fatigue, were tireless in helping the survivors of the *Laconia* to right capsized lifeboats, and in distributing coffee, cigarettes, and dry clothing.

Suddenly, screams of terror and agony rose from the water. Hartenstein, as the *U-156* approached, felt a wave of nausea sweep over him. The cries in English and Italian were those of men and women screaming, before they died: *Squales! Squales! Aiuto! Aiuto!* Help! Sharks! Sharks!

Schools of small sharks had discovered the hundreds of floating, exhausted, half-frozen human beings adrift in the swell, and they had attacked savagely. The final load of Italian prisoners taken aboard the U-boat were in a pitiable state, with pieces of their legs, buttocks and forearms eaten away by the predators.

"How many must have died this horrible death?" Hartenstein asked himself, agonizing over the tragedy of which he was the cause—a tragedy the extent of which he was coming to realize as the hours passed. "I could bear it," he confided to Mannesmann, "if it were not for the women and children. The Italians, after all, are soldiers. But these innocent people—I've done something tonight that I'll regret for the rest of my life."

From his vantage point on the conning tower, he watched his men among the wounded, working with the devotion which characterizes men of the sea of all nations. The chief difficulty seems to be to get the most seriously wounded survivors below, through hatchways only 2 feet wide.

"I've had hammocks strung all along the bulkheads," Mannesmann reported. "It looks like a hospital ship."

"Well done," Hartenstein answered in a tired voice. At that moment, Hartenstein—nicknamed "the Eagle" because of his hooked nose—bore no resemblance to the daring, carefree young officer he had been only two years before. He was only thirty-two, but extended submarine combat had taken a heavy personal toll, and he seemed old far beyond his years. His lined face, haggard eyes, and graying temples were those of a man of fifty.

The radioman's head appeared in the hatchway. "Message from headquarters, Captain."

Hartenstein took the piece of paper and read: "Inform me if ship has sent out distress signal. Are survivors in lifeboats? Give details on position of ship."

"As though I had nothing else to do," Hartenstein grumbled as he climbed down to the control room. Picking his way among the hammocks hanging from the bulkheads and the people sprawled on the decks, he made his way to the radioman and scribbled an answer: "Ship signaled exact position. I have 193 survivors on board, including 21 English. Hundreds more are still in the water, wearing life belts."

Hartenstein thought for a minute, then he added: "Suggest diplomatic neutralization of area."

Doenitz, after reading Hartenstein's message aloud to his staff, said, "I doubt that the enemy will accept Hartenstein's suggestion. They'd prefer to sink a U-boat, even if it is carrying some of their own people."

"Yes, that's obvious," agreed Hessler. "If they let a Grey Wolf get away, it might sink more of their ships later on."

"Even so, it's hard to believe that we're sitting around discussing the purely humanitarian aspects of this problem," Godt observed. "After all, according to the enemy, German U-boat commanders are all inhuman monsters. I'm afraid, in any case, that we'd be wasting our time."

"All right," Doenitz agreed, "we won't ask the Allies to agree to neutralize the area. But we'll have to continue our rescue operations until the French from Dakar and the Italians arrive to give Hartenstein a hand."

September 13, 5:34 A.M. After a satisfactory test dive, with two hundred people aboard, the U-156 surfaced and stopped its engines. Immediately, Hartenstein climbed topside. Despite the comparative cool of night, he removed his white cap and wiped the sweat from his forehead.

Dawn was beginning to break, and the first light revealed a sinister and tragic spectacle. All around, as far as Hartenstein could see, were overcrowded lifeboats, some with sails hoisted, and dozens of survivors still in the water, hanging onto lines from the lifeboats and rafts. Among the boats were dozens more of lifeless bodies, and the debris of the *Laconia*.

"I'll have to do it," Hartenstein told himself. "If it doesn't work—well, then I'll face the consequences."

He leaned toward the hatch and called the radioman. "Send out this message, in English: 'If any ship will assist the wrecked *Laconia* crew, I will not attack it, providing I am not attacked by ship or air force. I picked up 193 men, 4°52 South, 11° West. German submarine.' Send it in the clear, on 25 and 600 meters."

Through the aft and fore hatchways, the survivors began to emerge on deck, unshaven, listless, resigned. Only the U-boat crew had shaved that morning. It was Hartenstein's way. No matter what the circumstances, he insisted on neatness. And today, Sunday, even after a sleepless night, his men were as he wanted them to be.

Containers of hot soup and coffee were distributed on deck. Hartenstein saw one, then two, then five lifeboats cautiously approaching the *U-156*. He picked up the megaphone and called: "Come alongside! We have coffee and soup for you!"

Grappling hooks were thrown out and containers of boiling liquid were passed out among the survivors. Hartenstein saw their faces, flaccid with fatigue and fear.

A voice asked, in English: "We have a woman with us. Can you take her aboard?"

"Yes," Hartenstein answered.

The woman was lifted aboard, her hair and clothing dripping. At the end of her strength, she fell to the deck, trembling uncontrollably. Two sailors helped her down the hatchway. Hartenstein followed them below, and ordered the sailors to give her his own quarters and to bring her some tea. "It's certainly not the quality of tea that you find in London," he told the young woman, "but it's not all that bad. Now, lie down and rest. I'll send someone in for your clothes so that we can dry them."

The woman, surprised at such courtesy, managed to stammer, "Thank you, sir."

Hartenstein noticed that she was wearing an evening dress. "I'm sure it was a splendid dress before it got soaked," he ventured.

"Yes. We were having a dance when the torpedo struck," she answered in a thin voice.

The other eleven berths on the submarine were all occupied by British survivors, mostly officers from the *Laconia* and from the Royal Air Force.

Another Englishwoman, who had come aboard several hours earlier, came to speak to the newcomer as Hartenstein was leaving. He overheard her say: "The Germans on this submarine are human beings. Since I came aboard, some of the sailors have given me fruit and chocolate."

Hartenstein passed several of his crew picking their way through the narrow corridors, carrying bread and canned food.

Trying to piece together an intelligible account of the *Laconia,* Hartenstein decided to question some of the survivors. The first ones he interrogated were the British, through his engineer who spoke perfect English. Then he found an Italian sergeant who spoke fair German.

Hartenstein took him above, although he seemed quite weak. The man, it transpired, was from Venice. He was tall, fair-haired. His uniform was in tatters. There was a flesh wound in his right hip.

Hartenstein lighted a cigar, then said: "I'd like to know for certain what happened aboard the *Laconia.*" And, since he mistrusted both explanations and Italians, he added: "I want a clear account. No exaggerations. No dramatics. Do you understand?"

The Italian looked at him coldly. Hartenstein realized that he had offended the man. Well, he thought, that's too bad. This isn't the time to be gentle.

He stared back at the Italian. "I'm waiting."

"I don't know if you think my wound is exaggerated, Captain," the Italian answered, "but I got it from a bayonet. I don't know if you find it overly dramatic that my fellow prisoners and I were locked up in the ship's hole, which was hot as hell. Since boarding the *Laconia*, we were kept on bread and water —for three days. You may think I am exaggerating—"

"All right!" Hartenstein exploded. "That's enough of that! Keep it up and I'll have you thrown overboard, understand?"

It was the Italian's turn to lose his temper. Clenching his teeth, he hissed rather than spoke: "You're right. That was enough. After what we've been through, we deserve some consideration. Do you know what happened aboard the *Laconia* when you torpedoed her? As soon as we felt the ship listing, we tried to get out of our cells. The Poles or the English—I don't know which—had locked all the doors. In my compartment, we managed to break down the door. There were several hundred of us, all fighting to squeeze through the same narrow opening at the same time. When someone fell, the others trampled him.

"When we reached the deck, the Poles were waiting for us, with guns and bayonets. They tried to push us back, to keep us from reaching the lifeboats. That's when I was wounded. Everything was noise and confusion, but we could hear the prisoners who were still locked up begging to be released. For the rest of us, who were already on deck, there was only one thing to do. We had to jump overboard—without life belts, since there were none for us.

"But that wasn't the worst of it, Captain. Take a close look at the Italians who were saved. Some of them were bitten by sharks; but others were wounded in other ways while in the water. If you look closely enough at them, one after the other, you'll see that some are missing a hand. The English cut them off with a hatchet when these men tried to climb aboard the lifeboats."

"I don't believe you!" Hartenstein interrupted.

"You don't believe me? Then go below and look around your submarine. Go down and see, for God's sake, what you've pulled out of the water!"

"Shut up!" Hartenstein ordered. "I will not allow you to speak to me in that tone!"

The Italian turned on his heel and, without saluting Hartenstein, went to join his compatriots who were jammed together on the foredeck. Before going below, Hartenstein glanced at him, and saw that he was crying.

Hartenstein stood silent for a minute, staring at the sea as it rose and fell in the increasingly long swell. He saw the overcrowded lifeboats and rafts, and he saw the faces of the men in them as they stared silently, motionless, at the Grey Wolf. He thought of the atrocities and the horrors of the preceding night. And he confessed to himself that it was he who had been the cause of it all.

The sun had risen, and its rays beat down pitilessly on the survivors of the *Laconia*. After freezing during the night, they were now broiling. Long strands of skin were hanging from the backs and arms of many of them, and their flesh was bright red. Their lips were swollen and cracked, their bodies dehydrated, they lay half-delirious in their boats. Despite the water distributed by the submarine's crew, they were suffering terribly from thirst. Some of them, out of their senses, had drunk sea water and were in agony.

Toward noon, Hartenstein, using the megaphone, instructed the boats and rafts to gather together in groups, and to secure themselves by lines. He also organized shifts and, in turn, the survivors on the decks of the U-boat gave up their places to the people in the five lifeboats being towed by the submarine. These transfers were carried out under the merciless sun; and occasionally it was necessary to use force in order to displace those who felt safe on the U-boat deck and refused to move into the lifeboats. The latter had been damaged and were taking on water, and it was necessary to bail continuously.

In the midst of these operations, Hartenstein was increasingly nervous and worried. He feared that at any moment an enemy ship, or planes, might attack him notwithstanding the survivors on and around his vessel. He had stationed a sailor aft, armed with a hatchet, to cut the lines to the lifeboats in case of an attack. Even so, he was aware that if he was attacked, his ship and his crew would almost certainly be lost. With so many people aboard, the U-156 would require four minutes to submerge—a fatal delay.

Night fell once more. Toward 4 A.M., the U-156 dispatched a message to headquarters: "600 survivors saved. Dispersed among twenty-two lifeboats and rafts. Others have drifted away."

As the sun climbed in the sky, the hours became a nightmare for the survivors clustered around the Grey Wolf. The lifeboats and rafts became stages on which scenes of madness were enacted. The Italians and the British came to blows over the sharing of water and food. Some of the survivors were violently delirious, and their companions were forced to knock them unconscious in order to prevent them from jumping into the shark-infested water.

Occasionally, corpses, half eaten by the sharks and drifting on the surface, were thrown against the sides of the boats.

On the conning tower, Hartenstein sat, dozing. At 11 o'clock, a crewman woke him with a message from Doenitz: "French gunboats *Dumont d'Urville* and *Annamite*, French cruiser *Gloire* proceeding at full speed from Dakar. Your instructions for contact: rendezvous only during daylight hours; show national colors."

At 12:27, one of the watch called out: "Vessel to port, Captain!"

The alert sounded, creating a wave of panic among the survivors. Hartenstein, fearing the worst, peered through his binoculars. What he saw caused a wave of relief to sweep over him.

He smiled as he recognized the familiar silhouette of a Grey Wolf. A sailor on watch reported: "It's the *U-506*."

It took a few minutes for the *U-506* to come alongside the *U-156*. On the conning tower stood Commander Würdemann, smiling. After a few questions, Würdemann had a suggestion: "Let's share the survivors. How many do you have?"

"Two hundred and sixty-three."

Würdemann laughed. "How can you stay afloat?"

Although secured by lines, the two Grey Wolves were continually jostled by the swell, and the transfer of 132 weak and dispirited Italians was a difficult job. In the inevitable confusion accompanying the operation, Hartenstein caught a glimpse of the Venetian sergeant's head rising above those of his shorter countrymen. The sergeant looked toward the tower, and Hartenstein raised his hand in a friendly salute. The Italian looked away without responding, and shortly afterward was ferried over to the *U-506*.

Once the transfer had been completed, the U-boats separated. Each one took a different direction and began cruising the area in a search for other survivors. Hartenstein sent a message to headquarters: "Encountered *U-506*. Transferred 132 Italians. Am keeping 131 survivors, 55 Italians, 55 English of which 3 are women."

The watch searched the sea through their glasses. The heat was so intense, the glare so blinding, that their eyes ached continually. It seemed that the sea was boiling, and that steam, like a pale blue fog, was rising from the surface.

"Lifeboat dead ahead!"

After a brief maneuver, the deck crew threw out their grappling hooks and pulled the craft alongside the *U-156*. At first glance, it appeared to be empty; but when several members of the crew jumped aboard, they found ten men, shivering despite the heat, lying motionless in the water at the bottom of the boat. The water was cloudy, reddish, from the blood of an Italian whose arm apparently had been devoured by sharks. The man was dead. The others were not much better off. The corpse was put into the sea, and the crewmen struggled to get the others, who were unable to stand or to move on their own, aboard the submarine. In the surrounding water, a fleet of small, shining, black sails moved relentlessly: the fins of hungry sharks.

On deck, the German crewmen pried open the survivors' mouths and forced them to drink steaming coffee.

The rescue operation took over an hour.

By the end of the day, two more of the submarines diverted by Doenitz had arrived: the U-507, commanded by Schacht, and, a few hours later, the *Cappellini,* under Lieutenant Commander Marco Revedin. By then, Würdemann, in addition to the passengers he had taken aboard his vessel, had outfitted five life rafts with water, food, clothing, and medical supplies. The new arrivals exerted themselves to the limit to reduce the suffering of the survivors they found. Late that night, headquarters received a message reporting that Würdemann had taken aboard a total of 142 Italians, 9 women, and 7 children. Schacht had 129 Italians, one British officer (the second officer of the *Laconia*), 18 women, and 16 children. In addition, he was towing seven lifeboats containing 330 British survivors.

26

Thursday, September 16. 11:25 A.M.

"Engines at 70 degrees!"

All glasses turned immediately in the direction given by the watch. The plane drew nearer, larger. A four-engine Liberator.

Hartenstein was torn between fear and relief. The bomber might be coming to help in the rescue operation; or its mission might be to blast the submarine out of the water. He reached a quick decision. "Show the Red Cross flag," he ordered. "Hurry!"

With precise, disciplined movements, a sailor hoisted aloft

the flag which Hartenstein had had pieced together aboard the
U-156.

"All right, everybody off the foredeck. I want everyone on the
afterdeck—flat on their stomachs."

Aboard the *U-156* and in the five lifeboats secured to her
stern, where Italian Allies and British and Polish enemies were
packed indiscriminately, no one breathed. They watched the
plane overhead. They saw the white star on a blue field, the
legend *U. S. AIR FORCE,* when the aircraft turned at a low
altitude.

"Steurmann [helmsman]!" Hartenstein ordered. "Signal in
Morse code: 'This is a German submarine. We have English
survivors aboard. Are you sending help?'"

There was no response from the plane as it doubled back for
another pass.

An English survivor approached Hartenstein. "Let me send
them a message, Captain."

"Go ahead."

The Englishman rapidly sent out: "I am an R.A.F. officer.
Aboard we have survivors from the *Laconia.* Women, children,
civilians, soldiers."

The Liberator did not acknowledge the message. It began
to gain altitude and then disappeared into the distance.

"I'd give anything to know what's going to happen," Hartenstein muttered.

At 12:32, the watch announced: "Aircraft at 120 degrees!"

"Is it the same one?" Hartenstein wondered. "We'll know soon
enough."

The Liberator came in at an altitude of no more than 250
feet, its engines roaring.

"Goddammit!" Hartenstein swore. He could see the plane's
bomb bays swinging open. "*Ausserte Kraft voraus* [Full speed
ahead]!"

A hundred and fifty feet away, two columns of water rose,
followed almost immediately by two explosions. The men in

the lifeboats were thrown against one another by the brutal
percussion and by the submarine's sudden surge forward. Some
of them fell into the water, struggling and screaming. One
Englishman, clutching the side of his boat, raised one fist to the
sky and screamed: "Bloody fucking Yankee bastards!"

The Liberator turned for another run at the submarine from
whose deck still fluttered the Red Cross standard.

"Cut the lifeboats adrift!" Hartenstein ordered.

A crewman, hatchet in hand, obeyed immediately and cut
the lines. The boats smashed into one another, their lines inter-
twining; but the survivors had no time to untangle them, for
almost immediately a bomb fell near them. One boat was lifted
out of the water and capsized. Its occupants were scattered like
straws over a hundred feet of ocean.

Mannesmann raced to Hartenstein's side. "Captain, can we
fire on that bastard?"

"No!"

As the men from the overturned boat swam about, screaming
for help, the Liberator returned to the attack.

"Hard to starboard," Hartenstein shouted as the aircraft released two more bombs. One of the missiles exploded at the
level of the conning tower, and the U-156 rolled at a 45° angle
to port. Its prow was thrust violently beneath the surface, then
rose streaming water.

When Hartenstein looked up, the Liberator was heading
away, as though regretfully, with empty bomb bays.

Hartenstein lighted a cigar, wondering if he had been wrong
in not firing on the American plane. At 250 feet, his gunners
would have made mincemeat out of it with the first salvo.

"Leak in the forward compartment, Captain," Mannesmann
said.

The engineer reported angrily: "One of the couplings on a
diesel cooling tube is shot, Captain. The main periscope is bent.
The attack periscope doesn't turn. And the batteries are giving
off chlorine fumes!"

For the first time since the attack on the *Laconia,* Hartenstein lost his temper. "Clear everyone out of here!" he shouted. "I don't want to see one goddammed foreigner on this ship, and I don't care what his nationality is. Put them all aboard lifeboats. And open up the fore and aft hatches so we can air out this place."

Amid the loud protests of the *Laconia* survivors, some of whom had to be ejected forcibly from the submarine, the radioman reported: "Captain, our radio is on the blink."

"Can you repair it?"

"I hope so."

At 4:47 P.M., the *U-156* moved at slow speed at a depth of 190 feet. Hartenstein, holding a cup of coffee, stood motionless in the control room, suddenly overcome by the emotional burden and the fatigue of the past three days. He shook himself violently, like a wet dog, and pinched his cheeks to keep from falling asleep. He knew that his men were as tired as he.

"Sir," the engineer reported, "most of the damage has been repaired. All except the radio and the attack periscope."

"Good. Thank the men."

A while later, Hartenstein lay on his bunk, his eyes closed, talking to Mannesmann. The clean-up detail had succeeded in clearing the debris left by the *Laconia* survivors, and in scrubbing away the filth. Two-thirds of the crew were already asleep. Except for the hum of the electric motors, the *U-156* was a peaceful oasis.

Hartenstein, however, was discouraged. For the first time, Mannesmann saw the "old man" overwhelmed by events. He looked at the face usually so firm and authoritarian, and he suddenly realized the depth of the friendship which bound him to this man. The sight of the lines worn by war on that face aroused deep pity in him. Soundlessly, he rose and drew the canvas curtain which separated the cabin from the corridor.

From behind the curtain, he heard the captain's drowsy voice: "Mannesmann, have someone wake me at 9 P.M., please."

Mannesmann stuck his head into the cabin. "Yes, sir," he said softly.

"Mannesmann?"

"Captain?"

"Mannesmann, the *Laconia* which I sunk—the American plane that bombed us—you know, Mannesmann, men are bastards." Then he fell asleep.

The radio was not repaired until shortly before midnight. From the surface, Hartenstein was now able to communicate with Doenitz' headquarters and report the air attack: "American Liberator dropped five bombs despite lifeboats carrying survivors and Red Cross flag. Periscopes damaged. Have discontinued rescue operation. All survivors now in lifeboats. Am proceeding westward. Hartenstein."

Doenitz had not slept since the night of September 12. Except for those brief hours during which he reluctantly stretched out on his bed, he was too worried, too tense, to rest. Until the *Laconia* affair was brought to a conclusion, he remained in the map room, following the activities of the Grey Wolf in its rescue operation.

Now, he sat in his office, alone. He had just received Hartenstein's message describing the attack on his submarine, and he must reach a decision. It was a decision that he did not wish to make until he had analyzed all aspects of the problem and foreseen all the consequences of the solution. In a few hours, French ships would take aboard the survivors and the U-boats would be free to continue with Operation Polar Bear. That is, if everything went well. Except, Doenitz reminded himself, that we must never again allow ourselves to be put in this position. As a soldier, he recognized the military expediency of the Americans' decision to bomb the *U-156*. The destruction of the enemy, after all, was the first priority of combat. Now, however, Doenitz would be compelled to adopt the same tactics. With an air of finality, he sat at his desk and wrote out a message, fully conscious of the effect which *Triton Null,* as the communication was called, would have upon his own fate and that of his men. Then he summoned Godt, Hessler, and several other officers of his staff, and read aloud what he had written:

"Henceforth, it is forbidden to attempt to save personnel from torpedoed ships, to pull such personnel from the water for the purpose of transferring them to boats and rafts, to right capsized lifeboats, and to distribute food and water among survivors. Such rescue operations are directly contrary to the most elementary principle of war, which requires the destruction of enemy ships and enemy personnel."

"Shall I send this out now?" Hessler asked.

"No. Let Hartenstein finish his rescue operation. He needs only a few more hours."

Hessler tried to protest the delay, but Doenitz silenced him with an imperious gesture.

On the morning of September 18, the *Laconia* survivors from the *U-506* and *U-507* were hoisted aboard the *Gloire* and the *Annamite.* A few hundred yards away, their torpedo tubes toward the French ships, Hartenstein and Würdemann waited as the last of the Italians were ferried away. Then, the Grey Wolves submerged and, zigzagging to cover their tracks, they headed south.

During the entire day, the French ships cruised the area in search of drifting lifeboats. Darkness had already fallen when Commander Graziani gave the order to head back to Dakar.

A month later, on October 21, a British ship, H.M.S. *Saint Wistan,* sighted a lifeboat drifting aimlessly in the Atlantic. Aboard were four men, unconscious, barely alive, incapable of moving. These last survivors of the *Laconia* had somehow, miraculously, endured forty days of exposure in a lifeboat.

Their rescue brought the number of survivors to 1,111, out of a total of 2,732 aboard the *Laconia.*

27

Hermann Rasch ran up the steps of the nightclub in the rue Fontaine, closely followed by Oesten, his former commanding officer, and Nyssen, his second officer. Seated at a ringside table, the Germans scrutinized the seven half-naked dancers twisting and turning in approximate time to the music. The officers smiled. The girls appeared to be all that they were said to be.

A man in a dinner jacket bowed before them. "What will you have, gentlemen?"

"Champagne," Rasch answered. "Mmm."

He leaned back in his chair and lighted a cigarette. Oesten and Nyssen, on either side of him, kept their eyes on the dancers. Despite the sinuous gypsy music, despite the undoubted attractions of the dancers, Rasch was uneasy. That morning, Doenitz had summoned him to his office on Boulevard Maunoury. The interview had been brief, but the Lion had left no doubt as to his intentions. Rasch remembered the admiral's every word.

"Last night," Doenitz said, "at a reception, I met an uncle of yours. A Wehrmacht colonel. He mentioned to me that you have not spent a single day with your family in Germany since the beginning of the war. Is that correct?"

"Yes, sir," Rasch had admitted.

"Why not?"

"I've been too busy, sir. In Paris."

Doenitz did not smile. "How many days do you have left on the beach?"

"Seven, Admiral."

"You leave for Hamburg tomorrow morning."

"But that's impossible, sir," Rasch blurted out.

"I must have misunderstood you."

"I mean, sir, that I haven't a franc to my name. I can't go."

Doenitz rose and glared at Rasch. Then he opened a box

containing stacks of bills and took out a handful of them. "Here,"
he told Rasch. "Take this. Then pick up your ticket and go see
your parents. And try not to spend all your time thinking of
women."

Rasch had counted the money after leaving Doenitz' office.
Six thousand francs. He felt them now, rustling agreeably in
his pocket. "Don't forget to let me know when it's five o'clock,"
he said to Nyssen. "I have to catch that train, or the admiral
will kill me."

The champagne was served and, simultaneously, the officers
were joined by three "hostesses" employed by the club. These,
Rasch reflected, were equal in every respect to the dancers. One
of them began to stroke his blond goatee. Before abandoning
himself to the pleasures of this new encounter, Rasch touched
Nyssen's arm and reminded him: "Remember, I'm counting on
you. I have to make that train."

"Yes, sir," Nyssen replied, from between the breasts of the girl
sitting on his lap, "you can count on me."

But Rasch was still worried. Judging from the way the evening
had begun, it was certain that in only a couple of hours they
would all be dead drunk. He asked the girl to excuse him and
went to the bar, intending to call his hotel, the Ambassador,
and ask them to pack his belongings and have a military vehicle
sent to drive him to the train station. At the bar, however, Rasch
was stopped by a heavy man of about sixty who addressed him
in German. "I am the proprietor of this club. This is the first
time that officers of the *Kriegsmarine* have honored us with
their presence. May I offer you something to drink?"

Rasch glanced toward the telephone booth. It was occupied.
He accepted the offer, and the man ordered two drinks.

"My name is Vladimir. I am a White Russian," the man
explained. "During the first war, I was an officer in the navy of
His Imperial Majesty, the Czar."

"Oh? Were you in combat?"

"In the Black Sea. My ship was sunk."

"Bad luck," Rasch said politely as he emptied his glass.

"Very bad," the Russian said. "It was only a gunboat, you understand, and I came up against a German cruiser. They sent me to the bottom with the first salvo, damn it."

Rasch looked toward the telephone booth again. It was still occupied. "What was the cruiser's name?" he asked, not wishing to appear disinterested.

"I'll never forget that name, my friend," the Russian replied, ordering two more drinks. "Never! It was the *Greuben*—"

"The what?" Rasch exclaimed. "What was that name?"

"The *Greuben*. G-r-e-u—"

"Incredible!" Rasch shouted. "Fantastic!"

"What do you mean, incredible?"

"My friend," Rasch answered, "my father was captain of the *Greuben*. My father sank your ship!"

The two men stared at each other for a second, and then burst into laughter. The Russian threw his massive arms around Rasch and began to pound him on the back. "It really is incredible," he roared. "My friend, my club is yours—my dancers, my musicians, my girls, my wine cellar. You and your friends make yourselves at home! We're going to celebrate, the way we used to in Moscow in the good old days!"

The Russian pulled himself away from Rasch and made his way to the center of the dance floor, pushing aside the surprised dancers. He clapped his hands and, in a voice which drowned out the music, he announced: "Everyone out! Quick! We are closed for the night!"

The waiters and busboys looked at him in astonishment, then began to hurry their resentful customers through the doors.

"Dancers!" the Russian shouted. "Musicians! Waiters! Whores! Stay where you are. No one is allowed to leave!"

Vladimir accompanied Rasch to his table, where Nyssen and Oesten were looking around in wonderment. Rasch quickly explained what had happened as the Russian shook their hands vigorously. "What a celebration we're going to have," he roared. "What a celebration!"

One of the hostesses at the table seemed not to have been

infected by his excitement. "Mr. Vladimir," she said, "what are we going to get out of this?"

Vladimir seemed to explode with rage. He grabbed the woman's arm and shook her violently. "Bitch!" he roared. "Fool! How dare you think of money on a day like this?"

The woman began to cry. "Let her go," Rasch said drily. "She's right. They should be paid." He took a roll of bills from his pocket and, without counting them, held them out. "Here," he told the woman, "this is for you and your friends."

Vladimir, impressed, exclaimed: "Ah, you are a true gentleman!"

Suddenly, Rasch remembered his train. He looked at his watch. Midnight. He went to the checkroom and told the attendant: "I want you to let me know when it's five o'clock. It's very important." And he handed her a princely tip.

When he reached his table, Vladimir greeted him uproariously. "Listen," he said, "I've thought of a game. There are lots of women here, and all we have to do is choose which ones we want. That's not much fun. Let's spice it up. Your friends and I have thought of a way. We're going to fill ice buckets with champagne, and the first one of us to finish his bucket will choose the most beautiful girl in the place. All right?"

It occurred to Rasch that if he drank a bucket of champagne he would be in no condition to take advantage of the prize, but he agreed. The ice buckets were brought, and Vladimir, Oesten, and Nyssen raised theirs to their lips. Rasch glanced at one of the dancers—a girl with auburn hair and green eyes. She smiled. Rasch felt a mounting excitement. He raised his bucket and began to drink.

The orchestra played, and as the waiters set the table for an improvised supper, Vladimir leaped onto the dance floor and, with surprising agility for a man of his size, began whirling in a Russian dance. Nyssen and two of the dancers joined him, as the others clapped their hands in time to the music. Oesten rose to his feet, weaving, and waved the empty bucket over his head. "I won," he shouted. "I won!"

Rasch looked around dizzily. I hope he doesn't pick the one with the auburn hair, he thought.

Oesten looked over the women carefully, then chose a tall brunette with astonishing breasts. He beckoned, and the girl—her name was Michelle—threw herself into his arms.

In honor of the winner, the orchestra played a fanfare, followed by a drum-roll as Oesten and Michelle exchanged an interminable kiss then fell limply into a chair.

Vladimir returned to the table, dripping with sweat and puffing like a whale. He picked up his ice bucket and drained it in a single gulp.

Rasch watched in admiration. The Russian had drunk at least a liter of champagne; but he was still steady enough on his feet to gather a buxom blonde into his arms and carry her bodily over to a dark corner of the room.

Rasch rose unsteadily to his feet and approached the auburn-haired girl. He bowed and asked her to dance.

"My name is Christine," she murmured.

They returned to the table after dancing. Vladimir—still shouting—Michelle, Oesten, Raffaela, Nyssen, and two dancers were eating a meal of cold chicken and *pâté*. Two small tables had been placed alongside the larger table, and these were covered with bottles of vodka and Bordeaux. The musicians gathered around the table and, with an agility which delighted and astounded the three officers, they played without missing a beat while taking great swigs of vodka and eating pieces of chicken.

"Eat, drink, my friends!" Vladimir shouted. "For tomorrow we may die." Then he collapsed into his chair, dragging down the girl next to him.

Everyone joined in the bacchanal. The waiters, the busboys, the kitchen employees all shouted toasts and emptied glass after glass. In the checkroom, the attendant had curled up on a little table and was sound asleep, one hand clutching a chicken leg.

Rasch and Christine disappeared for a while, carrying a bottle of vodka. Then, as Oesten danced drunkenly around the floor, they returned and fell asleep on a narrow banquette running

along the wall. Rasch, always meticulous, had removed his
uniform jacket, folded it, and carefully deposited it on a chair.
In the dim light, the submarine insignia shone with something
less than its customary brilliance. It was covered with lip-
stick.

The musicians still played, but with less passion. Some of
them were snoring, stretched out in chairs and on tables. At one
table, a group of waiters were engaged in a heated argument
over a game of *belote*. On the table was a bucket with two
bottles of champagne.

On a small platform which served as a stage, Nyssen and one
of the hostesses were making love, passionately, noisily.

Vladimir, gulping champagne again, was singing a Russian
song.

"What time is it?" Rasch groaned.

"I haven't the slightest idea," Vladimir answered.

"I could use some coffee—"

Christine sat up lazily, embraced Rasch, ran her hand through
his hair, then stood. "I'll get some," she whispered.

Rasch tried to stand. A sharp pain flashed through his skull.
"Shit!" he swore softly. Then, weaving precariously, he picked
his way toward the table, picked up a piece of chicken, and
proceeded to eat it with his hands.

Vladimir, apparently inexhaustible, dropped the girl he was
holding and joined him. He poured two glasses of champagne
and handed one to Rasch, who made a face, and proposed a
toast: "To the memory of the *Greuben!*"

As soon as Rasch put down his glass, he remembered his
train. He looked at his watch. He noted with surprise that it
was 1 o'clock. He raised it to his ear. It was running. He still
had four hours to spend with Christine.

The girl returned from the kitchen with a pot of steaming
coffee, followed by haggard waiters carrying cups.

After swallowing his coffee, Rasch staggered to the dance
floor and, with Christine glued to him, moved groggily around
in time to the music. Oesten and Michelle joined them, and
Rasch noted that one of Michelle's breasts was exposed.

"Where's Nyssen?" Rasch asked Oesten.

With an effort, Oesten motioned with his chin. The second officer of the U-106 was fast asleep on the stage. On him, like a quilt, also dead to the world, lay his girl. Rasch sent a waiter to waken him; but Nyssen refused to open his eyes.

Hours passed. Again, Rasch dozed. He felt someone shake him, gently at first and then more roughly. He heard a voice, seemingly distant, repeating insistently: "It's five o'clock! It's five o'clock!"

The meaning of the words penetrated the alcoholic fog. He remembered his train. Painfully, his head throbbing, he rose to a sitting position. Next to him, Christine's half-nude body stirred weakly. He stood, and there was a pain like lightning in his skull. He moaned, then doubled over. It felt as though his stomach was on fire. "God! What a mess I am," he groaned.

The checkroom attendant gave him a cup of coffee. As he drank, he looked around. A violinist was seated on one of the tables playing a melancholy air. Everywhere there were bodies, singly and in couples, asleep, surrounded by empty bottles. He dimly remembered some of the events of the preceding hours. They had discussed politics with Vladimir. A dozen toasts had been drunk to victory. He remembered that, at some point, some of the men and women had taken off their clothes and bathed in champagne poured over them by the waiters . . .

"I have to use the telephone," Rasch told the attendant. She dialed the number of the Ambassador Hotel for him, and, with difficulty, Rasch explained to the desk clerk that he wanted his bags packed and sent to him along with a military vehicle. There was a short delay, then the clerk returned. "Your bags and the car will be there in five minutes, Commander."

Rasch spashed cold water on his face, combed his hair, and, after a look at his puffed face, put on his jacket. Passing through the kitchen on his way out, he saw Vladimir slumped over an enormous sink, asleep and snoring, as cold water from the tap ran over his motionless body.

Rasch shivered in the cool night air. He lighted a cigarette.

Then he saw the camouflaged headlights of the *Kriegsmarine* vehicle. He climbed in and slumped into the seat next to the driver. "Gare de l'Est," he ordered. The sailor looked at him and smiled to himself, but said nothing.

A few minutes later, the vehicle came to a halt. It was 6:10 A.M., forty minutes before train time. Rasch, carrying his suitcase, walked to the military police checkpoint. The two men on duty watched him in amusement as he fumbled in his pockets for his ticket and his pass. Several officers and enlisted men brushed past, jostling him roughly.

Finally, he found his papers and held them out to the military police. One of them, a sergeant, took the pass and scrutinized it. A neutral expression on his face, he handed it and the ticket back to Rasch. "I'm sorry, Commander, but your ticket is no good."

"What do you mean, no good? It was issued by headquarters! Can't you read?"

"I can read, Commander," the sergeant said coldly. "And I tell you that your ticket is no good, invalid."

"Invalid?"

"Yes, sir. This is October 27. Your train left on October 26."

On October 27, Radio London announced, during its 10 o'clock news, that the crew of the *U-532* had been captured to the southeast of Ireland after their submarine had been bombed and sunk by British aircraft. The U-boat captain, Lieutenant Commander Eck, and his officers would be brought before a court-martial and tried on a charge of having machine-gunned survivors of a tanker sunk by the U-boat. The announcer concluded with the comment: "By order Triton Null, Admiral Doenitz has ordered his U-boat pirates to murder Allied crewmen. When the day of reckoning comes, this will not be forgotten."*

* Lieutenant Commander Eck and his officers were tried, found guilty, and executed by a firing squad on November 30, 1945. On the other hand, the Nuremberg Tribunal brought no charges against Doenitz, or against other submarine crews, concerning the manner in which the Grey Wolves had conducted themselves in combat.

28

It was a stormy day, early in November 1942, when the wolf pack designated by Doenitz as "Battle Axe" joined battle with convoy SL-125. The convoy had left Africa, bound for an English port, and the wolf pack had been tracking it for many hours. The battle continued for several days, with the Grey Wolves attacking, then disappearing only to reappear a short time later and pounce upon their prey with renewed fury. The results obtained by the U-boats were remarkable. They were also an accurate indication of the destructive impact of the two submarine groups which Doenitz had stationed permanently in mid-Atlantic in order to take advantage of the lack of Allied air-protection for convoys in that area. Battle Axe's score was thirteen ships—85,000 tons of Allied shipping.

Yet, for all its success, Battle Axe had been duped by Fortune. In their eagerness to destroy the convoy, the submarines of the group had missed a much more important target, one which had been sailing only a few miles away from the convoy: a fleet of transport and cargo ships which would, in a few days, effect an Allied landing on the coast of North Africa.

For Doenitz, as well as for the German High Command, the Allied invasion came as a surprise. Yet, it confirmed the admiral's analyses of the situation. On November 8, he transferred his total submarine strength to Moroccan coastal waters. Once there, however, the Grey Wolves found themselves virtually helpless against an operation protected by an impenetrable wall of gunboats and destroyers and shielded overhead by massive air defenses. In the face of such overwhelming naval and air power, the submarines were compelled to remain submerged for such long periods that the noses and ears of the crews bled constantly. In addition to the physical discomfort, there was the constant fear that the slightest noise aboard the submarine would bring down a rain of depth charges from a nearby de-

THE CONFRONTATION

233

stroyer or gunboat. Yet, despite these circumstances, the U-boats performed with extraordinary success. The *U-150*, for instance, under Commander Kals, sank three American cargo ships in 75 feet of water, in the Fedala Straits. Commander Piening's *U-155* surfaced in mid-convoy and sent an aircraft carrier—the *Avenger* —and the *Estrick*, a troop transport, to the bottom.

Even such striking victories could do little more than inconvenience the enormous American fleet of 800 ships, divided into seven convoys, in its determination to disembark men and material on the North African coast. "Attack whatever ships it is most logical and most economical to destroy," Doenitz ordered his commanders. The commanders obeyed to the letter. They struck in mid-Atlantic; they sought out the enemy's weakest points in the Caribbean; off the Cape of Good Hope; in Brazilian waters; along the coasts of the Azores, Bermuda, Greenland, and Newfoundland. And, despite the fact that the favorable conditions of Clash of Cymbals existed no longer in American waters, the Grey Wolves obtained notable results. In the last quarter of 1942, the Allies lost 3,200,000 tons of shipping—575 ships—to the determination of the U-boat commanders. For the entire year, the score was 6,200,000 tons—which was approximately equal to the amount of shipping built by the Allies in that year.

An official of the British Admiralty did not exaggerate when, in December, he stated: "Never has the situation been so difficult." By the middle of that month, Great Britain had on hand only some 300,000 tons of liquid fuel; and her average consumption was 130,000 tons per month.

Doenitz, however, was not carried away by optimism. "In war," he declared, "success must be total. To smash the enemy is not an end in itself. It is true that November was our best month in 1942, and that we sank 220 tons of shipping per day for every U-boat in operation. But let's not forget that, in October 1940, that figure was 920 tons! This means that today we would need four times the U-boats we actually have in order to attain the same results. And even those results, as we know, were not decisive."

For the Grey Wolves, indeed, the time of the blitzkrieg had come and gone, and the new year of 1943 would prove to be the Stalingrad of the undersea war. Both sides were determined on a final confrontation; and both sides were forging new arms for that purpose. On the German side, technical improvements had increased the dive capability of the submarines. They could now dive to almost a thousand feet to escape depth-charge barrages —barrages which now employed increasingly powerful explosives. Torpedoes had also been improved, and a new magnetic-firing machine gun had finally eliminated (three years after the war had begun) the "mis-fires" of the first years. Antiaircraft capability had been increased by the addition to the submarines of a double (C-38) 20-mm. And finally, in August 1942, the German Navy's Chief of Communications, Admiral Stummel, had obtained a British radar device taken from a downed plane. By October, the Grey Wolves were equipped with a French invention, the Metox-Fu M.B.—a device capable of detecting radar waves at a distance of 35 miles, and which therefore afforded the U-boats a certain amount of time in which to make their escape.

But Doenitz knew that wars were not won by technological puttering. He became more insistent than ever that Berlin consider the request that he had submitted and resubmitted since 1939 and develop an over-all strategy which would accord absolute priority to a submarine striking force. Churchill, Doenitz knew, had already given the same priority to an antisubmarine striking force. Putting aside his Prussian pride, the Lion even appeared at Goering's headquarters and attempted to persuade the *Reichsmarschall* of the necessity for such a force. He cited the example of the Gulf of Gascony, pointing out that, in the first years of the war, that body of water had been a hunting ground for U-boats, but that now it was a veritable hell, dominated by the R.A.F., whose planes came and went with absolute impunity. "The Reich has no right," Doenitz concluded, "to leave its submarines without air protection and exposed to enemy attack."

Goering, smiling, placid, had then offered Doenitz twenty-four Junker-88s. "That's all I can spare," he said.

Doenitz took the planes. They had a very limited range, and could operate only over coastal waters. But, the admiral reasoned, they could at least make it easier on exhausted submarine crews returning to base.

On September 3, Doenitz returned to the attack and demanded that Goering supply him with a number of HE-177s, which were capable of operating up to 1,500 miles away from their bases.

"It is not possible at present," Goering replied, "to furnish air protection to submarines operating in mid-Atlantic. An aircraft of this kind would have to be capable of the same performance as an American bomber; and, unfortunately, we do not have the technological means at the moment to insure such performance." For lack of a "strategic" aircraft, which had been designed before the outbreak of war, the Grey Wolves were compelled to face, singlehanded, the might of the world's greatest air and naval powers.

But Doenitz was not ready to give up. On September 28, through the intercession of Grand Admiral Raeder, the Lion was admitted to the presence of the Führer himself. Hitler listened impatiently as his chief of submarine operations described how Allied air power now dominated the Atlantic—so much so that only the mid-Atlantic was open to unhampered U-boat action.

"It is impossible to believe, Admiral," the Führer interrupted, "that the enemy has gained control of the entire Atlantic."

Doenitz opened his briefcase and took out his maps. He spread them out on the long conference table and explained the concentric circles which demonstrated beyond doubt the expansion of Allied air power.

"Well, then," Hitler exploded, "what good is the Metox-Fu?"

"It allows us to dive," Doenitz explained patiently, "if we have time and if conditions are favorable. But, even if the U-boat does dive, it must remain stationary on the bottom, which means that it loses its mobility. And mobility is absolutely essential to our wolf pack tactic in attacking convoys. *Mein Führer,* there is only one effective means against enemy aircraft—"

"Yes, yes, I know," Hitler said in irritation. "You're going to tell me again about your invincible submarine." He reflected a few seconds, then added: "Very well. You shall have your famous *Walter* submarine!"

Doenitz left Hitler's office with his mission accomplished. But he took no satisfaction in that feat. He knew that the *Walter* would not be ready until 1944, and that, until then, his U-boats' only protection against enemy aircraft would be the Metox-Fu M.B. "Wholly inadequate," Doenitz concluded. "It operates only on a narrow band around a wave length of 150 cm. If the enemy ever leaves that band, our anti-radar will be completely useless."

Doenitz was aware of the danger, but even he had no idea of its extent. Indeed, no German scientist had an inkling of the revolution which was about to be carried out. The British had done the impossible. The new radar, to which they were putting the finishing touches, operated on short waves of 10 cm.

January 1, 1943. It had been snowing in Berlin for several days, and the blackened, crumbling façades of bombed buildings seemed alien to the white, silent city. Shaking the snow from their boots, the ranking officers of the High Command climbed the steps of the Chancellery and made their way toward the Grand Salon where, at precisely 9 o'clock, the Führer would appear to accept the New Year's greetings of his officers.

Hitler arrived on schedule. The yellowish cast of his skin, his blazing black eyes, his pinched lips told everyone present that the leader of the Third Reich was in a very bad temper. There was not a general in the room who did not wonder, in anguish, who would be the target of Hitler's anger.

Hitler took only a few steps into the room. His eyes moved over the silent officers standing stiffly at attention, and came to rest on Grand Admiral Raeder. "I wish to speak with you, Grand Admiral," he said. "Please come into my office. And you, Keitel, come with us."

Raeder, his step slow, heavy, followed Hitler from the room. His ascetic features betrayed nothing of his inner turmoil. He was already aware of the reason for Hitler's anger; and, from experience, he could foresee the violence of the scene about to take place. But he did not know what decision the Führer had reached, and this made him apprehensive.

No sooner had the door closed behind Raeder than the storm broke. "Grand Admiral," Hitler exclaimed in a strident voice, "I am extremely unhappy with your ships. They have brought ridicule upon the *Kriegsmarine!*"

On the evening of December 31, Hitler had learned from Radio London that a German squadron, based in Norway and led by the cruisers *Admiral Hipper* and *Lützow,* had attacked a convoy bound for Murmansk. The attack had failed. The squadron had been unable to stop the convoy. To Hitler, already exasperated by Russian resistance at Stalingrad and by the critical situation in North Africa, this new failure seemed the last straw. And Goering and Keitel, as usual, had dexterously turned the Führer's anger away from themselves and onto the *Kriegsmarine.*

For ninety minutes, Raeder stood pale and silent as Hitler covered him with insults and reproaches; it seemed an eternity to a man who had devoted his whole life to building up the effectiveness of the German Navy.

"Now, Grand Admiral," Hitler concluded, "do you know what I've decided? Since your ships seem to be useless in combat, I am going to have them scrapped! My decision is final, and it will be inserted into the official War Journal."

Raeder blanched under the insult. But Hitler did not give him a chance to reply. As *Marschall* Keitel watched impassively, the Führer went on: "Since your ships are useless, can you guess where their heavy guns can be put to good use? On land! On the Eastern front, and in Africa! And as for the ships themselves, we're going to make airplanes out of them—and yes, even submarines!"

Raeder, crushed, suddenly was overwhelmed by fatigue and discouragement. At sixty-seven, he felt too old to bear up under Hitler's insane rage. Always a daring tactician and brilliant strategist, he now felt his courage drain away. He could not summon the strength even to defend himself, to say that the German surface fleet, even though it had never won spectacular victories, had, nonetheless, with Hitler's approval, succeeded in immobilizing Britain's redoubtable Home Fleet.

When Hitler finally fell silent, Raeder, with a shallow bow, asked permission to speak to him alone. At a sign from Hitler, Keitel withdrew, and Raeder began to speak in a solemn, glacial tone. "My Führer," he said, "since you do not approve of the way in which I exercise command of the Navy, as you have just explained, I ask to be relieved of that command. I no longer have your confidence, and it is impossible for me to continue. I am an old man, and my health is no longer what it was. It is only to be expected that I be replaced by a younger man."

"Grand Admiral," Hitler interrupted, "your age has nothing to do with this. And I am not condemning the entire Navy. I simply cannot see the point in maintaining a large surface force. Your resignation at this time, when we are engaged in a struggle to the death on all fronts, would be an additional burden for me to bear."

Raeder, however, had made his decision, and he remained firm. "After what has happened," he replied, "my authority would be undermined. And it would cease to exist altogether if you scrapped the fleet."

Hitler, taken off guard by Raeder's decision to retire, was shaken. His lips pressed together, he paced back and forth in silence. Finally, he spoke: "Very well. January 30th is the tenth anniversary of my accession to power. It seems an appropriate date for you to submit your resignation."

The Grand Admiral was about to leave the room when Hitler stopped him. "I want you to give me the names of two officers whom you think could replace you," he said bitingly.

Such were the circumstances in which Doenitz, to his astonishment, was named supreme commander of the German fleet and promoted to grand admiral. His new flag, however, with its blue cross and crossed batons on a white field, did not fly for long on the Boulevard Maunoury. Once Grand Admiral Raeder had made his farewells in a final Order of the Day, Doenitz was required to leave Paris and transfer his headquarters to Berlin. There, with Godt (promoted to vice-admiral) as his assistant, he continued to exercise direct command over the submarine fleet. For Hitler had assured him: "I am no longer interested in anything but U-boats."

29

For the twenty U-boats whose conning towers bore the polar-bear insignia of the Northern Fleet, the winter of 1943 was an unrelieved nightmare. The interminable patrolling of the Arctic Sea, from Spitsbergen to North Cape and Novaya Zemlya, had a more devastating effect upon the submariners than the desperate battles of the western Atlantic. For these men banished to the great northern wastes, the chief danger was not the enemy, but the elements. When they returned, haggard, exhausted, to their Norwegian bases at Trondheim, Narvik, Bergen, and Kirkenes, and even when they went on shore leave, they required a long rest before they were able to forget the howling storms, the ice, and the atrocious, incredible cold.

In winter, the Arctic was a veritable hell: a hell of ice, a desolate abomination of unending darkness which tried the courage and endurance of the bravest and hardiest men. The submarine crews lived at the outer limits of human resistance in the white hell created by periscopes constantly rendered inopera-

tive by the cold; vessels wrapped in eternal, icy, paralyzing
sheets of fog; faces bitten and torn by icy needles of spray; decks
and superstructures which were nothing more than grotesque
masses of ice; swirling clouds of snow which kept visibility to
zero; compasses spinning wildly because of the proximity of the
Pole; and the wind, forever roaring at 125 miles an hour. Daylight was a brief glow on the horizon which told that it was mid-
day and that there was, after all, a sun still in the sky. Then, the
submariners were again plunged into infernal darkness, and
continued to hunt, groping like blind men in the impenetrable
gloom. And pity the man who forgot himself and removed a glove
to touch the railing of the deck: the skin of his hand remained
fastened to the frozen steel.

Doenitz opposed these sufferings, for he judged them useless.
He was against these sacrifices, for he believed that because
of the climate conditions, it was impossible for the twenty
U-boats of the Northern Fleet to operate as successfully in the
Arctic as in the Atlantic. "Victories," he said, "are to be found in
the vicinity of Iceland, where the convoys are formed, if not even
farther to the west." And, even in the Far North, escort vessels
now formed protective circles around convoys which the U-boats
found almost impossible to penetrate.

The Führer, however, was intractable. He insisted that the
entire Northern Fleet remain in the Arctic, searching for convoys bound for Russia. It was his conviction that the U-boats,
even if their success was limited by the climate, were capable
of reconnoitering and scouting targets for the Luftwaffe bombers
stationed in Norway. Moreover, he had arguments of his own
with which to harangue Doenitz. During the summer of 1942,
three convoys suffered serious losses in the Arctic—one of which
lost twenty-four of its thirty-five ships. Doenitz tried in vain to
explain to Hitler that it was impossible to realize such successes
during the winter months, but Hitler's mind was already made
up. "The presence of our U-boats," he told Doenitz, "however
little effective they may actually be, has a considerable psy-
chological effect upon the crews of enemy ships."

In a certain sense, Hitler was right. The presence of German submarines had a decided impact on the morale of Allied sailors. Aboard cargo ships and tankers, the men were so nervous that gunners and machine gunners fired immediately at anything which however vaguely resembled a periscope. Doenitz, however, was right in a more important sense. Convoys to Russia, protected by the Arctic night, reached their destination despite the most strenuous efforts of the Luftwaffe and the submarines. In January, convoy J.W.-52, comprising thirteen cargo ships and twenty escorts, and in February, J.W.-53, composed of twenty-two cargo ships and twenty escorts, both reached Soviet ports without the loss of a single ship.

Hitler's rage on these occasions knew no bounds. No one was spared—except Doenitz, whose sensitivity and pride Hitler feared and respected.

March 5. 5:20 A.M.

A wind had risen during the night and blew now with terrifying force. The decks and superstructure of the U-265 were obliterated by the snow, and everything—the gun and the machine guns as well as the decks themselves—were covered with a 4-inch layer of ice. The U-boat pitched and rolled among the waves, like some great serpent struggling to escape the walls of water which broke over it.

To Wolf Shafer, the officer of the deck, it seemed that even the hands of the ship's clock were frozen in place and that his tour of duty would never end. Like the other men on watch, he was transfixed by cold. He shivered violently and continually, and at times he had the sensation that an icy fluid had been injected into his spinal column. His own mother would not have recognized that tortured, livid face with its eyelashes and short beard encrusted with ice, its blue lips, its cheeks ravaged by the cold, its red eyes. For the moment, Shafer was busy counting the minutes left before the end of his tour of duty and the end of his suffering. With every leap and bound of the Grey Wolf, the security belt which was fastened to the railing jerked his body violently this way and that. His fingers, numb inside his thick rubber gloves, clutched the frozen steel of the railing. His face, with the neutral expression of a man overcome by total exhaustion, was turned toward the prow and he watched the two dark walls of water which rose and then broke over the deck as the U-boat plunged through the waves. The water splashed pitilessly over the decks and even over the conning tower. Shafer had given up trying to protect himself against the spray by turning his head. He submitted passively, with resignation, to the icy water which covered him from head to foot. When, periodically, the *U-265* rose on the crest of a wave, its prow at an improbable angle toward the sky, Shafer and the watch took advantage of that brief moment of relative visibility to peer through their glasses into the grayish white mist surrounding them.

After a wave had broken with extraordinary force over the U-boat, the hatch opened cautiously and Commander Harllfinger emerged. He hoisted himself onto the deck, and then waited for the next roll to throw himself against the periscope massive where, with considerable difficulty, he attached his security belt. Precariously, sliding and slipping on the icy deck, his arms waving madly in an effort to maintain his balance, he made his way toward Shafer.

"Nothing?" he shouted, his voice barely audible in the howling of wind and sea.

Shafer was shivering so violently that he could not speak. He shook his head.

Harllfinger was depressed and discouraged. For three days, the *U-265* had been tracking a convoy which, according to Luftwaffe information, was skirting the polar circle. So far, the chase had been fruitless, and Harllfinger was at wit's end to know how to locate a convoy in this incredible storm. He had never seen the sea and the wind combine with such destructive fury.

"If we don't sight them today," Harllfinger shouted into Shafer's ear, "we'll have to give it up. We're low on fuel."

"What do we do then?" Shafer asked. In this present state of exhaustion, he could not have cared less about convoys, and he was living only for the moment when he would be able to go below and gulp down a cup of boiling coffee.

"We'll circle around and head back to Bergen," Harllfinger yelled.

Shafer closed his eyes. "Thank you, God," he said to himself. The return to Bergen would be the end of two months of frozen agony, of fruitless tracking, of endless and useless searching.

At 6 A.M., the watch changed, and the relief climbed topside. Shafer unhooked his security belt and, the last man on his shift, started to climb down the hatchway. His frozen fingers would not hold, and he tumbled downward. An alert sailor caught him as he fell into the control room. The rest of his shift was already there, lying exhausted on the deck, incapable of moving. Tiny pieces of ice fell from their faces and clothing and melted slowly on the deck. Within the submarine it was 40°—a tropical paradise compared to the weather topside.

The other sailors helped the watch to remove their outer clothing and their rubber boots. Shafer and his men did not speak. As the numbness ebbed from their fingers, they began to move the encrustations of salt from the corners of their eyes and mouths and from their nostrils; and they listened to the storm raging over their heads.

Shafer went to his bunk. Wearily, he changed his clothing, then went to the tiny mess hall. Some of the men from his watch were already at the table. They were so hungry that they had not changed, and now they sat in silence, their eyes half closed, dulled by fatigue and by the sudden change in temperature. Their plates were attached to the stationary table, and they ate their eggs despite the rolling and pitching of the submarine. On the deck, loose objects rolled from side to side, piling up in one corner and then sliding into another—food, shoes, books, canned goods, pieces of broken dishes, broken eggs, slippers.

No one seemed concerned. It would all be cleared away when the weather improved.

The pitching and rolling of the submarine in the storm took its toll not only of the vessel's equipment but also of its personnel. Occasionally, the men were thrown from their bunks in their sleep. One of them suffered a broken arm, and Harllfinger would not let it be set because of the constant motion of the ship. "We'll have to wait," he told the sailor, "until it's a little more calm up there."

"How long will that be, Captain?"

"I'm afraid it's just beginning. The barometer looks like it's in free-fall."

Shafer was really not hungry. He stretched out on his bunk and savored the warmth which began to seep into his body. Whenever he returned from watch, he had the feeling that he was returning to life, and he relished the feeling with a deep, animal joy. He had had two cups of thick soup; and now, despite the regular noise of the diesels and the pounding of the waves on the hull, despite the voices and curses of the men and the incessant rolling of the Grey Wolf, he was drowsy. He smiled. He knew that, barring a disaster—it was always possible to ram into a rock or to encounter a floating mine—in a few hours the U-265 would be heading home. No doubt the storm would still be raging; but then, the sea seemed always easier to dominate when a ship was homeward bound. Hands clutching the railing around his bunk, Shafer slept.

The alert sounded ominously in the U-265 at 7:20 A.M.

"Vessel dead ahead!"

Shafer was on his feet in an instant, rubbing his swollen eyes. He rushed toward the control room, taking care not to lose his balance on the oily deck rendered even more precarious by the leaps and bounds of the U-boat in the storm.

One of the crew helped him into his leather suit, his boots, and his oilskins. His fur-lined gloves were still damp. He climbed the hatchway and, when he emerged into the open air, the icy wind burned his lungs and momentarily took his breath away. He shook his head, dragged himself upright, and, when the Grey Wolf's prow next plunged into a wave, lurched to his station next to the captain. Thinking that Harllfinger would give the order to dive at any moment, he did not fasten his security belt.

Harllfinger, however, had no such intention. He was in a frenzy of frustrated impatience. The U-265 was moving forward at full speed; but, with the incredible headwind which prevailed and the wall-like waves, she was unable to gain on the cargo ship. "Son-of-a-bitch!" he swore. "We'll never catch her at this rate—"

He was interrupted by a wave which broke with a roar over the conning tower. Spitting salt water, Harllfinger shouted in Shafer's ear: "In this weather, I can't tell if it's the beginning or the end of the convoy, or if this one is just a stray!"

"She's turning to port!" Shafer cried.

Harllfinger automatically raised his binoculars. Water ran from them. Cursing, he dropped the glasses and squinted intently ahead. He could barely discern the shape of the cargo ship. "Hell," he shouted. "You're right!"

The prey that the U-265 had sought for so long seemed about to escape under the cover of the fog and snow.

"Maximum speed," Harllfinger shouted down the tube.

"We're already at maximum speed," retorted the engineer, his tone leaving no doubt as to his irritation at the abuse to which his diesels were being subjected.

"Well, that's it," Shafer said. "The whole thing was for nothing. What a crock—"

Harllfinger did not alter his course, on the chance that the cargo ship might now make a starboard turn and return to her original course.

Suddenly, over the noise of the storm, Shafer heard a new sound: a steady, distant roaring.

"Aircraft to starboard," shouted the watch.

"They're at low altitude," Shafer observed.

"Well, we're not going to dive," Harllfinger decided. "They'll never see us in this pea soup." He knew the risk involved, but, judging from the direction from which the planes were coming, he was convinced they were Luftwaffe bombers.

Everyone looked up, but, in the fog and snow, there was nothing to be seen. The noise of the engines gradually grew fainter as the planes headed away from the Grey Wolf.

An hour passed. The *U-265* had changed its course and was now heading northeast in search of the cargo ship.

Suddenly, in the distance, there was the sound of an explosion. Everyone looked at one another in puzzlement and alarm. Then, gradually, through the snow and spray whipping across their faces, they detected the familiar odor of fire. Almost instantly, they saw it dead ahead: the cargo ship, so long pursued by the *U-265*, was in flames, her aft section already disappearing beneath the surface. The flames, instead of rising upward, were pulled downward by the wind and seemed to merge with the waves.

The *U-265* drew nearer.

"Over there, Captain! To starboard!"

Harllfinger and Shafer looked to starboard. They saw a lifeboat, pitching and rolling until it seemed it must capsize, rising and falling in the waves. Harllfinger hesitated only a moment. He ordered the helmsman to take the U-boat closer. As a seaman, he felt obliged, for the sake of his conscience, to make certain that there was no one in the boat. As the cargo ship's boilers exploded, sending up great geysers of steam, the *U-265* maneuvered to come alongside of the lifeboat. In the storm, it was impossible to throw grappling hooks from the submarine's foredeck. If a rescue operation became necessary, it would have to be carried out, somehow, from the conning tower.

The *U-265* was now 25 or 30 yards from the boat, maneuvering painfully to bring her port alongside the craft. Then Shafer saw them: four men, holding desperately to the lifeboat's grating, their terrified, oil-blackened faces turned toward the submarine. Shafer could see that one of them was bleeding from the shoulder. As nearly as he could make out, the man's arm was missing.

"Oh, my God!" one of the watch exclaimed in horror.

The lifeboat rose on the crest of a wave and seemed to remain motionless there for a moment. As Shafer watched, a figure stood upright in the boat—a woman. Her soaked dress adhering to her body, her hair flying in the wind, her eyes wild, she cried out; but her words were lost in the storm. Shafer could see that, against her breast, she clutched a small child.

The scene seemed to endure for an eternity of horror. Then the boat plunged into the waves and was hidden. When it reappeared farther away, its keel was all that showed above the surface.

There was silence on the deck of the *U-265*. The witnesses to the scene would have preferred to believe that they had been the victims of a hallucination. Yet, the proof of reality was there, the small dark form of the capsized lifeboat as it continued to rise and fall among the waves.

The *U-265* resumed its northeast course in the Barents Sea. As so often happens in those inhospitable waters, a fog rose suddenly, reducing visibility to a hundred yards.

"Ice dead ahead!"

The watch had given the alert too late. The U-boat reeled under the impact of the collision, and there was an ominous cracking sound. Fissures appeared everywhere in the coat of ice which covered the length of the steel hull. A few seconds passed before the engineer reported: "We're taking on water in the forward compartment, Captain. But it doesn't look too serious."

Harllfinger did not answer. He was scanning the huge blocks of ice ahead which were being driven toward his prow by the wind and the current. The ice was the color of lead, and the pieces were generally rounded and perhaps 3 feet in diameter. Their shape, Harllfinger knew, was caused by the adhesion of frozen sea water and snow. This slush-ice, as it is called, was a warning of much larger floes ahead. Some of the pieces were quite large, for as the individual blocks collided in the water they tended to adhere and form larger blocks. In the storm, and with reduced visibility, it was impossible to maneuver among such obstacles.

Harllfinger gave the order to dive and climbed down the hatchway. He struggled to secure the hatch. Everything was frozen, even the thick oil in the hinges. After a series of muttered oaths, the captain descended into the control room. The deck was covered by a thin layer of moisture—the melted ice from the men's outer garments—which, because of the relative warmth of the interior, was now evaporating and releasing a damp vapor. There was moisture everywhere; but the submariners were accustomed to this. What they never became accustomed to was the rash of boils caused by improper nutrition—the crews ate only canned goods—which was also responsible for numerous cases of scurvy and anemia.

Wolf Shafer leaned against the metal door of the forward gangway drinking a cup of coffee liberally spiked with alcohol. He waited until the captain had changed his clothes and drunk the coffee handed him by his orderly. Then he spoke: "Captain, the engineer says that at this speed it will take us at least ten hours to catch up with the convoy—that is, if there really is a convoy, and if we're going in the right direction."

"How's our fuel?" Harllfinger asked, wiping his lips with the back of his hand.

"We have enough for ten or eleven hours, Captain," the engineer answered. "That's the most we can spare if we're going to have enough left to get home."

"Well, then, we'll go on for another ten or eleven hours."

At 4:27 P.M., the U-265 made its first attempt to surface. It was unable to do so. When Harllfinger attempted to raise the periscope, it struck ice. No one said anything, but everyone knew that the batteries of the electric motors were almost dead and that it would soon be necessary to surface in order to recharge them.

5:00 P.M. Another unsuccessful attempt. There was still ice overhead. To save his batteries, Harllfinger reduced speed to 3 knots. At that speed, the batteries would be good for another 2 hours.

The *U-265* was now cruising at a depth of 45 feet. Harllfinger set the broken arm of the man who had been thrown to the deck and made a cast for it. Then he lay down on his bunk. He had been without sleep for four nights, and he had managed to stay on his feet only by swallowing quantities of caffeine tablets and capsules of stimulants.

Shafer relieved the captain and, every quarter hour, attempted to raise the periscope. On each occasion, he encountered ice. The crew exchanged worried looks.

6:15 P.M. The periscope, with its accustomed hiss, slid easily in its housing and broke the surface.

"It's clear!" Shafer announced. "Go wake the captain." He felt as though a great weight had been lifted from his shoulders.

"Engine noises," the radioman reported.

"Surface!"

As the submarine surfaced, it was struck by the full fury of the storm. Below, unsecured objects fell to the floor and were tossed from one side of the compartment to the other. A sailor fell to the deck, stunned by a can of food which struck him on the temple. A trickle of blood ran down his cheek. As his friends went to help him, Shafer and the watch were already topside. Visibility was about 2 miles. Looking aft, Shafer could see the enormous ice floe which had held the submarine beneath the surface for so long.

Within the past few hours, the violence of the storm had risen to such a pitch that it was now virtually impossible to navigate on the surface. Harllfinger, Shafer, and the watch, constantly pounded by walls of water, deafened by the incredible howling of the wind, felt as though they were witnessing the end of the world.

Harllfinger and Shafer held with all their strength to the railing of the conning tower as they were thrown from side to side. It was obvious that if the submarine remained on the surface there would be serious damage from the tons of water which crashed continuously over the decks. Still, it was necessary to recharge the batteries, and that would require at least fifteen minutes. Harllfinger placed his mouth against Shafer's ear and shouted: "It's crazy to go on. We don't have a chance of finding that convoy—"

Shafer, shivering violently, nodded. The captain was right. In this storm, and in these waves as high as houses, the U-265, with engines running at maximum speed, could move at no more than between 5 and 7 knots. It would obviously be impossible to intercept the convoy. He shouted back to Harllfinger: "I'd give anything to know where those engine noises were coming from!"

"Probably a ship that lagged behind, and I'll bet it's not far from here," the captain answered, wiping the water from his face.

Shafer did not reply. As Harllfinger was speaking, the U-265 had given a particularly heavy roll, and Shafer's left knee had struck the steel wall with shattering force. It felt as though the kneecap were smashed. With tears of pain in his eyes, Shafer cautiously bent the leg, repeating over and over: "Son-of-a-bitch! Son-of-a-bitch!" Slowly, the pain dissipated.

The engineer's voice rose through the tube. "Captain?"

Harllfinger leaned toward the tube, careful to keep a safe distance. More than one submariner had had teeth knocked out by the tube in rough weather. "What is it, Engineer?"

"Vessel to starboard, Captain!"

"A cargo ship," Shafer reported, looking through his binoculars.

The ship was slightly over a mile from the U-265, and seemed to be in serious trouble. Its rudder was damaged, and it was unable to keep its prow into the waves which now crashed against her flank with incredible force. The ship was rolling wildly and almost awash in the waves breaking across her decks. Shafer could not suppress a twinge of pity at the spectacle.

"Ready tubes 1 and 3!" Harllfinger shouted.

At that moment, even Wolf Shafer experienced revulsion. For the first time in his twenty years of life, he felt a true distaste for war.

Harllfinger maneuvered the submarine so as to align his tubes with the cargo ship's flank.

"Tubes 1 and 3 ready, Captain."

"It's not going to be easy," Harllfinger said to Shafer. "In this kind of sea, there's no telling where our torpedoes will end up."

He turned toward Shafer, surprised at his second officer's silence. He sensed that, for the first time, Shafer disapproved of what he was doing. And he understood. After all, it was one thing to attack an enemy who could escape, maneuver, use various stratagems. Combat, in such circumstances, was a challenge. But to finish off a disabled enemy ship was sickening, even though such an action was in accordance with the laws of war in all their horror and all their cruelty. Harllfinger felt the need to justify himself to Shafer. "In our place, they'd do the same thing!" he shouted.

Shafer remained silent.

Harllfinger maneuvered the U-265 against the pounding waves until its prow was facing the cargo ship's flank at 500 yards.

"*Achtung!*" he shouted.

Shafer could see activity on the target ship's deck. The submarine had been sighted.

"*Rohr ein—*" Harllfinger began, but he did not finish. A light began blinking dimly aboard the cargo ship.

Shafer decoded it automatically: "Help us." He turned to the captain.

Harllfinger was staring fixedly at the enemy ship within his grasp. His jaws were clenched tightly, as though to prevent him from completing his command, from uttering the single word that remained: *Feuer!* It would have sent the torpedoes speeding toward their target. But he could not bring himself to speak it. Angrily, to conceal the emotion that he felt, Harllfinger shouted to Shafer: "'Help us,' they say! What do they want us to do? Tow them?" He shook his head. "We'll have to finish them off." He leaned toward the tube at the instant that the light began again:

"Help us."

"Look, Captain!" Shafer yelled, clutching Harllfinger's arm.

Harllfinger felt his second officer's hand tremble nervously. He looked up in time to see the cargo ship lifted up on the crest of a gigantic wave, where it remained suspended for a moment, its propellers spinning wildly in the air. Then, as it descended, another enormous wave broke against its foredeck, at the level of the bridge. There was the sound of steel plates cracking like thunder over the sea, and a roar like an explosion. Before the horrified eyes of the men on the deck of the *U-265*, the ship broke in two parts and disappeared almost immediately into the waves.

Harllfinger, his voice unsteady, spoke into the tube: "We're going home."

On March 20, 1943, the *U-265* arrived at the port of Bergen. The officers and men emerged on deck, their faces thin and white, their eyes sunken, their uniforms hanging loosely on emaciated bodies. On hand was the commander of the base and his staff, with a brass band, to greet the returning crew.

The festive air which prevailed on the base was not entirely in honor of the safe arrival of the *U-265*. News had just arrived that, the evening before, a great battle off the Newfoundland coasts had been brought to a victorious conclusion. For four days —since the evening of March 16—a wolf pack of thirty-eight U-boats had been wreaking havoc among the ships of two convoys, the SC-122 and the HX-229. Despite a storm which raged throughout the battle, thirty-five cargo vessels were sunk, and an escort ship was sent to the bottom with a new type of anti-destroyer torpedo. The cargo ships totaled 231,000 tons of shipping—a great loss to Allied supply lines, which the British Admiralty described as "a very serious blow." The Grey Wolves broke off their attack only when increased air protection, including American Liberator bombers, which were being used for the first time in the Atlantic, made it necessary for them to dive in order to escape pursuing destroyers and aircraft.

Captain S. W. Roskill, official historian of the British Navy, has stated that the Germans had never been so close to disrupting communications between the New World and the Old, as during the first twenty days of March 1943. He points out that, in those twenty days, over a half-million tons of shipping disappeared forever—most of it in convoys. The crisis was so grave that the Admiralty began seriously to question whether the convoy system—which had been the cornerstone of British naval security for three and a half years—was indeed the best protection for cargoes and transports. The problem was that there seemed to be no other system available. And the Admiralty was brought face to face with the imminent possibility of defeat.*

The grand total for March 1943, when a hundred Grey Wolves prowled the Atlantic, was 107 Allied vessels—570,000 tons of shipping.

It was a great victory indeed, but Grand Admiral Doenitz could not enjoy it for long. One reason was a great storm which rose in the Atlantic, which prevented even the Grey Wolves within range of their targets from using their weapons. In his Berlin office, Doenitz read, in a mood of somber irritation, a report from the captain of the *U-260*, Lieutenant Commander Purkhold, which he had just received:

"March 28, 1943. Storm, sea 9, 8:30 P.M. Sighted a cargo, estimated at 8,000 tons, at about 4,000 yards. Remained to her starboard and decided on surface attack before night fall. Heavy swell and fog limited visibility to one or two miles.

* *The War at Sea*, Vol. I.

Fired torpedoes at 9:05 P.M. Missed, because I had under-estimated speed and angle of target. The angle had widened as a series of high waves caused me to lose sight of target. I continued, still wishing to attack before darkness reduced chances of finding ship again.

"Pursuit interrupted at 10:00 P.M. Proceeding at full speed into the wind, we twice took on water, which we cleared by using a hard rudder and our ballast tanks. Topside, the weather is incredible. After a half hour, the watch and I were half drowned. In a short time, we took on five tons of water through the hatch, the voice tube, and the diesel vents.

"The ship was navigating ahead of the wind, and I was com-pelled to lie to. The distance between us was increasing, and regretfully I had to give her up.

"The storm was so ferocious that the ship of the commodore in charge of the convoy capsized and all hands and material were lost."

But there was a reason other than the storm for Doenitz' depression. For the first time since the beginning of the war, an aircraft carrier was being used to escort the convoy sailing from Halifax. And, despite the storm, her planes were in the air and prevented the Lion's U-boats from coming near enough to attack the convoy. The only sector of the Atlantic—30° W–51° N—which had not been protected by Allied aircraft was now dominated by fighter-bombers from the carrier. From one shore to the other, the Atlantic was under constant surveillance from the air. And, for the first time, the famous "Atlantic hole," the graveyard of so many hundreds of Allied ships, was closed. It was now the turn of the Grey Wolves to be hunted. Henceforth, the convoys, from the time they sailed until the moment they docked on the opposite shore, would be protected by an ever-expanding system of air and naval protection.

During a Spartan lunch with Godt, Peter Cremer (who had now almost completely recovered), and Hermann Rasch, who had just been assigned to headquarters, Grand Admiral Doenitz, his face drawn and haggard, confided: "We are now at the

turning point of the war. I've just learned that the British and
the Americans, at a conference held at Casablanca, have declared, as a result of the losses they have suffered, that our
U-boats are their number-one enemy. So, we have been given
fair warning. In the months to come, we must expect to make
difficult sacrifices, and to fight desperate battles."

Cremer, usually so jovial and optimistic, answered softly, citing
Doenitz' old motto: "May God protect the German submariners."

Rasch put down his pipe and, with an effort at humor, remarked: "We're going to need all the help we can get if we're
going to have to fight airplanes."

There was an uneasy silence. In everyone's mind was the
memory of Hartenstein who, after a ferocious battle, had been
sunk in the Caribbean a few days before.

The grand admiral rose brusquely. "Well, gentlemen," he
concluded, "in a few months' time we'll know who has won the
Battle of the Atlantic."

As Doenitz believed, the British and the Americans had determined to break the backs of the Grey Wolves, regardless of
the cost. Mustering their phenomenal resources, they constructed
a veritable armada and prepared to launch a pitiless assault
against the 164 U-boats in Doenitz' Atlantic fleet.

Simultaneously, the new enemy of the wolf packs, the aircraft
carrier, passed to the attack. The Allies possessed two types of
carrier. First, there were the MAC ships, which were cargo-
ship hulls surmounted by a flat deck suitable for takeoffs and
landings. These ships, in addition to their regular cargo, carried
four Swordfish fighter-bombers. The second and most important
type were the Baby Flattops, or Jeep Carriers, which were the
first light aircraft carriers designed as convoy escorts. These
were vessels of 12,000 tons, designed to handle fifteen planes.
They operated hand-in-hand with a new breed of fast, heavily
armed destroyers equipped with the new radar device whose
wave length remained a secret from the Germans. Together,
the Baby Flattops and the destroyers made up what were

designated as "support-groups," or "hunter-killer groups," whose mission was to patrol any area in which a wolf pack was reported.

And finally, in November 1942, Churchill had found an opponent worthy of the Lion: Admiral Max Horton. Like Doenitz, Horton had been a submarine commander during World War I. Now, in charge of antisubmarine operations, he knew from experience the most effective means to be employed by the escort vessels, destroyers, and aircraft carriers which patrolled the Atlantic.

From his headquarters in Liverpool, Horton devised and implemented a new antisubmarine strategy. Until then, the small number of destroyers available did not allow them to pursue U-boats. Their role had been essentially defensive, and consisted in an effort to fight off attacking submarines without going too far from the convoys under their protection. Now, however, the number of destroyers was greatly increased, and this increase allowed the Allies to provide their ships with a double ring of protection. The first ring, consisting of the destroyers nearest to the convoy, had a defensive mission. But the second and more distant ring, composed of destroyers, frigates, and the planes of a Baby Flattop, were ordered to track down Grey Wolves and pursue them, for days if necessary, until they were destroyed.

Doenitz was correct. The turning point of the war had been reached. Now, the convoys were surrounded by an impenetrable shield. Henceforth, the experience, tenacity, courage, and inventiveness of his U-boat commanders would be of little use against the material and technical superiority of the enemy.

Statistics soon began to bear out Doenitz' worst fears. On May 4 and 5, in an engagement to the east of Newfoundland, fifteen U-boats sank twelve Allied vessels (totaling 55,000 tons) —but seven of the U-boats were sent to the bottom. On May 14, after spending four days tracking two convoys (the HX-237 and the SC-129), the Grey Wolves were obliged to submerge to escape a deluge of bombs and depth charges. Eleven of the submarines tried to approach the convoys and were detected with amazing accuracy. Even though pursued by the convoy's destroyers and by aircraft from the carrier *Biter*, the wolf pack, by carrying their daring to extremes, succeeded in sinking five ships, totaling 30,000 tons, they lost three of their own number.

When the U-boats attacked convoys SC-130 and HX-239, Allied superiority was even more crushing. The carriers, long-range aircraft and destroyer-escorts were all equipped with the new radar systems and with improved depth charges, and the convoys did not lose a single ship.

Everywhere in the Atlantic, ships of the Allies were locked in combat with Doenitz' Grey Wolves in a struggle of unprecedented ferocity, intensity, and extent. The U-boats were sometimes successful in the struggle, generally in the case of unescorted ships or by virtue of an audacity which bordered on the suicidal. But it soon became evident that, in every part of the Atlantic, the tide of battle had turned and the Grey Wolves were losing. In a single day—May 22, 1943—thirty-one submarines were sunk.

Every day, Admiral Godt's desk was flooded with frantic reports from U-boat commanders. The most recent item in that long litany of disaster came from Commander August Maus, captain of the *U-185*, which was operating off Cape Maisi to the southwest of Cuba:

"Detected by destroyers and aircraft and underwent heavy aerial bombardment. After crash dive, subjected to depth-charge bombardment at depth of 1,000 feet. Almost asphyxiated, we surfaced to recharge batteries and found planes still overhead as though they knew our precise position. We fought desperately with antiaircraft gun but situation was impossible. It was hailing, there was a strong swell, and we were taking on tons of water. If we had not dived we would have been sunk. Resurfaced in the morning. An American dirigible was overhead and dropped bombs. Obliged to dive and remain submerged throughout the day. Have sustained severe damage."

Grand Admiral Doenitz, writing about these tragic days many years after the fact, declared: "After four and a half years of continual combat—combat of a violence and intensity that posterity will find difficult to conceive—the air and surface defenses established by the world's two greatest naval powers had neutralized our submarines—thanks above all to their new radar."

Until mid-1943, the Grey Wolves had been predators. Now, they were the hunted rather than the hunters in the sea.

Part Five

THE HUNTED

30

As the black Mercedes sped through the streets of the city, the all-clear sounded in the capital of the Thousand-Year-Reich. Berliners began to emerge from the air-raid shelters, anxiously glancing at the sky as though to assure themselves that the Allied flying fortresses had indeed disappeared. The car drew up before the Am Steinplatz office building, and Vice-Admiral Godt, commander of the submarine service, emerged from the vehicle and hurried up the steps carrying a briefcase crammed with documents and handwritten notes. A few minutes later, he stood before Grand Admiral Karl Doenitz. Neither man smiled.

"Well, Godt," Doenitz began, "where are we?"

"I've spoken with Captain Meckel, sir. He's just completed a tour of inspection of the various branches of the *Kriegsmarine,* the Luftwaffe, and the arms-production installations. He's met with the outstanding specialists in detection devices."

"And?"

"They still haven't come up with anything definite. There was much talk about ultrared and infrared beams and ultrasonic devices. But nothing that you can really put your finger on. Every possibility has been explored thoroughly, but our technicians are working in the dark."

"We had better admit it, Godt. We're blind. Literally blind. The enemy apparently can read our charts whenever he wants to, and we can't even catch a glimpse of his!

"You know, Godt, we've had problems and failures in the past, but the determination and efficiency of our men have always enabled us to overcome all these difficulties. Now, it seems to me that the technical and material superiority of the enemy is so pronounced that we're going to have to revise our strategy. Our U-boats can no longer get near Allied convoys without being detected. They can't even attack at night. We have to face it, Godt. Our wolf pack tactic is now worthless."

"Where does that leave us, sir?"

"There are no alternatives. We're going to have to withdraw our U-boats from the North Atlantic."

"Where do you want to send them?"

"It seems to me that the best place would be to the southwest of the Azores. Maybe there they'll have more freedom of action."

May 31, 1943.

"Ah, there you are, Grand Admiral." Hitler's tone was cordial. He stood before his desk, heels together, hands clasped behind his back, leaning slightly forward. To one side of the Führer stood his aide-de-camp, Major Puttkammer, and Marschall Keitel.

Hitler, though nervous as always, appeared to be in good humor. He walked around his desk and sat, then put on his spectacles and began to read a note. He put down the paper, removed his glasses, rose and walked across the huge room to stand before a window which looked out upon a pine forest. Finally, he turned and smiled again.

"Forgive me, Grand Admiral. I forgot to offer you a chair. Please sit. You'll find those armchairs very comfortable. Keitel, Puttkammer—you sit, too."

The three men took chairs and, after a short pause, Hitler asked, "Exactly what is the situation of our submarines?"

"*Mein Führer*," Doenitz answered, his voice steady, "you know what kind of man I am. I've never tried to hide the truth from you, and I have no intention of doing so today. I must therefore tell you that the situation in the Atlantic has deteriorated greatly. Our U-boats can no longer attack Allied shipping. They are constantly hunted by the enemy, and the British and Americans have such superior means that our losses have increased alarmingly."

"Why is that, Grand Admiral?"

"Air superiority, *mein Führer*. An air superiority so overwhelming that it has become a nightmare for our submarines even to return to their Atlantic bases for supplies."

Hitler did not respond to this information. He sat behind his desk, somber and pensive. Finally, he spoke: "What are your conclusions?"

"Until the *Walter* submarine is put into service, our U-boat fleet will be unable to play a significant part in the war."

"Nonsense!" Hitler exploded. "That is out of the question! It is unthinkable for us to give up the Battle of the Atlantic, Grand Admiral. Even if our U-boats must assume a purely defensive role, they are still important to us. The enemy must still commit a great deal of material and troops to defending their convoys. If we withdraw our submarines, then their convoys will no longer be threatened and they will be able to transfer the material and men to other fronts!"

"Perhaps I expressed myself badly," Doenitz interrupted sharply. "In the present situation, it is impossible for our submarines to take any offensive action. They are neutralized—paralyzed. As soon as they move, they are detected and attacked."

"Do you still believe that the enemy has a detection device that we know nothing about?"

"It is no longer a belief, *mein Führer*. It is a certainty! And so long as we don't know how to counter that device, we will remain helpless against it."

"Well," Hitler asked, "what about the Metox-Fu M.B.?"

Doenitz opened his briefcase and took out a thick folder. "Here," he explained, taping the folder with his forefinger, "are reports written by my U-boat commanders when they returned to base, and also extracts from messages received from U-boats at sea. Let me quote from a few of them: 'Despite Metox, we have been attacked by Liberators in the middle of the night.' 'I have been attacked three times by aircraft which appeared directly overhead despite heavy fog. On each occasion, the Fu M.B. was fully operational.' 'Surprised by aircraft. Metox operating. Obliged to crash-dive.' 'I was recharging my batteries at night, in a dense fog, when several destroyers appeared dead ahead, making straight for us. We barely managed to escape.'"

In the oppressive silence which followed Doenitz' report, Hitler paced back and forth in the room. He stopped directly in front of Doenitz. "What are your suggestions?" he asked sharply.

"There are two solutions. Increase and accelerate submarine production, and accelerate work on our *Walter* submarines."

"Where do you expect me to get the steel and the labor? It takes almost our whole production to meet requirements for antitank guns, tanks, and aircraft. We desperately need men and material on the Eastern front. In spite of all this, I've already exempted your workmen from conscription. And, on March 6, I increased your allotment of steel by 45,000 tons per month."

"That is only five per cent of our total output, *mein Führer*. It's too little for a combat branch as essential as the submarine service."

Keitel and Puttkammer looked at the grand admiral, their faces a study in astonishment and apprehension. They were certain that Doenitz had gone too far, and that his candor would draw Hitler's fury down on his head.

The Führer, however, showed no sign of anger. Instead, he smiled, and in a reassuring tone said to Doenitz: "Very well, Grand Admiral. Go talk to Speer and set up a program." Then, with a gesture, he informed Doenitz that the interview was over.

Doenitz rose, saluted Hitler first and then Keitel. As he turned to leave the room, Hitler asked:

"How many U-boats did we lose this month, Grand Admiral?"

"Thirty-eight, *mein Führer*. That's the most we've lost since the beginning of the war." Then he added: "Our losses have just about tripled."

13

The spring of 1943 was the beginning of the end for the submarine service of the Third Reich. Even those which managed somehow to return unharmed and intact to their bases were no longer greeted by commanding officers and parades and brass bands. Instead, they crept furtively, almost fearfully, into ports devastated by Allied planes which seemed daily to multiply both in numbers and in striking power. It was not until they were safely inside the concrete bomb shelters of the submarine bases that the exhausted crews of the Grey Wolves felt secure.

In the officers' mess, the sole topic of conversation was the growing number of submarines destroyed at sea; and all such discussions ended and were summarized in a single sentence: Where is it all going to end? A cloud of uncertainty and discouragement settled like a blanket over the Atlantic bases of the U-boat fleet.

At Lorient, Peter Cremer stood at attention before the commander of the Western Fleet, Captain Rösing. "Cremer," Rösing said, "you're going to be our guinea pig. The grand admiral wants you and Guggenberger and Kuppish to sail together. You already know the mission assigned to your three U-boats. You're supposed to test our new antiaircraft weapons in actual combat conditions, determine how they can be used most effectively— and return to give us a complete report. You have one week before departure. I'm sure you'll make good use of that time . . ."

"Thank you, sir. I'll try."

Cremer, limping slightly, left Rösing's office and made his way to the pier where the U-333 was undergoing extensive repairs. The pier was swarming with workmen—French workmen, mostly—welding, hammering, and painting in a cacophony of shouts, curses, and singing.

Aboard, he found Schluppkoten, his boatswain, as well as Spanberg and Baumein. They had been waiting for him and were obviously delighted to see their captain on his feet again. Cremer, deeply moved, shook hands with them. Then, despite his weakened condition, he undertook an exacting inspection of the vessel from stem to stern, climbing up onto the conning tower, examining the foredeck, and shaking his head at the obvious lack of enthusiasm of the French workmen.

During the evening, at the officers' mess, Cremer was agreeably surprised to run into August Maus, captain of the *U-185*, who was passing through Lorient. After his return from the Caribbean, Maus had been ordered to the U-boat base at Bordeaux, which seemed a less attractive target for Royal Air Force bombers than Lorient. Maus would be at Lorient just long enough to collect his personal belongings, then he would be off on a mission the destination of which he had not yet been told.

The two men greeted each other warmly. Of all the young officials in the enormous mess hall, they were the only two "old-timers"—a fact which was evident from their worn, lined faces and the look of indefinable sadness which was always with them.

"Let's have a drink," Cremer suggested.

The two veterans sought out a table in a distant corner, away from the other officers, where they would be able to talk without being overheard. Though neither Cremer nor Maus mentioned it, they were both aware of the dangers of a free exchange of opinions in a roomful of youthful fanatics.

They ordered cognac and were in the midst of a pessimistic discussion of the situation in the Atlantic when Cremer saw Hermann Rasch enter. Rasch waved at them, and Maus gestured for him to join them.

"I just heard that you're going out on a mission," Rasch said. "I envy you."

"Where've you been keeping yourself, you bureaucrat?" Cremer asked.

Rasch shook his head. "I've just returned from a tour of our bases, looking for a downed British plane with its detection device intact."

Cremer and Maus were no longer smiling. "What did you find?" Maus asked.

"Nothing. Someone told me about a bomber that had gone down in the area, but it was nothing more than a junkheap. It was impossible to find anything in that pile of scrap."

The three men were silent. Rasch raised his glass and swallowed his cognac in one gulp. He scratched his chin with his thumb, and his lips puckered in a gesture familiar to Cremer and Maus. They knew that Rasch was trying to decide whether or not he could talk freely.

"Come on," Cremer urged, "you can trust us. It must really be serious if you have any doubts about that."

"Yes, it's serious. Well, it will be out in a few days anyhow. A few days ago, the grand admiral had a meeting with Albert Speer, the Minister of Armaments. They talked about the *Walter* submarine—"

"Are we going to get it?" Maus interrupted excitedly.

"No. At least not right away. But we're going to get something else. Something that's a big improvement over what we're using at present."

"What?"

"The trouble with the *Walter* is that its turbine engines haven't been perfected yet. On the other hand, its hull has passed all its tests with flying colors. So we're going to use that hull without the *Walter* engines—but with double the number of batteries we've been using in our old submarines."

"What exactly is that going to accomplish?" Cremer asked, frowning.

"Right now, our U-boats, when submerged, cruise at a maximum speed of 6 or 7 knots, and then only for forty-five minutes at a time. The rest of the time, we drag along at 3 or 4 knots in order to preserve our batteries. But with the new system devised by Walter himself—and this is a temporary solution, mind you—do you know what our speed will be beneath the surface?"

"I can't imagine."

"Eighteen knots for ninety minutes; 12 to 14 knots for ten hours; and 5 knots for sixty hours. And that's beneath the surface. It's still a long way from the turbine engine's performance, which will be over 25 knots per hour. But it's a big step forward. At those speeds, we'll be able to get near convoys without being detected, and we'll be able to get away from destroyers after an attack."

"What are we going to call it?"

"Type XXI. It'll be 1,600 tons. At the same time, we're going to start producing the type XXIII, 300 tons, to operate in the shallow water off the British coast. Submerged, it'll be able to do 12 knots."

"Thank God," Cremer said. "This is the first good news we've had this year."

"But that's not all," Rasch went on. "Doenitz shook up Walter so much that he gave birth to another idea: the *Schnorchel*."

"*Schnorchel?*"

"Yes. It's a Dutch invention, a periscopic tube twenty-six feet long which, when extended to the surface, will allow us to vent our diesels and to blow off gas. It's a sort of ventilator, actually, and we're going to use it on the type XXI. But we're also going to install it on our present U-boats, so that we'll be able to recharge our batteries without surfacing."

"It's about time," Maus exclaimed. "These last few months, we've been like turtles trying to fight off eagles. When are we going to get this new equipment?"

"Well, not before the spring of 1944."

"Shit! That means we're going to go through another year of getting the hell beat out of us," Maus groaned.

Cremer filled his glass and raised it. "We'll just have to hold on till then."

As he spoke, his left hand reached into his pocket and touched the tiny piece of shrapnel which he carried there. It was the piece which had been embedded in his spine during the battle with the *Crocus,* and which had paralyzed him until it was removed. He had kept it as a good-luck piece. And it had been pure luck that it had been found at all. For three weeks at the hospital at La Rochelle, the French doctors and nurses had seemed incapable of locating it. A doctor of the *Kriegsmarine* had happened to visit the hospital one day, on his way to a new station in Germany, and had spotted it instantly. Cremer, with grim amusement, recalled the exaggerated surprise on the faces of the French doctors, and their expressions of astonishment:

"I can't understand why we couldn't find it!"

"How on earth could we have missed it?"

"Congratulations, *Herr Doktor!*"

Cremer bore no grudge against the French at the hospital. War was war, and as long as he remained paralyzed there was one U-boat captain less to attack Allied shipping. The French doctors, in their way, were part of the Resistance, with Cremer as their target.

The waiter had just brought a second bottle of cognac when the air-raid siren echoed over the Lorient base. As the sound of the first bombs reached the mess, the other officers made their way casually down to the cellar. But Cremer, Maus, and Rasch remained seated.

"I've had enough of cellars that smell of mildew," Cremer complained.

"You're right," Maus said. "Let's stay here."

The three officers continued to pour cognac and drank steadily as the glare of incendiaries and exploding bombs occasionally filled the room with an unearthly light. Finally, thoroughly drunk, they rose and, with much stumbling against tables and chairs, they made their way into the street.

The bombing seemed unusually heavy. The sky was red with flames; and occasionally, among the explosions, the three men were able to discern the roar of walls collapsing.

Rasch was whistling Mozart's *Concerto for Clarinet,* while

Maus began a solitary game of football, using a pebble as the ball. Cremer walked slightly ahead of them, with his index fingers extended toward the sky, firing imaginary ack-ack guns at the flying fortresses overhead. Suddenly, he halted, turned, and, with a peculiar weaving, limping gait rejoined his friends.

"Listen," he said, "I have an idea."

A bomb exploded a few hundred yards away, showering dirt and gravel around them, but leaving them unharmed.

"Do you know Sophie?" Cremer asked.

Maus and Rasch shook their heads.

"Let's go see Sophie. She's the nicest, prettiest girl in all Brittany."

"If she's all that nice," Maus said, "I'd better not go. I'm about to get married. All I want right now is something to drink. I'm dying of thirst with all this dust—"

"Follow me!" Rasch shouted.

Stumbling through debris, lurching into one another, clutching one another's shoulders for support, the three officers picked their way through the streets, past the *Marina Heim,* the gigantic and miraculously undamaged, rest-and-recreation center for enlisted personnel. After walking in circles for an hour, they finally emerged onto the Avenue du Port. Most of the buildings along the street were in flames, and firemen and rescue teams were hard at work. No one paid any attention to the three German officers.

"Hell," Cremer moaned, "how am I going to find the house in all this confusion?"

They stumbled down the street, climbing over piles of rubble. Occasionally, Rasch said: "Maybe we should stop somewhere and get an hour's sleep."

"Forget it," Cremer answered. "We're going to see Sophie."

The sun was beginning to rise, and the first light of morning disclosed the full horror of the burning city. Over the ubiquitous flames hung a thick cloud of smoke and dust.

"There it is," Cremer announced proudly. "I've found it!" He pointed to a tall, narrow building which, somehow, had escaped destruction, its four stories rising defiantly toward the dark sky.

The three men entered the vestibule and pressed the elevator button as the all-clear sounded.

"How could it have gotten stuck there?" Maus asked in astonishment, pointing to the grill of the elevator cage. Cremer and Rasch looked. A human hand, its fingers spread, clutched the grill. Its bloody stump dripped blood.

"Disgusting," Rasch said.

Cremer took a closer look, sighed, then announced: "At least it's not Sophie's hand. It belongs to a man."

"That's nice," Maus mumbled.

Impatiently, Cremer leaned on the elevator button. There was no sign that it was working. He pressed again. Maus, pleading excessive thirst, suggested that they use the stairs.

"No," Cremer said. "Sophie lives on the top floor, and we'd probably fall asleep before we got there."

"Maybe someone left the elevator gate open," Rasch said. "You know how careless the French are."

"It's this goddam building," Cremer replied. "Nothing ever works here."

They heard hurried footsteps behind them in the vestibule. Three men, wearing French helmets and civil-defense armbands, approached the German officers in a state of great excitement. "What are you doing here?" one of them shouted. "Are you out of your minds—?"

He fell quickly silent when he saw the German uniforms.

"My dear sir," Rasch replied courteously in French, "we are not out of our minds. We are simply drunk."

The Frenchmen looked at one another furtively, obviously taken off guard by the decidedly unmilitary behavior of the German officers. They shifted from foot to foot as though they were barefoot on hot coals. Finally, the one who appeared to be the leader swallowed and said: "You can't stay here. It's too dangerous."

"Dangerous?" Rasch asked sleepily. "What's dangerous?"

"A bomb, sir. If fell down the elevator shaft and didn't explode. Lean over and look. You can see it."

June 7, 1943. At 5 o'clock in the morning, the *U-185* moved slowly into the mouth of the Gironde. On deck, everyone was alert. An extra man had been added to the watch. He was known as the "sun-watch," since enemy planes generally swooped down out of the sun.

Suddenly, one of the diesel engines began to vibrate and sputter.

"Look aft, Captain," the second officer said.

August Maus turned. A thick black smoke rose from the diesel. Then the engine stopped.

"Son-of-a-bitch!" Maus swore. "What's going on?"

The engineer's voice came from below: "Port engine inoperative, sir."

"Thanks for letting me know. I'm not deaf and blind," Maus replied in irritation. "Can we repair it?"

"I doubt it, Captain. I think it's burned out."

"All right," Maus sighed. "Half-turn. We're going back to base—on electric motors."

June 10. At precisely 10 o'clock, August Maus walked onto the pier where a French work crew was attempting to repair his diesel under the supervision of a suspicious German crew chief. Maus immediately noticed the air of tension in the shop. Something was wrong. He saw several men in civilian clothes, with soft hats, walking around, inspecting, asking questions, taking notes.

"They look like cops," Maus said to himself. He caught sight of his second officer walking rapidly toward him.

"Captain, they're waiting for you."

"Who's waiting for me?"

The second officer pointed to a group of men standing alongside the *U-185*. "They're specialists. They've been here since this morning, and they want to talk to you."

After a glance at his vessel, moving gently in its moorings, Maus walked to the group and introduced himself.

"Now, then, gentlemen," he said, "what did you want to talk to me about?"

"Sabotage, Commander," replied the most impressive of the men. "In dismantling your engine, we found tiny pieces of steel in the block. If you had run that engine at top speed for any length of time, it could have exploded and ripped open your hull. And you and your men would have become fish food."

"Good Lord," Maus replied heatedly, "you say it as though it were an everyday occurrence for us to find enemy saboteurs on our bases!"

"Commander, you're not the first victim of this kind of sabotage. Wherever we have men fighting, we have sabotage. We do everything we can to put a stop to it; and, believe me, we're not overly gentle about it. We know that here in Bordeaux there's a large spy and sabotage ring. The Gestapo has tried everything; but, so far, we've been unable to neutralize it."

"Listen," Maus said, "I'm not stupid enough to be completely unaware of the way you people work. I thought that all personnel, on our bases at least, were thoroughly screened."

"They are, Commander. But there's no way for us to keep the enemy from acts of terrorism. We'd have to keep the whole country under constant surveillance. Every single Frenchman who works in our installations, from the child serving Mass to the dishwasher, could be a spy or a saboteur. Every one of them. And the slightest detail could be an item of information valuable to the enemy. Even the crews' laundry that we hand over to the French washerwomen could give away the movement of our ships. And the amount of laundry from a particular ship can disclose its tonnage. We try to keep an eye on everything, Commander; but we can't do the impossible. Let me give you a bit of advice. If, when you're at sea, you see a pigeon, shoot it down!"

"What? You don't mean to tell me that—"

"Precisely. Every day, dozens of homing pigeons cross the Channel with messages."

One of the German technicians interrupted them. "Sir," he said to Maus, "you'll be able to sail tonight."

"I hope we're not going to have any more trouble."

"We've checked everything, Commander," the man said wearily, "at least everything that we have the equipment to check. We can't dismantle the whole thing. We'll double the guard around her until you leave."

"All right. We'll see," Maus replied, looking at the French workmen swarming over the U-185.

The next morning, at 4 o'clock, the U-185 was already in the open sea, following a southwesterly course. Overhead were three Junker-88s, providing air cover. They would remain with the submarine until nightfall. Maus had already opened his sealed orders and learned that his destination was Recife and the Brazilian coast.

"With a little luck," he said, handing the orders to the second officer, "we'll have decent hunting in those waters."

The next day, late in the morning, the U-185 was joined by four other submarines from Lorient and Saint Nazaire. The five Grey Wolves were to remain together until they were outside the Bay of Biscay, which was infested with aircraft of the Coastal Command. It was Doenitz' hope that his submarines' new anti-aircraft guns, and this new tactic of group navigation, would allow the U-boats to pass safely through enemy-controlled waters and, if need be, offer an adequate defense against air attack.

June 12. 7:17 A.M.

"Aircraft!"

Through his binoculars, Maus saw a Wellington bi-engine and two four-engine Halifaxes approaching rapidly. In a few seconds, they were upon the Grey Wolves. The encounter did not last long. Within a few minutes, the Wellington fled toward land, black smoke pouring from its fusilage. It was shortly followed by the Halifaxes.

"Well, it's starting," Maus said jokingly. But, in his heart, he was not as indifferent as he pretended. On earlier missions, it had seemed to matter little to him whether he survived or not. On this mission, however, he had every intention of returning in one piece. He was to be married on August 13, at Lübeck.

June 13. 8 A.M. A Sunderland, despite the concentrated fire of the five submarines, dived at the *U-564*, which was the last U-boat in the formation, and dropped depth charges. The aircraft did not have time to regain altitude before it was struck by fire from the *U-185*. It seemed to stop dead in midair, then exploded and fell into the sea.

Through his megaphone, Fiedler, captain of the *U-564*, informed Maus that he had sustained severe damage. He was unable to dive, he said, and had notified headquarters that he would have to return to base. An answer from headquarters arrived a few minutes later. A torpedo boat was being sent out from Bordeaux to escort the damaged U-boat back to base. Maus was ordered to escort the *U-564* to the rendezvous point. A short while later, Commander Fiedler and eighteen of his men were taken on board the *U-185*.

At 3:08 P.M., the men from the *U-564*, as well as a wounded gunner from the *U-185*, were transferred to the *Kriegsmarine* torpedo boat. During the operation, a Liberator appeared but was immediately attacked by five Messerschmitts and shot down after a short pursuit.

Maus, in a dark mood, gave the order to dive.

July 8. The *U-185* had been in Brazilian waters for two days. Maus' relentless search for enemy shipping was now rewarded. A convoy, the BT-18, was sighted, and the *U-185* successively sank a tanker, a Liberty ship, and a cargo ship.

As the ships went down before Maus' delighted gaze, his friend Peter Cremer was several thousand miles away, in Lorient, standing before the desk of Captain Rösing, commander of the Western Flotilla. The two men, after saluting, shook hands warmly. Cremer was the only one of the three "guinea pigs," sent out to test the new antiaircraft guns in combat, to have returned. Guggenberger had been sunk somewhere off the Brazilian coast, and Kuppish had disappeared in mid-Atlantic.

"I'm delighted to see you again, Peter," Rösing began. "Sit down and tell me about it."

Cremer cleared his throat. "Captain, this was a relatively short mission. But from the beginning of it to the end, my men and I all had the same feeling: that we would never come out of it alive. That this was going to be our last mission."

"Come on, Cremer. An old sea dog like you isn't going to let those British and American landlubbers get the better of him."

Cremer seemed suddenly old and tired. "You know, Captain," he said in a tone of obvious discouragement, "in the present situation, experience and daring have very little to do with anything."

"Peter," Rösing said in alarm, "I hope you're not going to tell me that even with our new antiaircraft guns we aren't better off than before."

"Oh, yes. We're better off. We can put up a better defense. We can shoot some of them down. But what are we doing, really, except postponing the inevitable?"

"But you returned!"

"Yes, I returned. But barely. On June 17, I was absolutely certain that we'd never make it. At a little after seven in the evening, we were attacked by a plane—a Martlet—which came roaring out of the fog at us. I waited for it to get close in before opening fire. Meanwhile, it was coming in to starboard, its machine guns blazing away, strafing the tower and the decks."

"Why didn't you open fire immediately?"

"Because I've noticed that if we begin firing too soon, our antiaircraft pieces run out of ammunition when the target is directly overhead. It's a hell of a situation. You don't feel like reloading the gun, you feel like jumping overboard.

"Well, when the plane was at about a thousand feet, I gave the order to open fire. The plane must have been hit by at least fifty rounds. I'm certain of it. And they were direct hits. But that didn't stop him. He kept coming right at us at an altitude of no more than 125 feet. When he was right on top of us, he dropped five bombs. They missed us, thank God, and landed a few hundred feet away. Then the plane left, probably because he didn't want another round with our guns.

"I immediately gave the order to dive, since I was afraid that there might be other aircraft in the area."

"And then?"

"We didn't have time to dive. Two bombers came out of nowhere and began circling at 6,000 feet. While I was trying to figure out why they didn't attack, three Mustangs came at us through the clouds—from three different directions so as to scatter my fire.

"You should have seen it. The surface was unusually green and absolutely calm, then suddenly I couldn't see anything but the splashing of machine-gun rounds. The conning tower got it too, of course. It looks like a sieve, in spite of its armor plate. Fortunately, my gunners are experts, and they managed to hold off the planes for a while. Eventually, two of the Mustangs got directly overhead. We got one of them, and it went down into the sea a short distance away. The other one was hit, but it flew over so low that I thought it was going to hit the conning tower.

"It had just flown past when two more fighter planes showed up; two Martlets. I looked up, and the two bombers were still circling overhead, like vultures.

"The Martlets began strafing us, and two of the men on watch and five of the gunners were wounded. Then, while we were waiting for men to relieve them, the bombers attacked, flying past, one behind the other, with their machine guns blazing. Five more of my men were hit—which left me with no gunners. My second officer ran to one of the guns and began firing, while I watched the bombers so that I could try to get out of there before they began dropping bombs. At what I thought was the right moment, I gave the order to prepare to dive."

"It was the only thing to do, Peter."

"Yes. But we still had to find a way to do it. The bombers passed over us at about 300 feet, and the first one dropped a string of bombs. The second one let go with some depth charges. As soon as I saw the bombs falling, we turned hard to starboard. It wasn't much of a maneuver, but it was all we could do. One of the bombs fell into our wake at about a hundred yards, and a depth charge exploded at 150 feet. The explosion rolled us over at a 25° angle. One of the wounded men fell overboard.

"Just as we were handing the last wounded man through the hatch, the two Martlets and the Mustang dived at us again. All I could think of was my encounter with the *Crocus*, and I was certain that I was going to end up stuffed with lead again. But this time, I was lucky. We kept zigzagging as they fired their machine guns. I gave the order to dive and then jumped down the hatchway just as the bombers dropped some flares—by then, it was getting dark—for another bombing run.

"I think we must have set a record for diving. I hadn't even secured the hatch when we were already beneath the surface. And I got off with nothing more serious than a cold shower."

"Well, at least you got off," Rösing said with an encouraging smile.

"Yes, Captain. But luck doesn't last forever."

"What are your conclusions, Peter?"

"They're very simple. First, even with our new antiaircraft guns, sooner or later every one of our submarines is going to be sunk by aircraft. Second, the enemy pilots are remarkably well trained and their tactics are excellent: the fighters come in and clear off the decks, then the bombers move in to finish off the submarine. I got away, and so I'm not complaining. But I know that it was a miracle. Third, the armor of the enemy's planes has obviously been reinforced. Our 20-mm. shells hardly seem to bother them at all."

Cremer's report was read and reread by Grand Admiral Doenitz. It confirmed, point by point, the information he had already received from other, less experienced U-boat commanders, and it led to the same inevitable conclusion: Allied air superiority was such that submarine warfare was no longer possible. To continue would inevitably lead to staggering losses of men and ships.

On the other hand, it was impossible to suspend operations in the Atlantic, even for a short time, while waiting for the new types of submarine to become operational. The enemy would only make use of the aircraft no longer needed over the Atlantic to increase its bombing of German cities. Moreover, if there were no German submarines in the Atlantic, the Allies would no longer be required to follow the convoy system and would thus increase by one-third their means of transporting men and material across the Atlantic from America to Great Britain.

Doenitz knew that there was no way out. The Grey Wolves would have to continue fighting, even though combat was tantamount to suicide. It was the only solution; and it was a solution dictated by despair. Doenitz discussed it with his staff, and they approved it. But the grand admiral wished also to know the reaction of the men actually engaged in combat, and he summoned to Berlin, for that purpose, the commanding officers of the various flotillas: Captain Lehmann-Willenbrook, commander of the 9th Flotilla; Captain Kuhnke, commander of the 10th; Captain Söhler, of the 7th; Captain Schulz, of the 6th; Captain Zapp, of the 3rd; and Captain Rösing, commander of the Western Flotilla. He explained the problem and its solution to them, and they, in turn, agreed to the necessity of continuing the battle, even though, as they were well aware, it was nothing more than a form of slow suicide.

32

August 11. Four hundred and eighty miles west of Ascension Island, the forward watch of the U-185 reported:

"Vessel dead ahead!"

Through his binoculars, August Maus recognized the U-604.

Eleven days before, off the coast of San Salvador, it had been attacked by a U. S. Air Force hydroplane. The attacker's four bombs had all detonated at the level of the conning tower, and there had been severe damage. With its ballast tanks punctured, one electric motor inoperational, and its periscopes disaligned, the U-604 could navigate only with the utmost difficulty.

In human lives, the toll had been even heavier. Two of the watch had been killed, two gunners wounded, and a helmsman had gone mad with fear. It had been necessary to tie him down in his bunk. The U-boat's captain, Horst Hoeltring, had received multiple shrapnel wounds.

Hoeltring, Maus knew, was a strange man. Very dark, with the build of a laborer, hard and muscular, he was nicknamed "the Gangster" because of his fondness for waving his revolver around at the slightest provocation. He also enjoyed a solid and well-founded reputation as a hard drinker. He was cast in the mold of the pirates of old; and his rough manners and disreputable appearance were in striking contrast to those of his fellow submarine captains.

Maus had been ordered by headquarters to rendezvous with Hoeltring and offer whatever aid he could. At a few minutes after five in the afternoon, the U-185 came alongside Hoeltring's vessel and began to ferry over supplies of food, fuel, and ammunition.

At 6:45 P.M., four distinct explosions ripped through the U-604: the scuttling explosives which the engineer had just taken aboard the damaged U-boat. In a few minutes, the U-604 disappeared beneath the surface.

August 24. 6 A.M. The U-185, having completed its mandatory test-dive, returned to the surface. August Maus climbed topside and quickly scanned the horizon through his binoculars. The sea was an emerald green, broken only by occasional whitecaps. Like sheep in a green field, Maus reflected contentedly, as he quickly computed the number of days before his wedding.

"Watch topside," he said into the acoustical tube.

As soon as the men on watch were at their posts, Maus went below. Hoeltring had just risen, and Maus nodded at him, noting that he already had his revolver strapped to his hip. I wonder if he sleeps with it, Maus thought as he stretched out on his bunk and closed his eyes.

As Maus dozed, a Hellcat fighter cruised nearby at 7,000 feet. It belonged to a squadron attached to the carrier *Core,* which patrolled this sector. The Hellcat's navigator caught a glimpse of something glittering in the sun, on the green surface of the sea. He pointed it out to the pilot. The plane gained altitude so as to avoid being spotted as the navigator raised his binoculars. "It's a submarine," he told the pilot, and then immediately notified the *Core.*

An answer came a few seconds later: "Maintain contact. We are sending reinforcements."

Exactly seventeen minutes later, two more Hellcats and two Avenger bombers reached the submarine's position and circled in the clouds which had begun to gather. Then with the fighter planes in the lead, the four aircraft dived toward the *U-185.*

Simultaneously, the alert sounded aboard the submarine and the gunners rushed to their posts. They were aiming their weapons when the first Hellcat cut them down with a burst of machine-gun fire. The second plane came in for a strafing run as Maus came up through the hatch. He was in time to catch the second officer as he fell backward, with one round through his throat and another through his chest. In a hoarse whisper, the man told Maus: "It wasn't the watch's fault, Captain. The planes were hidden behind the clouds, then they came out of the sun. You mustn't punish the men—" Then his eyes rolled back until Maus could see only their whites, and he was dead. Maus looked around. The men on watch had all been cut down by the second Hellcat. The second gunnery team was lying with the first on the foredeck, all dead or wounded. They had not had time even to fire their weapons.

The depth charges dropped by the first Avenger exploded,

one to port, and the other directly on the 105-mm. The gun was ripped from its mooring and thrown into the air, leaving a yawning hole in the deck. Under the impact of the explosion, the U-185 rolled and pitched wildly, taking on water. The crewmen who had been on the ladder on their way to man the guns were thrown screaming to the deck below. Maus, who had been knocked down by the percussion, dragged himself to his feet. Blood poured down his face from a deep cut on his forehead. He wiped the blood from his eyes and, clutching the periscope superstructure, called down the hatch to Ackermann:

"Chief! Can we dive?"

The engineer, coughing with every word, his voice unsteady, called back: "Impossible, Captain—"

Ackermann's voice was drowned out by shouts of terror and by the roar of water pouring into the aft compartment.

A few seconds later, Ackermann's head appeared in the hatchway. "The ship is finished," he gasped, "there's chlorine everywhere . . ."

Below, panic had erupted. Water was pouring into the compartments, and the chlorine gas generated by the drowned batteries was carried from one compartment to the next by the ventilating system and mixed with the black smoke pouring from a burning diesel. The terrified men, their lungs seared by the chlorine, unable to breathe because of the smoke, fought one another desperately in their struggle to reach the ladder leading up the hatchway.

In the weak, flickering light generated by the emergency system, Hoeltring saw one of his own crewmen fall to the deck, gasping for breath, his lips pulled back over his teeth. "I'm done for, Captain," the man moaned, coughing, terror in his eyes. "My lungs are on fire." He coughed, then spat blood. "Finish me off, Captain," he begged. "Finish me off."

Hoeltring stood over him, bent double by pain. His lungs, too, had been burned by the chlorine, and every breath he took seemed to rip open his chest. The man at his feet had closed his eyes and was moaning. A reddish foam was dripping from his lips onto the deck. Summoning his strength, Hoeltring took his revolver from its holster.

The sailor opened his eyes, saw the revolver, and understood. "Do it quick, Captain," he groaned, twisting in agony.

The shot was like an incredible burst of thunder within the *U-185*'s steel hull. The sailor's body was thrown several feet away from Hoeltring, who stood holding his revolver at arm's length. He looked toward the control room, where twenty men were fighting savagely, petty officers and seamen alike, using iron bars and wrenches as weapons, in their panic to escape to the upper deck. He leaned against the bulkhead, coughing violently, and his blood splattered against the bulkhead. Slowly, Hoeltring raised the barrel of his weapon, placed it carefully into his mouth, and pulled the trigger.

As he fell to the deck the prow of the *U-185* was raised from the water by an explosion, and tons of water rushed from the foreward compartment toward the ship's stern, carrying a dozen men along by its force. The U-boat's prow was raised even higher, and her stern began to sink slowly beneath the waves.

On the conning tower, Maus, struggling desperately to retain his footing, pulled his men one by one through the hatch and sent them to huddle at the foot of the tower on the foredeck. He shouted down the hatchway, ordering the men who remained below to remain calm. Finally, there were no more men on the ladder. "Is there anyone down there?" Maus yelled. He listened for an answer, and heard only the roar of water. He looked around. Only one of his officers was near him: von Kliege, the ship's doctor, who was trying to revive Ackermann. Maus shouted again: "Is anyone down there?" There was no answer.

A Hellcat swooped down, guns spitting at the submarine which was now no more than a ruin surrounded by columns of black smoke. Maus and von Kliege, supporting Ackermann between them, made their way, miraculously untouched by the shower of hot lead, to join the other survivors on the foredeck.

"Look!" screamed a terrified sailor.

An Avenger was coming at them at an altitude of 200 feet. They could see its bomb bays wide open. Then it was upon them.

With a roar of its engines, the bomber turned and, as the submariners watched in dumb amazement, began gaining altitude.

A savage cry of joy and relief rose from the sinking submarine. "They didn't bomb us!" some of the men shrieked. And some even shouted, "Long live America! Thank you, Yankees!"

Von Kliege, his voice trembling, said to Maus: "They're good men! Yes, good men! If they had dropped a bomb, they would've blown us to bits." Then he laughed, a weird, grating, animal laugh.

The aft section of the *U-185* was now almost entirely covered by water. In a few minutes, Maus knew, it would go down stern first. He took a long, last look at his ship; then, blinking to hold back the tears, he turned to his men. "All right, men, abandon ship! Get as far away as you can, and form a circle . . ."

Aboard the Avenger, the navigator was furious. "The fucking thing jammed!" he reported to the pilot, punching savagely at the bomb-release mechanism. "Jammed, goddammit!"

33

Maus counted the men as they jumped into the water. Twenty-seven. Then he jumped. It was not until he began struggling to rise to the surface that he realized he had forgotten to put on a life jacket. I won't last more than a few minutes like this, he thought in panic. The wound on his forehead burned, and for the first time he felt a numbing pain in his left wrist. Finally, his head was out of the water, and he took a deep gulp of air. Then he was dragged under again by the suction from the sinking U-boat. Once more, he struggled to the surface, then began paddling painfully, his wrist throbbing, toward a cluster of survivors bobbing in the swell a hundred yards away.

The men had joined hands or were holding each other by the shoulders to avoid drifting apart. When Maus joined them, von Kliege let go of the man next to him to make room for the captain. Maus clutched at the doctor and held on, exhausted.

"Good God!" von Kliege shouted. "You don't have a life vest!"

Maus could not speak. He simply shook his head.

"Hang on to me," von Kliege said.

The sailor to Maus' left put his arm under the captain's armpit and smiled weakly.

Overhead, an Avenger came in at low altitude and made a wide circle above the survivors as they watched in silent fear, wondering whether they would be strafed.

"He's signaling," Maus reassured them, spelling out the message which the Americans were blinking in Morse code: H-E-L-P I-S C-O-M-I-N-G.

"Help is coming," Maus translated for his men. "They're telling us that they're sending help! Hold on, men!"

A few weak cheers rose as the bomber disappeared into the west. The sky was empty once more, and the silence which now settled over the sea which had so recently echoed to the sounds of war was somehow depressing. The survivors felt suddenly alone, abandoned.

"Look," someone said.

A few of the men made an effort to raise their heads.

"Look," one of the sailors said to the man next to him who kept his head down.

"I don't give a shit," the man replied. "I don't give a shit about anything."

With an almost human shudder, the *U-185* raised its prow at a 90° angle and then slid into the depths. The water foamed violently, and a large bubble of air rose to the surface. There was the sound of a muffled explosion, and a fierce churning. A few bits of debris showered down into the water. Then there was silence. Some of the men cried.

"We forgot Adolf on board!" The man who shouted let go of his neighbors and began to laugh uncontrollably, a metallic, hysterical laugh. His shipmates attempted to grab him as he began drifting, but, still laughing, swallowing sea water, coughing and spitting, he paddled wildly beyond their reach.

"I'm going to get him—"

"Don't be an asshole! Stay here!"

By then, the sailor had put a considerable distance between himself and the circle of survivors, and he continued to swim, spitting, coughing, and laughing all the while.

A few moments later, another man became hysterical and began to try to break loose from the circle, using his fists to fight off the men around him who tried to hold him back. "I see a bar!" he screamed. "A bar! I'm going to get a beer! A glass of beer!" Waving his arms frenetically, he struck von Bothner, the second officer, in the face with his elbow, and began to swim away from the circle.

Maus, meanwhile, had fallen asleep in the water, supported by von Kliege on one side and by the sailor, Fritz, on the other. Now he opened his eyes and struggled to regain consciousness. His head throbbed, the pain in his wrist was excruciating, and it felt as though his back was covered with shrapnel wounds. Shaking his head, he began to tread water, in order to relieve the doctor and Fritz of his weight. Occasionally, he plunged his head into the water to keep himself awake.

Then he called to his crew: "Men, try to hold on! We all know that the hours we'll spend waiting to be rescued are going to be the hardest ones of our lives. But let's not lose courage. Soon, it will all be over—"

He was interrupted by a shout: "Otto is dead!"

Before anyone could react, Fritz, with incredible coolness, spoke. "Take off his life jacket," he said. "The captain doesn't have one."

The life jacket was passed from hand to hand until it reached

Maus, who struggled to put it on. Finally, he succeeded. "I feel a little more secure with this thing on," he told von Kliege.

The doctor did not answer. Maus looked at him closely. His skin was the color of chalk, his lips were blue; his eyes, closed. Maus shook him roughly, but he did not respond. "Doctor!" Maus shouted. "Wake up! You can't go to sleep! Come on, try to stay awake!"

Von Kliege opened his eyes, nodded, and then fell asleep again.

The torpor which had begun to settle over the circle of survivors was broken by shrieks of terror. The men raised their heads and saw the two men who had drifted away from the circle a few hundred feet away. They were beating the water frantically, screaming, disappearing and then reappearing.

"Sharks," Fritz whispered.

Maus saw the dark fins of the predators cut through the water which had now taken on a reddish tinge. There was a final cry of agony, and then an ominous quiet.

The fins reappeared on the surface several hundred yards away from the crew of the *U-185*, and everyone watched in terror as they moved in a circle around the survivors.

Night fell, and the darkness, combined with the proximity of the dreaded sharks, awakened a new sense of despair and fear in the survivors. Those who had the strength to struggle against despair clutched the hands or shoulders of the men nearest them. The night was an endless agony for all of them. Most had been wounded during the attack and were weak from loss of blood. Occasionally, one or another of the men succumbed to despair and wept or screamed. Several of the men died during the hours of darkness. From time to time, Maus talked to his men to keep them awake. Whenever he did, he repeated to them the phrase: "Anyone who falls asleep is a dead man." But, for the crew of the *U-185*, death held no terror. They had lost the will to resist, the will to live. They had given up all hope. They bowed their heads and awaited death with resignation, as their only means of escape.

Late in the night, Maus ordered everyone to pray aloud and to sing. Still later, he made them recite the multiplication tables as loud as they could. He wanted them to speak, to hear voices. Voices meant life, and silence was the acceptance of death.

Finally, dawn broke. In the dim light, Maus saw the black fins of the sharks. He looked at von Kliege. The doctor was dead. It was impossible to know exactly when he had died. Perhaps it was while they were praying. When fatigue surpasses the invisible threshold of human resistance, a man accepts even death with indifference; and it was with a feeling of utter indifference that Maus removed von Kliege's life jacket and set his body adrift in the sea. For a while, the doctor's body remained near the circle of men, occasionally drifting against one of them as though unwilling to be alone. Then it disappeared without anyone caring what had happened to it.

The survivors—there were now only twenty-one remaining— continued to float aimlessly in the swell. Their lips were parched and smarted in the sea water. No one spoke. No one bothered even to moan. The only sign of activity came from the sharks, who circled endlessly in search of more corpses.

According to the position of the sun, it was about 9 o'clock in the morning, and a thin fog had settled over the surface. Fritz shook Maus' arm, and the captain looked up wearily.

"Captain," the sailor said, "I think I saw a mast on the horizon, but I'm not sure. I'm so tired it may have just been a mirage. Maybe I'm going out of my mind like the others—"

"Where, exactly?"

Fritz pointed to the northwest. Both men stared at the line of the horizon.

"There," Fritz said. "Did you see it?"

"I think I did," Maus answered. He thought he had discerned a thin line dark against the sky; but he no longer trusted his eyes.

"Look! There it is again!"

"Yes, I see it! It's a destroyer! I'm certain of it," Maus exclaimed. He cleared his throat and somehow found the strength to shout: "Men!" Everyone looked up, as though astonished at the sound of a voice. "Men," Maus went on, "we're going to be rescued!"

The men looked at him without grasping what he had said.

"It's true! A destroyer's coming to get us. Fritz and I both saw it. Look for yourselves if you don't believe me. You can see its mast!"

As though animated by a new strength, the men raised their eyes and looked where Maus was pointing. An eternal minute passed during which fatigue and incredulity were so strong that the men refused to believe their eyes. Finally, one of them shouted: "It's true! I saw it! We're going to be rescued!"

Life seemed to flow back into the survivors' exhausted bodies. They began all speaking at once. Some of them wept and laughed at the same time. Then, the sound of aircraft engines was heard, and the men saw a plane approaching rapidly, very low over the water. They waved their arms frantically. The plane spotted them and passed directly overhead. Then it was lost in the fog.

"We've been spotted by the plane," Maus told his men. "It will give our position to the destroyer. In about an hour, we can expect to be rescued.

"As you know, we are going to become prisoners of war. I don't have to remind you that a captured soldier must tell the enemy only his name and serial number. They are going to try to get you to tell whatever you know, and especially to find out whether there are any other submarines in these waters. You are not allowed to give them any information which might lead to the loss of the men who are continuing to fight."

He was silent for a moment. He looked at his men one after the other, then he asked:

"Can I count on you to do your duty to the very end?"

The men answered in chorus: "*Jawohl, Herr Kaleunt!*"

As Maus had predicted, it took about an hour for the American destroyer to reach them. When the ship had stopped its engines at 50 yards from the survivors, an officer called from the deck:

"Who is the captain?"

Maus raised his arm.

"Come aboard," the officer shouted.

Gathering the remnants of his strength, Maus climbed painfully up the net hanging from the destroyer's starboard. Two sailors, wearing the white caps of the U. S. Navy, helped him over the railing. Water dripped from his clothes as he stood burning with fever, shivering uncontrollably, before two officers in immaculate whites. He saluted smartly, and the Americans returned his salute.

"*Kapitänleutnant zur Zee August Maus,*" he reported.

One of the officers, a commander, asked brusquely: "Do you speak English?"

"Of course."

"Good. We don't have time to waste, Captain. Are there any other German submarines in this area?"

"I am not allowed to answer that question."

The American officer glared at him. "Captain," he said, "I must tell you that if you refuse to give me the information I need, I am going to put you back into the water and leave you and your men to the sharks."

Exhausted, feverish as he was, Maus drew himself up to attention. He glanced over the side at his men who were swimming about, expecting to be taken aboard at any moment. He was bound to them by the comradeship of combat, of sufferings shared and victories won. And yet, despite his almost obsessive craving for hot coffee, dry clothing and a soft bunk, he did not hesitate. In a voice trembling with anger, he answered:

"I have nothing more to say."

The American looked at him in mingled anger and surprise. Then, turning to a young ensign standing slightly behind him, he said: "Tell those men to come aboard. And give them some coffee immediately. Be sure to separate the officers from the enlisted men."

Before walking away, he looked at August Maus once more and mumbled: "Goddam kraut-head!"

A short while later, in the infirmary, Maus found out that his left wrist was broken.

34

Wolf Shafer walked quickly along the track of the tiny station at La Baule, looking for the coach reserved for submariners on pass. His legs felt weak, and he was sweating lightly in the heat of the late-August sun.

"Wolf, Wolf!" a voice called. "Over here!"

Shafer looked up and saw an officer leaning out of a window of the train, waving at him. He waved back, then began walking toward the coach. He climbed the steps and pushed his way through the seamen in the aisle to the compartment reserved for officers. Baumein was alone in the compartment. Shafer threw his bag into the rack overhead and wiped his forehead. He and Baumein smiled. Although they were not actually friends, the two officers had run into each other occasionally in the officers' mess and on the docks at Lorient and Saint Nazaire. They were both twenty-one years old, and they belonged to the same promotion class.

"Well," Shafer said, settling into a seat and stretching out his legs, "this is really a first-class train. Why are they treating us so well?"

"This is no ordinary train," Baumein answered. "Guess who it belongs to."

Shafer shrugged.

"To none other than *Reichsmarschall* Hermann Goering. He's inspecting the Atlantic Luftwaffe bases."

Shafer emitted a low whistle. Then he lighted a cigarette, took one puff, and crushed it out in an ashtray. It was too hot to smoke.

The two men sat in silence for a while. Even the sailors in the aisles outside the compartment were unusually quiet. They leaned out of the windows trying to get a breath of fresh air.

"I thought you had already gone on leave," Baumein said.

Even in this heat, Shafer reflected, he can't keep his mouth shut for more than two minutes. "The second officer confined me to quarters for three days," he said aloud.

"Oh? What did you do?"

"I can quote the charge verbatim. It's one of the craziest things that's happened in this whole screwed-up war. It reads: 'He deliberately destroyed naval property by cutting up a suit of long woolen underwear and making a cap to wear on the deck of his submarine.'"

Baumein burst out laughing.

"What really makes me mad as hell is that I just about saved the life of that son-of-a-bitch," Shafer growled.

"Well, obviously you don't hold grudges."

"You can say that again. The bastard had just informed me of my punishment when we were attacked by aircraft. We were two days out of Saint Nazaire, waiting for a torpedo-boat escort. They came down on us before we knew what was happening. There were five of them, and there was nothing we could do. After fighting them off for about an hour, we had eleven men dead, and almost as many wounded. There were holes all over our hull. The submarine was taking on water aft, and the pumps couldn't keep up with it. The compartment was already flooded, so the captain ordered us to abandon ship.

"We jumped into the water wearing our life belts, and we had just formed our circle when the English strafed us again."

"The bastards," Baumein said, fanning himself with a news-paper.

"Yes. Well, we were in the water for about five hours. The torpedo boat had arrived just as we were abandoning ship, and of course the planes attacked it. We spent the whole time praying that the boat would be able to fight them off. I was holding up the second officer. He had been wounded and was unconscious most of the time, and his head kept dropping into the water, face-down. It was all I could do to hold him up and keep paddling so as not to drift away from the others.

"To make a long story short, the planes finally went away, and we were hauled aboard the torpedo boat.

"When they were taking that son-of-a-bitch down to the infirmary, he turned to me and said: 'Thank you, Shafer. But don't think you're going to get out of your punishment.' That's what he said, word for word. I felt like picking him up and throwing him overboard.

"And he kept his word. The fact is, we never did get along. He never passed up a chance to screw me up. Well, when we were back on the beach, I passed him on the dock one day. He had his arm in a sling. I just couldn't resist it. I told him, 'The next time, you'd better find another sucker; because if it's up to me, I'll let you drown.'"

"What did he say?"

"He turned white as a sheet. I know his arm hurt like hell. But he said, 'Shafer, I'll get even with you for this. You'd better hope you never cross my path again.' Actually, there's not much chance that I will. By the time he's ready for duty again, I'll already have sailed."

The minutes sped by. Baumein dozed. Shafer was absorbed in a French novel, *Les Petites Alliées*, which Rasch had told him to read in order to improve his French. They were not far from Angers when a group of English fighters swooped down, guns blazing, on Goering's train. The train raced ahead for several miles; then, with much screeching and grinding, it came to a halt. Baumein's suitcase fell on his head, cutting open his forehead.

Nearby, bombs began to explode, shaking the coach alarmingly. Shafer could see the sailors outside his door jumping out the windows. Some of them were running toward a nearby clump of trees, and others huddled against the side of the train away from the explosions. Shafer and Baumein—the latter's face covered with blood—leaped through the window of the compartment and ran toward a ditch. They reached it just as a plane roared over, dropping a string of bombs which detonated and showered the two officers with dirt and rubble.

"Where the hell are our antiaircraft guns?" Shafer wondered. He raised his head and looked at the last coach of the train—actu-

ally a flatcar on which a double 20-mm. had been installed. He
saw the bodies of several gunners lying there, hanging over the
side. Baumein saw them too. They ducked as a fighter screamed
past, the rounds from its machine guns raising small clouds of
dust only a few feet from their ditch.

"I'm going," Shafer said. And before Baumein could reply, he
jumped up and began running toward the track. He stumbled
once, and then continued on all fours, throwing himself flat when
the fighter returned for another pass. As he lay there, his arms
folded over his head, he reflected that the British were poor
shots not to have hit the train yet. When the plane had passed
over, he began running again toward the flatcar. He reached it
and threw himself under the platform at the same moment that
two fighters released their bombs. The explosions were much
nearer the train this time. Shafer looked back, and saw Baumein's
body rise into the air and then fall back to the ground and lay
motionless. Further on, he say a high-ranking Luftwaffe officer, in
his shirtsleeves and stockingfeet, making a mad dash for a nearby
thicket. He was a man about sixty, with a protruding stomach.
As Shafer watched, the officer was struck in the side by shrapnel.
He rose on tiptoe, his arms flailing, then fell heavily to the
ground.

Around Shafer, all hell seemed to have broken loose. There
were screams, cries of pain, shouts, explosions. Shafer wondered
if perhaps Goering himself were on the train. If he is, he told
himself, the flames and the heat will melt some of the fat off of
him.

He stuck his head out from under the flatcar and looked up.
The fighters were gaining altitude preparatory to another dive at
the train.

Shafer rolled over, pulled himself upright, and raced up the
metal ladder to the gun mount as the roar of the planes grew
progressively louder. Without looking up, he threw himself across
the bodies of the dead gunners and held onto them with all his
strength. There were two explosions which shook the entire
length of the train, and machine-gun rounds ripped across the

flatcar. Twice, Shafer felt the bodies beneath him jump under
the impact. He raised his head and saw the two fighters pulling
out of their dive. In an instant, he was behind the guns, thanking
God fervently that his training at Cadet School had included in-
struction in the 20-mm. He was in luck. They were fully loaded.
He spun the double gun around, aiming it upward just as the
first fighter passed overhead. The second was approaching
rapidly, ready to release the load of bombs under its wings. Shafer opened fire, and experienced an immediate sensation of relief,
a lessening of nervous frustration at his own helplessness. It was
replaced by an overwhelming rage.

Shafer saw a wide streak of black smoke shoot out of the
fighter's belly, and he shouted wildly in triumph as the plane
crashed into a thicket a few hundred yards behind the train. He
felt the hot blast of the explosion on his face and hands.

His victory had an unexpected consequence. Three sailors ran
out of the woods toward the front of the train, where there was
another flatcar armed with antiaircraft guns, about a hundred
yards ahead of Shafer's. He did not have time to see whether
they reached it. Once more, fighters were diving at the train,
following closely one upon the other. With a coolness that
astonished him, Shafer waited for the first one to come within
500 yards, and then began firing. He did not care about the fire
from the planes' machine guns whistling around him. He thought
of nothing but shooting down the planes. A bomb exploded a
hundred yards behind him, and Shafer thought the flatcar would
be overturned by the blast; but he continued firing, holding fast
to the gun's grips so as not to be blown off the car. His attention
was entirely on the second plane which was coming in very low
and concentrating its fire on the flatcar.

Shafer watched as the plane grew rapidly larger, apparently
impervious to his fire. He heard the machine-gun rounds coming
closer, and it occurred to him that he would probably be dead
by the time the plane was directly overhead. Then, as the fighter
seemed about to reach him, masses of black smoke began to

pour from its fuselage. For a split second, Shafer saw the horror-stricken face of the pilot. Then there was a deafening explosion.

A second later, Shafer heard the guns on the forward platform open fire. The three remaining planes made a half turn, gained altitude, and sped away.

In the area surrounding the train, people began to stir, to rise to their feet, fear still in their eyes. Shafer barely looked at them as he ran back to the spot where he had seen Baumein fall. He found the officer lying face down in the dirt. At first, Shafer saw no blood and thought that Baumein had only been stunned by the explosion. Then he turned him over and saw the gaping wound in his shoulder. Baumein heaved a deep sigh. Shafer stood up and called to some sailors nearby to carry the wounded man aboard the train.

As they were moving Baumein, Shafer head a series of harrowing screams. He turned and saw the Luftwaffe officer, surrounded by doctors and nurses, shrieking like a madman. The piece of shrapnel had gone through his side and ripped open his abdomen, half eviscerating him. His hands were clasped over the bloody wound, and he was shouting: "Don't touch me! Don't touch me!"

Shafer joined the group around the officer as one of the doctors said, "I'm going to give you a shot of morphine, Colonel."

The colonel's face was livid and covered with sweat, and his eyes were open wide and staring—like those of a corpse, Shafer thought. "Hurry, Doctor, hurry," he moaned. "Please! I can't stand the pain. I can't—" Tears flowed down his cheeks.

Shafer walked slowly away, the sight of the old man weeping, as his hands attempted to hold his intestines in place, indelibly graven in his memory.

In the compartment, he found Baumein, his shoulder bandaged, fast asleep.

Late in the evening, a few minutes before the train arrived in Paris, the door of the compartment was thrown open. Shafer,

who had been dozing, sprang to his feet as a Luftwaffe general
and two colonels crowded into the compartment.

"You are Lieutenant Wolf Shafer?" the general asked.

"Yes, sir."

"Excellent. Lieutenant, the *Reichsmarschall* is deeply cogni-
zant of your courage during the attack. Thanks to your initiative,
the train was saved. Thus, the *Reichsmarschall* has awarded you
the Iron Cross of the Luftwaffe and has ordered me to present it
to you."

Solemnly the general turned and walked to the door of the
compartment, where an officer placed the decoration in his out-
stretched hand.

Smiling, the general returned to stand before Shafer and
placed the red ribbon of the *Eisenkreuz* around the neck of the
young officer, who remained speechless with astonishment.

Before they left the compartment, one of the colonels said:
"You are the first submariner ever to be decorated by the Luftwaffe."

There are some men who are pursued by misfortune, and Wolf
Shafer was convinced that he was one of them. Three weeks
later, when he returned to Saint Nazaire after his leave, the first
person he saw was his second officer; and the man seemed even
less cordial than usual. To make matters worse, his arm was no
longer in a sling—which meant that he was once more available for sea duty. The final blow was delivered immediately.

"Lieutenant," the second officer announced coldly, "I have news
for you."

Shafer swallowed and braced himself for what was to come.

"We are sailing in three days. I'm your new commanding officer.
I've been looking forward to telling you so, personally."

"Yes, sir," Shafer stuttered, utterly crushed.

The officer's cold eyes grew wide as they noted the decoration
hanging from Shafer's neck.

"What is that?"

"The Iron Cross, sir."

"Where did you get it?"

"It was conferred on me by *Reichsmarschall* Goering, Captain. I—"

"Since when does a submarine officer accept decorations from the Luftwaffe?" the captain asked harshly. "Remove it immediately, Lieutenant! You'll wear the Iron Cross only when you earn it aboard a submarine. In the meantime, you will remain confined to quarters for eleven days when we return from our mission. That will teach you to have more respect for your uniform than to wear such junk!"

35

December 5, 1943. Hermann Rasch, his cap beneath his arm, came smartly to attention before Grand Admiral Doenitz as an orderly closed the door behind him.

"Sit down," Doenitz ordered. "Sit down, all of you." As Godt, Rasch, and Meckel, Doenitz' communications officer, found chairs, the grand admiral came from behind his desk and joined them. His fingers strummed the armrest of his chair for a few seconds; then, as was his habit, he came directly to the point.

"Rasch, the mission I have in mind for you is extremely important to all of us. Certainly, it is the most delicate mission that you'll ever be asked to undertake; and I'm depending on you to succeed."

Rasch looked closely at Doenitz. Since his assignment to the Special Detection Research Group headed by Admiral Stummel, he had seen the grand admiral only rarely. Now, looking at the lined face, he tried to find evidence of the personal tragedy of which every submariner was aware, but to which Doenitz never referred. The grand admiral's two sons had both been lost at sea. The elder had gone down with his submarine in the Channel; and the younger had been buried at sea in the Atlantic. Yet, the face seemed as strong and inscrutable as ever; thinner, perhaps,

and certainly tired. But there was no indication that the Lion had
lost either his energy or his determination.

"Here it is, Rasch. The Wehrmacht is holding two British airmen in Paris. We all know that the enemy has a new detection
device called radar; but we have no idea on what wave lengths
it operates. Your mission is to find out from these two officers
what we need to know.

"It's not going to be easy. If you're going to get these men to
talk, you're going to need patience, an understanding of human
psychology, an ability to put understanding to work for you, and,
above all, time.

"The trouble is," Doenitz said harshly, "we don't have much
time. I've had a rather unpleasant meeting with the Führer and
Himmler about these men. The head of the Gestapo is demanding that we hand the two prisoners over to him for questioning.
I don't have to tell you that I was strongly opposed to this step,
and that I pointed out that any information concerning radar
was the business of the Navy rather than of the police.

"Naturally, *Reichsführer* Himmler protested vehemently. Especially when I said that I doubted whether any Gestapo officer
would be able to understand the problems involved in submarine detection.

"Eventually, the Führer decided in my favor; but we are allowed only two weeks to question the prisoners. If they haven't
talked by then, they must be handed over to the Gestapo. Moreover, the Führer granted Himmler's request that the naval officer
in charge of our interrogation give the Gestapo a daily progress
report.

"So, Rasch, it's up to you."

December 4. 10 A.M.

The SS guard stepped aside to let Rasch precede him into
the sitting room of a private house on the Avenue Foch. "I'd
prefer you to remain outside," Rasch told him as he walked past.
The guard looked at him quizzically, then shrugged, as though
to say that all sailors were peculiar anyhow, and closed the door.

Two men were standing in the center of the room, bareheaded, their arms at their sides. They both wore fur-lined leather jackets. "Typical Englishmen," Rasch told himself. One was tall, thin, slightly stooped, with heavy eyebrows which met over his nose. "My ex-wife would have said it's a sign of a jealous nature," Rasch reflected. His eyes were small, round, gray; his nose, long and straight. His forehead protruded slightly. "Not very intelligent, but stubborn," Rasch concluded.

The other man was of medium height, rather squat, with dark hair and light blue eyes. He had a long, drooping mustache, worthy of a Mongol emperor, which he stroked constantly. The first man was a sergeant major; the second, a lieutenant.

His inspection completed, Rasch saluted. The two prisoners exchanged glances, but did not return the salute. "To them I'm just another dirty kraut," Rasch reminded himself.

He put down his briefcase on a small, highly polished table of white wood and then sat down. "Why don't you sit down?" he said politely in English. "There's no need for you to stand."

The British airmen sat. The tall, thin sergeant major crossed his legs.

Rasch took out his cigarette case and extended it, first to the lieutenant, then to the enlisted man. "We don't smoke anything but Virginia tobacco," the lieutenant said sarcastically.

"Of course," Rasch answered. "I should have remembered. He took a package of Players out of his jacket pocket and held it out. "Is this your brand?"

The lieutenant grunted, but took a cigarette. The sergeant major did likewise. Rasch took one for himself, then lighted the three cigarettes. He put the package of Players on the table.

"Now," he said, "I'm going to begin by asking your names."

The two prisoners looked at each other as though to say, "Here we go again."

"Lieutenant Philip Edward Charles George Pittwall," the officer answered.

"Which of your given names do you prefer to be addressed by?"

"Philip."

"All right. And you?"

"Dick Finnecker."

"Where are you from, Lieutenant?"

"I'm a pure-blooded Londoner. My family's lived there for generations."

"A beautiful city," Rasch said.

"Not so beautiful now, after your bombing," Pittwall replied.

"Hamburg was once beautiful too," Rasch said drily. "Your planes have changed it considerably. And you, Sergeant, where are you from?"

"Southampton. But I was living in London. And I can't talk about the condition of Southampton, because it would provide military information for your propaganda," Finnecker growled, glaring at Pittwall.

The lieutenant, anxious to redeem himself, said loudly: "Look here. It's no good wasting your time and ours. If you think we're going to give away military information, you're mistaken."

"The truth is," Rasch said, "it's not military information that I'm after."

"No? What is it then? A recipe for porridge?" Finnecker said laughingly.

Rasch turned to face Pittwall. "I was a submarine commander," he explained. "I won't try to deny that your planes made me break out in a cold sweat on more than one occasion. As a technician myself, I'm interested—eager—to know how you're able to locate us with such precision."

"Well, it's no use counting on us to tell you," Finnecker interrupted, taking another cigarette. "I prefer Woodbines," he added.

Rasch decided to change the subject. "Do you have a family?" he asked Pittwall.

"Yes. A wife—a brunette with green eyes; very unusual type. And two little girls; one is eight, the other is five."

"And you, Sergeant?"

"Just an uncle. He's a constable in a small town. You remind me of him."

Rasch looked at his watch. It was 11:15. He concluded that the first session had gone on long enough.

On December 8, at 3:15 A.M., Rasch sat in the same room watching the two prisoners enter. He had had them awakened. They were unshaven, and their eyes were still swollen with sleep. They sank groggily into chairs, and Pittwall yawned widely.

"We're not going to be friends for long," Finnecker said angrily, "if you're going to start waking me up in the middle of the night!"

"I'm sorry to have disturbed you," Rasch said, "but I was passing by when it suddenly occurred to me that you might be willing to satisfy my curiosity."

"It bothers you, doesn't it?" Finnecker grinned, leaning forward. "Well, we don't intend to tell you a thing."

"That's too bad."

"Yes, too bad for your bloody submarines."

"No, Sergeant. Too bad for you."

"So, that's it!" Finnecker shouted, slapping his thigh and laughing uproariously. "Did you hear that, Lieutenant? They're going to make things unpleasant for us!"

"Let me tell you why I say it's too bad for you, Sergeant. It's because you may soon have to deal with a man much less patient than I. Good night, gentlemen."

General Oberg, commanding officer of the Gestapo in France, sat stiffly behind his desk. His tiny eyes shone behind his steel-rimmed spectacles, and the light from the chandelier reflected from his shaved scalp. He looked up sharply at Rasch, who had come to make his first report.

"Well, Commander, where do we stand?"

"Nothing yet, sir."

Rasch remained stiffly at attention, and Oberg did not ask

him to sit. The two men stared at each other for a moment. Neither experienced the slightest sympathy for the other. To Rasch, Oberg appeared to be exactly what he was said to be: brutal, determined, ruthless.

"Do you think you'll have results soon?" Oberg's voice was rough and tinged with irony.

"I'm going to try, *Herr General*. In any event, I still have thirteen days."

"Yes, thirteen days completely wasted," Oberg roared. "I can't understand what you're doing here! The Gestapo never meddles in naval affairs. That's your business, not ours. Our business is to interrogate people and make them talk—even if they're mute. That's our job! And we can do it better than you can!"

"It's a question of methods," Rasch began calmly, then immediately regretted having spoken. I must be out of my mind, he chided himself. He's going to write up a report on me and really screw me up.

"Yes, Commander Rasch, that's right," the general replied coldly. "But let me ask you something. Is it better to treat two men roughly, even brutally, in order to extract a secret which might save hundreds of lives—the lives of your friends in the submarines, especially—or should we handle them with kid gloves, not get the secret, and resign ourselves to the death of your men?"

"I cannot answer your question, *Herr General*," Rasch said in an icy tone.

"You do not *want* to answer, you mean. You disguise your hypocrisy under your ridiculous code of knightly honor. Make your headquarters open its eyes, for God's sake! Chivalry was for the Middle Ages! But remember that torture was raised to a fine art during those same Middle Ages.

"The end justifies the means. Always! You can't win if you let yourself be burdened with scruples. And with your attitude, you navy men, you're heading straight for disaster. Your U-boats will all end up at the bottom of the sea! All of them. Not one of them is going to come back! All, *kaput!*"

Rasch felt the blood drain from his face. With a tight grip on his mounting rage, he interrupted Oberg's tirade. "Sir, these are matters which should be taken up directly with Grand Admiral Doenitz," he said calmly. "I am merely obeying my orders. Do I have your permission to go, sir?"

Oberg, in his fury, had sprung to his feet. Now he fell back into his chair and dismissed Rasch with a gesture of his hand. "Go," he said. "Go to the devil, for all I care." Rasch was at the door when he added: "Tomorrow, here in my office, at the same time. And with the same results, I'm sure."

Rasch questioned the prisoners the next afternoon, and again late at night. The two British airmen smoked more of his cigarettes, talked endlessly and openly about football, about their families, about their old girl friends and their drinking bouts. But when the subject of radar arose, they smiled and smirked and remained silent.

Rasch left them at 2 o'clock in the morning and had his driver drop him off at the Schéhérazade. He sat alone at a table and ordered a bottle of very expensive, very bad champagne. Then he opened his notebook and began to read the information which he would use to write his final report as soon as he returned to Berlin:

"9. The prisoners were not happy to see me. They accused me of barging in on them at all hours of the day and night.

"10. Our relations seemed better today. Pittwall and I discussed literature and painting. He's passionately fond of classical music. Even Finnecker is less resentful now.

"11. I saw the British airmen five times today, the last visit being at 11 P.M. I brought a bottle of cognac, and we got drunk and sang some songs together. The guards were flabbergasted. The prisoners still refuse to talk about their radar.

"12. A stormy meeting with General Oberg. He was furious about the cognac last night. He demanded that I turn the prisoners over to him. I refused.

"13. Since I am getting nowhere, Oberg's resentment grows stronger with each passing day. Today, he made me take a Gestapo captain along when I visited the prisoners. Needless to say, they were not happy about this. They still don't realize what they're facing if they don't talk soon. I'm exhausted, and I'm beginning to be discouraged.

"14. They're leading me around in circles. I'm aware of it, of course. Even so, they talk freely in my presence, and I have the impression that they are more trusting and less arrogant.

"15. I've finally convinced Oberg that his Gestapo captain was ruining my chances of finding out what we want to know. Pittwall is sick in bed with a fever. I talked to Finnecker alone, but he told me absolutely nothing, except what we already know: that men and material in large quantities are being concentrated in the British Isles. When I said, 'Our submarines have cut off your supply lines,' he answered proudly: 'You think so, do you? You'd drop dead if you knew how much we've already unloaded in men and material!' Finnecker is not very intelligent, but he is very stubborn. Once more, it is obvious that it is useless to try to interrogate the prisoners separately. When they're apart, they're on guard even more than when they're together.

"16. Oberg is in a rage. He is a really vicious man. Sometimes I have the feeling that he's a greedy cat eager to eat the mice after playing with them for a while. Finnecker talked to me today about the long-range, four-engine planes being delivered by the Americans. He boasted about their maneuverability and their armor. And he dwelt at length on the amount of rations that they carry. Like many very thin people, Finnecker thinks only of eating.

"17. Finally! Today, for the first time, the two prisoners—Pittwall is well again—talked to me about their radar. I don't know what to think of what they told me. Our conversation went something like this:

"'We Germans also have radar,' I said.

"'Ours is better,' Pittwall answered quite seriously.

"'I can't deny that,' I said. 'But you can't be far ahead of us. I'm sure that our scientists will catch up with yours.'

"'I doubt it,' Pittwall told me. Then he said: 'Your radar operates on a wave length of 2.5 meters.'

"I said that it did.

"'Well,' he went on, 'ours operates on wave lengths that you know nothing about.'

"'You mean even less than 2 meters?'

"'Much less.' Pittwall smiled, delighted at my incredulity.

"'Less than a meter?'

"He laughed and said: 'Much less.'

"'What is it, then?'

"Dick Finnecker had not said a word so far. Now, he said: 'Your scientists will tell you—as soon as they find out.'

"I could have strangled him.

"18. I told Oberg about my partial success, and he seemed less contemptuous and less angry than usual. But he said: 'That doesn't really tell us much.' Our meeting lasted only a few minutes. When I left, he told me: 'Those men are going to be turned over to us in two days. I'm willing to let you set the stakes if you want to bet that, by the end of the first night we have them, we'll know everything that there is to know about British radar.' During the afternoon, I visited the prisoners again. Because of what had happened during the previous meeting, I was accompanied on this occasion by Captain Hamm of the *Kriegsmarine,* and by a Luftwaffe captain. I did not like the idea of the three of us confronting the prisoners, but I was too tired to protest. Our interrogation of the prisoners got nowhere.

"19. At 2 A.M., I had the prisoners awakened and brought to the sitting room which had become our regular meeting place. They were still half asleep when they entered, and I immediately sensed a certain coolness on their part. I told them that I had only two days left with them, and that, after that, they would be in for some hard times. Pittwall answered, in a serious tone, that he thought he understood what I was saying, and he thanked me for telling them. As for Finnecker, he seemed to understand nothing at all, and stood there yawning.

"At 7 A.M., the telephone rang. I jumped out of bed and answered. It was an officer from headquarters, telling me that the Luftwaffe base at Oberursel had in its possession a radar which had been salvaged from a British plane shot down over Rotterdam. The only problem was that the device was not in working order. I was very much excited by this information, and I asked the officer to have the device sent to me immediately at *Kriegsmarine* headquarters in Paris—explaining that I wanted it fixed so that, as much as possible, it would appear to be in perfect working order. I also asked him to notify Grand Admiral Doenitz and Admiral Stummel. Then I went back to bed. I did not visit the prisoners that day. Instead, I slept so soundly that I did not even hear Schnee when he came into my room and tried to wake me. He left me a note: 'Are you dead?'

"20. Oberg was furious with me for not having reported to him yesterday and said that he would report me to headquarters. I don't give a damn. Tomorrow, my job will be over—one way or the other. I didn't tell Oberg about the radar apparatus I'm expecting. I had dinner with Schnee. He is extremely impatient for our new U-boat, the XXI, to become operational. He's convinced that it will revolutionize submarine warfare and allow us to regain control of the Atlantic."

On December 21, an official vehicle pulled away from *Kriegsmarine* headquarters on the Place de la Concorde, sped up the Champs-Élysées and around the Arc de Triomphe. Hermann Rasch was in the rear seat. Next to him on the seat was a cardboard box.

When the automobile pulled up in the Avenue Foch, Rasch hurried up the steps of the house carrying the box. He set it down carefully on a table in the sitting room.

Pittwall and Finnecker were led in a few seconds later. Like senior members of a private club, they went immediately to their accustomed chairs. As soon as they were seated, Rasch beamed at them and said, as lightly as he could: "My friends, I'm happy to tell you that there won't be any more questions!"

"Well, we're going to miss you," Pittwall answered, making an effort to match Rasch's tone.

"You've given up trying to make us talk?" Finnecker asked.

"It has nothing to do with you," Rasch said. "Do you know what's in this box?"

The two men looked at him in puzzlement, and Finnecker's enormous eyebrows rose in a perfect arch as Rasch slowly opened the box and lifted out the radar.

"Good Lord!" Pittwall said. "You've got it!"

"Yes, we have it, finally. All we have to do now is take it apart and examine it. Then we'll know exactly how it works."

"Where did you get it?" Finnecker asked roughly.

"We salvaged it from one of your planes. Now listen to me. I'm going to make you a proposal." Rasch walked away from the table and stood silent for a moment. He was about to play his trump card, and he was aware that everything depended upon the next few minutes and upon the ruse—suspiciously similar to blackmail, he knew—that he was about to employ. The deceit involved, and particularly his role as a virtual blackmailer, aroused a feeling of profound self-contempt in Rasch; but he knew that there was no other way to obtain the information so vital to the survival of the submarine service.

"You know that it will be only a few hours, or a few days at most, before our scientists know the wave length of your radar device. In any case, it will be too late for you. Believe me; I'm being absolutely frank with you. We've spent the last two weeks together, and I've come to know you. I'm not out of sympathy with what you're trying to do. I hope that, if our circumstances were reversed, I'd behave in the same way. That's why I'm telling you that unless I can tell my superiors tonight that you've given us the information we want, you're going to be turned over to interrogators who are totally free of scruples."

"You mean your bloody Gestapo?" Finnecker asked.

"Yes."

The two Englishmen looked at each other. Rasch saw that, for the first time, they were worried. "Till now," he explained, "you were safe, because you were in the Navy's custody. I want you to understand that there's no longer any point in refusing to talk. It's not only useless, but it's also going to make things extremely unpleasant for you. Before we had this device," Rasch went on, his voice earnest and sympathetic, "your attitude was perfectly correct. But now it's pointless. There's no longer anything for you to hide."

There was a profound silence in the room. Rasch was afraid that the two men would hear his heart pounding in his chest. He kept repeating to himself, like a litany: "God, let them talk! God, let them talk!"

"If we tell you what you want to know," Pittwall asked, cracking his knuckles, "what are you going to do with us?"

"A *Kriegsmarine* vehicle will take you immediately to a prisoner-of-war camp. I'm not telling you that you'll have an easy time of it there; but at least you'll be safe from—from other things."

Dick Finnecker walked over and looked closely at the radar device. Finally, he asked: "Could the lieutenant and I talk this over, alone?"

Rasch nodded. He picked up the radar and left the room. As soon as he appeared in the hallway, the SS guard asked: "Shall I take them away, Commander?"

"No. Not yet."

Rasch lighted a cigarette and began pacing back and forth before the door, conscious that what was being said at that very moment would determine whether hundreds of his comrades in the service would live or die. He looked at his watch. Five minutes had passed. That was long enough, Rasch decided. Then, suddenly, he had an overwhelming desire to put off finding out whether his trick had worked. "That's stupid," he told himself. "Waiting isn't going to solve anything." He dropped his cigarette on the floor, crushed it with his heel, and walked to the door. He handed the radar to the guard, saying, "I'll pick it up when I leave."

When Rasch entered the room, Pittwall was stroking his mustache nervously and Finnecker was standing with his hands in his pockets.

"Well?" Rasch asked.

"Do I have your word of honor," Pittwall asked, "that we won't be turned over to the Gestapo?"

"I give you my word as an officer."

Pittwall looked at Finnecker, who nodded.

"Ten."

"Ten what?" Rasch asked, thinking that this might be a trick.

"Ten. Our radar operates on a centimetric band, and the length of its waves is ten centimeters."

"But that's impossible," Rasch exclaimed.

"It may be impossible for you," Pittwall said drily, "but that's what it is, nonetheless. Our scientists have perfected a precision instrument."

"How does it work?"

"A rotating antenna picks up even the smallest objects and reproduces them with extreme accuracy on a screen. As soon as one of your U-boats surfaces within range of the device, it shows up as a dark spot on the screen."

"One more question, Lieutenant," Rasch said. "Are all your planes and escort ships equipped with this device?"

"All the bombers and fighters of the air branch of Coastal Command have it. So far as ships are concerned, I think that the new ones have it."

Rasch was silent, wondering how it would ever be possible to discover a means of neutralizing such a device. The sound of Finnecker clearing his throat brought him back to reality. He looked up. "Gentlemen, the time has come to say goodbye. A vehicle from headquarters will be here for you in a few minutes. I wish you both the best of luck."

The three men looked at one another, astonished to discover

that they were genuinely moved. They shook hands, and Rasch left the room.

He was going down the stairs when the guard called out, "Sir! You've forgotten this thing." Rasch took the "radar" and left. An hour later, he was on the telephone to Berlin.

Grand Admiral Doenitz, now that he knew the reason for the loss of over a hundred U-boats in the past three months, lost no time in calling a meeting of his staff in the *Am Steinplatz* building.

"Our scientists have been telling us," he told his officers, "that a centimetric detection device was absolutely impossible. Well, we have proof that they were completely in error. This does not mean that we're in a position to neutralize that device; but at least we now know what is involved, and we won't be working in the dark.

"We also know why the devices that were supposed to detect the detectors—I'm referring to the Metox, of course, and to the Borkum—were ineffective."

Doenitz turned to Captain Meckel, his communications officer. "What, in your opinion, can we use to counter this centimetric radar?"

"We have two devices, the 'Fly' and the 'Mosquito,' which, in a few months' time, will be operational. They'll be able to register any detection signal, from the high-frequency range to decimetric waves. With these devices, our submarines will know immediately if they've been detected, and they'll have sufficient warning to be able to escape."

"Yes," Doenitz murmured, "they'll be able to escape. But they won't be able to attack. What I had most feared has been realized, beginning last July. Enemy shipyards are turning out ships faster than we are sinking them. Until this past spring, we were sinking 600,000 tons of shipping every month. Since the beginning of fall, that average has fallen to 180,000 tons per month. This year, the enemy has lost only 300 vessels—1,842,000 tons of shipping.

"I'm convinced that we have only one chance of recapturing the initiative; and that is for the *Walter* submarine to become operational."

The grand admiral seemed suddenly old, tired. The lines on his face seemed to deepen as the officers of his staff watched.

He went on in a low voice: "I had expected to have our first type XXIs in service by spring. However, the bombings have upset our production schedule, and now I am told that the *Walter* submarine—the only means we have to make the Grey Wolves invincible once more—will not be ready until the end of the year.

"Gentlemen, only God knows what is going to happen between now and then."

36

Some 4,000 Allied combat ships and more than 1,600 aircraft were now patrolling the Atlantic. Throughout the Atlantic, confrontations between the U-boats and the Allied patrols became more and more one-sided. During the first two years of the war, the Grey Wolves had come and gone as they wished, with impunity, anywhere in the Atlantic. After an attack, they remained to observe the death agony of the victim; and, occasionally, even to film it. By the beginning of 1944, however, the only way in which they could attack was to fire their torpedoes from afar and trust to luck for a strike. They did not dare remain in the vicinity to see whether the target had been hit, but dived immediately to make their escape.

There was no longer any doubt as to who ruled the Atlantic. And, to make matters worse, the new T-5 torpedoes, far from tilting the balance in favor of the U-boats, constituted an additional threat to their survival; for it happened not infrequently that a T-5 circled back and struck the submarine which had fired it. The most distressing factor, however, was the long hours of anguish and terror which the Grey Wolves were compelled to endure as they lay, motionless and silent, on the bottom while

Allied ships and aircraft prowled endlessly above in search of them.

In his log, Peter Cremer noted:

"It is impossible for us to get near a convoy during the daylight hours. Most of the time, we lay on the bottom, listening, our lights extinguished in order to save our batteries, and with all of us remaining in our bunks to conserve oxygen. One can imagine that state of our nerves as we lay there in darkness, listening, without a moment's relief, to the ping-ping of the sounder, the explosions of the bombs and depth charges, and the vibrations of the destroyers' propellers overhead. We live in a state of constant terror—so much so that I sometimes fear for our sanity. I wonder how long the men will be able to hold up in this situation. There is terrific tension aboard, and no way to relieve it. I keep waiting for them to crack, and I can't blame them if they do.

"Our garbage is beginning to give off a pestilential stink, and the level of carbon monoxide is alarming. We now stay submerged twenty hours a day. This is a great trial for us. So as not to be detected, and in order to give the men some relief, I frequently disconnect the electric sounder, the gyroscope, and the Metox, so that they are at least spared its continual noise. In consequence, we often do not know where we are, and we are in constant danger of hitting bottom and damaging our propellers and rudders, or of springing a leak. It is hard for someone who has not experienced it to realize how much we are suffering."

With the Allies dominating the Atlantic, the chances of survival of the Grey Wolves in combat were now one out of five. Before, they had been three in five.

The U. S. Army truck sped through the Arizona desert, maintaining its speed despite the bumps and potholes in the dirt road. It slowed only when it drew near the highway intersection; and then the stacks of logs and the sacks of "sawdust" in the back began to stir, and two heads appeared.

"Now!"

Clumsily, the men extricated themselves from the truck's cargo, then crawled on all fours toward the tailgate and looked out. There was no one to be seen. Without hesitating, they climbed over the tailgate and jumped to the ground, rolling in the dust. They lay still until the truck turned onto the highway and accelerated.

The two men stood up and dusted off their gray and maroon uniforms. They began walking, frequently glancing over their shoulders. When they reached the highway, they turned southward and walked more briskly. The sweat poured down their faces, but they did not slow their pace or speak.

After three hours of steady walking, a city appeared in the distance, its outlines blurred by a light, late-afternoon fog. The men exchanged a smile, but did not stop until they reached a sign reading: CITY LIMITS—*PHOENIX*.

"Well, here we are," August Maus sighed, wiping his forehead.

"Yes," Guggenberger replied, "but that was the easy part. The trick will be to get away with it."

The two men looked at the low houses, colorful stores, and billboards lining the street. "There are houses," Maus commented, "but there's nothing behind them. Just desert."

They entered Phoenix at 6 P.M., and a few minutes later they were standing before a ticket window in the small railway station.

"Two tickets to Nogales," Maus said.

"I'll sell them to you," the agent—an elderly man—replied without looking up from the counter, "but there's no train until tomorrow morning."

"I thought there was an evening train."

"Sorry. The schedule was changed two days ago."

Maus and Guggenberger looked at each other in consternation. By morning, the guards at Camp Papago would have discovered that they were missing, and the search would be on.

"Is there a waiting room?" Maus asked.

Still without looking up, the agent replied: "Not unless you want to build one yourself, sonny."

They walked outside and considered going to a bar for a drink, but decided that it would be too risky. If they got involved in conversation with anyone, it would be obvious that they were foreigners. Their English was far from perfect.

"This really is a crock of shit," Guggenberger fumed. "What are we going to do now?"

Maus, the more levelheaded of the two, thought for a moment. "It seems to me," he said, "that the best thing would be to wait for darkness and then try to hitch a ride on a truck."

"That sounds like a good idea," Guggenberger agreed. "But what are we going to do until then? It looks like everyone in this place has a car; and everybody knows everybody else. Two strangers on foot are going to look very suspicious, don't you think?"

After some discussion, Maus and Guggenberger decided to find a place to hide until nightfall—which, given what they had seen of Phoenix, would not be easy. They were standing in the main street, and the only street, of the town. There were few pedestrians, and the occasional shopkeepers standing on their stoops looked at them with undisguised curiosity. A few of them said "hello" to the two German officers; to which Maus and Guggenberger mumbled responses. They walked to the end of the street, and then turned around and walked back, looked around desperately for somewhere to hide.

"It would be just my luck to get caught now," Maus grumbled, dragging his feet, his hands thrust deep into his pockets. Since his capture on August 21 of the preceding year, he had thought of nothing but escape. But he had had to wait for a favorable opportunity, and until he had been transferred to Camp Papago, the circumstances were never precisely right. He had spent two weeks aboard the aircraft carrier *Core*, after being picked up in the Atlantic by a destroyer. After disembarking at Norfolk, Virginia, he had learned that three of his crew had died since the rescue, all of chlorine poisoning: Ackermann, the engineer, and two seamen.

Maus had then been separated from his men and taken by train to an interrogation center near Washington. He was there for three weeks, during which practically every day was taken up by questioning. He discovered, to his surprise, that the Americans knew more than he did about U-boats—their codes, organization, and supply methods at sea, and even about such private matters as where Maus spent his vacations before the war.

In mid-September, Maus had been transferred to a transient center in Tennessee. There, he was delighted to find one of his best friends, Captain Guggenberger, who had been one of the "guinea pigs," along with Cremer and Kuppish, testing Doenitz' new antiaircraft weapons. Earlier, Guggenberger had been reported missing, and Maus had assumed the worst. The camp was crowded with bored Luftwaffe and Wehrmacht officers and men, and Maus had been reunited with his own crew from the U-185.

One morning, all submarine personnel were ordered to fall in, and then were driven to a railway station and put on a train to Camp Papago. Maus had been hard pressed to hide his excitement once he arrived in Arizona. He often awoke in the middle of the night and talked for hours with Guggenberger about escaping. The Mexican border was only 150 miles away; and Maus had friends in Mexico who would help the two men board a neutral ship bound for Europe.

Both Maus and Guggenberger had taken their men into their confidence. It was necessary to do so, since the men had access to the civilian clothing stowed in the wardrobe of the camp theater. Some of the seamen passed onto the two officers the money given them by American guards in exchange for small personal services rendered; and this was the money that Maus had intended to use to buy train tickets to Nogales. It was only a few miles from Nogales to the border, and Maus and Guggenberger intended to finish the journey on foot, under cover of darkness.

When the army truck had arrived at Camp Papago to deliver part of its load of wood, the seamen on loading detail had concealed the two officers in the back of the truck.

And now, Maus reflected, they were stranded in a small town, surrounded by openly curious people—all because of a change in a train schedule. A Godforsaken place, where it was warm even during the winter, and where there wasn't even a decent place for a man to hide.

"Let's walk to the end of the street again," Maus suggested, "then we'll go into a drugstore and get a cold drink and a sandwich. Maybe we'll even feel better; and it will be better than having all these people staring at us."

"What if we don't have enough money left to get to Nogales?"

"I was just thinking about that. It might be better for us not to go to Nogales now. It's too close to the border, and once they found out that we've escaped they're going to be watching the border. Even though it'll mean more walking, I think we'd better get off the train before it gets to Nogales."

"You're probably right," Guggenberger said. "In this heat, I could use a cold beer."

They crossed the street and passed in front of a drugstore.

"I can taste it already," Guggenberger said, smacking his lips.

"Didn't you see the sign inside the store?" Maus asked.

"What sign?"

"They don't sell beer. Only milk and lemonade. What a country!"

They had walked a few hundred feet past the drugstore when Guggenberger whispered: "Let's get out of sight. A police car is coming this way."

As luck would have it, there was an alleyway only a few feet ahead of them. At the end of the alley was a fence. "Come on," Maus said, "let's go over the fence."

They had just ducked into the alleyway and began to run when the police car screeched to a halt behind them, blocking the entry. An enormous man, wearing a cowboy hat and with a star pinned to his massive chest, got out of the automobile and shouted: "Hey, you! Stop!"

Maus glanced over his shoulder and saw a revolver in the sheriff's hand. Next to the car, a deputy stood holding a carbine.

The two Germans froze.

"Where do you gentlemen live?" the sheriff asked.

Maus, who barely reached the officer's shoulder, looked up into his face, swallowed, and said hoarsely: "Tucson."

"Tucson, huh? Nice place. I guess you've got some sort of identification?"

"No. We forgot it," Guggenberger blurted out.

The sheriff motioned toward the car with the muzzle of his pistol. "You don't talk English too bad, for a couple of Germans," he said. "Let's go. All aboard for Camp Papago. The holiday's over, boys."

They climbed into the car and the deputy started the motor. "Sir," Maus said in his most polite voice, "before taking us back to the camp, do you think we could stop somewhere for a drink? You'd be our guests, of course, you and your deputy."

"All right. But if you try anything, young feller, I'm going to have to drill you full of holes." And to give substance to his threat, the sheriff waved his pistol toward Maus' stomach.

The police car stopped in front of a small bar, and the four men went in and took seats at the bar. Maus and Guggenberger each bought a round of Bourbon. The bartender asked for their autographs, and then bought everyone a round on the house. When they left the bar, the two prisoners of war felt considerably better.

An hour later, Maus was in a tiny cell. Next to him, in an equally small cell, was Guggenberger. They would be there for fourteen days on bread and water, the punishment decreed by the camp commander.

The two recaptured prisoners were not unduly resentful of their punishment. They consoled themselves periodically with a flask of Bourbon, a gift from the sheriff.

At approximately the same time that August Maus was serving time on bread and water, his fiancée was informed by the Red Cross that her future husband had survived the sinking of the *U-185* and was now a prisoner of war in the United States.

37

The sirens signaled the all-clear over Flensburg. New ruins were now piled on those of yesterday and new columns of black smoke, occasionally broken by bursts of orange flame, rose toward the lead sky of April. Ghostlike figures picked their way cautiously through the smoke and dust and the mountains of debris toward the gutted ruins of apartment buildings. Occasionally, the wailing of ambulances and fire engines was heard; and when it grew faint in the distance, there was only the roar of the flames, the crash of crumbling walls, and screams of pain and terror.

Wolf Shafer emerged from the concrete shelter of the base. He felt on his face the biting, hot air which follows a bombing. His eyes teared, and he began to cough.

Around him, the base was a scene of destruction. The barracks were in ruins, the crane and hoists scattered about like toys, automobiles and trucks overturned. Here and there, wounded men dragged themselves through the debris, groaning.

Shafer, coughing, began to walk as rapidly as he could toward the docks. Shafer's first impression when he arrived was that an earthquake or a tidal wave had struck. Torpedo boats, speedboats, and larger vessels of various sizes and tonnages were floating on their sides or half sunk with their bows toward the sky. And, on all sides, there were columns of acrid black smoke and constant explosions.

Then, Shafer saw it. The *U-368* was lying on its side, moving in the swell. There was a gaping hole in its side through which tons of water had poured. It was like a giant animal, mortally wounded.

"The bastards," Shafer muttered as he ran toward the *U-368*'s pier, climbing over piles of gravel and debris, until he stood a few feet away from the submarine on which, two days later, he was supposed to sail.

He looked around. At other piers, the *U-368*'s sister ships had suffered the same fate. Shafer was not surprised. Germany had only a hundred sheltered piers for her U-boats, scattered over several ports. They were all occupied; and the other submarines were thus exposed constantly to the Allied bombings which every day were becoming more intensive.

Shafer dug through the rubble and pulled out a large plank. He dragged it to the edge of the pier and, with an effort, raised it and let one end fall onto the *U-368*. He walked across the plank and stood on the starboard flank of the vessel. Moving cautiously, so as not to slip on the oily hull, he made his way toward the conning tower, which was listing at a 45° angle. He leaned over, but was unable to make an estimate of damages because of the cloudy water. He stood upright and steadied himself against the periscope superstructure. His hand moved caressingly over the smooth steel. It was as cold as death. He looked up at the sky, at the clouds moving rapidly against the heavens as though fleeing the sight of such devastation. Tears ran down his cheeks, and Wolf Shafer wept without shame. He wept over his dead ship; but above all he wept for his country, whose final defeat he saw now looming inexorably.

In the month of April 1944 twenty-nine Grey Wolves had disappeared. To submariners, the Atlantic had become a vast, gray tomb. "On the graves of seamen, roses do not bloom," Doenitz' men sang as they sailed out on missions from which they knew there would probably be no return. "And on sailors' graves, there is no edelweiss."

June 6, 1944. A sergeant, a large white MP painted on his helmet, knocked politely and then entered the small room.

"Commander August Maus?"

Maus looked up from his bunk and put down his book.

"Would you follow me, please?"

Lazily, Maus rose, tucked in his shirttail, and asked: "What's the matter?"

"There's someone to see you."

Maus could not understand who would possibly visit him in Camp Papago. He glanced through the open window. The large open field, which served as a recreation area, was deserted. It was a sign that the heat outside was intolerable. He decided not to wear his jacket.

He followed the sergeant outside and along the barracks, walking close to the building so as to remain in the shade. When they reached the camp headquarters, the sergeant opened the door and Maus entered. The outer office was stifling. Two clerks, their desks in the sunlight from the windows, tried to work as sweat poured down their faces and onto the papers before them. Their uniforms were drenched. No one at Camp Papago, guards no more than prisoners, could find relief from the summer heat, and everyone spent the days in a state of subhuman torpor.

Maus saw a man in civilian clothes sitting in a corner. His face was pink in the heat, and his hair was plastered to his head with sweat. Yet, he wore a jacket and vest, and a prim bow tie protruded from the wings of his starched collar. My God, Maus wondered, how can he stand it? He felt rivulets of sweat running down his back.

"This is Commander Maus," the sergeant informed the man. Then he disappeared—doubtless to get a cold beer, Maus reflected enviously.

The civilian rose and made a polite bow. "I belong to the Swiss Red Cross," he said, extending his hand. "I am attached to the embassy in Washington."

Both men smiled.

"I think we could both use something to drink," the man said.

"A good idea."

The Red Cross delegate spoke to an orderly in English. Maus noted that his accent was distinctly British. Then he told Maus to take a chair, and sat down opposite him. "Let's wait until we have our drinks," he said smilingly, "before we discuss why I'm here."

The visitor's typical Swiss-German accent amused Maus somewhat. He tried to guess, somewhat apprehensively, what could have happened to cause a representative of the Red Cross to come from Washington to Arizona. He had more or less decided that it must be bad news about a member of his family in Germany when the man, alert to the expression on Maus' face, raised his hand reassuringly. "Don't be concerned, Commander," he said. "The reason for my visit is that I am bringing good news."

Maus inhaled deeply. Good news. What on earth could it be?

The orderly brought two glasses on a tray, and a bottle of light beer. The men filled their glasses and took a swallow. Then the Swiss opened his briefcase and, still smiling, removed a sheet of paper. "There is a young lady in Germany," he explained, "who is very impatient to have you sign this instrument." He held out the paper.

Maus took it and read rapidly. It was a marriage contract issued by the office of the Mayor of Berlin. In addition to the official seals and signatures, Maus noted that it had also been signed by Gabriella, his fiancée. He was familiar with the contents of the document, which had been designed to facilitate the union of servicemen abroad or at sea with their fiancées at home. All it needed was his own signature, and he and Gabriella would legally be man and wife.

"If you sign," the Red Cross delegate explained, "I will send a telegram to your wife tomorrow, from the Swiss Embassy, informing her that everything is in order. The instrument itself— as well as a copy of it, since we never know what will happen to mail nowadays—will be sent to our embassy in Berlin. From there, it will be sent to the mayor's office, and they will notify your wife of its safe arrival. Now, Commander, are you willing to sign this document and to enter into matrimony with Gabriella?"

"Certainly!"

"Are you willing to become her husband, for better or for worse?"

"The worse is now. I'm hoping that the better will come later."

A few days earlier, a peculiar ceremony had taken place in the Nuptial Hall of the Berlin City Hall. The enormous room was a shambles. Its windows, destroyed by bombs, had been boarded over, and its walls and ceiling were cracked and peeling. Before a massive wooden table, a young woman was seated in a leather chair reserved for the bride. Next to her was a matching chair, that of the groom. On the seat of the latter, propped against the backrest, was a photograph of August Maus, in full uniform and wearing his decorations. To the mayor's question as to whether she would take *Kapitänleutnant zur See* August Maus as her lawful husband, Gabriella, her eyes brimming with tears, answered softly, "Yes."

"In order for the ceremony to be complete," the mayor concluded, "we must await the answer of the groom, who is not present. Please sign the register."

Gabriella rose and, her hand trembling, scrawled her name.

"Please sign also this paper, which you must take to the Swiss Embassy. It will be sent to Commander Maus. As soon as it is sent back, duly signed by him, you will be husband and wife."

The ceremony was over, and as the mayor rose, the air-raid warning sounded for the third time that morning.

At Camp Papago, August Maus had already received the congratulations of the American officers at the camp. The commanding officer had given permission for the submarine officers to organize a reception in the officers' mess to celebrate the marriage of their comrade. By way of exception, the Americans had supplied several bottles of California wine, some whiskey, beer, fruit juice, preserved fruit, and an assortment of sandwiches. The enlisted men had also been invited, and the reception was a great success. The voices of the men, singing and shouting, drowned out the roar of the electric fans.

Guggenberger raised his glass of Bourbon, its ice cubes clinking, and yelled drunkenly, "I propose a toast to Commander Maus! Today is a historic day for all of us!" A great hurrah rose in the room, and dozens of glasses were emptied. It was 6 P.M.

Five hours earlier, across the American continent and across the Atlantic, five thousand ships had dropped anchor off the coast of Normandy as four thousand planes passed overhead in majestic formation. The Allied invasion of France had begun.

38

Several days before, on June 1, 1944, Grand Admiral Doenitz made an entry in his operations journal: "It is particularly difficult for our submarines to determine the positions of ships and aircraft responsible for the protection of convoys. More than in any other branch of the service, the success we have enjoyed until now has been due to the spirit of our crews, a spirit characterized by aggressivity, tenacity, and self-sacrifice. Now, however, the chances of success are greatly reduced. Indeed, the odds are great that a submarine will not return from a mission. In these past few months, only 70 per cent of our U-boats have returned safely to base."

In January, Doenitz' headquarters had been moved to Koralle, a post, comprising an assembly of barracks, several miles from Berlin. This was done upon Hitler's insistence, because of Allied bombings of the capital. Hitler was convinced, on the basis of reports he had received, that the Allies were preparing to land somewhere on the Continent.

Now, that dreaded day had arrived and Doenitz, after much hesitation, had sent a message to the thirty Grey Wolves of the Landwirt Group (comprising fifteen U-boats, equipped with *Schnorchels* from Brest, and fifteen from Lorient and Saint Nazaire), which were assigned to challenge the colossal Allied invasion fleet. The message read:

"Submariners, every enemy ship being used for landing troops, even if it is carrying only fifty soldiers, is an opponent worthy of total commitment. You must attack, even when attacking exposes you to almost certain destruction.

"If you reach the main body of the landing fleet, you must attack regardless of factors such as shallow water or enemy mines. Nothing—*nothing*—must stop you.

"Every man and every weapon that the enemy is unable to put ashore diminishes his chances of success. In inflicting losses upon the enemy, a submarine accomplishes its most important mission and justifies its existence, even if it is destroyed in so doing."

During a visit from Admiral Godt, Doenitz, for the first time, showed signs of depression. He knew that his message would send men to their deaths. He also knew, although he did not acknowledge it, that the supreme sacrifice which he demanded of his crews would be in vain. There were times when he was vividly conscious of the loss of his two sons. Their death had affected him deeply. When Germany had been victorious, their sacrifice had seemed to serve some purpose. But now, it seemed useless, a waste.

During his visit, Godt commented that U-boats were Germany's only remaining means of achieving important successes with the loss of only a handful of men. The Army, in order to eliminate an equivalent amount of tanks, artillery, and men, would have to sacrifice an infinitely greater number of men.

"Yes," Doenitz replied. "And that is precisely why we must go on. We must go on, and continue to accept losses which are disproportionate to our successes—however difficult it may be for us to bear such losses. It requires a firmness of purpose, however, which I find it more and more difficult to muster."

During this conversation, the two men were walking in the camp grounds. Doenitz suddenly stopped short; and, in a voice inexpressibly sad and yet angry, he said to Godt: "If only they had listened to us! Since 1936, I've been begging them for a strong submarine fleet; but they ignored me. When war broke out, I asked for a massive program of submarine construction—but they wouldn't listen. Those fine gentlemen of the High

Command were all deaf. All they could think about was their senseless determination to win the war on the ground. Then I began fighting to get the *Walter* submarine; and, again, I was a voice in the wilderness!

"Now, we are going to have to pay the price for our mistakes. And it's a high price, Godt. A very high price. We have no right to make mistakes in war."

In May 1939, Doenitz had written to Hitler that the Third Reich was not ready to confront Great Britain. The Führer had answered that he would do all that he could to avoid war. "If not," he had added, "*finis Germaniae.*"

Now Doenitz recalled Hitler's prophetic words. "*Finis Germaniae,*" he told Godt. "We have reached that point."

The Landwirt Group, despite its daring, did not succeed in approaching the Allied landing fleet. The thirty U-boats had hardly left their base when a hundred and twenty bombers of the Coastal Command—the aces of Britain's antisubmarine warfare—attacked and forced the Grey Wolves to remain submerged. Even those U-boats equipped with *Schnorchels* were unable to break through the formidable aerial barrage, which was supported on the surface by groups of destroyers. And thus, Operation Landwirt, designed to blunt the strength of the attack which the Wehrmacht would have to counter on land, failed. By the time that Doenitz' headquarters had recalled the U-boats, their losses were extremely heavy: only ten of the submarines returned to base, and these had all been damaged, more or less severely, by depth charges, bombs, and machine-gun fire. The other twenty had been sunk.

June 26. The men of the *U-482* lay in their bunks, their pupils dilated in the feeble light of the emergency electrical system. Their nerves stretched to the breaking point as they listened to the explosions which shook their ship from stem to stern and reverberated through its narrow hull. For the past four hours, they had been required to remain virtually motionless in their bunks, breathing the recirculated air from which the carbon monoxide had been filtered by the air purifier. The engineer was in the center compartment, controlling the flow of air. With increasing frequency now, he was releasing oxygen into the air from the submarine's reserve supply. The U-boat's captain, Lieutenant Count von Maritschka, was also in the control room, sitting motionless at the base of the periscope. His arms were folded across his chest, and his face was a mask of calm indifference. From time to time, he raised his arm to wipe away the blood which flowed from his nostrils and mixed with the sweat. It required the greatest effort on his part to maintain his placid exterior. Within, his stomach was knotted in fear. He glanced at the boxes stacked the length of the bulkhead, then looked quickly away, as though to spare himself the sight of the 9,000 antiaircraft shells, 380,000 machine-gun rounds, and the dynamite that the U-482 was carrying to the besieged port of Cherbourg.

For four hours, a group of destroyers had been hunting the Grey Wolf to the northeast of the island of Alderney. They had already launched hundreds of depth charges—von Maritschka had stopped counting when he reached 300—which were considerably more powerful than those previously encountered by the U-boats. Every explosion made the submarine leap and bounce on the rocky bottom 750 feet beneath the surface; and every explosion could have detonated the U-482's cargo and blown the U-boat and its crew to smithereens. The explosions followed one another unremittingly, at well-spaced intervals, and lost themselves in the clanging of the destroyers' propellers whirling overhead.

Now, the lights dimmed still more. "The batteries are just about dead, Captain," the engineer reported.

Von Maritschka stood, swaying. His head pounded. He felt a wave of nausea sweep over him—the beginning of asphyxiation, he reflected. He looked around, trying to distinguish the features of his men in the semidarkness. Almost everyone was bleeding from the nose or ears. Some of the men, in order to keep from screaming, were biting on pieces of cloth. Some were only half conscious. A few of the men were holding their hands against their ears. Soon—it was only a matter of minutes, the captain knew—they would begin to lose consciousness entirely; and then, gradually, the U-482 would sink into the lethargy which precedes death.

Von Maritschka looked at his watch. It was 9:10 P.M. Soon, it would be dark at the surface.

Von Maritschka's head felt as though it were gripped by hot tongs. His vision was clouded. Through the thickening fog of unconsciousness, he was suddenly aware of a change. Something was different. He struggled to his feet, shook his head. Then he realized what it was. The noise of the destroyers' engines was growing fainter. They were going away.

"Periscope depth!" he shouted.

All heads turned toward the captain. Every man wondered: Would there be enough energy left in the batteries to rise to the surface? The indicator needle was almost at zero. But they heard the electric motors engage, faintly, almost inaudibly. The U-482 stirred on the bottom. Air whistled into its ballast tanks. The Grey Wolf, at the end of its strength, rose slowly toward the surface.

It had been several minutes now since anyone had heard propellers overhead. Luck, almost miraculous luck, had saved the desperate, bleeding, semiasphyxiated crew of the U-482 and pulled them back from the very edge of death. But they were too weak from lack of oxygen to rejoice. They performed their duties like robots, relying on instinct rather than on reason to propel their vessel to the surface.

"Periscope depth," the engineer announced weakly.

"Raise periscope and Schnorchel."

The long, cigar-shaped tube broke the surface. The "Tunis," a new detection-receiver, which registered the presence of enemy ships, was attached to its squat black head.

"Diesel engines, ahead," von Maritschka ordered, and the rhythmic pounding of the diesels began. The engines expelled their gases through the *Schnorchel* and, by the same means, gusts of fresh, life-giving air were drawn into the submarine. At the same time, by means of the tube, the batteries were being charged.

As life returned to the *U-482*, von Maritschka scanned the horizon. The sea was empty; and—another stroke of luck—calm as a lake. Von Maritschka sighed in relief. He recalled vividly his first mission with a *Schnorchel*. There had been a heavy swell, and, despite the ingenious efforts of the engineer, it had been impossible to keep the air vent open. In consequence, the submarine's oxygen had been quickly consumed by the diesels, and the diesel fumes, with a high content of carbonic acid, had filled the ship with a blackish smoke in a matter of minutes. He and his men had almost suffocated, and he had had to take the U-boat to the surface immediately.

Now, however, all went well. The *U-482*, carrying its dangerous cargo, skirted the coast and approached Cherbourg. Suddenly, just off Cape La Hague, the strident screech of the Tunis began. It was only a preliminary warning, an indication that there was an enemy ship in the distance; yet, von Maritschka saw a look of terror once more cross the faces of his men. He looked through the periscope and cursed softly. Then he ordered, "Rudder hard to port! Diesels, full speed ahead!"

He looked at the engineer and at his second officer, and, in a tone of utter discouragement, said: "We're heading home, God willing."

The two officers looked at him in amazement.

"The port is filled with Allied ships riding at anchor," the captain explained wearily. "The fact that there are so many of them is the only reason we haven't been picked up by their radar."

"What does it mean, Captain?"

"It means that Cherbourg has fallen. Probably the whole of Normandy is lost."

The American breakthrough at Avranches, on August 4, followed by the Allied landing in Provence on August 15, forced

Grand Admiral Doenitz to reach a decision which he had post-poned as long as he could. He would have to give up the Atlantic bases in France from which, for four years, the Grey Wolves had sailed out to prowl the sea and spread destruction among the Allied convoys.

Orders were given accordingly, and on September 23, the last submarine, the *U-267*, sailed from Saint Nazaire. After a difficult journey, most of which was spent submerged, the U-boat joined the flotillas based in Norway and at the German ports on the North Sea.

Ironically, it was in the same month of August that the largest convoy of the war, comprising 167 tankers and cargo ships, and carrying a million tons of equipment, crossed the Atlantic. It reached its destination without losing a single ship, although it was escorted by only seven destroyers. The Grey Wolves, it seemed, had lost their teeth.

Part Six

THE EXECUTION

39

It was 4:07 A.M., and the tiny fishing port a few miles from Bergen was covered by that blue darkness peculiar to Norwegian fjörds during the summer months. A German patrol had just completed its rounds and was returning to barracks. The soldiers had not seen a living soul during their tour of the village.

As the sound of the soldiers' boots grew fainter and faded into the distance, the silence was broken only by the sound of the sea lapping at the boats of the fishermen.

A man's head rose cautiously in one of the boats and scrutinized the shore. "All right," the man whispered in English. "The krauts are gone."

From within the boat, another man asked: "Are you sure?"

"Yes."

A third voice was heard. "All right, let's get moving. They're going to be here soon."

Three men, wearing dark clothes, their faces blackened with cork, rose and began stripping away the heavy fishing net which camouflaged the boat. Within a few minutes, the sleek lines of a British torpedo boat were revealed.

"Olgar, check the torpedo mechanism," the officer-in-charge said.

"I'm doing it now, Lieutenant."

"Good. Gursson, start loosing the lines, and get ready to start up the engines. Good Lord! I wonder what's keeping them?"

From the far end of the fjörd there came the muffled sounds, scarcely audible, of engines.

"There they are," Olgar said, cupping his hand to his ear. He was filled with a strange inner excitement mixed with indefinable fear.

"Thank God."

The engine noises were nearer now.

"They'll be here in twenty minutes."

"I've loosed the lines, Lieutenant. We should get the engines warmed up."

The lieutenant stared into the darkness. The sounds were growing steadily louder.

"Cast off," he ordered.

Gursson deftly disengaged the torpedo boat from the line of fishing craft where it had been hidden. As it drifted on its own momentum into open water, he leaped onto the bridge and turned the bow toward the entry of the port.

As though the German ships had increased their speed, the roaring of their engines was now rapidly growing louder and echoing along the cliffs surrounding the fjörd.

"I think they'll be here in two or three minutes, don't you, Gursson?"

"Yes, sir."

"You understand exactly what you're supposed to do? As soon as the krauts are in front of us, we pull out."

"Don't worry, Lieutenant. I know."

"The torpedoes are O.K.?"

"Everything's ready, sir."

Several minutes passed.

"There they are!"

The long, low profile of a light cruiser suddenly appeared before them, followed, at 200 yards, by a lower, sleeker shape: a U-boat.

The three British seamen felt their hearts pounding. Their teeth clenched, their eyes squinting in the dim light, they watched the submarine draw nearer.

"For Christ's sake!" the lieutenant shouted. "The bastard's diving! Ahead, full speed! He's trying to get away!"

The roar of the torpedo-boat's engines cut through the night as it leaped ahead, raising a foaming wake. The distance between the two vessels narrowed rapidly, but already the U-boat's bow was under water. The lieutenant's hand tapped Olgar's back once, twice; and two torpedoes sped across the dark waters of the fjörd.

The watch aboard the light cruiser saw the wakes of the torpedoes, but he did not have time to give the alarm. An explosion echoed across the fjörd, and a column of water rose from the surface. When the water was calm once more, there was no trace of the U-240.

The British torpedo boat sped out of the fjörd and headed westward, toward the North Sea.

So far as discipline was concerned, Commander Harllfinger was known as a strict officer. Many of his fellow U-boat captains, for example, never secured the watertight doors separating the three compartments, even during an attack. It was their opinion that it had a demoralizing effect upon the crew to lock seamen in the forward and aft compartments, out of sight of the control room. To be sure, there was a risk involved. If there was a major leak in any one of the compartments, the entire ship would be flooded and everyone drowned unless the flow could be quickly sealed off.

Harllfinger was well aware of the effect upon morale of closing off the compartments, but he preferred to follow security regulations to the letter. Thus, when the U-240 was struck aft by the British torpedo and tons of water poured into the submarine, only the compartment containing the diesels and the electric motors was flooded. The center and forward compartments remained completely free of water.

Nonetheless, the U-240, without power and weighed down by the water she had taken on, sank. Or rather, it drifted downward, stern first, so gently that the men, who had been thrown to the deck by the explosion, were able to stand and move about, despite the steep angle, by holding on to any fixed object they encountered in the darkness. No one seemed yet to realize the seriousness of the situation. It had all happened in the twinkling of an eye, and the crew was still too shaken for the first signs of panic to make themselves known.

Only two minutes had passed since the torpedo had struck. It was 4:29 A.M.

When the first narrow beams from the men's flashlights passed over the disabled control panels, a man—Shafer recognized the voice of the navigator—shouted in terror: "We're sinking!"

From the forward compartment, cut off from the control room, there came shouts and cries for help. Then there was a violent impact. The shock resounded like a giant gong through the two compartments. The men were thrown to the deck once more, clutching their ears. They felt as though they were imprisoned inside a giant drum.

Shafer turned his beam onto his watch. It was 4:32 A.M.

At that moment, the *U-240* was plunged into a silence which was, if anything, more frightening than the impact itself. Silence, coupled with darkness. No one spoke. Then the shouts from the forward compartment began again, this time accompanied by a pounding on the door.

"Open it," Harllfinger ordered the navigator. "And for God's sake, stop trembling. That's an order!"

Wolf Shafer's voice, strong, vibrant, came out of the darkness. "We're not sinking any more. We must be resting on a rock. Let's not lose our heads. We may still be able to get out of this."

The engineer flashed his light on the main depth-indicator. It seemed to be working, and the needle oscillated gently over the figure "50." "If it's really 50 meters," he said, "we have a chance."

A dozen flashlights swept across the control panels. Harllfinger knew that he would have to make an immediate decision. It was 4:35 A.M.

"All right," he said, "everyone listen to me. Whether or not we can get out of this is going to depend on every man keeping his head. At this depth, we can abandon ship with our masks. But if even one man screws up, it's going to be the end for all of us. If you follow my orders exactly, we have a chance."

Harllfinger was silent, searching for the right words. His men crowded around him in the darkness, waiting for the "old man" to save them.

"Here's what we're going to do," Harllfinger went on. "The engineer will open the main hatch. Before any water comes down into this compartment, a huge bubble of air is going to rise to the surface very quickly. Three men will be able to rise with the bubble. They won't need masks. *But*—those three men are going to have to be very careful not to go through the hatch together. If they do, they're going to block the hatch, and that will be it so far as the rest of us are concerned.

"This is what the three men will do. I want them to climb the conning tower ladder one after the other and to hold on with all their strength. Then, when one man sees the man above him pulled out through the hatch by the bubble, he is to let go and let himself be pulled out.

"As to the three men—the first one has to be the engineer, since he knows how to get the hatch open in spite of the water pressure. We'll decide who the others will be later on."

Harllfinger looked around. In the darkness, he sensed rather than saw the tense, attentive faces of his crew.

"Now," he continued, "the rest of us are not going to have an easy time of it. We're going to have to wait till the center compartment is completely filled with water. Until then, absolutely no one is to move under any circumstances. When it is full, Lieutenant Shafer will release the buoy carrying the knotted rope to the surface—the rope that we're going to climb.

"Before we begin, I'd like to remind you of two things—things that our lives depend on. First, be careful, when you go up through the hatchway, not to hit the hatch. You could break your neck, or crack your skull. Second—this is very important, and requires that no one lose his head—remember to inflate your life belts very slowly, so that you won't rise too quickly. Otherwise, there's the danger that your lungs will burst because of the water pressure.

"That's all I have to say. Lieutenant Shafer will tell you in what order to leave the ship. I want you to go out in single file.

But I don't want you to go until you're certain that the man above you is already through the hatchway. I'm going to stand at the bottom of the ladder, and when I give you a shove on the back, I want you to go—and not before."

After a moment of silence, Harllfinger added: "And good luck, men."

It was 4:44 A.M. The men stood motionless and silent in the center compartment. Many of them trembled uncontrollably. No one could put out of his mind that, in a few minutes, he would be in the open water far below the surface, and that the slightest error would kill him. There was a universal and unreasoned urge to remain in the submarine and accept certain death rather than to face the terrifying prospect of the ascent to the surface. But no one gave in to that urge. The men had all reached that state of utter resignation which makes them incapable of doing anything other than following orders.

Wolf Shafer flashed his light over the faces of the crew. "You," he said, "you, then you . . ." Sometimes he skipped a man to return to him later. He knew the men well, their strength and their weaknesses. He also knew that in this situation the slightest hesitation, a split-second of panic, might well be fatal. Therefore, the order he established for the men to leave the ship followed a pattern. He interspersed the calm, stolid members of the crew with the more volatile and emotional ones, so that every man who might break at the last minute was both preceded and followed by men who could be relied upon to handle the situation. He had not forgotten to include Harllfinger in his calculations. As captain, of course, he would be the last man to leave the ship—the last of twenty-five; for the other seventeen members of the original crew were in the aft compartment, crushed under tons of water.

"Stüssen and Klein," Shafer said, "you'll go up with the engineer in the bubble." These two men, Shafer had surmised, were the two who might crack if they were forced to remain in the compartment while the sea poured in. He could see from their expressions how near to panic they were already.

The two men followed the beam of the flashlight and began to climb the ladder. The engineer was already at the top, directly under the hatch, waiting for Harllfinger to give the order.

"Shafer," Harllfinger said.

"Yes, Captain?"

"I want you to leave in the middle of the group."

"But, Captain—" Shafer began.

"Do as I say, Shafer," Harllfinger interrupted.

The second officer shrugged and took his place in line. A trembling voice behind him said hesitantly: "Lieutenant? Sir, I'm number thirteen. I have a feeling that if I'm thirteenth, I won't make it. Will you change places with me, sir? You don't mind?"

"All right, Altena," Shafer agreed, and let the sailor get ahead of him in line.

"Put on your masks," Harllfinger ordered.

It was 4:56 A.M.

Harllfinger took his place at the foot of the ladder. "Engineer," he shouted, "open the hatch!"

The water that came through the hatch at first was no more than a gentle flow as it struck the deck. The men watched it in terror as it began slowly to spread. "Good," Shafer thought to himself. "It means that the engineer was able to get the hatch open."

Then, suddenly, the flow became a roaring cataract pouring through the hatch and into the compartment, swirling, foaming, rising with incredible speed to the men's ankles, knees, chest, and finally covering them entirely. The more nervous of the men instinctively pressed forward toward the hatch to escape as quickly as possible from the nightmare.

Shafer unexpectedly felt Harllfinger's hand on his back. He gripped the ladder and pulled himself upward, straining against the mass of water pressing against his shoulders. As he reached the hatch opening, he felt an irresistible force drawing him upward. Clutching the mouthpiece of his oxygen mask between his teeth, he looked up and turned in order to remain squarely in the center of the opening immediately above his head.

Shafer was barely through the hatch when he realized, in terror, that he had not remembered to take hold of the knotted white rope intended to mark the decompression stages to be observed on the way to the surface. He looked about frantically; but the blackness was impenetrable. He reached out with his right hand. Almost immediately he lost his footing and his left hand released the ladder. He was drawn upward and crashed with great force against the rim of the hatch. The pain was so sudden and so intense that he was certain his hip had been splintered.

At the same time, the fingers of his right hand closed around the rope. He felt the panic subside. Carefully, he allowed a trickle of air into his life jacket, then shot upward before he could get a firm grip on the rope. His ears ached sharply, and he felt that his skull would burst. He inhaled greedily through his tube, then once more fed a small amount of air into the life jacket. Again, he seemed to leap toward the surface, and he was certain that his eardrums would burst. The rope sped through his fingers, and it seemed forever before he came to a stop.

He felt a body brush past him on the rope. Someone was inflating his life jacket more rapidly and was rising faster. Too fast, Shafer knew, but he did not care. The pain in his head was so intense, particularly in his ears, that he was almost past caring about himself. He told himself that he would never have the strength to make it to the surface.

Then, suddenly, he was overwhelmed with terror. He was convinced that his oxygen tube was twisted shut and that he would drown. He shook his head in the water, attempting to disengage the tube, forcing himself to resist the temptation to remove the mouthpiece. Even in his panic, he was conscious that this would mean certain death. Then, when it seemed that his lungs would certainly burst, he felt air pouring through the tube. He realized, with almost hysterical relief, that as he clutched the rope, he had squeezed the tube between his forearm and his chest, cutting off his supply of air.

He was about to let more air into his life jacket when he stopped short. "No," he told himself, "I can't do it. My head and my eardrums won't be able to take another jump like that last one. I'll just have to go up the rope."

He had no idea of how far it was to the surface, how long he would have to remain in the chilling, numbing water. He did not know, and he did not care. His mind was occupied with a single thought; he must continue to climb, slowly, carefully, so as not to worsen the pain in his skull. But the pain was stronger than he. He felt a wave of warmth flowing from his ears and nose, and it was as though a thousand white-hot needles had pierced his skull. Instinctively, he released the rope and raised his hands to his head, pressing them against his ears. And, immediately, he shot toward the surface.

Shafer opened his mouth, spat out the mouthpiece, tried to scream. At that moment, he reached the surface and was thrown 3 feet out of the water. Before he fell back, he yelled, a long, bloodcurdling, inhuman scream.

After the explosion which had sunk the *U-240*, the light cruiser had come to a full stop and lowered her lifeboats to pick up survivors. One of the boats was only a few yards from the spot where Shafer surfaced. He lay screaming and splashing in the water when he felt strong hands grasp his arms. He was pulled from the water and put down gently in the bottom of the boat. A sailor held out a bottle of rum. Shafer shook his head and sat up. Blood was dripping from his nose and his ears, and he was gasping for breath.

He looked around. Next to him, there were two bodies. He touched them, but they did not move. He did not know whether they were alive or dead. He looked at the water around the boat. He could see lifeless bodies here and there in the fjörd, kept afloat by life jackets. But some of the men in the water were alive, shouting and flailing their arms. Every few seconds, another man appeared on the surface, and immediately began screaming. Shafer, despite his exhaustion and pain, smiled at the thought that they were for all the world like infants emerging, crying and kicking, from the wounds of their mothers.

Suddenly, only a few feet away from the lifeboat, another body broke the surface, rose into the air, and then fell back.

"My God," whispered the boatswain next to Shafer.

The body floated on the surface without moving. Shafer noted that the head was at a peculiar angle. The lifeboat drew nearer and the body was pulled from the water. Shafer recognized Harllfinger's features in the dim light of dawn. Somehow, the captain had struck the hatch when leaving the ship. His neck was broken.

It was 5:17. Of the twenty-five men who had left the submarine, only eleven were taken aboard the cruiser. They were bloody, exhausted, and in great pain. But they were alive. Altena, the superstitious sailor who had exchanged places with Shafer, was not among them.

40

During these fatal months of 1944, Admiral Doenitz' submariners learned every week of the deaths of friends and comrades at sea, and they lived with the knowledge that the next Grey Wolf reported missing might well be their own. Yet, their daring in combat was undiminished; and they were spurred on by an American communiqué, a copy of which was found aboard a downed U. S. Air Force bomber: "The following is a typical list of our losses when a U-boat sinks two 6,000-ton cargo ships: forty-two tanks, eight 152-mm. guns, eighty-eight 87.6-mm. guns, forty 40-mm. pieces, twenty-four armored cars, fifty self-propelled machine guns, 5,210 tons of ammunition, 600 rifles, 428 tons of spare parts for tanks, 2,000 tons of supplies, and 1,000 cans of fuel. It would require 3,000 air raids for the enemy to do the same amount of damage."

What really sustained the submariners, however, was their expectation of a miracle. Everywhere, in the new bases, in the barracks and in the officers' clubs, in the training camps as well as aboard the submarines at sea, everyone hoped, constantly and in spite of everything, that the new weapons on which Germany's scientists were working would finally be delivered and turn the tide of battle.

Indeed, the new models—the types XXI and XXIII, equipped with the *Walter* hull—were already being tested in the Baltic. Commander Schnee, who was in command of the *U-2511*, the first such submarine to be tested, enthusiastically assured his fellow officers that "It's an absolutely extraordinary ship. With it, we can pursue and attack while submerged. It's going to make us masters of the Atlantic again."

Schnee's enthusiasm was not entirely unfounded. The type XXI, because of its more powerful batteries and its sleeker hull, cruised at a maximum speed of 18 knots—which was sufficient to outrun any destroyer. The *Schnorchel* system made it possible to remain submerged for as long as two months. Its antiradar device was extremely sensitive. And, finally, for the first time electronic calculators were installed in the control room and provided information on range, speed, and bearing—which made it possible for a U-boat to fire its torpedoes at a depth of 100 feet.

Allied bombs, however, continued to devastate Germany's cities, demolishing her factories, destroying her ports and shipyards and wreaking havoc with her transportation system. It had been hoped that the type XXI would become operational in the spring of 1944. Now, it was postponed until the spring of 1945.

As Germany burned and her armies fell back on all fronts, Doenitz' men somehow allowed themselves to be lulled by dreams and hopes which bore no relationship to reality. There was much talk of an electrically powered *Walter* submarine, of a bomb of incredible power, and especially of rockets far more powerful than the V-1 and V-2 which were to be fired at American cities from U-boats.

"We must tighten our belts and hold on," commanders told their men, "so as to give our scientists and workmen the time they need to produce these weapons." Until that day arrived, it was essential that there be no retreat. "At the present time," the U-boat captains told their crews, "we may not be able to win victories; but we can at least die trying."

On October 2, 1944, at 9 A.M. a battered old *Kriegsmarine* truck pulled up less than a mile from the port of Neustadt, a small village not far from Lübeck. Twenty sailors and a chief petty officer climbed out. Then the truck drove off, black smoke pouring from its exhaust.

The men looked around. They were standing in the middle of a sandy, windswept expanse of land. There was no vegetation other than a few tufts of grass, scorched by the salt air. The men stared glumly at the long wooden barracks before them. There were no stairways, and no panes in the windows. "What a dump," one of the men muttered. "It looks like it's about to fall down." As though in protest, the doors of the building banged loudly in the wind.

Here, nonetheless, was where the twenty-one men were to live, with the three boxes of canned goods and the sausages they had brought with them in the truck. There was not a single bottle of beer among their provisions.

Hermann Rasch stood facing the men, noting the expressions of disgust and anger on their faces. Rasch himself had changed a great deal. His innumerable missions, combined with a lung condition due to chlorine fumes, had aged him far beyond his years. He was still slender—thin, now—but his features had lost all traces of youth. He was only twenty-six, but his forehead was wrinkled, there were lines around his eyes, and there were deep creases around his mouth which, when he smiled, gave him a look of bitterness. The preceding summer, he had met a girl and become engaged to her. Yet, even this did nothing to dissipate the profound melancholy which was with him constantly. He had only to walk into any officers' club, whether at Kiel or Wilhelmshaven, Berlin or Flensburg, to be reminded of countless friends and shipmates lost at sea, and to be overwhelmed by infinite sadness at the thought of such useless sacrifice of human life. Still, he never forgot that he was a German officer, and he was determined to do his duty till the end. His face was lined, his blond hair now was laced with gray; but he had lost nothing of his air of authority, and his voice was as commanding as ever.

Now, looking at the men before him, he was mindful of the sacrifices, the suffering and the heroism of his former shipmates, and the sight of these recruits, unhappy because their quarters were dilapidated, angered him.

"What did you expect to find here?" he shouted at them. "A castle, with maid service and dancing? If it's comfort you're looking for, then you have no business in the Navy. If you can't put up with hardship at nineteen or twenty years of age, then you're good for nothing except being killed by bombs."

Some of the sailors blushed.

"You see the condition of this building," Rasch continued. "You're going to get it into shape. Fast. You're going to take this place and make a camp out of it! There will be other men coming here soon, and I want it to be ready for them.

"You had better know it from the start: you're in for some tough training, and only the best men are going to make it. But I can promise you one thing: those who do make it are going to be *men*. They are the ones who are going to be assigned to the *See-Hund* division."

At the time that Hermann Rasch was trying to awaken enthusiasm and determination in his men, there were very few people in Germany who had ever heard of the *See-Hund* (sea dog). Indeed, the *See-Hund* did not actually exist except on paper, though construction on a number of them was under way in the shipyards of Danzig, Kiel, and Cologne. Only Doenitz himself, Admiral Godt, a few officers of his staff, and Hitler himself, naturally, were familiar with this new "secret weapon."

The *See-Hund* was essentially a two-man submarine, carrying two torpedoes. It was powered by a diesel (truck) engine on the surface, and by an electric motor when submerged. It had a speed of 9 knots, and could cruise without refueling for six days.

Several days earlier, Rasch had been summoned to Koralle by Grand Admiral Doenitz. After a warm handshake, Doenitz had told Rasch immediately what he expected of him.

"As you know," he said, "in 1941 the Channel lost its strategic importance for us, and we no longer used our conventional units to patrol it. Now, however, it has once more become a combat zone of the first importance because it is the supply line of the forces invading France. We must therefore return to the Channel.

"You know the problems we face there. There are mines, nets, acoustical buoys—and, above all, Allied supremacy in the air. All of this makes it impossible for us to commit our conventional units to the Channel.

"The only way that we can effectively help the Wehrmacht and relieve the pressure of the Allied offensive is for us to send in nonconventional submarines—miniature submarines capable of infiltrating Allied shipping, harassing the enemy—and even venturing up the Thames.

"These new vessels are already off the drawing board. We call them *See-Hund*. Their small size will make it possible for them to avoid detection by enemy radar. They're also extremely quiet when submerged. Therefore, they won't be exposed to depth-charge attacks.

"In eight weeks, we will have 250 of these new submarines. So, we have eight weeks in which to train crews, physically, psychologically, technically, and tactically, to man them.

"I want you to handle this for me, Rasch. You will have absolute authority. The first group of volunteers is going to arrive in a few days, and your training camp is going to be near Neustadt. There's nothing there now. Not even a telephone. You'll have to do the best you can. It is impossible for me to give you anything; not even a single chair. We have nothing left. I don't give a damn how you go about getting what you need. That's up to you. Just remember: it's absolutely essential that we have trained, efficient crews for the *See-Hund* in eight weeks."

During his first inspection of the barracks, Rasch noted with satisfaction that his men had somehow managed to get the building into respectable shape. Everything had been scrubbed and polished. There was, of course, no furniture; not even a single bed. And there were still no panes in the windows. But the roof had been repaired with scrap lumber; and wooden hasps had been installed on all the doors.

His hands behind his back, Rasch walked between the two rows of sailors standing at attention. He inspected the men carefully, one after the other. And finally he smiled. "Very good," he said. "At least it's now fit to live in. Our problem is that we have absolutely no supplies, and no way of getting any. Headquarters has more important things to worry about than our lack of furniture. So, if we're ever going to be comfortable here, we're going to have to do everything ourselves.

"The grand admiral has left it entirely up to us to get settled here. So, it seems to me we ought to take advantage of the freedom he was given us. Chief!"

"*Jawohl, Herr Kapitän*," the chief petty officer answered, clicking his heels.

"I think it's time to see if these young sailors are as resourceful as seamen are supposed to be."

"*Jawohl, Herr Kapitän.*"

"I want you to break the men down into small groups with special missions. To start with, we're going to need beds and tables, and pots and pans. You see what I'm driving at—"

"*Jawohl, Herr Kapitän.*"

"Obviously, I'm not talking about buying things. There are no funds available. But I don't want any trouble either. I'll cover for you as much as I can; but that doesn't mean that you have permission to go out and rob churches."

"May I ask a question, *Herr Kapitän?*"

"I'm listening."

"According to regulations, we should assign some of the men to guard duty. But I'm going to need all of the men if we're going to get this job done."

"You're right. Take all of the men. I'll stand guard," Rasch said as he left the building.

The motorcycle made a sharp turn at full speed, balanced precariously on the wheel of its sidecar, and screeched to a halt in front of the barracks. Rasch was sitting on the new steps, reading a magazine. He looked up, and barely managed to suppress a smile. He rose and walked to the sidecar which was loaded with pots and pans, cans of paint, cartons of beer, and a gramophone. On top of the piles were two enormous rolls of iron wire.

"Where did you get all this?" he asked.

The young sailor jumped from the motorcycle and stood at attention before Rasch. "I don't know, sir," he answered, bursting with pride.

"You don't know?"

"No, sir. The chief and some of the men brought it all in."

"And—the motorcycle?"

"The chief saw it parked in the street. He asked me if I knew how to drive it, and I said yes. So, he told me to go get it. I did, and when I brought it back, they piled all this stuff into the sidecar and secured it."

"What's all this paint for?"

"The truck, Captain."

"What truck?"

"The truck they're bringing back, sir."

That evening, Rasch drove to Lübeck for dinner with his fiancée. When he returned, and walked into the barracks, it was impossible for him to conceal his astonishment. "If they get thrown out of the Navy for this," he told himself, "they'll always be able to make a living as thieves."

He walked up the aisle. There were beds—twenty of them, but, as yet, without sheets. There were tables, chairs, and even a rocking chair. Candles glowed softly from elaborate candelabra. Two massive armoires stood against one wall. And, of course, there was the gramophone, which had stopped playing when Rasch entered.

"Well," Rasch told himself, "we still don't have dishes and curtains, but I expect we'll have them soon." He noted that some of the panes had been replaced in the windows, and that the others had been covered with new boards. He looked down and saw an Oriental rug almost covering the entire floor. "If we had girls," Rasch smiled to himself, "it would look like a harem."

The short, squat chief clicked his heels. "All present, sir," he reported "—except for three men."

Rasch, not wishing to appear surprised at anything, asked indifferently, "Where are they?"

"They're painting the truck, Captain. Blue. It was red, and that's not the right color for a navy truck."

"Obviously," Rasch agreed.

"Sir? May I show you your quarters?"

The small room at the end of the barracks had had its missing door replaced by a pair of colorful screens. Rasch had a difficult time keeping a straight face as he looked around at the massive, canopied bed, the two armchairs, the chest, and the rug. "My compliments, Chief," he said.

There was no answer, and he looked at the petty officer. To his surprise, the man had his eyes down and was blushing violently, relishing his commander's approval.

Rasch, slightly embarrassed, said, "But that's not all, Chief. There are more things you'll have to get tomorrow, and the days following, too."

"Why, Captain," the chief stuttered. "We're taking a big risk. It's not that we're afraid; but it would help if we knew exactly what sort of stuff you want. Because—"

"Because what, Chief?"

"Well, at the rate that we're stealing stuff, there are bound to be complaints, and all the police in the area are going to be on our trail."

"Good. Very good. That's what I want: complaints."

"I don't understand, *Herr Kapitän*. Stealing isn't a sailor's job. It's fun for one day; but to do it every day—"

"I'll explain it to you, Chief," Rasch said. "When the police find out—and I'm sure they'll find out soon—that everything that's been stolen has ended up here, they'll notify *Kriegsmarine* headquarters. There'll be an investigation. The brass is going to ask for explanations. When they do, I'll tell them that we're willing to make restitution—on condition that the Army gives us what we need out of their own supplies. Do you see?"

"Well, *Herr Kapitän*," the chief said, grinning broadly, "if all our officers were as smart as you, we'd have won this fucking war long ago!"

"I'm not so sure of that, Chief. But thanks for the compliment. And good night."

That was the only night in his whole life that Hermann Rasch slept in a canopied bed. The next afternoon, his hopes were realized. Three long black automobiles pulled up in front of the barracks and disgorged several high-ranking naval officers and several policemen in plain clothes. There was a demand for explanations, which Rasch gladly furnished. Finally, it was agreed that the camp would receive the supplies which it needed. At the last minute, Rasch added a new condition. Even that was agreed to, and he was promised two cooks.

Two days later, he inspected the barracks again. It was now furnished according to regulations. Behind him, Rasch heard the boatswain mutter: "It's not nearly as nice as it was before."

The barracks of the training camp at Neustadt were warm and comfortable. There were training fields now, and lines of trucks; a training ship of 6,000 tons; two cargo ships; 250 *See-Hund* minisubs; and 2,000 men who had survived the rigorous training out of the 20,000 who had volunteered for duty aboard the new submarines.

It was Christmas Night, 1944, and the blacked-out camp was celebrating the Nativity. Each building had its Christmas tree, and the submariners were enjoying their holiday. They knew that it might be the last that they would have for a long time; perhaps forever. In the address which he had delivered to his men, Rasch had informed them that they would see action very shortly.

The British, Americans, and Russians were at Germany's frontiers, and a ring of steel was closing inexorably around the Thousand-Year Reich. The year had seen some successes for the U-boats. The *Schnorchel* had permitted them to take to the Atlantic once more, and to attack Allied shipping. Moreover, the U-boats were now armed with a new remote-controlled torpedo, the L.U.T., which was effective in 95 per cent of the cases in which it was used. But these victories, encouraging as they were, seemed meager compared to those of the earlier years of the war. And they in no way diminished the incredible losses suffered in that terrible year of 1944, which had seen the destruction of 257 Grey Wolves.

4

The fighters and bombers of the Allies were now absolute masters of the sky over Germany. Over 650,000 tons of bombs had rained down on the cities of that nation, and the Reich was nothing more than one vast ruin. To the east, the army of Marshal Gregori Zhukov, spearheading the Russian offensive, was making for Frankfurt an der Oder and Küstrin. The Americans under General Omar Bradley, and the British under Field Marshal Bernard Montgomery, were preparing to cross the Rhine. The military situation was deteriorating alarmingly, and the Wehrmacht was now simply an immense mob of starved, exhausted, ragged men in full retreat.

As the Allied noose tightened, the Third Reich came to a standstill. Railway and highway communications were paralyzed, destroyed by Allied bombs. Long columns of civilians, fleeing the advancing Red armies, streamed out of the east, making for the putative safety of the western part of the country.

Still, there were seventy Grey Wolves at sea, attacking Allied supply lines between the British Isles and the French mainland and between Iceland and Soviet ports in the north. Thanks to the *Schnorchel* and to the new remote-controlled torpedoes, there were some successes. In October 1944, off Halifax, Commander Dubratz' *U-1232* sank four convoy ships, for a total of 25,000 tons. And, in the last quarter of 1944, the score of individual U-boats was equal to that of August 1942. In February 1945, the first type XXIII submarines went into service and began patrolling the western coast of Britain. The communiqué issued at the end of the Yalta Conference duly noted the apprehension of the Allies at "the possibility that German submarines may once more become a serious threat to our shipping in the North Atlantic"; and Churchill asked Stalin to speed up the Russian offensive aimed at German ports on the Baltic.

The Allied leaders had good reason to be concerned. Everywhere in the Atlantic, the crews of the Grey Wolves were fighting with suicidal desperation and audacity—so much so that the Americans referred to them as "blond kamikazes."

February 2, 1945. The first bomb fell at the end of the pier, striking and demolishing the water tank. The second fell on a group of refugees who were running in panic, clutching their bundles and suitcases, toward a tunnel. They were all killed. All that was left was a crater in the ground, and a litter of bodies and personal possessions. The other bombs were scattered over the railway center of Elbing, cutting down men, women, children and soldiers indiscriminately, lifting great locomotives and boxcars into the air and then releasing them with a mighty crash.

For several days, Germany's eastern province of Pomerania

had trembled before two Russian armies. The first, under General Wassiliewski, was making for Koenigsberg. The second, commanded by General Rokossowski, after cutting to the center of the province and destroying the German Army of the Vistals, had turned northward. Before them, hundreds of thousands of soldiers and civilians were fleeing toward Danzig and Kolberg.

Wolf Shafer lay on his side alongside an overturned boxcar, watching the Russian planes turn overhead like vultures seeking their prey. He did not move. Experience had taught him that, in a few seconds, they would return for another bombing run.

The roar of the planes' engines grew louder, and Shafer surmised that they had completed their turn and were now coming in at a low altitude—not more than 6,000 feet, he concluded. For some reason, the antiaircraft guns were now silent, and the bombers were free to come and go as they wished.

Instinctively, Shafer moved closer to the wooden boxcar, knowing that it offered no real protection. He folded his arms over his head and waited. The bombs came whistling down, and the earth trembled. He dug his fingers into the ground. Then—he did not know how long it was—the bombs stopped, and the planes went away.

Shafer raised his head and saw a sight which, through repetition, no longer shocked him. The rails were twisted and broken; fires were burning everywhere; every building in sight was in ruins. And from everywhere there came the screams of human beings in agony. The train which had brought Shafer from Pillau was a total wreck.

He stood up and began walking toward the sound of voices. He had gone only a short distance when he met a Luftwaffe general escorted by four military policemen.

"Stop!" the general ordered. "Where are you going, Lieutenant?"

Shafer snapped to attention. "Lieutenant Wolf Shafer, sir, assigned to the U-boat flotilla at Pillau. I have been ordered to report to the Flensburg base."

"For what reason?" the general asked.

"My submarine was destroyed in an air raid, *Herr General.* I'm on my way to take delivery of another one."

"When did you leave Pillau?"

"Two days ago, sir. But the locomotive kept breaking down, and we were under constant air attack."

"I see. Well, you're not going to be able to go on. It will take at least thirty-six hours to lay down new track and put together a train."

"*Herr General,* it is essential that I get to Flensburg."

"I tell you it's impossible," the general snapped. "Are you deaf, for God's sake, or stupid? It's going to be at least two days before you can leave here! Meanwhile, Lieutenant, report to the military authorities of the city. You had better know from the beginning what the situation is. Tanks from Russian advance units have already reached the outskirts of the city. It's absolutely necessary to turn them back. We cannot allow them to reach the railway line. Until your train is ready, you will be given command of an infantry company. We are short of officers at present, and I will send someone to relieve you as soon as I can. Do you know how to handle a *Panzerfaust,** Lieutenant?"

"*Jawohl, Herr General.*"

It snowed. For two days and two nights, Wolf Shafer crouched in a foxhole with his *Panzerfaust* at the ready. From time to time, artillery shells exploded nearby. Nonetheless, the occasional patrols he sent out returned with encouraging news: there was no sign of Russian advance units.

Still, Shafer was not optimistic. He could hear the intermittent roar of Soviet artillery, and he knew that the Russians were preparing for an attack.

At 7 P.M., a Luftwaffe captain appeared at Shafer's foxhole, an expression of profound distaste on his face. Shafer had just finished a cup of *ersatz* coffee which had left a vile taste in his mouth.

---

* Antitank gun.

"I'm supposed to relieve you, Lieutenant," the captain said. "They asked me to tell you that your train will leave in one hour."

Shafer climbed out of the hole, his hands and feet numb from the cold, and began walking hurriedly. He was still a hundred yards from the railway station when he saw and heard a crowd of soldiers and civilians standing around a track, shouting angrily. Facing them was a troop of soldiers, rifles with fixed bayonets at the ready. An SS captain was shouting orders, and people were milling about frantically, shoving one another, terror on their faces. As Shafer watched, the crowd grew in size until it comprised about five hundred people, all of them gesturing threateningly at the small group of soldiers.

"Remain calm!" Shafer heard the SS captain shout. "We're going to distribute soup and bread. Don't come any closer!"

Even as the captain spoke, the crowd continued growing. The captain blew three times on his whistle. More soldiers came running and charged into the crowd, striking right and left with their rifle butts. The refugees began to scatter in confusion. Shafer heard several shots.

He sensed rather than saw what was going on, and turned away in disgust. A voice next to him in the darkness made him jump: "Ah, there you are, Lieutenant."

Shafer turned, squinting, and saw the Luftwaffe general whom he had encountered two days earlier. He was freshly shaved and his uniform was clean and neatly pressed.

"There seems to be a disturbance, *Herr General.*"

"Yes, a disturbance," the general said in a tired voice.

"What's happening?"

"Those people over there panicked because the train is not going on to Stettin. Instead, it's been ordered to proceed eastward, to Koenigsberg."

"Then how am I going to get to Flensburg, sir?"

"You'll have to go back where you came from. Surely the Navy needs you."

"But—"

"No buts, Lieutenant," the general replied in exasperation.

"Hurry up and get on the train. It's over there, on a track they slapped together this afternoon. You can't miss it, since it's the only train there is. Good luck, Lieutenant."

Shafer saluted, then stumbled off in the dark, over piles of debris and through craters, until he saw the train. He stopped short. The entire train was composed of a dilapidated locomotive of antique vintage and two coaches. The coaches were filled with soldiers—apparently reinforcements for the garrison at Koenigsberg.

Shafer hoisted himself into the second coach and picked his way down the aisle through the soldiers. They were all reservists, none of them less than fifty years old. Their faces were sullen, and they were silent as they sat or stood jammed together in the seats and the aisles.

"Well," Shafer said in an attempt to revive their spirits. "You men don't look too happy."

"We're supposed to be happy because they're sending us to be shot by the Russians?" a voice asked rhetorically.

Shafer did not reply. He used his feet to push apart two men lying on the floor, and then lay down between them. He pulled his cap down and closed his eyes. He was asleep in a few seconds, for the first time in four days. His last thought before dropping off was that Germany was indeed lost if she had to depend on men like these to stop the Red Army.

Shafer awoke the next morning at dawn to the sound of a Soviet fighter buzzing the train. The pilot was merely amusing himself. It was as though he would not condescend to fire. Nonetheless, the train came to a halt. Shafer saw through the window that they were in open country. There was not even a tree to hide behind.

"The stupid sons-of-bitches," one of the soldiers shouted. "They're going to get us bombed!"

Another man shouted, "Why don't they stop this fucking war? What are they waiting for—for us to be killed?"

Suddenly, Shafer was filled with rage. He sprang to his feet and struck the man who had shouted. Another soldier came at him, but Shafer hit him in the face before he could even speak, and the man stopped dead in his tracks.

As though by magic, there was a sudden silence throughout the coach. Shafer heard only the chugging of the locomotive as it emitted tiny puffs of smoke.

"Let me through," Shafer snarled, pushing aside the soldiers in the aisle. He opened the rear door of the coach and jumped down onto the track. He saw a trainman do the same, then bend over and inspect the track. Shafer called to him, and the man— an old man, Shafer saw—walked slowly toward him.

"What's the matter?"

"The track has been cut."

Meanwhile, the sergeant in charge of the detachment of soldiers had come running up and came to attention before Shafer. "Get those men out of the train," Shafer ordered. "We're going to walk."

"Jawohl, Herr Leutnant."

As the reservists poured from the coaches, Shafer walked over to the two engineers, who seemed to be engaged in a discussion of the situation.

"Are you going to come with us?" he asked.

"No. We're going to wait until they repair the track, Lieutenant," the older of the men replied. "At our age, we can't walk very far. At least we'll be warm in the locomotive."

The detachment of soldiers began walking through the snow with Shafer at their head, toward Koenigsberg which lay some eight miles to the east. They had barely reached the highway when they heard the sound of airplanes.

"Scatter and get down!" Shafer shouted, then threw himself flat on his stomach in a field along the road. He shivered in the snow.

The bombers dived down at the defenseless train. They made one pass, and there were two explosions. The locomotive and the two coaches were blown into the air. Shafer thought of the two old railroad men who had wanted to stay warm in the locomotive.

"Let's get moving," he shouted, and the double line of soldiers re-formed on the road. They had walked a little over two miles when a military vehicle came to a stop a few yards away. Two military policemen got out. Shafer by now had had enough of the reservists, and had only one desire: to get back to his flotilla. He ordered the policemen to drive him to Koenigsberg.

"What about these men?" one of the men, a sergeant, asked, obviously reluctant to abandon the reservists to the mercy of the enemy.

"Let them take care of themselves," Shafer replied. "In any case, I don't think they'd be of much help to our soldiers in Koenigsberg."

Koenigsberg resembled an ancient ruin rather than a modern city. There was hardly a building that had not been gutted. The streets were impassable because of the holes and the rubble. Somehow, Shafer was able to find a *Kriegsmarine* truck en route to Pillau.

It was only 25 miles from Koenigsberg to Pillau, yet it took the truck more than three hours to cover that distance. The road itself was a disaster; but worse than the road were the mobs of refugees trying to make their way to the port. It was impossible even to estimate how many people there were. Shafer, seated between the driver and his assistant, could not tear his eyes from the faces of the men, women, and children who made up that tide of humanity, faces expressionless with shock, fatigue, and despair. Occasionally, some of the refugees signaled frantically at the truck. Sometimes, some of them clutched at the doors. But, with a skill acquired from experience, the driver and his assistant forced them to let go by rapping their fingers with a large key.

The truck never stopped. It continued rolling, sometimes on the road, sometimes through flat fields. The driver, as though trying to justify himself to Shafer, explained: "We can't stop, Lieutenant. If we do, we're done for. These people are crazy with fear. If a truck stops, they attack it. They fight to climb aboard. A couple of days ago, they turned over a truck that stopped."

Shafer saw Pillau from a distance, as the road turned to the left and slanted gently toward the port. Then he saw the port itself. Before its gates thousands upon thousands of men and women of all ages were crowded in the piercing wind, pushing and fighting among themselves to get through the gates and aboard a ship—any ship that could take them westward, away from advancing hordes of Russians. As they struggled, Russian artillery rumbled in the distance; and Russian planes circled overhead. Periodically, the planes dived and strafed the refugees, leaving gaping holes in the mob which were quickly filled.

The truck made its way with great difficulty through the surging mass of people. The sailors at the gates used their rifle butts to clear a passage for it to enter the base. When it pulled up before the headquarters building, the driver heaved a sigh of relief and said, "God! They give me the creeps more than the Russians do."

A few minutes later, Wolf Shafer stood before Captain Shuhart, commander of the flotilla. Shuhart kept rubbing his forehead and his eyes, as though to force himself to stay awake despite his extreme fatigue.

A dozen other submarine captains were standing or leaning against the wall opposite Shuhart's desk, their faces dull with fatigue. In the silence, Shafer heard the sounds of the mob outside the gates, screaming, shouting, fighting to invade the compound and take by force the few ships moored there.

"Well," Shuhart said, making an attempt to smile. "Wolf, I didn't expect to see you back so soon. What happened?"

Shafer gave him a brief account of his trip. When he had finished, everyone listened for a moment to the howling of the refugees at the gates.

Shuhart looked at his watch. "Gentlemen," he began, "I've asked you here because I've received new orders from headquarters. The front has moved again. It is coming closer. The Red Army is now about 70 miles from Koenigsberg. The Wehr-

macht is making a stand in its new positions, but they're expected
to fall back again at any moment.

"In these circumstances, we've been given a new mission: a
difficult mission, and, in some ways, a cruel one. We are going to
have to evacuate some of these poor people and take them to our
western ports. We have only a few ships, and, obviously, we
can't take them all. And, of course, time is short. We don't have
time to make up boarding lists—which means that we're going
to have to be completely arbitrary about who goes and who
stays. It's going to be hard on us, and we're going to have to be
strong, even brutal. We're going to have to separate families,
knowing that some of them will never be reunited. But we can't
do otherwise.

"Tonight, the hospital ship *Pretoria* is going to dock. As soon as
it does, we're going to start loading her. Shafer, you're in command of the detachment who are going to choose those to go
aboard.

"I'd like the *Pretoria* to be able to leave during the night, so
as to be out of range of Russian planes by daybreak. You stay
aboard her, Shafer. Maybe this time you'll be able to get to
Flensburg."

February 6, 1945. 2 A.M. Word had spread through the shivering refugees that a ship was going to take on some of them
and carry them to the west. Slowly, silently, thousands came
and stood outside the gates in the freezing weather. Then, they
waited, calmly for the most part, apparently resigned to whatever
lot would be theirs. From time to time during that long and
terrible wait, a voice cried out, "A dead man!" The crowd parted
momentarily as the corpse slid down into the snow, then closed
again. There was an occasional shout, or a scream, quickly
muffled.

Shafer was not deceived by the apparent apathy of the refugees. He knew that, as soon as the gates were opened, they
would become a raging mob. He knew what had happened at
Gdynia, Hela, and Danzig. In the latter port, it had been

necessary for the soldiers to open fire upon their fellow countrymen.

6:15 A.M. The *Pretoria* finally docked, after a long delay due to the difficulty of obtaining fuel. Large detachments of submariners were posted at the foot of each of the two gangplanks to control the flood of human beings which would be loosed when the gates were opened.

Shafer repeated his orders to his men, then added: "Above all, don't let yourselves be overrun. Stand your ground! If you have to, use your rifle butts."

Then he climbed the gangplank. On deck, a dozen more submariners stood guard, weapons in their hands.

"Here they come," one of the sailors shouted. Shafer heard a noise like distant thunder in the darkness. The sailors who had been stationed at the gates were swept aside by the onrushing mob.

A man standing next to Shafer said: "If they get through, we're going to be squashed flat."

The captain of the *Pretoria* shouted into his megaphone in an attempt to make himself heard: "Don't go near the edge of the pier! If you fall into the water, you'll be crushed against the ship! Don't go near—listen to me, for God's sake—!"

No one paid the slightest attention. The mob was beyond listening, beyond reason. It was hysterical, momentarily insane, obsessed by the thought of escape.

Shafer's throat was dry. How could he possibly hope to control these people? They had already reached the foot of the gangplank and had massed along the length of the pier, fighting like animals for place. And they were still coming. As far as Shafer could see into the darkness, there were terrified, desperate human beings. Screaming refugees fell or were pushed into the water by the dozens. No one noticed except the men standing on the deck, who could see them moving frantically in the water before being crushed between the pier and the ship moving gently in the swell.

At the gangplanks, a pitched battle raged between the sub-mariners and the refugees. Rifle butts struck out indiscriminately, heads were cracked open, and there were screams of pain. In the surging crush of human bodies, dozens of the refugees died from lack of air, their eyes wide, their mouths open in a final gasp. They could not fall, and the corpses were carried upright among the bodies of the living.

At a given moment, the sailors at the foot of the gangplank retreated in disorder to the deck. There was place for 2,000 refugees, at most, aboard the *Pretoria;* and there were some 5,000 people battling for those places. At the gate, two machine guns had been hurriedly installed, and the guards fired periodic bursts over the heads of the mob to keep it at bay while the gates were secured. As soon as the machine guns fell silent, the attack began again.

Finally, all but 400 spaces had been allotted on the ship, and there were still several thousand people on the pier fighting desperately for them. Shafer and his men, with great difficulty, succeeded in fighting their way down the gangplank to the pier, and there they began choosing at random those who would be allowed to board. They separated wives from their husbands, children from their parents, despite the heart-rending cries which they did not hear and did not want to hear.

At 9 A.M. the shouts of the refugees were drowned out by the roar of diesel engines as seven Wehrmacht trucks, preceded by two automobiles, turned onto the pier. The crowd fell suddenly silent and opened to allow the vehicles to approach the *Pretoria.* Soldiers wearing helmets jumped from the trucks, pushed back a few curious civilians, and formed a protective circle around the trucks.

"What's going on?" a sailor asked Shafer.

Shafer shrugged, watching in astonishment as a detachment of musicians and an honor guard emerged from the trucks. Orders were shouted, and the musicians formed ranks. Shafer saw a Wehrmacht major at the foot of the gangplank, and heard him say: "Let me through. I must speak to the captain of this ship."

The major ran up the gangplank and brushed past Shafer and his men. They watched him as he disappeared onto the bridge. When they turned back to the pier, they saw two caskets being unloaded from the trucks and placed carefully on the ground. The honor guard had unfurled four flags, which were now flapping noisily in the glacial wind.

The major emerged from the bridge and returned to the pier. He spoke to the occupants of the two automobiles, and Shafer saw ten high-ranking officers climb out and walk stiffly toward the caskets. He noted that their highly polished boots glistened in the morning light.

Just then, the second officer of the *Pretoria* appeared on deck. "What's happening?" Shafer asked.

"Those are the caskets of Marshal Hindenburg and his wife. The Führer doesn't want them to fall into the hands of the Russians. He says it would be a dishonor to the German Army."

"What?" Shafer whispered indignantly. "Those two coffins are going to take as much place as twenty people standing. Are we going to let people die in order to save a couple of corpses?"

The second officer's responses was drowned out by the band as it struck up the German national anthem.

Wolf Shafer, despite the love which he felt for his country, experienced a surge of revulsion. At the same time, he felt astonishment at the reaction of the refugees. Only a few minutes earlier, they had been battling with a savagery inspired by panic. Now, they were silent, standing motionless, on the pier as well as aboard the *Pretoria*, as the strains of *Deutschland über alles* rose serenely over the port.

When the anthem was over, there were a few terse orders. As taps sounded and the honor guard presented arms, soldiers carried the two caskets aboard the hospital ship. The soldiers had just reached the afterdeck when fighter planes, bearing the red-star insignia, appeared overhead. The refugees surged toward the gate, trampling one another in their terror. The honor guard fled, dragging their flags in the dust; and the musicians ran, brandishing their fifes, drums, and trombones. The pier was deserted by the time that the antiaircraft shells began to explode in the sky.

The captain of the *Pretoria* immediately gave the order to cast off. The lines were loosed, and the gangplanks raised with a grinding of pulleys. A few men rushed out onto the pier then, waving their arms and shouting desperately as the ship pulled away. The refugees on deck looked down and held out their hands to those who had been left behind.

All the shipyards and training centers on the Baltic had either fallen to, or were threatened by, the Soviet offensive, and the Grey Wolves were at the end of their rope. In the face of the tragedy about to overwhelm the German people, Doenitz ordered his U-boats to confine themselves to ferrying refugees from the ports of the east to those of the west. Their mission was no longer to attack, but to evacuate as many as possible of the people of eastern Germany. All seaworthy commercial and fishing vessels were requisitioned for this purpose.

So far as the U-boats patrolling the North Sea and the Scottish coast were concerned, no one at headquarters knew what had become of them. Their radio silence prevented Admiral Godt from knowing their situation. The only information which reached Godt's headquarters came over Radio London.

February 14. Shortly before 10 P.M., the *Pretoria* dropped anchor in the Gulf of Stettin, and Wolf Shafer learned from the military police that a train would leave shortly for Hamburg. He and a dozen submariners crossed Stettin and forced their way onto the train already jammed with refugees.

It was about 200 miles from Stettin to Hamburg, and the train, with its many coaches and its ancient locomotive, proceeded slowly, stopping during the day and traveling only under cover of darkness. In the daylight hours, the passengers hid themselves in forests as Allied planes swooped continually over the railroad. Occasionally, a fighter came in low for a look at the stationary train, fired a few token rounds, and then roared off, as though to signify that the archaic locomotive and its dilapidated coaches were not worth the time that it would take to destroy them.

The second night of the trip, in a compartment near Shafer's, a woman began screaming. As the screams grew louder and more frequent, Shafer awoke and went into the corridor.

"It's a woman in labor," someone told him. "No one seems to know what to do."

"I'll go see her," Shafer said.

The compartment was permeated by the odor of unwashed bodies and human sweat, and it was filled with a crowd of curious men who stood watching the woman twist and turn in agony. Shafer ordered the spectators to leave, and as they filed out, grumbling, he made the woman stretch out on one of the wooden benches.

"Are you a doctor?" she asked as he stroked her forehead.

"Yes. Well, almost," he assured her. "Don't worry. Everything will be all right. This isn't the ideal place to have a baby, but we'll manage."

He looked down at his hands. They were filthy. He called one of his men. "Get me a bottle of schnaps," he ordered. When the bottle was brought, he took a deep swallow, then washed his hands in the liquor, under the reproachful stare of the sailor. Finally, he opened his pocket knife and washed the blade.

It was almost 4 A.M. when he left the compartment, dizzy with fatigue. A dozen pairs of eyes looked at him expectantly. "It's a boy," he told them. "He's all right."

It seemed to Shafer that he had just fallen asleep when a hand shook him. He opened his eyes reluctantly. A white-haired woman was standing over him. "I'm sorry to have to wake you, Lieutenant," she said, "but we need you."

"Why?"

"Two coaches up, there's a woman in labor."

"Good God!" Shafer moaned. "This isn't a train. It's a maternity ward."

About noon, a short distance from Lauenburg, the woman—a young blonde with the high cheekbones characteristic of Prussians—gave birth to a son. The train was stationary, and everyone else was lying outside on the snow-covered field, in the biting wind, waiting for darkness. The infant's angry cries assailed Shafer's ears as he wiped the blood from the mother's stomach and applied military bandages. He covered her with his soiled overcoat and wrapped her feet in rags. He stood, shivering in his uniform jacket, his teeth chattering, as the infant continued to scream.

"He's in good voice," he said to the mother.

She smiled weakly in gratitude, then looked down at her son who was wrapped in a shawl donated by an old woman.

Shafer heard the unaccustomed sound of laughter, followed by curses. He looked up. "I'll be right back," he told the woman reassuringly, and went out into the corridor.

Through the window, he saw four sailors slipping and struggling in the snow as they tried to half lead, half push a terrified cow toward the train.

"Where in God's name did you get that?" he shouted, forgetting the cold and his fatigue as he laughed uproariously.

"Well, we went looking for some milk for the children," one of the sailors explained, panting. "We found a farm a couple of miles from here, but it was deserted. Then we heard this cow mooing. She was hidden in a thicket nearby. We brought her back, thinking we had found a steady supply of milk. But she's afraid of the train. As soon as she saw it, she stopped and tried to go around. I've never heard of a cow who was afraid of trains."

Shafer walked around the cow. "Well, she's not the fattest cow I've ever seen," he observed, "but she's better than nothing. You've done very well, men. In fact, she's a real prize."

As Shafer watched his men tie the cow to one of the coaches, it occurred to him that their pea jackets looked strangely lumpy. He walked nearer to them, his face a study in suspicion. The sailors looked up at him and smiled innocently.

"Come over here," Shafer ordered.

The sailors, wide-eyed, obeyed and lined up before him.

"Empty your pockets."

"But, Lieutenant—"

"None of your bullshit. Empty them."

The four men, their expressions conveying their conviction that they were the victims of a grave injustice, did as they were told. Each man had a bottle of schnaps.

"You goddam drunks," Shafer growled. "I should send you all to the Russian front."

"The way things are going," one of the sailors answered jokingly, "we wouldn't have to move from here. It should catch up with us pretty soon."

Shafer had no time to reply. There was a scream, followed by another and another. A man came running out of a clump of trees, his shabby coat blowing behind him in the wind.

"Lieutenant," he gasped. "There's a woman—"

Shafer blanched. "Don't tell me she's—"

"Hurry, Lieutenant. She's having a baby."

42

March 19, 1945. From his headquarters at Koralle, Grand Admiral Doenitz launched his final submarine offensive: Operation Sea Wolf. Seven Grey Wolves, equipped with *Schnorchels*, sailed from their Norwegian ports bound for the American coast. British Intelligence was immediately made aware of their departure, and Admiral Ingrand dispatched four Support Groups in pursuit. In a few weeks, five of the U-boats had been sunk; but the *U-805* of Commander Bernardelli, and Commander Bode's *U-858*, escaped. For fifty-one days, neither the Germans nor the Allies knew what had become of them.

March 30. The Red Army laid siege to Danzig and Gdynia and reached the Gulf of Stettin. The beleaguered German garrisons offered furious resistance as German ships, under continual air and artillery bombardment, continued to evacuate thousands of refugee civilians and wounded military personnel.

April 14. Twenty-one German divisions were surrounded in the Ruhr and surrendered to the Americans.

April 16. Soviet armored divisions reached the suburbs of Berlin.

April 22. Under Hitler's orders, Grand Admiral Doenitz transferred his headquarters from Koralle to Camp Forelle, near Plön in Holstein in case the Reich should be split.

April 27. Crouched in a muddy foxhole south of Harburg, Wolf Shafer heard the rumble of advancing tanks. In the darkness, he stretched out his hand to make certain that his *Panzerfaust* was within easy reach.

Since his return from Pillau, he had been assigned to an antitank company commanded by Peter Cremer. The unit was composed of U-boat crews whose submarines had either been sunk by Allied bombs or had been unable to put to sea because of lack of fuel. Three nights earlier, Cremer and a handful of men had succeeded in infiltrating British lines and had destroyed almost forty tanks and armored cars. This daring raid had momentarily slowed the progress of the Second British Army. Now, however, British troops had pushed to within 12 miles of Harburg, and Shafer's unit was fighting a desperate battle. Shafer himself, in various skirmishes, had destroyed six tanks.

The submariners' navy uniforms, dirty and torn beyond repair, had been replaced by the regulation field gray of the

Wehrmacht. Shafer's skin itched under the rough cloth, and he scratched frantically in the darkness. Then he leaned backward and rubbed against the soggy wall of his foxhole. He shivered in his damp uniform, and his waterlogged boots squished disconsolately whenever he moved.

The company had been deployed in three extended lines, each one about a hundred yards behind the other. Far to the rear, there was a mortar section composed of pilots without planes.

Shafer heard someone approaching from the rear. He turned, sliding his revolver from its holster.

"It's me—Peter," Cremer whispered.

"You scared the shit out of me."

Cremer laughed softly. "Is everything all right?"

"No. I think I have fleas."

Cremer laughed again. "Lucky! At least you're not alone." Then his voice grew serious. "I think there might be some action tonight. The Tommies are getting tired of us and they're going to try to break through."

The rumble of the tanks was closer now.

"I think they're four or five hundred yards away now," Cremer said. Then he patted Shafer's back and ran, crouching, to the next foxhole.

Shafer waited for several minutes. Then he saw them: an endless line of massive black shapes moving through the night. Calmly, he slid a round into the antitank gun.

The British artillery had stopped its systematic shelling a half hour earlier. Shafer could not see very well, but he had no doubt that everything around him had been destroyed. The earth was covered with shell crater.

The first tanks were now 150 yards away. Shafer raised the long tube. "I'll fire at a hundred yards," he told himself. He waited three seconds, counting: 1, 2, 3. There was an explosion, and the weapon thrust back against his shoulder. The Churchill tank directly before him burst into flames. In the reddish light, he saw the hatch open and one man, then a second, jump heavily to the ground. He had already reloaded the *Panzer-faust*.

The tanks opened fire, but their shells whistled overhead and exploded far to the rear; perhaps on the third line, Shafer guessed.

He raised his weapon again, took aim as well as he could through the smoke and dust, and fired. "Shit," he said aloud. "I missed." But there was no time to try again. The tank was no more than 25 or 30 yards away, thundering toward him. And there was no time for Shafer to climb out of his foxhole. More terrified than he had ever been in his life, he threw himself to the bottom of the foxhole and curled up in the fetal position as the earth trembled under him. The left track of the tank passed not more than 3 feet above his head, and it was as though all the din of war at that moment assaulted his ears. Great clods of dirt showered down on him, and he was certain that he would be buried alive. He sprang up in panic—but the tank was already far past the hole. He coughed violently and was unable to breathe for what seemed an eternity. The taste of dirt was in his mouth as he reached for his antitank gun and placed it on the edge of the trench dug by the tank's track. Another tank was coming toward him. Standing in the foxhole, exposed from the waist up, Shafer took aim at the precise moment that the tank's machine-gun tower swung toward him. He saw his round explode against the forward part of the tank, and simultaneously a terrible pain tore through his stomach. He let the *Panzerfaust* fall and clutched at his abdomen. A thick, viscous liquid ran through his fingers. He heard screams, orders shouted, detonations. He saw men running toward him; and, before he lost consciousness, he wondered if he would die there, with his entrails exposed. His vision dimmed, and a violent chill passed through his body, followed by a new spasm of pain. Then all was darkness.

When Shafer opened his eyes again, he saw a white spot, dimly, as through a fog. He closed his eyes. There were a hundred needles of pain in his skull. He opened his eyes again. The white spot seemed clearer now. It moved; and its movement made him dizzy. He dropped his lids, and the universe was stationary once more. But, despite the sensation of floating in empty space, despite the bitter, almost acid taste in his mouth, he was determined to know where he was. Again, he raised his lids, and the effort involved seemed gigantic. The white blur began to take on definition. It was a doctor. Shafer tried to speak, but nothing came out of his mouth.

He saw the doctor observing him closely, holding a syringe and a small bottle.

"Where am I?" Shafer articulated finally and with great difficulty.

"In a British field hospital," the doctor answered in laborious German.

"Am I a prisoner?"

The doctor smiled in amusement and nodded as he filled the syringe. "If you want to remain a prisoner instead of becoming a corpse," he added, "then you'll have to lie still." He bared Shafer's arm and rubbed it with an alcohol-soaked cotton ball. "It's pure luck that you're here at all. When they found you, you looked dead; and they threw you in with a pile of bodies. If you hadn't moaned at precisely the right time, you'd be in a mass grave somewhere at this very moment."

He plunged the needle into Shafer's arm and watched the liquid as it drained from the syringe. Then he withdrew the needle, swabbed Shafer's arm again, and, before leaving, said: "Don't worry. You'll have a nice, flat stomach from now on. We took out a few yards of intestine."

April 30, 1945. The Thousand-Year Reich neared its end. On every front, the once mighty Wehrmacht had been defeated and was in full retreat. Germany's highways were filled with endless columns of refugees, both civilian and military, from the incessant artillery and aerial bombardment.

At Plön, Grand Admiral Doenitz had announced to Admiral

Godt, Captain Hessler, his son-in-law, Captain Lüdde-Neurath, his aide-de-camp, and Albert Speer, Hitler's Minister of Armaments, that he had no intention of surviving the annihilation of the German people. As soon as it became impossible to continue the evacuation of refugees from the East, and when it became clear that there was nothing more to be done, he intended to seek out death at sea, in a final battle.

Such was the grand admiral's state of mind when, in the course of the morning, he received a coded telegram from the Berlin Chancellery: NEW TREASON UNDER WAY. ACCORDING TO ENEMY RADIO, REICHSFÜHRER [Himmler] HAS OFFERED CAPITULATION THROUGH SWEDISH INTERMEDIARY. FÜHRER DEPENDS ON YOU TO PROCEED AGAINST ALL TRAITORS WITH SPEED OF LIGHTNING AND HARDNESS OF STEEL. BORMANN.

When the first astonishment at Bormann's message had passed, Doenitz felt the need to reflect before arriving at a decision. He walked with Godt and Lüdde-Neurath toward the beach, slowly and in silence. Suddenly, he stopped, looked at his two officers, and then exploded: "Those people in Berlin have lost their minds! They're completely insane! What do they mean, 'with speed of lightning and hardness of steel'? The *Reichsführer* has the police force and the SS at his disposal. And what do I have to oppose that? My sheep dog. All of our men are either busy with the evacuation, or have been assigned to the land forces. We have absolutely nothing!"

Later, in his office, Doenitz announced his decision. "Gentlemen," he told his staff, "I'm going to meet with Himmler. It's the only way to find out what's in his mind. Lüdde-Neurath, telephone the *Reichsführer* and arrange an appointment as soon as possible."

As the aide-de-camp tried to contact Himmler, Doenitz noted a scowl on the face of Admiral Meisel. He smiled and said, "Come, come, Meisel. What's on your mind?"

Meisel cleared his throat and glanced at Godt and Hessler. Then, seeing that Doenitz was becoming impatient, he replied: "Grand Admiral, we're concerned about your safety. The

Reichsführer is a dangerous man, and his people are capable of anything. If there should be any—any unpleasantness, your sheep dog won't be much protection."

"What do you suggest?"

"Let Commander Cremer and his submariners escort you to the meeting."

"Very well, Meisel. You may be right."

Lüdde-Neurath returned to announce that Himmler would meet with the grand admiral early in the afternoon, at the police barracks in Lübeck.

"I hope that, for once, Cremer won't be late," Doenitz muttered as he left the room.

Toward noon, a strange sight appeared on the streets of Plön: Peter Cremer, on a bicycle, leading a group of puffing, sweating submariners also on bicycles, some of them riding in tandem.

"This is all the transportation we could find," Cremer explained to Lüdde-Neurath. "That's why we're a little late."

"You're going to accompany the grand admiral to Lübeck," the aide-de-camp explained.

"On bicycles?"

"Put your mind at ease, Commander. We'll find a truck for your men. And you'll ride in the grand admiral's car."

Cremer sighed with relief, then gulped down a full glass of schnaps handed him by one of his men.

It was almost 6 P.M. by the time that Doenitz and his escort returned to Plön. The roads were practically blocked by military convoys, and by wounded soldiers and refugee civilians. A British plane, diving and strafing the road, had added to the confusion.

The discussion with Himmler had taken place at the SS landing field, and it had been extremely courteous on both sides. The *Reichsführer*, a smile playing at the corners of his lips, had categorically denied any attempt at contact with the Allies through Sweden. He had expressed total agreement with the grand admiral's conviction that it was absolutely necessary to avoid doing anything which might, through political discord, throw the country into chaos. At the end of the interview, Himmler had risen and, hands folded across his chest, he had asked Doenitz whether, if Hitler appointed him—Himmler—as his successor, he could count on the grand admiral's support.

"I will support any legally constituted government," Doenitz had answered drily.

As soon as he had reached Plön, Doenitz' first act was to have Admirals Dummitz, Meisel, and Godt report on the military situation, which was desperate. The meeting, attended by Albert Speer, was interrupted by Lüdde-Neurath, who entered excitedly waving a telegram.

"A message from Berlin," he announced. "It was in the secret *Kriegsmarine* code."

Doenitz took the paper nervously, wondering what it was that Berlin now wanted him to do. As he read, astonishment spread over his face:

GRAND ADMIRAL DOENITZ: IN PLACE OF THE FORMER REICHS-MARSCHALL GOERING, THE FÜHRER HAS DESIGNATED YOU AS HIS SUCCESSOR. WRITTEN AUTHORIZATION IS BEING SENT. IMMEDIATELY TAKE ALL MEASURES REQUIRED BY THE PRESENT SITUATION. BORMANN.

Doenitz held out the message to the men in his office. Speer, who had not spoken until then, mumbled vague congratulations and asked what the grand admiral intended to do.

"I accept," Doenitz replied decisively. "As you may know, I should have much preferred that this responsibility fall on someone else's shoulders. I have never been part of that *clique*. I have not even seen the Führer since July 20. But I must accept, since it is my duty to bring this war to an end."

Wearily, he turned to his aide-de-camp. "Ask the *Reichsführer* to come here this evening. Tell him I have a communication of the utmost importance for him."

Then he turned to his staff. "I must know for certain that he is not going to attempt to interfere," he explained. "With such a man, anything is possible."

A few seconds later, Lüdde-Neurath returned and reported that Himmler refused to meet with the grand admiral.

"Call him back," Doenitz said, his voice shaking with anger. "This time, I'll speak to him myself."

The conversation was short. Himmler agreed to come to Plön, and he would arrive around midnight.

Again, Peter Cremer was made responsible for protecting the grand admiral, and he stationed twenty of his submariners, armed with machine guns, around Doenitz' headquarters building. The men were scattered among the trees and in the bushes, with orders to go into action when they heard Cremer's whistle. Cremer himself, with a pistol tucked into his belt, sat in the headquarters mess hall with Lüdde-Neurath, chatting with the six SS officers, all armed to the teeth, who had accompanied the *Reichsführer.*

In an office nearby, Doenitz, sitting at his desk, held out Bormann's telegram, saying: "Please read this."

The chief of the Gestapo and the SS turned pale as he read, but quickly regained his composure. He rose and bowed to Doenitz, then spoke in a slightly hoarse voice: "Grand Admiral, may I express my sincere congratulations. The Führer is right. It is up to a soldier to put an end to the war."

He fell silent for a moment, and seemed lost in thought. Then he went on: "Are you willing to allow me to become the second man of the Reich?"

"Certainly not, *Herr Reichsführer,*" Doenitz replied.

"May I know why?"

"Of course. The government which I intend to form must include no one with political commitments. You have such commitments. In the event of negotiations, the enemy will not accept you as a spokesman for Germany."

For an hour Doenitz listened to and answered Himmler's arguments. Finally, the *Reichsführer* submitted to the inevitable. He rose, clicked his heels, gave the Nazi salute, and walked rapidly from the room.

During the entire interview, Doenitz had not moved his hand

from a pile of papers stacked on his desk. Beneath the papers was his revolver.

Later that night, Doenitz summoned Marshal Jodl and Marshal Keitel to Plön for a briefing on the military situation. They arrived several hours later. Their reports were in agreement: Germany no longer had any forces available to oppose, let alone to stop, the Allied armies.

Lüdde-Neurath, in recalling those bitter hours, wrote: "For the grand admiral, death would have been the simplest solution. He had no longer anything to lose. His two sons had been killed in battle at sea. His life's work, the submarine fleet, had been destroyed."

Doenitz, however, did not consider suicide. "Suicide," he had once explained, "can be interpreted as a confession of guilt. But I have nothing to feel guilty about."

During the afternoon of May 1, at 3:18, another message arrived for Doenitz from Berlin. It began with these words: FÜHRER DECEASED YESTERDAY AT 3:30 P.M. TESTAMENT OF APRIL 29 APPOINTS YOU REICH PRESIDENT.

May 2. The British forces reached Lübeck, thus cutting off both the Army of the Vistula and the civilians surging toward the West, fleeing from the Red Army. As Doenitz himself said, it was now necessary to obtain Field Marshal Montgomery's permission before these millions of German refugees could take refuge in Schleswig-Holstein. And, in order to obtain that permission, the new German chief-of-state would have to undertake negotiations immediately. Doenitz therefore busied himself with the appointment of a delegation to meet with Montgomery.

Cremer appeared in the operations room, his features drawn with tension. "British armored units are only a few miles from here," he said tightly. "My men and I will try to hold them off. For heaven's sake, clear out of here!"

The cabinets containing the headquarters files and documents were locked and hurriedly loaded onto trucks, and

Doenitz' staff drove toward Murwik, a small town north of Flensburg. The mob of refugees, the military convoys loaded with wounded soldiers, and the continuous attacks by British planes, made the journey a long and dangerous nightmare.

Several hours later, Peter Cremer, having destroyed two British tanks, crumpled to the ground, his stomach ripped open by shrapnel.

Doenitz, before leaving Plön, had locked himself in his office to read, for the last time, the latest reports he had received. Germany was in its final agony. Her industrial might had been wiped out by Allied bombs. Her reserves of munitions, fuel, and food were totally exhausted. All communications were paralyzed. Everywhere, the Wehrmacht was in the final stages of disintegration and had been crushed by the numerical and material superiority of the enemy. There were still pockets of resistance in Holland and Denmark, at Lorient and La Rochelle, in Kurland and Prussia. But these, Doenitz knew, were nothing more than a useless spilling of blood. The surface fleet had been crippled during its evacuation operations. And the people of Germany had reached the outer limits of human endurance.

When Doenitz reappeared before his staff, his face had regained its customary impassiveness. He had made his decision: surrender was inevitable. Therefore, it must be accomplished without delay.

At 9 P.M., on the Levensau Bridge, over the Kaiser Wilhelm Canal at Kiel, Doenitz met with Admiral von Friedeburg, chief of the delegation to the British, Vice-Admiral Wagner, and General Kinzel. It was a short meeting. Doenitz concluded his instructions by repeating to von Friedeburg: "Try to get Montgomery to agree to a partial surrender in the North sector; but above all, persuade him to give safe-conduct to civilian refugees and to retreating military personnel. I know that we are in no position to bargain. We are beaten. Nonetheless, do your best for the sake of our people. And may God go with you."

On the way back to Murwik, Doenitz slept in the rear seat of his car. He did not awaken even when the automobile was strafed by a British fighter. When he arrived at headquarters, he shaved, drank a cup of synthetic coffee, then went into his office. He remained there until dawn, waiting impatiently for word from Admiral von Friedeburg.

May 3. In the middle of the morning, there was a sudden cessation of Allied air raids. It was a sign, Doenitz hoped, that his delegates' first meeting with Montgomery had borne fruit. His face lined with fatigue, he said to Godt: "Perhaps this is the beginning of the end of our people's suffering."

After a quick visit to Doenitz to report on his progress, von Friedeburg returned to Montgomery's headquarters, on May 4, to sign the surrender of the North sector. The capitulation was to go into effect on May 5, at 8 A.M. But it contained a stipulation that was a bitter pill for Grand Admiral Doenitz and his men.

"Field Marshal Montgomery," von Friedeburg had reported, "gave me to understand that he had no objection to the continued evacuation by sea of refugees from the East. But he has insisted on one condition: that our fleet not scuttle itself when hostilities come to an end."

"It is contrary to the traditions and honor of the Navy," Doenitz said sadly. "But, since our only and final objective is to save as many lives as possible, tell Montgomery that I will do as he says."

A few minutes later, the order to cease fire was communicated to all submarines.

When Doenitz' U-boat commanders read that Operation Regenbogen (Rainbow)—the scuttling of the fleet in case of defeat— had been canceled, they refused to believe it. Lüdde-Neurath was swamped by telephone calls. A group of submarine commanders called upon him personally for verification. "Yes, it's true," the aide-de-camp assured them. "The grand admiral has given his word to the British. And don't forget, we will need our ships up to the last moment to rescue our wounded soldiers and our people in the East."

A young captain interrupted him. "That's true as far as surface vessels are concerned," he said. "But submarines are useless for that kind of mission. I can't believe that we're going to turn over our U-boats to them, intact!"

Lüdde-Neurath lost patience. It was late. In a nearby room, the grand admiral was finally getting a few hours of sleep. "These young idiots are going to wake up the admiral with their shouting," he told himself.

"Listen!" he roared at the commanders. "If I were captain of a U-boat, I wouldn't need anyone to tell me what to do!"

The U-boat captains looked at him in silence. The aide-de-camp's words had only one meaning so far as they were concerned. They clicked their heels, saluted, and ran out of the room.

The boatswain's whistles sounded throughout the barracks, and the same orders were given in each squadroom: "On your feet! Formation in five minutes!"

Shortly afterward, the long silhouettes of the last Grey Wolves slipped their moorings for their final voyage. Operation Regenbogen had begun. At Cuxhaven, the two electric *Walter* submarines, built in desperation and intended to revolutionize the war at sea, were the first to be destroyed. The others went down in the open sea, their standards flying. Some of the U-boat captains went down with their ships in order to wipe out the humiliation of defeat.

Field Marshal Montgomery, a man with a sense of fair play, took no reprisals against the cities of Germany for the self-immolation of the Grey Wolves. "I expected it," he told his aide-de-camp. "I should have been surprised if they had done otherwise."

43

"Oh, the bastards!" Rasch growled. "They're really close this time. Too close!"

The shell exploded 400 yards from the camp at Neustadt, and

the barracks shivered in the blast. Men ran out into the streets, shouting. The roar of the artillery was now uninterrupted, and so near that it was audible above the screaming air-raid sirens.

"It seems that they're concentrating their fire on Neustadt," said one of the officers near Rasch. "I wonder what they think they'll be able to destroy here, other than a few fishing boats."

"It sounds more like they're shelling Lübeck," Rasch answered. "Good Lord! If only we knew what was going on!"

Neustadt, cut off from the rest of Germany, had not heard of the latest developments. Everyone knew, of course, that things were going from bad to worse; but no one knew any details. The camp had no telephone or telegraph. There was not even a radio. They knew Grand Admiral Doenitz had become President of the Reich; but this information came from a local peasant whom one of Hermann Rasch's sailors had engaged in conversation. Eventually, official confirmation of the fact was brought by a bicycle courier from Lübeck.

"Get my car ready," Rasch ordered. "I'm going to go to Lübeck and find out what's happening."

A rumbling from overhead caused everyone to look upward. But, because of the low-lying clouds, no aircraft were visible.

"So far as you gentlemen are concerned," Rasch told his officers, "my advice is to stay in the air-raid shelters. I suspect there's going to be some heavy bombing."

An hour later, Rasch's vehicle came to a halt 200 yards from *Kriegsmarine* headquarters. It was impossible to go on. The road had disappeared under a mass of rubble which, in places, was almost 30 feet high. Rasch and his driver had passed numerous detachments of soldiers running to take up new positions in the city. One of them, without stopping, shouted at them: "The British are at the south end of the city!"

There was not a single civilian in sight. The entire population of Lübeck had taken refuge in cellars and air-raid shelters.

"Let's go," Rasch told his driver. "And don't forget to take the key. All we need is for someone to steal our vehicle."

Rasch drew his pistol as soon as he left the car. The sailor with him carried an automatic rifle at the ready.

The sentry boxes before the headquarters building were overturned, and the gates were wide open. The two men entered cautiously and looked into the guardroom. It was empty. They climbed the stairs. All the doors along the corridor were either ajar or open. Here and there, piles of ashes showed that files had been burned. Desk drawers were lying on the floor, and chairs and desks had been overturned.

Rasch walked into the admiral's office. Everything was in disorder. "Shit!" he told the sailor. "He's gone. They're all gone!"

"What's going to happen now, Commander?"

"I haven't the wildest idea. They could at least have told us, the bastards!"

He saw a box, tied with cord, protruding from behind a cabinet. He tried to rip away the thin cord but cut his palm on it.

"Give me your knife," he ordered the sailor.

"Maybe it's secret files," the man answered, opening the blade and handing it to Rasch. "They were so much in a hurry to get away that they forgot them."

"That would surprise me," Rasch said, sniffing. "Besides they don't smell like files."

He cut away the cord and pulled open the container, then let out a low whistle of satisfaction. Neatly stacked in the carton were twenty boxes of cigars.

"The admiral retreated without his reserves," Rasch observed. "Put them in the car."

"Do you think they might have forgotten some liquor?" the sailor asked excitedly.

"Maybe. But we don't have time to look. We'd better get back."

As soon as he was back at Neustadt, Rasch issued orders to evacuate the camp immediately. "The British are in Lübeck," he explained, "and they're liable to be here at any time. I want everyone out of here by five o'clock."

By 5 P.M., the bombings had stopped. Rasch's 2,000 men were already aboard ship, distributed among three light cargo ships, twenty-four vedette boats, and the seventy *See-Hund* submarines moored in the tiny port which the British had not yet bothered to bomb. The submariners had taken everything aboard with them: their beds, dishes, pots and pans, drinking water, and food for six months. Doenitz had been right: Hermann Rasch had a talent for organization.

For two days, this strange armada sailed northward without incident. On May 7, later in the afternoon, Rasch dropped anchor at Flensburg. He shaved, drank his coffee, and put on a clean white shirt which his orderly had just ironed. Then he went up on deck. "Tell the others that I've gone to head-quarters," he told the orderly. "I'll be gone for about an hour."

He paused to look at his fleet, pitching lightly in its moorings. From one of the ships there came a message, in Morse code, from someone using a flashlight: "To the captain: We have fresh fish. Do you want some?"

"Tell them yes, for God's sake!" Rasch said, as he walked away. This apocalyptic voyage seemed more and more to be turning into a picnic, he mused.

Twenty minutes later, he stood before Captain Luth, former U-boat commander and now commander of the flotilla. "Sir," he reported, "I have two thousand men and seventy *See-Hund* submarines, all ready for action."

Luth's face turned scarlet. "Are you insane?" he roared. "They're bombing the hell out of us every night. We can't even leave the shelters. And you tell me that you're here with two thousand men and seventy submarines? What do you expect me to do with you, for Christ's sake?"

"Sir, you forget that my *See-Hunds* have already sunk more than a hundred thousand tons of shipping. They can still be of service—"

"Listen," Luth said brusquely. "The biggest service you and your gang of pirates can render is to get the hell out of here."

"Very well, sir. Since you don't want us, I'll go somewhere

else." Rasch drew a cigar from his pocket, lighted it, and turned
to go.

"Just a minute, Commander!"

"Yes, sir?"

"Where did you get that cigar?"

"I found it. Pure luck."

"Isn't that strange," Luth said. "Cigars haven't been available
for months. Then you come out of nowhere—with cigars. I've
had an admiral on my back for the past three days, screaming
and yelling because his supply of cigars was lost!"

Rasch returned to his ship and ordered his officers to meet
him on the pier. In the gathering darkness, he explained his
plan: "Since they're bombing at night here, we're not going to
stay. We're going to sail to the Danish side of Jutland. The
British don't seem to be bombing there. I know the Gulf of
Flensburg pretty well. I used to spend my vacations there
before the war. There won't be any problem with navigation.
All you have to do is follow me. And have a nice evening,
gentlemen."

Two hours later, the small fleet dropped anchor off a small
fishing village. It was a clear night, and Rasch's men, from their
ships, could see the explosions from the bombs falling upon
Flensburg. It was 5 A.M. before Rasch managed to get to sleep.

His orderly awakened him shortly afterward; "Captain, there
are some Danish fishermen who want to talk to you."

Rasch yawned widely, dressed, and went on deck. A fishing
boat was tied up alongside. Five men were in the boat; and one
of them was holding an old hunting rifle.

"Are you in command of these ships?" the armed man asked in
bad German.

"Yes. What do you want?"

"You and your ships are our prisoners," the man said, raising
his rifle.

Before Rasch had time to think of an answer, one of his
sailors picked up a garbage can and emptied it over the fishing

boat. The Dane dropped his weapon and put his arms over his head to protect himself. The boat hurriedly moved a few yards away. "You're going to pay for this," the man shouted, shaking an enormous fist. "We'll be back with reinforcements, you sons-of-bitches—"

A sailor jumped onto the forward deck and swung the machine gun in the direction of the fishing boat, which now beat a hasty retreat.

"It's becoming unhealthy here," Rasch grumbled. "Pass the word to raise anchor."

As the ships prepared to get under way, a volley of rifle shots came from the shore nearby.

"I could throw up when I think that we're running away from those filthy old men," Rasch's helmsman said in disgust.

"Shut up, Karl!" Rasch snapped.

Shortly before noon, on May 7, the fleet once more dropped anchor in German waters, in the tiny port of Eckerfeörde.

On the same day, at Rheims, Marshal Jodl prepared to sign the instrument of general surrender to the Allies.

And, on the same day, the Grey Wolves based in Norwegian ports, and those which had found shelter in the Baltic, received the following message:

"Submariners.

"We have been through six years of submarine warfare. You have fought like lions. The crushing material superiority of the enemy confined us gradually to a more and more limited space. It has now become impossible for us to pursue the battle from this last base which remains to us.

"Submariners, you have fought heroically and with unprecedented courage. You will now lay down your arms intact and unsullied. We will remember with reverence our fellow comrades whose deaths bear witness to their loyalty to our Führer and to our country.

"Comrades! For the good of our country in the times to come, preserve the spirit which has enabled you to fight so valiantly and so effectively.

"Long live Germany!

"Grand Admiral Doenitz."

On May 9, at 1:40 A.M., another message was addressed by Doenitz to the Grey Wolves still at sea:

"Submariners! After a heroic and unprecedented struggle, you will now be called on to make the greatest sacrifice for your country by carrying out unconditionally the following instructions. Your obedience will spare Germany much suffering." The message went on to order all ships to surface and, showing a blue or black flag, to proceed immediately to the nearest enemy ports. There, they were to surrender.

The day before, at Bergen, shortly before the arrival of the British, the Grey Wolves operating out of that port had been disarmed. The crews were at attention on deck, the officers on the conning towers. The senior boatswain signaled, "Strike the colors." Tears streamed down the cheeks of the men as, after six years of war and suffering, the battle standards of the Grey Wolves were lowered slowly, flapping sadly in the wind.

44

May 4, 1945. 8:00 A.M. The *U-2511*, the only type XXI submarine in existence, lay at 250 feet to the west of Fair Island. Commander Adalbert Schnee, Engineer First Class Eberhardt Suhren, and the entire crew, were in a state of excited enthusiasm.

Two hours earlier, their radio had picked up four sonar echoes simultaneously. "It can only be a group of submarine chasers," Schnee concluded. "The time has come to see if our new toy is as good as we think it is."

The *U-2511* was cruising at 3 knots, and the sonar echoes grew rapidly louder. The enemy ships were very near. Aboard conventional submarines, the crew would have braced itself for the beginning of a depth-charge barrage.

"Let's go," Schnee ordered. "Full speed."

Suhren echoed the order. The hum of the electric engines increased in intensity and the needles of the speed indicators leaped forward.

"Sixteen knots," Suhren reported joyfully. "That's as fast as a corvette or a frigate!"

The U-2511 changed course slightly. The sonar signals decreasing rapidly, grew faint, and finally ceased altogether.

"Fantastic!" Suhren exclaimed, pounding the navigator's back until the man almost collapsed. "That's the first time that a U-boat has ever gotten away so easily!"

The crew cheered madly.

"With this ship, men," Suhren continued, "we'll more than be able to hold our own against the Tommies. When you think of how we used to be sitting ducks—and now all we have to do is press a lever and we're out of range! I can't help but remember all our comrades who don't have the type XXI yet."

The U-2511 was cruising with its *Schnorchel* above the surface when Grand Admiral Doenitz' message arrived announcing Germany's surrender. The men looked at one another in utter disbelief. Their incredulity turned to anger at the thought of putting down their weapons at the very moment when they had finally been given the new weapon for which they had waited so long.

"What are we going to do?" the second officer asked, his eyes glistening with rage. "Are we really going to surface and surrender?"

"We will obey," Schnee snapped, in a voice which indicated that he would allow no discussion.

The U-2511 made a half turn and set a course back to Bergen. No one spoke. A terrible sadness hung like a pall over the ship.

"Well," Schnee said softly, "this is the end. All that we did, all that we suffered—it was all for nothing. There won't be any parades and triumphal arches for us. There won't be anything for us. We've been beaten. We don't know yet what humiliation is. Now, we're going to live in humiliation. We've been free, here in the depths of the sea. Now, we're going to be caged like animals in a prisoner-of-war camp."

In the forward compartment, one of the men began to play his harmonica. A sweet, sad melody floated through the ship.

"Tell him to shut up, for God's sake," Suhren said angrily.

"Propeller noises!" the radioman reported.

"Periscope depth! Quick!"

The periscope broke the surface. "It's a British cruiser with an escort of four destroyers," Schnee told the crew.

Schnee was overwhelmed by a wild desire to fire his torpedoes one last time. The U-2511 had not yet been detected, and the cruiser was only 500 yards away and coming closer. Within a few seconds, it would be directly in Schnee's line of fire.

Schnee heard a voice, which he recognized with difficulty as his own, give the order: "Ready tubes 1 and 3!"

"1 and 3 ready, sir!"

Schnee's finger tightened convulsively on the periscope levers until his knuckles were white. The cruiser was now directly ahead, ideally exposed, as no enemy ship had ever been, to U-boat attack. Schnee had only to give the order; to speak the single word that would loose his torpedoes.

His fingers dropped from the periscope.

"Goddammit!" he cried. "Goddammit!"

At almost the same time, aboard the U-977, Commander Heinz Schaeffer was addressing his crew. The U-977 had also just received the order to surrender.

"Comrades," he said, "the enemy wants us to surrender our ship. They say that our superiors have surrendered. But I don't think we should obey orders issued by the enemy. It seems to me that we should continue on course, but without taking any offensive action. There will be no attacks on enemy ships.

"We have enough fuel and enough food aboard to spare ourselves the humiliation of captivity. I suggest that we head for

Argentina. Every man is free to choose for himself what he wants to do. And I'm certain that you will all conduct yourselves with the dignity that one expects of a submariner.

"We are going to take a vote. Those who want to return to Germany will be put ashore along the Norwegian coast. We'll give you life rafts and food."

Out of the forty-two men aboard the *U-977*, sixteen chose to return home. They were all fathers of families. As soon as they left the ship, the *U-977* began the Atlantic crossing. The voyage took sixty-six days, all of it spent beneath the surface. It was the longest crossing of the war.

"Surface!"

A few seconds later, the hatch opened. Commander Bernardelli emerged on deck and peered through his binoculars. There was nothing in sight. The watch appeared and took up their stations. There was a light wind, and a fine spray played over the deck. Bernardelli found it refreshing.

The navigator appeared on deck and took his bearings. Bernardelli watched him in silence for a few moments. Then he looked around at the sea, strangely and beautifully calm on this spring day.

The navigator went below, and Bernardelli lighted a cigarette. It was 6 A.M., and dawn was breaking. It was a dangerous time of the day; the time when aircraft patrolled the skies with their radar. It was also the time to renew one's supply of oxygen; and the time when fatigue weighed most heavily on everyone, when everyone's reflexes were at their slowest.

The radioman's head suddenly appeared through the hatch. His features were set in an expression of utter stupefaction.

"Captain—"

"What is it, Sparks?"

"Captain, we've surrendered."

"Don't be an ass," Bernardelli said harshly. "That's impossible!"

"I just picked up a message from the grand admiral to all units at sea."

Bernardelli took the sheet of paper from the radioman and read.

The *U-805* was 350 miles from New York and was carrying twenty-three torpedoes.

He handed the message back to the sailor. "Inform the enemy of our position," he ordered quietly. He turned to the watch officer: "Run up a blue flag."

Turning toward the bow of his ship, his hands clutching the steel railing, Bernardelli stared at the water ahead. The men on deck saw tears on his cheeks, heard him murmur: *"Verdamnter Atlantik!"**

Shortly afterward, the *U-158* which, like Bernardelli's *U-805*, had escaped the British support groups and reached American waters, surrendered. It was only 180 miles off the Delaware cape. Grand Admiral Doenitz' final offensive against American shipping had ended.

May 10. The khaki jeep screeched to a halt at Eckerfeörde, and the small British flag affixed to the fender drooped on its staff. An English colonel, his blond hair neatly combed, his blond mustache newly trimmed, emerged from the vehicle. He looked down to ascertain whether his trousers were wrinkled; then, twirling his stick, he walked toward the port where Rasch's fleet was moored. His footsteps echoed on the boardwalk. When he reached the long, gray vedette, he stopped and looked up at the German officer leaning against the railing, his arms folded, his white cap pushed back on his head.

Politely, the colonel asked in German: "Are you the captain?"
"Jawohl."
"Very good. The war is over, you know."
"I know it."
"Then, of course, you are prisoners of war."
All around Rasch, sailors and even a few officers had gathered,

* Damned Atlantic.

curious to see a British officer in the flesh. They concluded that they had a characteristic specimen before their eyes.

"Tomorrow morning, Captain," the colonel went on, "you and your men must go to the POW camp at the mouth of the canal. And, of course, you must leave your vessels here."

"Halt!" Rasch ordered, raising his arm.

As he waited for his officers and men to catch up to him, he heard the grumbling and curses of the men as they stumbled into one another, and the sound of packs being dropped to the ground. For an hour they had been marching in the darkness, carrying their beds, their tents and their clothing, their cases of food and drink; marching along the Eckerfeörde canal in search of the prisoner-of-war camp.

"Well, we're not going to spend the whole night looking for that blasted camp," Rasch said. "Let's stop here. Pitch your tents, and get some sleep. If the British want to make prisoners of us, then let them wrap their barbed wire around us."

It was not until late in the morning that a jeep and a truck of soldiers pulled up at Rasch's camp. The British soldiers stared with an air of faint surprise at the sailors sitting around their fires, eating their breakfast, and at those fishing and wading in the canal.

An officer jumped from the jeep and darted among the tents, picking his way through men stretched out in the sun.

"Where is your commanding officer?" he asked angrily.

A sailor gestured toward Rasch.

"Who are you?" the officer demanded.

"Us? We're prisoners of war," Rasch answered.

"But this is not a POW camp!"

"Then suppose you build us one," Rasch replied.

The British officer glared at Rasch, but he did not know quite what to do. This was a situation which required a decision at a higher level. Generally, prisoners were taken to a camp, rather than camps being constructed around prisoners.

8

Rasch's orderly brought him a bottle of beer. Politely, Rasch offered one to the conqueror, who refused.

"Listen," the officer said, "while waiting for a decision from my superiors, consider yourselves under confinement within the moral bounds of your camp. Do you understand?"

"I understand."

"You are not to go beyond the camp. You must remain in the space between the canal and the road. Those are the moral walls."

The officer turned on his heel and walked away. When he reached his jeep, Rasch called to him: "Colonel!"

"What is it?"

"Be careful. Don't smash your jeep against one of our moral walls."

"Don't worry. There's a gate here, morally speaking!"

Two nights later, Rasch bade his men farewell and wished them good luck. Then, accompanied by his dog and three of his officers, he leaped over the moral wall and escaped. Some of his men had heard that the enlisted men and noncommissioned officers were to be demobilized by the British, but that the officers would be confined in regular POW camps.

"We always know when we're going to be locked up," Rasch said, "but we never know when they're going to let us go. I'm going to meet my wife at Timmendorf."

A month later, Rasch and Jutta—they had been married in March 1945—were in hiding in a sparsely furnished room in a small fishing village.

One morning, Jutta learned that, at the Neustadt camp, the British were releasing even the officers. Rasch therefore decided to report to the camp.

"I'll see you tonight," he told Jutta. But they did not meet again for eight months, until February 7, 1946. The British sergeant who interrogated Rasch at Neustadt had him arrested when he discovered that Rasch was the man who had organized the *See-Hund* division. When Rasch protested, the sergeant said, "The *See-Hunds* were a branch of the SS, you bastard."

Rasch was then transferred to the political internment camp at Neumunster. There, he was finally brought before an Allied military tribunal, tried, and found "innocent of any political activity." He was then released.

During his confinement, his weight had dropped from 160 pounds to 100 pounds. His ragged uniform jacket—which was all that he had to show for six years of service and which had been stripped of all insignia of rank—hung on him like a sack.

A few days earlier, at Munsterlager, a POW camp an hour out of Hamburg, August Maus was released. He had been repatriated from Arizona a week before. As Maus walked through the great wooden gate, the British guard winked at him. "There's a pretty girl waiting for you," he said.

Gabriella was indeed there, shivering in the snow, almost invisible inside her coat, her face buried in the collar.

Maus ran to her, shouting her name. She looked up, puzzled. She did not recognize the gray-haired, wrinkled man who was calling her. When he reached her and said, "I'm August," she burst into tears, then threw herself into his arms.

Dear Madame,

Even though I do not know you, I am taking the liberty of writing you a few lines. I hope that my presumption will not increase the sorrow you must feel at the news you have received.

I am Commander Holm, of the Royal Navy. I was aboard the destroyer *Crocus*, which sunk the submarine commanded by your son, Peter Cremer.

I shall always retain a vivid remembrance of the heroic struggle and resistance of your son.

I am aware of how greatly your country and your people are suffering. If I can be of service to you, or if I can help you in any way, even by sending packages of food, I should be grateful if you would let me know. It would be an honor for me to do anything that I can to ease the pain and the sorrow which you must bear.

I await the pleasure of your answer.

Yours respectfully,
s/Commander Holm

Peter Cremer's mother, after opening the envelope containing Commander Holm's letter, called out: "Peter, Peter, come here. There's a letter in English, and I can't make out a single word."

Peter Cremer limped into the room and took the letter from his mother. He read it and was greatly moved.

"What is it, Peter?" his mother asked, in that tone of infinite gentleness which she employed when speaking to the son who had been miraculously restored to her.

"It's nothing, Mother," Cremer answered gruffly. "It's from a friend."

There was a man who, throughout the war, opposed the Third Reich with all his strength and all his courage. His name was Winston Churchill. Here is Mr. Churchill's tribute to the men of the Grey Wolves:

"Thanks to a prodigious effort, and despite their enormous losses, sixty to seventy submarines remained in action until the very end, and their crews kept alive in their hearts an indestructible hope that the war at sea would turn in their favor. The final phase of our assault was carried out in Germany's coastal waters, and many submarines were destroyed in the bombings. Nonetheless, when Doenitz ordered them to surrender, there were no less than forty-nine submarines still at sea. Such was the intensity of the effort on the part of the Germans; and such was the indomitable courage of the crews of their submarines."

EPILOGUE

The final score of the submarine war was as follows:

Of the 2,200 Allied convoys which crossed the Atlantic, the Grey Wolves sunk 2,779 merchant ships, for a total of 14,119,413 tons of shipping, and 148 war ships.

630 U-boats were lost.

ACKNOWLEDGMENTS

Without the aid of former U-boat commanders of the Third Reich, it would have been impossible to write this book.

These men gave generously of their time, and they consented to describe to me their adventures, their experiences in combat, and their memories.

They did so without passion, and without fanaticism, but with that simplicity and lucidity which characterizes men of the sea, and in that spirit of detachment which is made possible by the passage of time.

Heartfelt thanks are due to those officers, petty officers, and seamen who have shared with me the hours of victory and those of sadness out of their lives.

My special gratitude goes to Commanders Peter Cremer, Reinhardt Hardegen, August Maus, Herman Rasch, Wolf Schafer, Adalbert Schnee, and to Lieutenant Commanders Dietrich von dem Borne and Volkmar Koenig.

I also wish to thank Joachim Ahme, who gave me access to the archives of the Association of German Submariners; to Petty Officer-Navigator Wilhelm Spahr, who was one of the few survivors of Commander Prien's U-47, the men of which were the heroes of Scapa Flow; and to Petty Officer-Radioman Josef Kassel, one of Commander Kretschmer's crewmen, who, as a prisoner of war, learned of the escapes of the U-570 from members of its crew.

Finally, I owe a special debt of thanks to Grand Admiral Doenitz, who agreed to speak with me one winter morning. Snow covered the tiny village where the former chief of the Grey Wolves now lives in retirement. In the house where he lives alone, the Lion spoke with deep emotion of the men whom he led in combat. I am profoundly grateful to him for his kindness.

Jacques Lux, former captain of *La Thétis*, was gracious enough to read the manuscript of this book and to make available to us the benefit of his experience as a submariner. Our special thanks to him for his advice.

* * *

The following works were very useful in the writing of this book:

Grand Admiral Doenitz: *Dix Ans et Vingt Jours.*
                                      La Guerre en Quarante Questions.
Winston Churchill: *The Second World War.*
Jean-Jacques Antier: *Histoire Mondiale des Sous-Marins.*
Claude Chombart: *Les Sous-Marins.*
Wolfgang Franck: *Les U-boote Contre les Marines Alliées.*
Léonce Peillard: *L'Affaire du Laconia.*
Terence Robertson: *Le Loup de l'Atlantique.*
Heinz Schaeffer: *U-977.*

P